DEVELOPMENT OF THE FILM

DEVELOPMENT OF THE FILM

AN INTERPRETIVE HISTORY

ALAN CASTY

SANTA MONICA COLLEGE

HARCOURT BRACE JOVANOVICH, INC.
NEW YORK   CHICAGO   SAN FRANCISCO   ATLANTA

ISBN: 0-15-517622-6

Library of Congress Catalog Card Number: 73-2179

Printed in the United States of America

Picture Credits and Copyright Acknowledgments

Cover art: Ms. Petie Brigham, Woodstock, New York

From *Archeology of the Cinema* by C. W. Ceram. Harcourt Brace Jovanovich, Inc., 1965: p. 4
Museum of Modern Art/Film Stills Archive: pp. 18, 26, 46, 50, 59, 65, 75, 76, 78, 85, 228, 326, 406
D. W. Griffith Productions: p. 29
Rosa Madell Film Library: pp. 30, 35, 36, 37, 42, 44, 45, 111, 113
Paramount Pictures Corporation: p. 54
Janus Films: pp. 55, 108, 117, 124, 127, 241, 243, 263, 268 (detail from *Beauty and the Beast*), 278, 294, 308,
    309, 335, 337, 390, 395
Metro-Goldwyn-Mayer: pp. 58, 62, 71, 131, 177, 182, 195, 282, 379, 383
A Nero Production: p. 67
Universal Pictures: pp. 72, 145, 189, 193, 210, 211
A Tobis-Paris Production, Presented by Captain Harold Auten: p. 81
United Artists Corporation: pp. 87, 153, 175, 311, 381
By Permission of the Harold Lloyd Estate and the Harold Lloyd Foundation: p. 90
Courtesy of Raymond Rohauer: p. 93
Warner Bros. Pictures, Inc.: pp. 98, 141, 160, 178, 206 (© 1941), 219, 225, 227, 256, 268 (detail from *A Clock-
    work Orange*), 289 (© 1970), 350, 353, 367, 373
MCA Enterprises, Inc.: pp. 120, 201, 258
Audio Brandon: pp. 122, 317, 318, 323, 324, 345, 347, 388, 393, 400
Metro-Goldwyn-Mayer/The Bettmann Archive: p. 131 (marginal photo)
A Gainsborough Production, Presented by Gaumont-British: pp. 134, 135
RKO Radio Pictures, A Division of RKO General: pp. 139, 168, 179, 233 (© 1941), 234
Warner Bros. Pictures, Inc./The Bettmann Archive: pp. 142, 151
Twentieth Century Fox Film Corporation: p. 156
Culver Pictures: pp. 163, 199, 236, 274, 306, 369, 376
Columbia Pictures Corporation: p. 186
RKO Radio Pictures/The Bettmann Archive: p. 197
By Permission of Alfred Hitchcock: p. 204
Contemporary Films/McGraw-Hill Book Company: pp. 215, 253, 261
Richard Feiner and Company, Inc.: p. 251
A Michelangelo Antonioni Film, Distributed by Cinemation Industries: p. 281

Picture credits and copyright acknowledgments are continued on page 426.

**FOR
JILL**

PREFACE

The unique congress of art and commerce that is the motion picture has never been more perplexing, frustrating, yet amazing. This is how it appears at present—early in 1973; yet glancing back, the written evidence indicates that at every stage of its development, the film has seemed to be at a point of crisis, always on the verge of settling the problematic issue of its inbred contradictions, one way or the other, but never doing so. The surpassing wonder is that out of the welter of cross-purposes, the dynamics of this congress have nurtured the creative progress of an art —public, popular, commercial, yet touching with sensitivity and shaping with a dexterity of form both the glimmering surfaces and the deepest pulsings of the life of our times.

This book essays an interpretation of the progress of film as an art form, ordering the flux of its history from the perspectives of the present and of a particular viewpoint, shaping a usable past, one that has pattern and meaning, one that can help us understand where we are now and how we got here. While any pattern must to a degree be selective, it need not distort. In seeking an open, flexible patterning, I have tried to strike a number of balances between the objective material, important in itself, and the interpretive hypotheses that give it meaning. Some of these balances will be indicated in what follows, but the controlling one lays equal stress on assessing and understanding individual works of film-making —the vital core of any history of this art—and on setting the terms of the contexts that can best guide us to how an individual film works, to what it means and what it does.

The point of view that shapes these contexts for the understanding of discrete films and film-makers stresses *development*. I use the term to indicate not only the process of advancing or expanding into a state of the art that effectuates more and more complex combinations of its possibilities, but also the nature of the process. That nature is to grow out of and extend, rather than replace, to reassemble basic constituents, although with the obvious discovery and introduction of new elements along the way. This pattern that shapes the progressive reordering of the elements of the art stresses the dynamics of interaction—the interaction between one period and another, the interaction between the shifting cultural and business contexts within a period and the developing work of film-makers, the interaction between stages of development and the individual works within a single career.

The overall pattern that I pose for this development involves a flexible three-stage dialectic of fundamental approaches to the film—from the period of D. W. Griffith's *The Birth of a Nation* to the present. The fundamental styles of these three stages of development are seen in interaction with each other; but each and all are also seen as deriving from the interaction of the film-makers and their times. I examine these styles on the basis of the ways they variously balance the terms of two of the central equations of film esthetics: content-form, representation-expressiveness.

At the deepest level, these styles are ways of structuring feelings and ideas, of structuring attitudes toward man and his world as well as attitudes toward the state of the art. But always, within the constantly split personality of the medium, these meaningful structurings must coexist with the effects of a different order of demands, of the movies as money-making mass entertainment.

The first stage of the development of film style, treated in Part 1, is the period of discovery and of silent films. The defining characteristic of the style of this first stage lies beyond the intrinsic imitation of reality found in the film image from the start. The structuring of form of this period does not, generally, deny the realistic representationalism of the film image but uses it for varied types of heightening, intensifying expressiveness, producing an art of hyperbole of both form and content.

Even within the silent period, there were countercurrents toward a more modulated form of literal representation. But it was not until the discoveries of the sound period, the political and social crises of the thirties and forties, the shifting of attitudes toward artistic taste and audience expectations that the consolidation of the Realist style took place. But again during this period—treated in Part 2—there were important and influential individual assertions against the dominant current.

In the contemporary period (Part 3), now the longest in the history of the film, the demands inherent in complex cultural tensions, issues, and changes have been met by what I have called the open style. This consists of a new synthesis, possibly temporary, still uncertain, a new complexity in the mixing and balancing of tendencies toward both representation and expressiveness, and a new set of relationships between content and form.

Within the general stylistic outlines of the parts, the individual chapters take into account the important shapes and directions of national situations and movements, the impact of technical advances, the constant interplay with commercial trends and fashions, the significance of the rise and development of genres. But at the core is the single film-maker, the single career, the single film. While I do attempt to take into account the important, but unfortunately hazy, interaction of the various contributors to the finished work, I inevitably focus on the director. For despite the complications of the technology and systems of production, and all theories aside, the lasting, significant films seem to be those that show the imprint of the director, though, to be sure, with varying—often revealingly varying—degrees of control. Within all the shaping patterns and contexts, the history of the film must be the story of film-makers and their works, singly and in the developing canon of a career.

The perspectives of my approach and the limitations of space—not to ignore those of my own bias and knowledge—have dictated certain key exclusions, points of balance, and emphases. While all three periods are treated thoroughly, the largest part of the book is devoted to work of the last 25 years. Conversely, the precursors of *The Birth of a Nation* are treated only to the degree that they clarify the state of the art by 1915. My position is that, from the perspective of what is valuable in assessing and understanding the present, the recent past assumes great importance. More subjectively, it is my feeling that the contemporary period has seen more widespread excellence and single works with greater total effect—more complex interplay of content and technique—than have previous periods.

While I do relate the films of other cultures to the central axis of European-American film-making, I do not treat them with the thoroughness of works within what is the central cinematic and cultural tradition of my audience of readers and viewers. Similarly, within the American orientation of most of my readers and myself, I have in some instances allotted American films and film-makers more space than comparable Europeans. But those generally are instances—such as certain of the genres—in which American developments have been particularly influential.

While I have dealt with some documentary films and some underground experimental films when these have directly touched upon the main thrust of my arguments, I have in the main restricted the discussion to what we might call fictional, or dramatic-narrative, films within the main channels of the production and distribution systems. The others are best approached, I feel, in more specialized books. On the other hand, while I have discussed events, developments, and influences in the spheres of technology and business when they have been important in influencing the art of the film, this book is not a history of production and distribution systems or of technical developments. Those, too, would be other books.

Finally, within periods, within national and stylistic movements, within the careers of single directors, I have aimed at a somewhat shaky, and finally, I suppose, impossible balance between a comprehensive picture of the factual pattern and the kind of detailed discussion of key works that is the most fruitful approach to the pattern. When in doubt, I have sacrificed names and dates for a bit more interpretation so that along the way there are bound to be some omissions. Still, while I feel that a sense of the plot and a description of the sensory concreteness of the visual image are vital, I have nonetheless had to retain briefer references to some films than I would have liked in the hope of capturing at least the flavor or feel of items that are significant in filling out a pattern. Similarly, I have often had to focus on a limited selection of a director's total output, while suggesting the total thrust of his work.

Useful bibliographies are available in a number of places; I have chosen to use the space that might have supplied another one for the kind of interpretation that is more distinctly my own.

I am obviously in debt to the many writers on the film who have helped shape my own understanding of its history. I owe them much—beyond the limits of this book. I have not attempted to surpass them with new, surprising discoveries; rather, I hope to have built upon the foundations they laid a patterning of the available data that can contribute to the understanding of film. More direct thanks are due the readers of the original manuscript, who saved me from many a misstep and pointed the way toward a sharper focus; to the editors of journals, who pinpointed necessary changes in earlier versions of some of the material here, which they were kind enough to use; and to the editors at Harcourt Brace Jovanovich, who somehow managed to put all the pieces back together again.

ALAN CASTY

CONTENTS

CHAPTER
TWENTY-FOUR
New Worlds of Entertainment and Art
406

Index
412

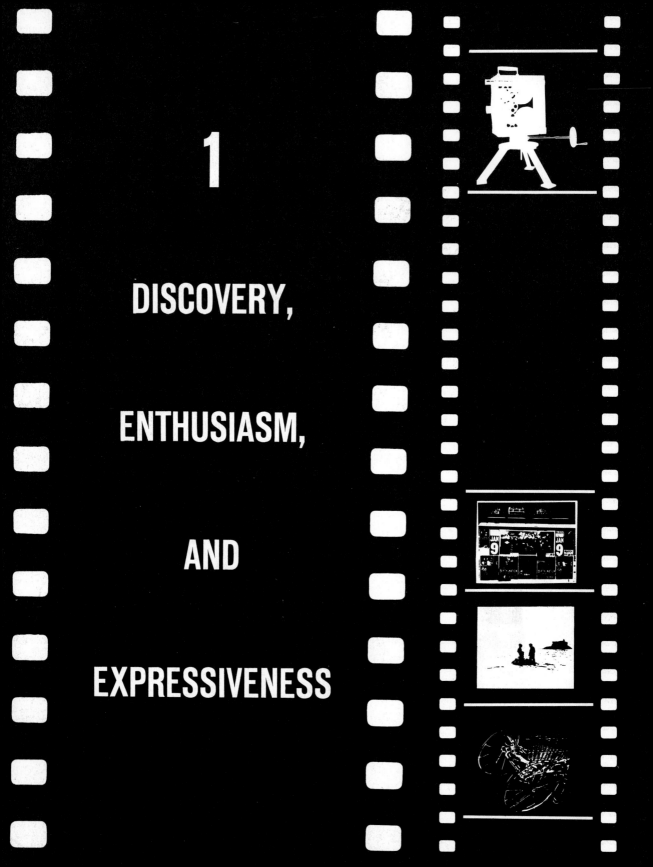

1

DISCOVERY,

ENTHUSIASM,

AND

EXPRESSIVENESS

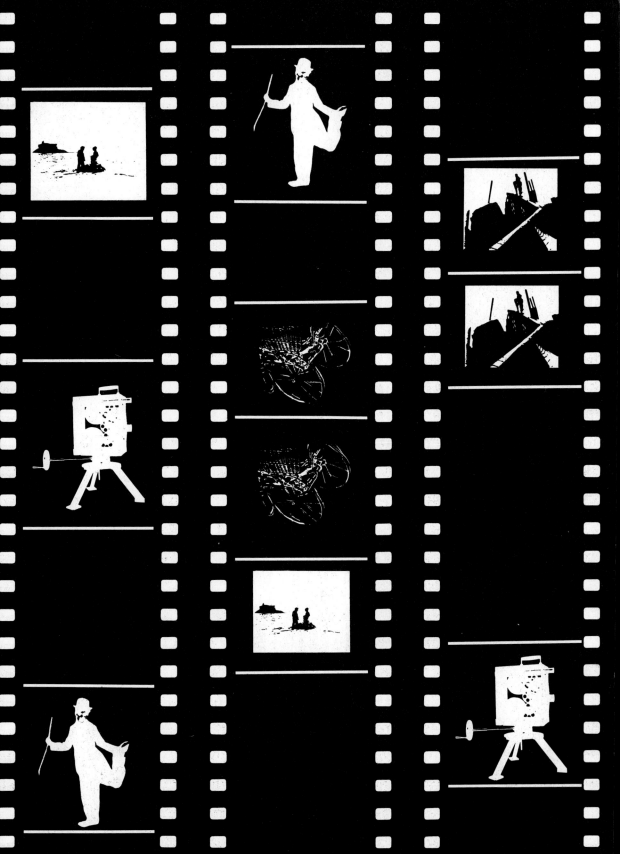

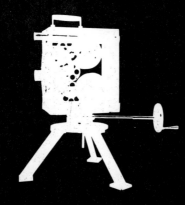

CHAPTER ONE

TOWARD A STYLE FOR THE TIMES

The title itself had an almost uncanny aptness. For David Wark Griffith's first full-length feature, *The Birth of a Nation*, was in many important ways the true birth of an art. For the first time, it brought together in a dramatic narrative all that was being discovered about the essential characteristics of the motion picture. And it fused these in a distinct style, a style that reflected both a man and his times—so deeply, perhaps even excessively, was Griffith attuned to the cultural and social assumptions of the period, the moral and esthetic expectations of its audiences. His film was a precocious summing up of all the possibilities and weaknesses of this first period of enthusiasm and discovery. It would also become a revealing archetype of the motion picture that would continue to reach for the resonances of art but at the same time find its greatest popularity, and make its money, through the power of romantic sensation.

The filmic language that *The Birth of a Nation* so thunderingly and silently spoke in 1915 had been evolving for several decades. In these years, the essential nature of film art was being discovered; in the years after 1915, most of the emphasis was to shift to the uses of these discoveries—what to do with what film was.

It was obviously not necessary to discover, in the years before 1915, that a film was visual and that it moved. Yet, often by trial and error and mainly without formal theoretical definition, film-makers of the earliest years of discovery were concerned with exploring the obvious—with what it meant to have visual images that moved. The implications of what turned out to be so complexly obvious can be traced through six important threads of discovery that came together in the emphatic knot of *The Birth of a Nation*.

BEGINNINGS: BEFORE *THE BIRTH*

The
Lumières

With the first brief films of Louis Lumière and his brother Auguste in 1895, the obvious began to become significant—though still in the most rudimentary form. What mattered most to the Lumières, what was understood best by them, was not the movement or subsequent manipulation of the strip of film itself but the movement within the shot from real life that could be captured tellingly and accurately in a visual image. In *Arrival of a Train at the Station*, the camera is placed to capture the impact of a train steaming in toward the audience; in *Bathing Beach*, waves move toward the audience and break on the shore; in *A Boat Leaving Harbor*, a boat is rowed away from the camera against the motion of the water toward it; in *The Baby's Lunch*, a closer view is presented, this time of the action of a mother, father, and baby as the child is fed.

The Lumières made movies with a single, uninterrupted flow of film through the camera, almost always from a single camera position. In these movies, the medium is transparent: What enters—never to leave—is the tangible presence of physical reality. But it was still beyond the Lumières' conception to pursue the implications: Film is an art in which physical reality —whether a baby's messy bib or a towering mountain—becomes more than the subject of the formal elements; it is palpably, tangibly felt as present *in* the formal elements; it becomes one of them. The physical world becomes dynamic, dramatic—both means and end. Approaches to this phenomenon, strategies in the use of it, play a central part in shaping the development of the film.

The method of the Lumières is an example of an early elementary exercise of a basic, constant tendency of film-makers—the attempt to imitate, capture, represent normal commonplace reality with as much accuracy and as little obtrusive filtering through the medium or the film-maker as possible.

Méliès:
Turn
of
the
Century

A contemporary compatriot of theirs, Georges Méliès, can be said to have been the first to explore the opposite basic pole in the production of films. For the typical short film of Méliès is more an exercise in imaginative expression, fantasy, and spectacle—to get beyond the commonplace to the wonderful and awesome—than an attempt to represent reality accurately. Méliès sought pure artifice—sought to manipulate the materials of the film image in what he called "artificially arranged scenes." And yet the comparison between the Lumières and Méliès is more complex, a first illustration of a central variable equation in film art. Méliès's imaginative manipulations do also seek to give to the images of magic and myth the sense of reality that a film image can give to everything; the Lumières' unobtrusive representation does carry with it some expressiveness, does invest physical reality with a kind of wonder and awe.

Clearly, though, a difference does exist between the two pioneers; an advance has been made. Though it is more than a matter of subject, the choice of subject is meaningfully related to the approach. Méliès begins with stage magic—in, for example, *Conjuring* and *The Vanishing Lady* (both 1896) and *The Magical Box* (1897); he moves on to narratives of fairy-tale transformations—as in *Cinderella* (1899) and *Red Riding Hood* (1901)—and then to the spectacles of *Faust* (1906) and the *Arabian Nights* (1905), to monsters and devils, to his most complete and successful spectacle of suprareality, *A Trip to the Moon* (1902). In all of these, he has recognized the importance of the movement of the filmstrip itself, beyond the movement of the content of the shot and image. He does more than record movement in space and time. With his camera and printing tricks, he provides the first real examples of the film's ability to surmount space and time, to manipulate physical reality with greater freedom, to control it; to make space and time (and action through them) more fluid and flexible, more changeable and dynamic. He is tinkering here with core elements of the film art; but, focusing on magic, he does not explore to any great extent their technical possibilities or further dramatic significance.

Typical of his partial discoveries was his use, mainly for magical effects, of a kind of pseudo editing—juxtaposing disparate images by stopping and starting the camera. In *The Vanishing Lady*, for example, the camera is stopped while the lady is onstage, started again when she is gone; when the film is projected—in one continuous sequence, uncut—she vanishes in mid-sequence. Again and again Méliès is to use the device, as in *A Trip to the Moon*, when the moon people, the Selenites, vanish, or when an umbrella becomes a mushroom. Often the device is combined with others: In *The Magical Box*, masking part of the camera lens gives the effect of a boy split in half. In numerous films, double exposures produce magical effects. They are often combined with stopping and starting the camera, reducing the lens aperture, or shifting lighting—sometimes to produce dissolves, a simultaneous fading out and fading in.

While many of his dissolves were used to produce magical effects, some (again reaching a peak in *A Trip to the Moon*) were used to link one scene to the next. In this way Méliès found a technique and form for certain advances in dramatic construction, but these narrative developments were as limited as his technical embodiment of them. Earlier, Louis Lumière had actually used a rudimentary dramatic continuity and climax, especially in some brief comedies: In *Watering the Gardener* (*L'Arroseur Arrosé*, 1895), a small boy steps on a hose and stops the flow of water; the gardener, puzzled, looks at the nozzle; when the boy takes his foot off the hose, the gardener is sprayed. Méliès, in turn, was to develop scenes with a dramatic line and was to go on to combine a number of these brief episodes in a sequence: 20 in *Cinderella*, 30 in *A Trip to the Moon*. But still, each scene was composed of a single shot photographed against a single painted backdrop by a stationary camera (with allowance for the effect of stopping and starting, as described above.) In turn, each was a self-contained vignette, with no continuity of action from one shot to another or between shots linked by a dissolve. The material was, on the one hand, theatrical (photographed stage fantasy with camera tricks) and, on the other, dramatically static. But film language was definitely being spoken, if haltingly, and with touches of the kind of humor that would continue to bring some of the greatest pleasures of moviegoing.

ACCELERATION: THE FIRST TWO DECADES

In the many short comedies—European and American—of the first decade and a half of the century, exploitation of the visual pleasures of movement was most markedly accelerated. This was primarily movement within the shot; the short comedies were not particularly distinctive in advancing the manipulation of time, space, and action through the manipulation of the moving reel of film or of the camera. But the movement shown was of great vitality. In the chases, confusions, accidents, encounters, and tumblings, the frenetic action was particularly suited to exploring the uses of objects, large and small, of physical reality in dramatic relationships with human beings. These comic encounters between man and man, and man and thing, also served to increase the emotional involvement of the audiences in the dramatic action.

Feuillade   Much the same emphasis was found in the noncomic but dramatic short films of the period, with a stronger play on sentiment and less physical vehemence. Particularly unusual among these were the moody adventure serials of the French director Louis Feuillade, beginning with the series on *Fantômas* (1913), the evil master of disguises, and climaxing with that on *Judex* (1916–17), the caped fighter for justice. It may well be that only Griffith's films of these years explore and use so fully certain resources of the cinema. While someone like Edwin S. Porter may have explored the realms of editing more extensively, Feuillade's work has a more advanced form of dramatic tension, greater textural density, a fuller amplification of mood. His expressive use of details of setting and his dramatic and emotional use of lighting are rivaled only by certain moments in Griffith. In Feuillade the factuality of the realistic world of objects and settings is made to function in striking juxtaposition with a mysterious and evil world of wonder and fantasy. The result is the first full sense of a director's creation of *mise en scène,* that ambience, part expression and part representation, produced by the lighting and patterning of the objects and settings that surround and immerse the actors.

Porter   Nonetheless, of the pre-Griffith directors it is Edwin Porter—working earlier than Feuillade—who takes the most important first steps and indicates most clearly the possibilities of handling the movements, space, and time of physical reality by manipulating film and camera. However partial, tentative, sporadic, uncumulative his innovations were, they were innovations in both drama and film technique.

While it is most frequently said that Porter's steps led particularly to the establishment of cinematic editing, it is important also to examine the conception of dramatic content to which the new kind of editing was applied. Porter's method was inductive, empirical: Dramatic needs led to editing innovations. In *The Life of an American Fireman* (1902), he obviously wanted to show pictures of material that would excite and thrill his audience, but he arranged this material in a dramatic structure typical of the direct, unsophisticated popular drama of the time. The film had immediate initiation of conflict, development of tension through action, crisis, even a last-minute complication, and final resolution. Compelled by the time limits (five minutes) of a one-reel film to compress his material, he ended by giving the dramatic content truly filmic treatment—condensed, selective, elliptical. No scene is a full, separable set piece, and he needs only seven of them to present his total story line. Even more important, he selects only the briefest materials for each scene, and the arrangement of these selected details also helps build the drama. In the best example of his cinematic selection, Porter establishes that a fire chief has a premonition of a fire, then dissolves to a brief close view of an alarm box in the street, and then to a man using it to turn in an alarm.

Despite this one close view, Porter was not, here or subsequently, to proceed very far with close-ups nor with cutting and change of shot within a scene. Most of his scenes would continue uninterrupted. The last scene of *Fireman,* however, is a notable exception. Though he still calls it one scene in his scenario, Porter dissolves from the exterior of the burning building to the interior and then back again to the exterior. Once he has shifted, he holds longer than Griffith would, not using the full implications of cutting—but a start has been made.

In the slightly longer *The Great Train Robbery* (1904), this particular breakthrough into editing is carried further. Each of the 14 scenes is still kept intact, each an uninterrupted long shot. The scenes are again carefully selected to build the drama with a minimum of footage, but this time the sequence carries itself forward by its own logic: There are no dissolves or titles between scenes. Moreover, at the point of the train robbers' getaway, Porter cuts away from them to action at a telegraph office and then at a dance hall, as the posse is summoned. The synthesis of the two separate lines of action is then made in scene 12. We see the robbers dashing down a hill toward and then past the camera, and then the posse following at the same angle—all shot uninterruptedly from the one camera position. Condensation and selection have here been joined by a primitive parallel editing—with time, space, and action manipulated and surmounted through the freedom of film.

While Porter would continue to use the devices, his own limited awareness of what he had come upon can be illustrated by two subsequent films, *The Ex-Convict* and *The Kleptomaniac* (both 1905). In the former, Porter wants to contrast the life of an ex-convict with that of a rich manufacturer who refuses to give him a job. While the film does show scenes from both lives, it does not capitalize on the possibilities of intense, direct juxtaposition of details from the two sets of scenes. Similarly, in *The Kleptomaniac,* the contrast between rich and poor is kept parallel but separate: first, a sequence of a rich woman caught stealing; then, a sequence of a poor woman arrested for stealing a loaf of bread. The two are brought together only in the third sequence, when they are seen in the same courtroom.

Early Griffith

In this pre–*Birth of a Nation* period, only the short films of D. W. Griffith explored the possibilities of these editing devices with a deepening understanding of their emotional and dramatic expressiveness. There are few extant samples of any Griffith theorizing in print about principles or techniques of his motion pictures. There are only the pictures themselves, about 200 (more than 300 others have been lost), of which roughly 80 percent are the one- and two-reel pictures he made between 1908 and 1914. In these, most frequently with his long-time associate G. W. "Billy" Bitzer as chief cameraman, Griffith hit upon method after method of controlling the materials of the drama and the audience's response to them; he recognized more fully the dramatic purposes to which techniques used sporadically by others might be put.

Although editing techniques may have been his most notable contribution to the forming of a filmic language, there were other discoveries. Among these was the manipulation of light, making lighting more than a utilitarian necessity by treating it as dynamic and dramatic, expressive in its own changeable shades, tones, and combinations, expressive in the ways it could play upon actors and objects, interplay with them. Again, as we have seen in the case of others before Griffith, it was a matter of using an aspect of physical reality to surmount that reality, of turning material into medium, of maintaining it as material and medium at the same time. As early as *A Drunkard's Revenge* (1909), he climaxed the typically bathetic tale of a drunkard's reform with a scene lit by the glow from a fireplace, casting shadows, creating highlights on the actors' faces in a way neither conceived nor risked by anyone before him.

His use of lighting for dramatic expressiveness was integrally connected with his greater concern for and inventiveness in the placement of the camera, its movement during a shot, and the angle of the shot. His concern for camera angle also involved a greater attention to the arrangement of the people and objects within the shot. Quite early, Griffith began to emphasize moving the camera during a shot, panning or tilting while the camera was stationary, or, for greater impact, placing the camera on a moving object. By 1911, his *The Lonedale Operator* revealed numerous placements that changed during the course of a shot—principally placement on a moving train, which Porter had also used, and which became one of the favorite movie-thrill clichés of its time. So successful was the trick, for example, that Griffith retold the same story of the rescue of a girl telegraph operator in *The Girl and Her Trust*, emphasizing even more extensively shots of one moving train by taking them from another moving train.

Less sensational, but much more significant were his experiments in placing the camera to achieve varying distances from and varying emphases on subjects. First, the medium shot, with cutting and moving in to a shot of one actor only, in *For Love of Gold* (1908). And then, in *After Many Years* (1908), an even closer view, a more emphatic, selective, manipulative view—the close-up—of an actress' face (to evoke her feelings as she awaits the return of her husband), inserted with quite positive effect between long shots. Griffith soon extended this breakthrough in cinematic selection of detail to physical objects, making *things*—along with movement, space, time, and light—dynamic, expressive elements in the human world of the film drama. Most frequently, close-ups were the tools for plot development and suspense: in *The Lonedale Operator*, a close-up of the wrench with which the girl is holding the desperadoes at bay and which, to them (and to the audience as the result of an earlier long shot), looks like a gun. But on occasion the surrounding world of things was used for the more sophisticated purpose of making tangible and visible the intangible states of human emotion; in *The Avenging Conscience* (1914), for example, Griffith cuts from close-up to close-up: from a pencil tapping to a clock pendulum swinging to a pair of nervous hands.

This kind of attention to the placement of the camera and the selection of the material within the shot involves a broader discovery: that it is indeed the shot of which the basic alphabet of film language is composed, that film-making consists of analyzing the materials into separate shots and then reconstructing them, editing them into a reconstituted patterning of physical reality. The switching to close-ups and medium shots thus led to breaking up the materials within a single scene. Griffith proceeded even more dramatically, contriving striking effects through contrast editing, the immediate alternation of contrasting scenes or details within scenes: In *A Corner on Wheat* (1909), he cuts from a scene of the wheat king's lavish banquet to a title ("Little thinking of the misery and suffering his so-called genius has induced"). Then to a "still" shot (the actors held still for 12 seconds) of a line of the unemployed, unable to buy bread because of an increase in prices; and then back to the frenetic movement of the banquet. His greatest success —and the hallmark of his developing style—was achieved with parallel editing. In many situations, but especially in his famed last-minute rescue sequences, he controlled and blended space and time in combinations that fully realized for the first time this dramatic potential of the screen. In the climax of *The Lonely Villa* (1909), he alternates between the robbery at the villa and the husband rushing home to the rescue, intercutting between the two in ever shortening intervals, that is, with less footage for each successive segment. Here Griffith does more than show actions occurring simultaneously at two different places. He extracts from time its emotional impact—emphasizing its role in the plot action. He impedes actual time by his cutting, yet accelerates the excitement of time by increasing the tempo of alternation between the two locations. By the time of *The Lonedale Operator*, he was extending his favorite device to the three-way intercutting that he was to employ in his major films.

The subjects and themes of the short films of these years also foreshadowed features that were to be typical of Griffith—especially just before *Birth*—and the period in general: the extremes of sentiment and situation, the conflicts of physical action, the tendency toward spectacle.

This suitability of the screen for spectacle was most widely capitalized on by the last of the contributing elements we might briefly look at: the European films of the second decade of the century, with classical and historical subjects, larger casts, larger sets, and longer playing-times. In France, Sarah Bernhardt appeared in *Queen Elizabeth* (1912), and the screen was full of the panoramic tales of other famous ladies in *Camille, Cleopatra, Gypsy Blood, Theodora.* In 1912 and 1913, the Italian industry brought forth the largest and most successful of the spectacles—*Quo Vadis, Cabiria,* and *The Last Days of Pompeii.* But for all their epic intentions, these films were in the main static and stuffed—mere pageants, stage drama on a vast scale, their exaggerated histrionics unredeemed by visual movement and rhythm, their spectacles unfulfilled in cinematic terms.

EMERGENCE OF A FILM STYLE

It was Griffith who was to bring this tendency toward spectacle, as well as the other newly discovered characteristics of the film, to their first full and unified fruition in a film style. The style that Griffith would forge was one of the most distinctive and personal of his times; his films bore a signature. Yet it was a style that was typical of his times and grew out of the discoveries in film technique that we have been tracing. For an individual artist's style— whether intuitive or conscious, however distinct or even idiosyncratic—bears significant relationships not only to those of his contemporaries but to a pervasive style of the times, the intricate fabric of a culture.

If style in art may be said to be the total, comprehensive manner of expression, it must also be said that it is more than a matter of certain conventions in the use of techniques and materials of a medium. It is also a matter of subjects for the medium, of motifs and concerns, of the intricate relationship of form and content. For true style is not merely formal. It is a way of embodying in form (in the sense of giving body to) a way of seeing life and responding to it. It is a way of using the outward appearances of life to capture and reflect an individual or collective sense of the inner character of life.

Style is a structuring of feeling and idea; the particular structuring developed in a style cannot help but influence ways of seeing and constituting life. It is true of the public, whose ways of seeing and responding are so strongly shaped by the prevalent structurings of art, and it is also true of artists and craftsmen themselves. Although the conventions of a style may arise from a way of seeing, they may in turn restrict and limit, may even distort the kind of felt life that can become the content of that art. In this reciprocal relationship, the opposite problem may also arise: The limitations of a way of seeing and thinking about life can dictate restrictions in the conventions of form and style that develop.

The Esthetic Nature of Film

As we trace this reciprocating encounter between content and form, conception and style, through the history of the film, we must keep in mind, then, that if style is a structure of feeling and idea, the feelings and ideas involved are about the art itself as well as about life. In this first stage of discovery in film art, the style that develops derives from both a response to the life style of the times and a response to, an attitude toward, what was being discovered as the essential characteristics of the film. The true nature of the film was what worked.

The empirical pioneers had been finding what worked. In more theoretical terms, this was the language with which they had been making the film silently speak. The motion picture is a visual medium with movement—movement of materials within the frame, movement of sequences of frames through the camera and projector, movement of the camera itself. With these characteristics, the film can produce accurate representations of physical reality, but it can do more.

It can transcend and manipulate the physical world, reconstituting it for the sake of a greater subjective expressiveness. It can turn light—both raw material and medium—to its own ends, can make it dynamic, suggestive, dramatic. Even more important, it gives man an exciting grasp of—and thus freedom from—space and time. Space itself is made dynamic and dramatic. Space is not only the arena in which movement takes place; it moves, is fragmented and transformed, it disappears and returns. Time, too, loses, on the one hand, its uninterruptible continuity or inevitability and, on the other, its frustrating elusiveness. It can be controlled; it can be stopped, slowed, accelerated, reversed, skipped, repeated, fragmented into simultaneity. And the intricate relationship between space and time becomes itself more graspable, subject to manipulation. In motion pictures, the passage of time is sensed through what is seen of space; whereas space is experienced in terms of the time in which it is allowed to be glimpsed. Similarly, the action that occurs in space and time—the movement within the frame—also becomes subject to manipulation, contributes to a greater expressiveness.

These recognitions about the nature of film coincide with certain contemporary tendencies in philosophic thought, in the physics of Einstein and others, and in other arts. The philosophy of Henri Bergson, for example, is deeply involved with the relationship between the flow and flux of raw life and the mind of man. In stressing the subjective nature of perception, Bergson develops concepts about the intermingling of elements of space and time. In particular, he stresses the kind of subjective simultaneity that exists for us as perceivers, as we seem to experience all of our experience—of space, time, and action—on a single plane; in an important sense, all takes place at the same time. Modernism in literature, in Proust and Joyce, for example, gives stylistic body to these same concepts, as do stylistic developments, such as the Cubism of Picasso and Braque, which transform reality in painting.

In the film, these techniques of transformation developed a paradoxical relationship to the raw materials of physical reality. One term of the paradox is that the film finds in the physical world its natural subject. No other art can so accurately and completely represent so much of the physical world. In fact, the fidelity is so nearly complete that there is debate over the implications of considering the film as *recording*—which implies a thoroughly neutral processing of physical data—or as *representing*—in which there is, however small, some intrusion and transformation. But—the other major term of the paradox—film can be more than a passive processor of the physical world that is its subject. It turns that subject into a formal element of the medium: The racing train so accurately reproduced is also a diagonal element in the composition, the darkness of its cars and smoke a component of the pattern of lighting. It also changes the physical stuff of the world into elements in the dramatic structure of the work. It gives meaning to things, whether environments or objects; it uses them to provoke in the audience a sense of the ideas and emotions of a character or the mood of a situation.

As a result of this paradoxical relationship, two basic tendencies have developed in the making of films. One has been absorbed with techniques that can most fully produce the illusion of reality—techniques and conventions of Realism. The other has attempted to do more than record accurately the data of reality; it has attempted to use those realistic images for other or additional purposes—whether in fantasy or in expressive transformation of that realistic base. Much of the emphasis of this history of film will turn on the varying relationships between the two tendencies.

These early years made it quite clear that in its major strain the film would develop as a dramatic art. Distinct as its form is from that of stage drama, the film is a means of dramatizing, and thus revealing, the conflicts of men in the world. It presents these conflicts with the immediacy, the sense of presentness, the necessary externalization of the inner world into objective forms that are traditional characteristics of the drama. As drama, then, it has a particular and unique relationship with audiences; it develops certain kinds of expectations in the film-maker about an audience, and, in the audience, it generates expectations about such matters as genre, conflict, dramatic structure, character development, and forms and degrees of identification and empathy with characters.

STYLIZATION AND EXPRESSIVENESS

A period of discovery is stimulating, and these were exciting discoveries about an art of great force. The first general film style, the response to this early stage of discovery—however it was influenced by other cultural and personal pressures—was bound to reflect this excitement. This enthusiasm and zeal encouraged an early tendency toward stylization, an emphasis on techniques that would display the full technical resources of the medium, that would produce a heightened expressiveness.

The tendency toward stylization, the style of expressiveness, did not, in most instances, produce an inward-turning art, an art that turned from an open relationship to an audience (as was the case with contemporary forms in the more sophisticated arts such as literature and painting). Rather, at this youthful stage, there was a shared expectation on the part of creators and audiences that the full resources of the medium would be explored; there was a shared enthusiasm that led to forceful manipulation of the less knowledgeable, but eagerly receptive, audience. The expectations of this audience had been shaped by the theatrical style that had dominated the popular stage from the middle of the nineteenth century. Despite the developments in serious stage Realism and Expressionism, the popular drama had continued to develop an increasingly strident theater of sensations, openly titillating its audiences with flamboyant acting, panoramic spectacles and action, mechanical wonders of setting and staging, emotional extremes of melodramatic plot manipulations. The stage had gone as far as it could go in this direction; the movies would go further.

With this seemingly natural, unproblematic connection between the exclamatory tendencies of form and the equally exclamatory conceptions of subject matter, early film stylization did not produce a divorce of form from content. In the major developments, no extreme tilt toward form occurred.

Nor did the stylization generally produce (despite certain important exceptions) a major break with Realism. Rather, there was a tendency toward something *more* than realistic representation, not something other than realistic representation. In this period, the tangible reality of the film image was valued yet taken for granted in the zeal for employing the medium's technical resources. The realistic image was not to be denied or contradicted; it was to be used. The basis for this use had again been established by the popular stage, for it had been regularly, and often incongruously, employing pictorially realistic settings and stagings in the rendering of its exaggerated, escapist romantic conceptions. On the screen, as the realistic image was put to more varied and often more sophisticated use, the early mixture of the tendency toward Realism and the impulse toward expression produced techniques for directorial expressiveness, not, as was the case in the major tendency of the thirties, techniques for releasing content, for letting it reveal itself.

Chief Exponents: Eisenstein and Others	The most extreme position and the most complete and sophisticated theoretical discussion of these early tendencies are found in the writings of Sergei Eisenstein, but similar statements abound in the writings of others. In a valuable final document—still on his desk at his death in 1948—Eisenstein restated the principles he had steadfastly held throughout his long career, which had begun with *Strike* in 1924. He wrote of his long-time effort to go beyond the raw materials of physical reality:

> I wrote about this long ago and practiced it still earlier, always proceeding from only one principle—destruction of the indefinite and neutral existing "in itself," no matter whether it be an event or a phenomenon, and its subsequent reassembly. . . .

His constant position had been "that mastery here means ability to develop each element of the expressive means to the utmost. . . ." Earlier he had insisted, "The essence is in shooting expressively." In this final piece, Eisenstein applies the same principle to mastering and transforming color:

Just as the recreating of a boot had to be separated from the boot before it became an element of expressiveness, so must the notion of "orange color" be separated from the coloring of an orange, in order that color may become part of a system of consciously controlled means of expression and impression.

In many years of theoretical writing, Eisenstein's compatriot V. I. Pudovkin was to echo the same principles. For Pudovkin, film techniques were "means of expression" to give new, significant life to "dead objects." Particularly the tool of technique was "intensification," an increasing, a heightening, a greater expressiveness: Realistic detail is important, not as "a slavish imitation of naturalism," but rather "to augment the potential expressiveness of the film's content."

Even tendencies in the twenties toward a greater Naturalism were colored by expressiveness. In a 1961 interview, when Josef von Sternberg was asked for his essential preoccupation as a *cinéaste,* he replied, "To find the means of expressiveness, to discover its possibilities. What interests me is expressiveness achieved by means of technical investigation." In his definition of style in a letter of 1962, he echoes other terms we have been using:

Generally speaking, all art is an exploration of an unreal world. Style is the inevitable result of imposing control on the elements with which creative work concerns itself. It is not necessarily a confining of form, but it results from a search for abstraction not normally contained in presenting things as they are.

The emphases were similar among early film critics and theoreticians. By the twenties, influential continental critics such as Ricciotto Canudo and Louis Delluc were stressing the expressive values of the visual esthetic (in the Italian term, *visualismo*), accentuated, admittedly, by the absence of sound but rising more importantly from the crucial aspect of the film itself—visual movement. In America, as early as 1917, Kenneth Macgowan was asserting that the promise of the movies as an art consisted in "the creation of expressive atmosphere" through the use of such techniques as lighting, sequence, and the close-up. Extolling the possibilities of the medium in his book *The Art of the Moving Picture* (1915), Vachel Lindsay asserted that its "flashes of lightning" would make the film "the prophet-wizard of our progress, not by slavishly, mechanically imitating reality but by achieving intensity, acceleration, symbolic implications." In a more sophisticated theoretical treatise of the twenties, Hugo Munsterberg also emphasized the screen's potentiality for "overcoming the forms of the outer world, namely space, time, and causality, and adjusting the events to the forms of the inner world. . . ." In *The Photoplay: A Psychological Study,* Munsterberg argued that the director should "sever every possible link" with commonplace reality, for "the highest art may be furthest removed from reality."

Munsterberg went much further than most of the practitioners of the young art in seeking so complete a break with commonplace reality. Most, like Griffith, were content to deal with reality in heightened terms, expressive ways. Most, like Griffith, left little in the way of theoretical documents. With their work, however, they left a stylistic consensus, a particular weighting of the terms of two basic artistic equations—one of technique and content and the other of tendencies toward expressiveness and tendencies toward imitation or representation. As we begin with Griffith and then follow the path of the development of film styles, we will be noting the changing weights, the significance, of the terms of these two equations.

CHAPTER TWO

GRIFFITH
AND
THE
EXPRES-
SIVENESS
OF
EDITING

By the time of the production of *The Birth of a Nation* (1915), Griffith had seen that on film a dramatic situation—whether an intimate scene or a panorama—was most powerfully experienced in a sequence of shots; that the expressiveness of the sequence of shots was a result of selection—of materials in the shot, of distance from them, of the angle from which they were shot, and of lighting and camera movement—and that this expressiveness was also the result of ordering, arrangement, the reconstitution of material through editing.

Changes in the production and distribution system in America allowed Griffith to bring these new approaches to a vast audience. The time was ripe for an American film of feature length, intense dramatic emotion and audience identification, and epic sweep of action and spectacle. For years a group of nine production companies, known as the Motion Picture Patent Company, and their affiliate distribution center, the General Film Company, had not only controlled the American film industry but had steadfastly denied the economic feasibility of longer films. With the eventual breaking of the trust's stranglehold on the industry, the new dynamics of the economic situation opened the way for the feature film. Distributors like Carl Laemmle, whose Independent Motion Picture Company eventually became Universal-International, and William Fox, whose complex organization eventually evolved into Twentieth-Century Fox, also became producers. Adolph Zukor founded Famous-Players, which evolved into Famous-Players-Lasky. Feature Play Company was organized in 1914; Paramount Pictures Corporation, under the control of W. W. Hodkinson, solidified the distribution of the multireel pictures of a number of producers. The new dynamics produced expansion—of studios and production schedules, and the stars to go with them; of investments and costs; of new and larger theaters (some 20,000 by 1916). The feature film would become the lure that would fill the theaters, pay the bills, bring the profits. Even so, there were still those who scoffed at the length (12 reels) and the cost ($125,000) of Griffith's *Birth*, but its impact and financial success were immediate and monumental—despite instances of protest and rioting.

It is hard to assess the role that the film's racial bigotry played in this success, though the subsequent and continuing praise of the film, even by liberal critics, would add credence to the judgment that its primary appeal was the impact of its emotional expressiveness, not its specific thesis. Griffith was concerned with what would make the audience feel, what would move the mass sitting in the darkened theater. This devotion to exaggerated emotionalism as the essence of drama was reflected in his hyperbole of subject, his largeness of scope, his exclamatory use of emphasis in depicting it. His world on film would be a world of intense high points, of irreconcilable poles of emotion.

On one level, his work fused form and content: The expressive extremes of his technique were well suited to the extreme melodrama of the contents. But on a deeper level, the fusion is, finally, a false one. For the two extremes feed on each other, glut each other, until the superior element, the technique, is marred. Or, when unmarred, it must be extricated from the weaknesses of content and viewed arbitrarily and artificially, without the interacting wholeness of the highest levels of art. In a like manner, Griffith's films are concerned with a realistic depiction of detail—even imitating historical photographs down to the smallest physical data. But detail must serve other ends—the heightened expression of emotion or idea—and again there is a lapse, a gap, between one element of the film and the impression of the whole.

INFLUENCES AND RESOURCES

The thesis that shaped *Birth* was a direct, specific expression of Griffith's family background. The film's attack on Reconstruction and Negroes in general, its heroic justification of the rise of the Ku Klux Klan are surely inheritances of his youth in the South. But more than racial or political prejudices were nurtured there. Griffith's father, a doctor, was wounded three times in defense of the romantic ideals of the Old South, his vision of which he never ceased expounding. He declaimed Shakespeare in public with a booming voice (thus his nickname, "Roaring" Jack Griffith). Griffith's sister read aloud to him from the romantic poets. The results were a blend, not untypical, of the hardness of antagonistic prejudice and the softness of idealistic moralism. The insistent caricatures of Blacks in *Birth* were really no different from Griffith's treatment of all his villains, whatever the specific subject. The unblemished purity of the women of the South, the noble heroism of the White men were found in the heroines and heroes of all his films. His was a world without mixtures—of black and white in more ways than one—a world of certitudes absolutely expressed. And with a booming voice. It was the world of nineteenth-century melodrama.

Eisenstein was the first to examine the significant relationship between Griffith and Charles Dickens, although Griffith's references to Dickens to support his own use of parallel editing had appeared earlier. In "Dickens, Griffith, and the Film Today" (still one of the most intricately wrought and persuasively argued pieces ever written on the film art), Eisenstein particularly focuses on the similarity of Griffith's technique—the use of physical detail and close-ups and especially the use of abrupt shifts of scene to build tempo and emotion. Although he remarks in passing on similarities of content, attitude, and world view, he does not penetrate far enough. For what we have in Griffith is the surface of Dickens—that which made him so popular because it touched only the nerve ends of the public—but not the wit or penetration, the insight into complexity, and the emotional depths that underlay the surface simplicities, the types, the sentimentalities of situation and emotion.

What is left is the energetic rendering of the shell: Griffith's cinematic embodiment of sentimental emotionalism; naive, simplistic conflict and tension; and character stereotypes.

Stage Melodrama

These sentimental simplifications and episodic rendering of many scenes had long been a popular staple on the stage. It was this late nineteenth- and early twentieth-century stage melodrama that established the patterns of expectations shared by Griffith and his audiences. The theater of Henry Irving, Scott MacKaye, and David Belasco, among other producers and directors, had imparted to the young film industry the impetus of its own movement toward more and more surface realism—conceived as the presence on the stage of real objects and settings. It had moved toward the rendering of impossible spectacle—locomotives, fires, sawmills, ice floes—and had developed rapid scene-shifting and a flourishing of physical action in fights, chases, and last-minute rescues.

But it had done more. It had provided the film-makers and the audiences who would smoothly make the transition from stage melodrama to film with a pervasive, habitual conception of dramatic oversimplification of character, emotion, conflict, and theme.

Griffith, along with others, was to move beyond this melodrama in terms of the inventiveness, the verve and vitality of tempo with which he rendered the melodrama. He would apply it more seriously and sincerely to grave problems of the world. But even here his themes were more simplistic *theses*, naively applied, without the depth of conception or powers of self-analysis to see the contradiction in following the sensationalized bigotry and prejudice of *Birth* with an equally sensationalized attack on bigotry and prejudice in *Intolerance*. In 1944, in a late and rare statement of his aims, Griffith replied to a question about what makes a good film:

> One that makes the public forget its troubles. Also, a good picture tends to make folks think a little, without letting them suspect that they are being inspired to think. In one respect, nearly all pictures are good in that they show the triumph of good over evil.

Progressivism

This approach to human problems—in terms of clear-cut, absolute distinctions between the forces of light and darkness—was the legacy of melodrama. But it also was a typical popularization of the ideals and attitudes of the Progressive Era in the first decade and a half of the century in America. More than a political movement, Progressivism seemed to capture a national tone: an innocent, optimistic faith in progress and human potential, in the efficacy of change; a moralistic seriousness, a no-nonsense soberness; a mixture of sentimental idealism and gruff, athletic confidence. Theodore Roosevelt was the type writ large. The movies, it was felt, were to be, in Vachel Lindsay's phrase, the prophet-wizard of the new millennium. Lindsay was one among many who stressed the role of the movies in uplifting society. An especially instructive voice of the times was that of Louis Reeves Harrison, an influential spokesman within the industry and the critic for the *Moving Picture World*. With insistent regularity, Harrison repeated his belief that we —especially in America—"seem to be at the dawn of enlightenment" and that it was the film that would hasten that dawn, with "its cultivation of the social muscle," its ability "to affect the manners and habits of the people, to cultivate their taste for the beautiful, to soften harsh temperament by awakening tender sympathy, to correct primitive egotism and avarice, to glimpse history and travel, to nourish and support the best there is in us."

The expressive style of Griffith, and of the period, reflected these attitudes —the innocent enthusiasm of discovery and Progressive meliorism, extreme polarizations and finger-pointing emphasis of melodrama and moral absolutism. Like the histrionics and mannerisms of the acting that has become one of its most bothersome aspects, Griffith's approach was a bold and bald iconography of broad gestures. His parallel editing most fully exemplifies his personal version of this collective style and its relationship to the conglomeration of attitudes—emotionalist, melodramatic, Progressive, reactionary, absolutist—that he brought to his films. Emotionally, it produced the extremes of tension and emotion that he sought, the roaring climaxes of his favorite narrative structures. Technically, it freed the film from the limitations of time and space. But even more important, it intensified the facile, absolute oppositions of his plot conflicts; it became the visual structure for his feelings about a world of totally distinct but directly opposed forces, of irreconcilable poles of good and evil. It is a split world, but clearly, neatly split. For all the rapidity and variety of his parallel editing, it is clearly oriented, sharply demarking, ordering editing. Unlike the rapid editing of today—and its context of relativity and ambiguity—it does not seek to blur, or overlap, or dislocate.

THE BIRTH OF A NATION

In *The Birth of a Nation*, some of the parallel editing produces contrasts in relatively static and undeveloped material, contrasts that give visual expression to the ideological simplifications: A shot of old people at home praying, intercut with shots of trenches piled high with bodies; a shot of the Southern girl Margaret being proposed to by a Northern soldier, followed by a shot of her brothers being killed; then a shot of her refusal.

But the major instances of parallel editing involve the development of dynamic, dramatic action in sequences of shots that manipulate space, time, and movement. In the re-creation of the assassination of Lincoln, a sequence of some 55 shots alternates, with varying tempo and selection, between the stage, the audience, Lincoln in his box, the hallway behind, the balcony, Lincoln's guard, and John Wilkes Booth in the gallery, on the balcony, in the hall, in the box, on the stage.

It is more characteristic for climaxes in Griffith's parallel editing to fuse two or three separate but simultaneous actions. This kind of cross-cutting between actions separated in space had become an integral part of panoramic stage melodrama, even as far back as the plays of Dion Boucicault, such as *Arahna-Pogue* and *The Octoroon* in the 1860s; but stage melodramatists could match neither the extremes of Griffith's manipulations nor his scenic flexibility, selectivity of focus, intensity of climax. In Griffith's work, the triadic pattern was strikingly recurrent at peak moments. The pattern is revealing: the two antagonistic forces of the world in combat over natural innocence, over the very soul of the world. Within the three-way pattern, there are often further embellishments. In the evil Gus's chase of Flora through the woods (in *Birth*) and the attempt of Ben to save her (this time with an untypical lack of success), there is not only cutting between the three but an effective alternation of long shots and close shots of Flora's frantic, wild course. In other cases, the three-way tension is achieved by cutting between an innocent one and a force of evil who are in one place, and then between them and the force of good at another place.

In the climactic double rescue in the same work, Griffith first alternates shots within two similar but separate situations, then fuses them for the climactic three-way pattern. First, at the mansion of the villainous mulatto leader, Lynch, the threat of his forced marriage to the good, sweet, and white Elsie is intercut with shots of the Klan gathering. After about 65 shots, we switch to the good Camerons besieged in a cabin by wild, evil Negro militia, again intercut with the gathering of the Klan, their number swelling. In the third part of the sequence, we alternate between all three places—the mansion, cabin, and Klan—as the Klan achieves the rescues and rides through the streets of the town. In the latter stages, time is markedly impeded and suspense built by delays at the points of rescue and by the breakup of the action into close shots of many component details, while tempo is accelerated by the increasing brevity of shots and rapidity of alternation between the three points of focus.

This intensification and expressive heightening of reality are effected by other means as well. The film has a visual richness, a purely visual excitement, as much from the number and variety of devices as from their individual effectiveness. It is a film more of devices and of movement—within shots, by camera, or between shots—than of perfection of composition of shots. Even in the climax just discussed, the composition of the shots of the Klan bursting upon the militia in the streets is not the equal of the momentum achieved by the editing. Among the many other devices of shooting, printing, or editing, noteworthy is Griffith's selective editing—the breakup of a scene into separate shots of varying content, angle, and distance from the subject. As a result, the film has some 1,375 shots, as compared to less than 100 in most comparable European spectacles. Yet this breakup of the scene into shots does not produce fragmentation or refraction; it is ordered so as to build the clear-cut emotional and ideological conflicts and support the insistent points of emphasis within the scene.

This emphasis is most often achieved through Griffith's important develop-

The Birth of a Nation

ment of the expressiveness of the close-up. Again, these close-ups confirm; they do not dislocate or fragment. They vary widely in the sophistication of what they sought to express and how they expressed it, being typically less sophisticated when they were most strongly icons of good and evil. A tight close-up of the gun in the hand of John Wilkes Booth is illustrative of the baldness of some of the emphases, while a wonderful, sudden bust shot of a Confederate soldier, in the midst of longer shots of a battle, emphasizes in much more sophisticated form the passion and fury of the battle. Shot from behind a cannon, the nose of the cannon projecting into the frame, he is captured, with a yell on his face, in the act of thrusting a Confederate flag into the Union cannon's mouth. For expression, physical objects are treated symbolically, again with varying sophistication: a close shot of parched corn in the South; the hands of the good "Little Colonel" caressing a bird; an ecstatic Elsie embracing a bedpost.

INTOLERANCE

For Griffith, a thematic connection and continuity existed between this tale of unjust travail imposed on the South by the North (as well as the unjust attacks made on him by some after the release of the film) and his next film, *Intolerance*, released in August 1916. For in the latter he would portray the more universal basis of his position—a protest against intolerance and injustice, a cry for love and justice—and he would portray this by interweaving four separate plots in which the good people are beset and, in three of the four cases, destroyed by the evil, intolerant ones. The flaws in his conception of the connection between the two films or in his working out of the universalized thesis in *Intolerance* are revealing but in one important sense irrelevant. For, to clear away reams of forced high seriousness offered by critics and historians, there are probably few who have ever responded deeply to this film in terms of the kind of metaphoric arc of meaning between immediate detail and theme through which significance rises from a work of art.

It is a film of paradoxes—beyond those ironies intended by Griffith. Its grandiose conception weighs it down. Its thesis is too broad and vague. Its four plots don't clearly develop the thesis in a consistent manner: In the modern plot, the most extended of the four, the term "intolerance" might apply to the actions of the lady do-gooders but not to the bosses who mistreat workers, the police who shoot the workers down, the criminal who misuses the girl and boy, the boy who, through bad luck and sheer stupidity, twice gets caught holding a gun, the court that stupidly sentences him to death for murder, or the ludicrous coincidences of the murder itself. Its sheer flood of detail gets in the way of even maintaining a response to the plots as plot, especially when so many of the plot details are bathetic, banal, oversimplified. Yet this very grandiosity gives the technique its challenge, gives Griffith the opportunity to carry it out with a plastic vitality, a flow of movement, an audacious inventiveness that, especially in the last third of the movie, is, for all of its artificiality, awesome.

The key is again parallel editing—on a monumental scale. The basic structure embodies Griffith's intuition of the space-and-time fluidity of film technique. Throughout, he juggles all four plots simultaneously, intercutting from one to the other. Through roughly two-thirds of the film, the segments devoted to each plot are several minutes long, although there are some exceptions, and there is some parallel intercutting during a segment between actions that occur within that plot. As the climaxes of the four plots approach, he begins to cut more rapidly from one plot to another. But in three of the four he also begins to use more intercutting *within* the plot, creating his characteristic three-way, chase-and-rescue pattern. (From the fourth plot —Christ moving to his crucifixion—relatively few shots appear.) Thus, in the last third of the movie, the three-way structures *within* each of the three plots are in turn part of what is basically a three-way structure *among* the three plots. The result is an intricate interleafing, as an element in one plot is juxtaposed against a similar element in another: Evil ones in Plot A gather, evil ones in Plot B gather; good guys in Plot B wait, good guys in Plot C wait.

In the contemporary episode there is actually a double chase as well, or a chase in two movements. In the first movement, the boy is being readied for execution by hanging, while the girl speeds in a racing car to catch the

Intolerance

governor, who is seen on a speeding train. Griffith cuts back and forth among these three elements, and then he cuts to a parallel three-cornered situation in the French Huguenot plot. Here the girl and her family are inside their house, the besieging army in the streets, her lover racing across the city to save her. Again, Griffith cuts back and forth among the three elements and then cuts to a parallel three-cornered situation in the Babylonian plot. Here, the Babylonians are celebrating a previous victory, while the evil hordes move on the city and a young servant girl races in a chariot to warn the Babylonians. Again, the three-way cutting, and then back to the three elements of the contemporary plot.

At the successful climax of the first movement of the contemporary rescue —the stopping of the train—Griffith achieves his most striking juxtaposition of shots. Without the intervening title that he often uses in his transitions between the plots, he cuts from a shot of the girl's happy success to a shot of the Huguenot girl being stabbed by her tormentor. From this point on, the continuing suspense of the race back to save the boy (and intercutting between the two points) is interleaved with the tragic final stages of the two other plots. With reversed contrast, the last shots of the defeated Babylonians are followed by the successful last-minute rescue of the boy. By this point the acceleration produces a flurry of images, with shots of shorter and shorter duration within each sequence and a resultant acceleration of alternation between sequences. By fragmenting space and action into component details, this acceleration produces a corollary sense of impeding time as well.

The virtuosity and excitement of this sustained crescendo of editing burst the bindings of ideological and esthetic conception; still, the basic stylistic structure underlies them. For all the visual fireworks, the images still build the conventional rhythm of emotion and linear progression of the dualistic narrative. In *Intolerance,* however, Griffith does use contrast editing with a sharper, ironic sense of counterpoint. The ironic reversals reinforce the clear-cut oppositions, rather than undercutting with any skeptical ambiguity: for example, between plots, the trial of the boy and the trial of Christ; within a plot, the workers visited by the "Vestal Virgins of Reform" to save their souls and (in the next scene) the workers denied work and shot down by the militia. Immediate visual juxtapositions reinforce the situational irony: the lavish home of the boss and the plain room of "The Dear One"; "Babylon's greatest noble" served wine with great pomp at the feast and "The Mountain Girl" milking a goat in a poor section of Babylon to get a drink for herself.

The selection of close-ups is one last indication of the mixed nature of the film's multitude of effects. A sudden cut to the eyes of one actress, another to the lower part of an actress' face, a shot in the shadows of the face of Mae Marsh ("The Little Dear One") as she returns to her child and darkened room after the trial, the brief shot of her stoic face at the verdict—these are in sharp contrast to the many facial close-ups of banal, exaggerated expressions. The shot of Mae Marsh in the courtroom is immediately followed by the famous close-up of her hands, twisting together, gripping tightly in anguish—the two shots together expressing her character, her state of mind and heart. But it should not be forgotten that the selective nuance of these two close-ups had been preceded by dozens of other shots of her face and hands, intercut with shots of the boy, as she encourages him during the trial, twisting her handkerchief, biting the end of it, blinking her eyes, essaying a flickering smile again and again and again. In Griffith's world of Armageddon, even the quiet nuance is shaped into the hyperbole of the booming voice.

REPETITION AND DECLINE

Somehow, in the film's excessiveness lay its wonder, and its weakness. The same might be said of its creator. And so it might be understood, to some degree, how and why, with *Intolerance,* Griffith had already reached his high point. The exuberance of technical discovery and a deep sincerity had more than kept a balance with the limitations of his conceptions. But now his advances in technique were haltered by the limitations of the uses to which he would put them. Even the style of his subsequent films seemed to collaborate with the reductive conceptions, restricting the kinds and degrees of felt life that could become the content of the work. The harsher Naturalism of a film like *Isn't Life Wonderful* (1924) showed some traces of wrestling free, and even within the hardening pattern there were major exceptions; but in the main, exciting extremes gave way to repetitious exaggerations, or even to surprisingly dull, awkward, seemingly careless compositions and patterns of editing. Among the numerous subsequent films Griffith directed, several might be mentioned to indicate some of the higher and some of the significant points in the pattern of decline.

The basic content was the same: the dear, pure hearts of the world beset by the forces of evil, whatever their particular name or uniform. In some, the personal tales were again interwoven with historical spectacle of some sort, but never again with the lavishness of *Intolerance.* In *Hearts of the World* (1918), the expected villains are the Huns, the contrast editing juxtaposes German atrocities and pure sweetness, German debauchery and the death of a French mother; the climactic rescue is made by French, English, and American soldiers. In *Orphans of the Storm* (1921), it is the French Revolution (with allusions to the evils of the Russian Revolution), using many repetitions of technique, some quite striking. *America* (1924) transfers the entire pattern to the American Revolution.

The same need to repeat what had worked produced similar reapplications of these techniques even to movies of smaller dramatic scope, including two of the best, *Broken Blossoms* (1919) and *Way Down East* (1920). In *Way Down East,* the obligatory rescue of the harassed dear one is from an ice floe drifting toward a waterfall; for all its repetitiousness, it has a fine sense of movement within shots and between them. In *Broken Blossoms,* the parallel-edited rescue attempt fails; moreover, not only does the innocent girl die, but there is a further turn to the pattern: The Chinese lover, Cheng Huan, kills her brute of a father and then himself.

More than the ending was powerful and distinct. There was something in the situation of the harassed waif, sheltered and loved by a kind Chinese storekeeper (only to have her father crush the blossom of the dream), that reignited a creative sincerity in Griffith, that overbalanced the bathos and sentimentality. The stylized acting is probably the best consort performance in a Griffith film. Richard Barthelmess made excellent use of his slender body—arching, poised, head tilted, tense but tender—and a sweetness of face captured in numerous close-ups. The franticness of Lillian Gish's sweetness oppressed is climaxed by an amazing scene in which (photographed partly from above) she spins wildly around and around in a tiny closet while her father smashes the door with an ax, and the lover rushes, too late, to save her. Donald Crisp's brute is tremendously physical, constantly on the move; even a shot of his angry face is given a sense of physical energy as Griffith cuts from a close-up to a tighter close-up to an extremely tight close-up.

Although Crisp's boxer-father is still too capitalized a brute, and other characters, too, suffer from stereotyping, the work as a whole has a sincere simplicity and a tangible, intimate tenderness that give a special grace to the metaphor of Griffith's favored dramatic pattern—the triadic battle. The three-way struggle in this film, however, is not confined to the climactic chase but is manifest in the basic structure: the gentle heart and the violent brute battling over the natural, unformed innocence of the world. But this time the final progressive affirmation is denied; and so is the usual pat smoothing and flattening of the figures of goodness. Barthelmess's Chinese storekeeper is bent and saddened by the corrupting effects on the Oriental of life in the West; Gish's natural impishness is inhibited, erratic, fearful. Thus, this typical variation on the triadic pattern has a much more than usual impact. The first section sets up the oppression of both good hearts; the second, the

Broken Blossoms

temporary and chaste idyll of love, is given a poignant density by its sense of an opening and blossoming of emotion, a more dynamic modulation within characters than Griffith normally captured; the third violates and destroys the sanctuary.

In the second section, Griffith uses parallel cuts between Cheng Huan's room and the boxing ring to build a distinctive contrast in atmospheric lighting and decor, rather than to create tension or excitement. This use of lighting is part of a basic technical shift in the film: Griffith often lets mood and action build on their own time within a scene, holding many scenes and shots longer than was usual for him. There is still much of the usual exclamatory editing and the iconographic pointing of close-ups, but there is more emphasis on manipulating mood through the use of elaborate details of decor, tinting of the film stock according to setting, softly blurred focus, and most of all, through heavily orchestrated patterns of black and white, shadow and light. It is all too much, but it has its own organic texture. It is Griffith's consummate evocation of naive, maudlin sentimentality; hyperbole still, but strangely muted in the midst of its excesses. It might have led Griffith into new textures for capturing the feel of the fragility of purity and love in the world, but he was unable to build on that precarious edge of muted hyperbole or go beyond it. He could, it seems, only go backward. He had struck a form adequate to his limited vision, but once the spark of discovery waned, there was something reductive and deadening in the locked-in interplay of the two.

It has often been said that the later neglect of Griffith was the first of many cynical and unwarranted Hollywood rejections; true as this may be, he was also a man who had lost his time and his touch. His insistently, even frantically, repeated structures of feeling were no longer his audience's; in a way they were no longer even his own.

CHAPTER THREE

THE
RUSSIANS
AND
EPIC
MONTAGE

Griffith's combinations of form and content had developed into one form of the epic style—one of the major tendencies of cinematic expressiveness in the period of silent films. "Epic," however, must be understood in more than its popular sense of a spectacle with a lot of scenery, actors, and action.

THE EPIC

Sweep and scope, to be sure, are common ingredients in the traditional, more serious usage of epic—whether Homeric or Brechtian—for traditionally, epic suggests a form in which narrative incident is stressed, and especially narrative with panoramic scope and diversity of setting, time, and action. But mere quantity of surface spectacle is only one ingredient; it is intention that shapes the serious epic. There is in the serious epic a raising, an elevating, an enlarging of the materials to the level of epitome—whether ideal, sentimental, or evil. There is a tendency toward the ceremonial, a celebration or exaltation of the characters as human beings or as representatives of a nation's history or social system, or as representatives of certain ideas, principles, or emotional states. Thus, in epic narrative we tend to encounter types, figures larger than life, heroic. But for all the heightening and intensifying as a means of expressing something beyond the verisimilitude of the dramatic materials themselves, there is, as we have seen in Griffith, a base of realistic phenomena, objectively rendered, without the subjective distortions of other expressive styles like Surrealism or Expressionism.

While this expressive intensification is most commonly associated with grandeur of sweep and of scope of action, there is also the possibility, in a phrase of Eisenstein, "to exalt the pathos of everyday existence." Those of Griffith's films that are on a smaller dramatic scale can be seen as attempts to invest his sentimental types with a kind of intimate epic grandeur, but most frequently the attempt rings hollow because of the emptiness, or at least insufficiency, of the conception and content.

America
and
the
Continent:
The
Spectaculars

In the decade following Griffith's first successes, it was the hollow ring and slick surface of spectacle that predominated, that turned the possibilities of an epic style into an entertainment genre. In America there were the spectaculars of Rex Ingram (much in Griffith's debt) and Thomas Ince, the sex and bible fantasies that were to be the trademark of Cecil B. De Mille for decades, MGM's spectacle of twenties' spectacles, *Ben Hur*, directed by Fred Niblo. In Italy producers continued, rather vainly, to resurrect their past glories. In France Abel Gance gave this cinema giantism its most artful rendering and its most exciting visual flair with his *Napoleon*, complete with a curving screen on which three images could be projected simultaneously. It was with this kind of titillation that cinematic expressiveness best seemed to fit the mood of the twenties in most countries.

31

Soviet
Russia:
Revolutionary
Theater

But not in Soviet Russia. Here the expressiveness of the film was seen as the ultimate instrument in serious revolutionary theater. In 1919 Lenin had proclaimed, "Of all the arts the most important for us in my opinion is the film," and, with the nationalization of the Soviet cinema, an intense examination of the esthetic, psychological, and sociological possibilities of the film had begun.

The early Soviet film-makers were fascinated by the ways in which the film's reproduction of the surfaces of reality could be manipulated to penetrate to the meaning and dialectical patterns beneath. Many were particularly concerned with applying this approach to the raw events of actuality rather than to fictionalized drama. Even the early re-creations and dramatized social analyses of Eisenstein can be seen as a rather special version of documentary.

Lev Kuleshov was the earliest theorist on the direct manipulation of actuality through reconstitution in film form, but the most fervent and prolific was Dzhiga Vertov. Beginning in 1919, Vertov announced his theories of the scientific, objective method of capturing real life on film. This "objectivity" precluded fictionalized drama but not manipulation. The point was not to copy what the eye could do but to use the machine to go beyond what the eye could do in organizing the meaning of reality. Vertov wanted, he said, a "candid camera" to catch people in full actuality. "But," he also insisted, "it is not enough to show bits of truth on the screen, separate frames of truth. These frames must be thematically organized so that the whole is also truth." The organization would come through editing, particularly, as in Eisenstein, through juxtapositions—montage—that revealed the dialectical connections. Vertov and his group, working with freshly shot film and with compilations of previously shot film, expanded their influence throughout the twenties, making more and more longer films even into the sound period, at which time highly experimental montages of sound elements were joined to the process. In his later films, Vertov moved beyond the rapid-fire rhythms of his earlier works to more flexible patterns. In *Three Songs of Lenin* (1934), he reached an emotional lyricism that gives a new grace to the didacticism of the work. Designed to show the benefits to the women of Uzbekistan of Lenin's teaching, the film combines individualized footage on the women with documentary material on the advances made, blending the visuals with a sound track of both poetic commentary and everyday voices and songs of the area.

As Griffith's conception of film form and content had been influenced by cultural context, so was that of the Russians, but with more deliberate consciousness, more intellectual analysis. Content and purpose were to be shaped by Marxist ideology, but so too were approaches to film technique. The Soviet epic film was to be a film of collective life, collective actions, collective values—whether in times of crisis or in times of everyday existence, whether with the submersion of individual characters in the mass (as in Eisenstein's early films) or with a focus on individual characters as representative of the mass (as in Pudovkin and Dovzhenko). It was to be film that would express the ideals of a society, the emotional climate of a society—express them and shape them. It would deal with physical reality, would accurately and objectively render it, but would imbue it with meaning in terms of the principles of historical materialism. It would not be a handmaiden to reality but would—by a thoroughgoing exploitation of film's ability to control and reconstitute space, time, and action—manipulate it into meaning, and so manipulate the response of the audience. To achieve this, the Russians emphasized montage, a rapid succession of related shots, as the core of film art.

EISENSTEIN: MONTAGE AND DIALECTICAL MATERIALISM

It was Eisenstein who was to apply the principles of dialectical materialism—thesis, antithesis, synthesis—most rigorously to the techniques of editing. Yet even here, with this heavy application of intellectual analysis, it is interesting to note that, by all accounts, the editing style that evolved matched his personality and temperament—vigorous, energetic, forceful, even aggressive. However important the other aspects of film-making, for Eisenstein, at this stage of his career, editing was the "dynamic principle" that fused and fulfilled the rest. "Each montage piece," he emphasized, "is not something unrelated, but becomes a particular representation of the general theme." In turn, "the interconnection of elements [is] dictated by the film-maker's attitude to the phenomenon, which, in its turn, is determined by his outlook." Because Eisenstein's own outlook was based on the principles of dialectical conflict, he saw the film as the prime artistic means of capturing those "moments of culmination and substantiation that are in the canon of all dialectical processes." He asked:

> By what, then, is montage characterized and consequently its cell—the shot?
> By collision. By the conflict of two pieces in opposition to each other. By conflict. By collision.

His first four films especially (more than his later sound-films) embodied these principles most emphatically. He gave form to moments of historical conflict by juxtaposing images in relationships that would produce a synthesis, a significance beyond the individual parts. In turn, these would be built into larger blocks of conflict and synthesis of didactic meaning. With this approach—in which all elements "become part of a system of consciously controlled means of expression and impression"—the aggressive manipulation of material supersedes the full development of credible dramatic scenes. The plastic, physical properties of the images become the didactic tools.

Even in the best work of Eisenstein, we find naive oversimplification of dramatic materials for the sake of the iconography, the symbolic dialectic of the images, and an excessive repetition and proliferation of the plastic, visual materials themselves. For example, in the first section of *Potemkin* (1925), Eisenstein focuses on the bad food aboard the battleship as the symbol of the devolving historical conflict, culminating in the breaking of a dinner plate. But there is not enough dramatic development; rather, an ornamental shorthand of juxtapositions—sailors, meat, maggots, officers, cook, bread, plates—is repeated excessively in hundreds of shots, carefully varied yet overinsistent. In contrast, the very opening produces its symbolic collision in just five shots, alternating images of waves crashing on a jetty and flaring up and waves (from an opposite direction) crashing into and through rocks on the shore.

Eisenstein's editing—the juxtaposition of colliding images to produce meaningful relationships—incorporates as well other carefully considered elements of his style. For example, these early films are especially characterized by constant agitated movement—not only in the manipulation of time and space in sequences of shots but by action within the shots as well. This double movement is carefully controlled to produce a rhythmic tempo to match and support the point of didactic development. Individual images in Eisenstein, despite his declared emphasis on editing, are composed with great care and tend toward ornamentation and proliferation of detail. With the collaboration of his cameraman Eduard Tisse and his long-time assistant Grigory Alexandrov, Eisenstein goes far beyond Griffith in the telling selection of details to be included in the shot, in the lighting, angle, and distance of the shots, and in the esthetic and dramatic balancing of forms, masses, and movements. These compositions frequently are intended as metaphor, with varying kinds of symbolic vehicles of expression—for example, the direct contextual detail of the meat or plate to indicate the evils; the more oblique reference of the waves to forecast conflict; the emotional imprint of form or movement, such as sailors rushing to the right, sailors rushing to the left to embody rising revolutionary consciousness. All these individual compositions and montage sequences are further incorporated into overall structures of intellectualized precision.

While Eisenstein was not concerned with realistic imitation for its own sake, he was even more strongly opposed to the kind of subjective distortions and expression of inner states of consciousness sought by stage and film Expressionists. He was clearly influenced by the nonrealistic theatrical devices of the Russian director Meyerhold, of France's gory Grand Guignol, of the Japanese Kabuki. But like Bertolt Brecht, in his conception of a didactic epic theater, Eisenstein employed the various devices of expressive exaggeration and manipulation for depiction of an objective historical reality. He was not concerned with inner consciousness, but with the character type, the representative figure within the collective whole. "The theory of the type," he noted, "is the tendency of our time," the means of depicting its social truths.

Strike
and
Potemkin

The first filmic test of his theories was *Strike*, released in Russia in 1924 but not distributed elsewhere. The film is typical of the kind of Agitprop drama that was to become even more prominent in the thirties: A worker is unjustly persecuted, his fellow workers finally unite in protest, the bosses send the police to break up the demonstration violently. In it Eisenstein begins his own development of the editing experiments of Kuleshov and the creative documentaries of Vertov. He constructs a system of character types to represent various forces within the society, raises an individual case to the level of collective action and significance, and particularly in the last sequence of the film, reveals the imaginative vigor of his editing style. In this depiction of the slaughter of the workers, he not only breaks up the materials

Strike

into telling details but alternates these details with the slaughter of a bull. Thus, at the very end we see quickly in sequence the bull's skin being stripped off, 1,500 bodies lying at the foot of a cliff, two skinned bulls' heads, a hand lying in a pool of blood, a huge close-up of the eye of the dead bull.

Jarring images of slaughter, to evoke in microcosm the evils of a society, become the amazing climax of *Potemkin,* his next film; this juxtaposition of indirect metaphor he will employ elsewhere. In *Potemkin* the climactic attack on the Odessa Steps is part of a carefully modulated structure of dialectical tensions and resolutions consisting of five major sections, each of which provides a set of variations on the central theme of oppression conquered through brotherhood and action while contributing to a cumulative climax and resolution. The five parts are composed of juxtaposed moods and tensions: (1) oppression and nonviolent conflict, with a final gesture of breaking the plate; (2) physical violence and triumph on the ship, but death; (3) mourning, but building to affirmation and resolve and unity; (4) peak of violent oppression, but awakening of resolve; and (5) fear of attack by the fleet, the fear dispelled, and final unity. Thus, each part has a similar internal pattern—a building of tensions followed (after a carefully chosen moment Eisenstein called the "caesura") by the exploding of the tension.

In Parts 3 and 4 the pattern is developed with the greatest complexity. In Part 3 the slow mourning of the crowd on the jetty builds to exhortations to rebellion, countered briefly by a reactionary; he is overwhelmed, and the scene continues to intercuts of unified resolve on the ship and ashore. In Part 4, for many the high point of Eisenstein's virtuosity, the dialectical progression is intensified. In the first third of the sequence, he continues to intercut between the joyful sailors on the *Potemkin* and the crowd on the shore: the thesis. But "Suddenly" (as used in a title) a third element is added—the Cossacks appear at the top of the steps on which the crowd is thronged: the antithesis. The Cossack attack on the crowd forms the major sequence of Part 4; but at the climax of the devastation of the attack, there is a turn to the synthesis: Further revolutionary action is produced as the sailors on the *Potemkin* fire the big guns at the theater, which is the headquarters of the Cossacks. In the last shot of Part 4, the theater is destroyed.

In the Cossack attack sequence itself, the principles of the style—montage as collision—are displayed in the intercutting. Within the basic pattern of conflict—Cossacks moving down the stairs against the people—a number of further variations are played: the frenzied rush of the masses and the slow, ordered violence of the Cossacks; individuals shot and falling intercut over and over with the downward rush of the fleeing mass of people; a lone mother intercut going upward against the downward rush of the masses; the mother bearing her child upward against the descending line of troops; the mother upward, the troops downward through the static residue of dead bodies; Cossacks on horseback charging the crowd at the bottom of the steps, people fleeing back up, the foot soldiers relentlessly coming down, individuals fall-

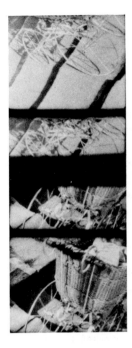

Potemkin

ing, the lone mother going upward, a baby carriage inexorably rolling past still, dead bodies. All these are in powerful intermixtures of long shots, medium shots, close-ups, with many repetitions of similar shots as motifs. They accelerate in tempo, with the decreasing duration of individual shots and the subsequent sense of the elongation of time that results when actions are broken into component parts. Everything culminates in the final microcosmic collision: a Cossack swinging his sword, an elderly woman in pincenez glasses, in extreme close-up, gushing with blood from the blow of the sword. At this close-up, Eisenstein cuts to the third dialectical phase (synthesis) with a medium close-up of the guns of the battleship.

Ten Days That Shook the World For all its inventiveness and power, this kind of montage of collision still rises from an analysis and reassembly of the component parts of literal action in space and time, if—as in Griffith—at more than one space and time. In *Ten Days That Shook the World* (1928; originally known as *October*), the technique of juxtaposition of shots to create a new synthesis was to get a more complex basis: the juxtaposing of disparate images, as in the earlier intercutting between the two literally unrelated slaughters (see above) in *Strike,* but with far greater variation, subtlety, obliqueness of reference, and downright excessiveness.

Ten Days is a paradoxical film. It has less overall unity, less purity through condensation to lucid epitome, more of the clutter of newsreel documentary. Part of this sense of a welter of not-quite-controlled materials results from the nature of the material—the quantity of details of the events that brought the Soviets to power that are crammed into the film. Part of it results from political interference that caused much reediting—most egregiously, the elimination of Trotsky from the history of the October Revolution. But part of it results from the very attempt at a newer, more complex form, with some consequent discrepancy between part and part, part and whole, approach and material. Still, the discrepancies should not be exaggerated; it is a volcano of astounding visual effects, a grandiose experiment in ideological persuasion.

In it Eisenstein seeks to go beyond the control of emotions that manipulation of time, space, and action can produce; he seeks to control "the whole thought process." Through intellectual associations created by the juxtaposition of images, he seeks to produce the same kind of overpowering "dynamization" (his own key term) that could be achieved by juxtapositions from within the context of actions. The results are not unlike the kind of association bridges built by James Joyce in his innovative works or the dense patterns of comparison and allusion in modernist poetry like T. S. Eliot's *The Waste Land.*

The film, then, goes even further than *Potemkin* in superseding the reality it deals with, using the form of images to produce cinematic effects that go beyond the physical reality reproduced by the image. It should be stressed, however, that much of *Ten Days* does continue in the same vein as *Potemkin*, reassembling the components of literal action. The most important example of this literal reassembly technique is the montage in which the attacking police cut off the demonstrating workers from their homes by raising a drawbridge. The shots of the police assaulting the workers are not only intercut among themselves, but tension is tightened by cutting rapidly and before individual movements are complete. These shots are, in turn, intercut with shots of a dead girl and a horse and cart at the apex of the bridge. Both finally fall as the bridge opens but not before dozens of different and repeated shots of them, in hectic juxtaposition with the other actions, explode the moment, then recompose and expand it, finally bringing it to an intense focus of emotion and significance: the essence of what the action, the opening of the drawbridge, feels like and means. In this way the individual part becomes a synecdoche, a basic poetic device in which a part stands for the whole—in this case, rising from the development of a full dramatic situation.

Throughout *Ten Days*, Eisenstein also uses the device of single shots that are to sum up major actions not actually developed in detail: Rifles wave in the air—the army goes over to the Bolsheviks; officials click their telephones in vain frustration—the Kerensky government has lost control.

In addition, strictly formal elements are raised to the level of intellectual and emotional association: To show the dead waste of the czarist regime, he uses a series of "stills," static shots of lavish architectural ornamentation, taken from low, distorting angles; in a different context, a low-angle shot of people hauling a cannon into position makes the enormous difficulty of their task more striking.

In some cases, these "stills" are a component of the film's most daring innovation, the juxtaposition of shots from outside the dramatic context to produce an intellectual allusion that comments on the material within the dramatic context—basically a simile. For example, a sequence of static shots of various religious symbols and statuary is used to discredit the religious tradition. These "allusion" shots of course also contain movement: harps and balalaikas being played, intercut with treacherous Menshevik harangues. (Eisenstein later felt that this was too oblique; on the other hand, he felt that the juxtaposition of spinning bicycle wheels with shots of the motorcycle battalion joining the Bolsheviks was intrinsic to the situation and did capture the exhilaration of the moment.)

The most extended sequence (263 shots) of these brief allusion shots occurs in the satiric depiction of the weakness of Kerensky and the moment of his downfall. A toy peacock is brought to life to imitate the strutting Kerensky. Similarly, a destroyed statue of the Czar is recomposed. A sequence of shots from ever greater distances dwarfs Kerensky in a large, ornate room. A decanter he uses has a top shaped like a crown; this is intercut with a factory whistle screaming steam. Church spires are tilted and inverted, in alternations with the religious effigies mentioned above. A series of 15 shots—of Kornilov (an antirevolutionary general), Kerensky, busts of Napoleon, and grotesque religious effigies—merge associations for them all. Finally, Kornilov, on his horse, moves his troops; a revolutionary tank hurls forward over a ditch; Kerensky throws himself on the Czarina's bed; the bust of Napoleon lies shattered on the ground.

One of the chief problems in the film is this attempt to treat simplistic ideas with complicated and elaborate devices. (Jumping far ahead, one might find the same kind of excessiveness in the later polemical films of Godard.) As a result, the devices, the plastic properties of the film images, seem too much apart—despite Eisenstein's intention—from the literal historical data and their interpretation.

Old and New In some ways, Eisenstein's final film of this silent period, *Old and New* (1929; also called *The General Line*), can be seen as an attempt to reduce that gap, although it also marks an attempt to develop an even more subtle form of montage—the montage of overtones. It is not that the content of the film is more complex—it is a celebration, without complication or ambiguity, of the collectivization of farming—but while the beauty and subtlety of its techniques still overbalance its ideology and dramatic material, they are nevertheless more in harmony with them. One can respond at several levels to the film as a paean of praise, not only to a system but to a people. Possibly this last distinction has a good deal to do with the difference between it and *Ten Days*.

While still bound to the data of actuality, Eisenstein is here free to choose and invent details for the actual incidents filmed. He focuses on several representative personal conflicts—peasant versus kulak farm-owner, atheist versus religious enthusiast—and principally on the attempts of a peasant woman, Marya Lapkina, to get the people to accept and work for the New. But the plot details are the least important element. More important is the creative general mood and desire of a people, in a series of lyrical songs or movements that nonetheless do build a cumulative whole.

Eisenstein wanted to turn from the peak crises of revolt "to exalt the pathos [in an older sense of deep emotion and spirit] of everyday existence" by "rendering down its deep meaning to the essential forms through which it is manifested." This involved not only the selection of essential epitomes but also the "aesthetic character of the presentation." Old and New is still esthetic and intellectual; its means, however, rise totally from within the literal dramatic context.

Eisenstein hoped that the images would produce unconscious, or subliminal, responses even while the spectator was following their literal import. This was part of his developing theory of visual overtones, a further gradation of subtlety in montage. It is a complex and elusive theory, neither thoroughly clear nor convincing. In the main, it seeks to foster and control "the collateral vibrations" that rise in addition to the dominant tones, the dominant indications, both literal and suggestive, of shots, singly and in juxtaposition. All "provocations or stimuli" present in a shot are given their due, are developed in orchestration. One sequence of shots, thus, can be doing several jobs at once beyond its initial literal level of representation. Eisenstein, for example, explains how seven separate but interdependent lines of effect are interwoven, not one after the other, but simultaneously and alternately in one sequence of shots: It begins with a pan shot from the top of a church down to the dust and then follows a line of people in religious procession coming in from the fields and ending groveling in the dust.

The sequence is typical of the application of the theory of visual overtones in Old and New, for the literal representation is clear, the emotional effect strong, however much one responds to the lines of effect created by the overtones of the purely plastic components of the shots.

It is, for one thing, a truly lovely film. The new, more sensitive panchromatic film allows Tisse and Eisenstein to create more accurate and subtle tones and greater depth of focus in the sweeping vistas of sky and land used as motifs throughout the film; the compositions generally avoid the clutter of detail sometimes collected by Eisenstein.

The vistas are united with the dramatic material, so that skies, sun, clouds, fields, hills, dust are integrated with human desires and conflicts. Typical is the sequence showing the failure of the religious ritual to bring rain in contrast to the sequence depicting the successes of the harvest and its parallel rainfall. In the same way, individual details of practicality are raised to a mystic level by a heightening that is more lyrical and less insistent than in the earlier films—often touched with an empathic good humor that is new for Eisenstein: the more typically elongated first success of the milk separator, the lighthearted development of the successful mating of the bull and cow. The wholehearted innocence of the way the peasants throw themselves into the wheat-reaping contest is rendered in appropriate basic strokes—a single mowing movement from one side of the frame to the other, and then the reverse, accelerating with the shortening of the segments: a new tone for fundamental parallel cutting. In the finale, as the single new tractor pulls the peasants' cart up the hill, their joy as they follow behind is captured not only in their own movements but in the happy dancelike rhythm achieved by the kinds of shots alternated and the varying speeds of the alternation.

Still, in sum, there is a nagging sense of disproportion between means and contents, a gap between the extreme refinement of technique displayed and the simplification of the materials. There is still a kind of reductive sentimentality here, though more intellectually sophisticated and consciously ideological than in the case of Griffith. It was not, however, the simplifications of ideology that continued to bring Eisenstein into conflict with the Soviet bureaucracy. In their view it was an intellectual and esthetic dilettantism that obtruded upon ideology. This conflict was to continue and intensify for years and reach its climax in the controversy—which we examine later—over his *Bezhin Meadow* (1935) and his subsequent recantation. In the meantime, this conflict and other forces, including Eisenstein's misadventures in America, were to make *Old and New* his last silent film and only fully completed film for ten years.

PUDOVKIN: LINKAGE

Pudovkin, too, was to find himself embroiled in controversy with the authorities, though never to the degree of crisis reached by Eisenstein. The cause was the same—the fear of estheticism overriding the Soviet Socialist truth of the material. In the twenties and early thirties, Pudovkin was to approach film-making with the same theoretic rigor as Eisenstein, though in later years his work revealed less distinctive and less experimental approaches and techniques.

Pudovkin's basic agreement with Eisenstein is found in all of his critical and theoretical writing. "And thus the material of the film director," he would insist, "consists not of real processes happening in real space and real time, but of those pieces of celluloid on which these processes have been recorded." Especially through editing, the director transforms: "The film assembles the elements of reality to build from them a new reality proper only to itself." Nevertheless, he differed from Eisenstein in certain basic ways of carrying out this expressive, intensifying approach. Through his early work with Kuleshov, he began to emphasize what he called "linkage" rather than "conflict" or "collision" as the basis of montage. Even when contrast was employed, the general purpose of editing was to build, piece by piece, a selective continuity of action and emotion, rather than to illustrate *a priori* concepts with juxtaposed images. Although his work and Eisenstein's often did not differ that greatly (especially in action sequences), a distinct overall difference did develop.

Mother

That difference centered on a greater stress and focus on individual characters treated more like the characters of conventional dramatic structure, the individual being representative of types, forces, conflicts in the situation. The montage linkage, then, was particularly meant to express the emotional responses and shifts in consciousness of the characters, through associations, rather than to express intellectual notions through emotional means. Thus, his films had more in common with the tendencies toward realistic narrative in the latter twenties than did the films of Eisenstein.

Mother   In *Mother* (1926), based on the Gorky novel and the first of Pudovkin's three great films of the twenties, he and his script collaborator Nathan Zahrki shaped the overall pattern of the action to follow a rhythmic scheme of four sections, alternating in mood and tempo, much in the manner of an Eisenstein structure. But within this scheme, the action was developed along more conventional story lines, dramatizing the acceleration of revolutionary consciousness and action within a son and the subsequent spread of this fervor to his mother, both finally dying for the cause of the new life. The representative nature of the individual actions is further strengthened by merging them with the historical events.

While even camera angles are chosen to express the theoretical points (shifting from shooting down toward the mother to shooting up at her to mirror her growing stature), Pudovkin works toward reducing the amount of detail in the composition and restraining the Eisensteinian hyperbole of symbolism. The shot that captures the impact on the mother of the father's death is typical: The corpse, covered by a white sheet, is at the center of the frame. Barely visible behind the corpse is a small candle with the mother immobile beside it, seated toward the rear of the composition, almost one with the dark gray wall, which is broken only by a small window and a plain light fixture; then she is joined by two other women—one in black on one side of the coffin, her shadow on the wall, the other in dark gray, like the mother, and standing next to her—both also immobile.

The key instances of associative editing center on expressing the emotion of a character—the sudden happiness of the imprisoned son shown by interspersing shots of the very corners of his smile with shots of nature's gaiety and finally a child laughing. Dynamic editing to heighten and intensify group actions is also used; earlier, Pudovkin had studied Griffith's *Intolerance* extensively. Pudovkin's editing of action is often keyed to movements within the shots or to responses to movements, much in the manner of editing devised by G. W. Pabst in the late twenties or by Hollywood editors generally.

The End of St. Petersburg and Storm over Asia

In *The End of St. Petersburg* (1927), Pudovkin and Zahrki again attempt to merge an individual tale of a young man's growth of political consciousness with the sweep of the historical event—this time the coming to power of the Soviets. But now the collective epic assumes dominance, and much of the resulting montage and symbolism seems closer to Eisenstein's. Still, there are many examples of Pudovkin's more austere symbolism capturing the emotional states of characters by rigorous concentration on selected details: A glass of tea, for example, in a worker's house is used to show the emotional tensions of the character (because it remains undrunk); the passage of time (as the steam from the tea lessens); the worker's poverty (by the solitariness of the glass on the table); even, finally, intensified resolve (by its being hurled through a window). On a larger scale, the selection and juxtaposition of images in the battle scenes are particularly powerful and transcend in human impact the Soviet ideology embodied in the script—as in one sophisticated advance on Griffith-like intercutting, the juxtaposition of battle images with the frantic rush of movement at the stock exchange.

Storm over Asia (1928) is Pudovkin's most bravura visual production, mixing extensive ornamental explorations into Asian local color with increased hyperbole of cutting and symbol. It is a propaganda fairy tale in which a Mongol trapper is cheated, develops revolutionary consciousness, is shot, saved at the brink of death so that he can become a puppet of the British, but then turns on his imperialistic managers. Its greatest hyperbole is its final sequence, in which the Mongol literally tears apart a building, jumps on a horse, is abruptly joined by endless streams of rebelling Mongol horsemen, all of them suddenly becoming a tremendous storm that reduces to debris the rule of the imperialists. Its best moments are still the small detailings of individual actions like the beautifully selected series of images that lead up to the shooting of the Mongol by a single British soldier.

**The End of
St. Petersburg**

DOVZHENKO: TIMELESS CURRENTS

The poetic hyperbole of the ending of *Storm over Asia* was something that Alexander Dovzhenko, the third towering figure of early Soviet cinema, could have managed more deftly, more lyrically, more deeply. For though he too dealt with the subjects and themes of Soviet progress (and though he was personally the most political of the three), his film touch was the most passionately sensitive in responding to the spirit and emotion of the people and their land—transformed by Soviet progress, yet still rooted in deeper, timeless human and natural currents. Parts of Eisenstein's *Old and New* are the closest parallel to the emotional lyricism and imagistic freedom of Dovzhenko's work. This freedom of imagery came from an audacious building of associations and a blending of an amazing variety of approaches: epic sweep and intimate moments of spirit, realism and fantasy and satire, didacticism and intense personal lyricism, allegory and history, unique leaps of montage and logical progression of editing, individual compositions of beauty and mystery.

Arsenal
and
Earth

An opening sequence in *Arsenal* (1920), the earliest of his major works, captures the Czarist domination of the Ukraine in a series of brief, disjunctive images—Czar, one-armed ex-soldier, mother and children, dying wheat field, old horse—climaxing with a series of intercut beatings of horse and children. But then the unique leap of association: The soldier falls to the ground, self-defeated, and when he rises finally the horse says to him, "It's not me that you should beat, Ivan." A horse talks again later, part of an enigmatic sequence that intercuts images of a widow waiting by a ready, gaping grave with soldiers urging onward horses that bring home a coffin from the front.

Deeper than the politics in this and Dovzhenko's other films is the sudden upsurge of joy in the life of simple people and the inevitable alternation of pain, both moored to a life in which death is ever present. These themes, and their relationship to man's life in tune with the forces of nature, are more fully and lovingly symbolized in *Earth* (1930). The political themes are here reduced to a simple thread of continuity—the peasants' demand for a tractor and the subsequent fearful reaction of the landlord kulaks. Its richness, however, lies in the power of its truly felt images, whether simple and direct or allegorical—the giant close-up of a young girl's face rising from the bottom of the frame to the clouds above, right next to a large sunflower doing the same—and in its sudden, surprising turns of sequence or mood. It opens on a lovely image of an old man dying, but happily biting into a fresh apple; as he is carried to his grave, the branches of an apple tree caress his face. The irreducible mixture of death and ongoing life is at the core of the film; even its political climax leads to this, in one of Dovzhenko's most magically flowing and strangely shifting sequences. After a scene of lyrical love and communion, young Vassily walks home in the soft light surrounded by swaying wheat. Overcome, he too begins to sway, breaks into a dance, which is suddenly captured in slow motion. As he twirls to the top of the frame, he falls, victim of a kulak bullet. His fiancée tears her clothes in anguish, but those in the funeral procession are calm, one with the natural setting, unconcerned with a priest praying at a church, untouched when the guilty killer appears, first boasts of his killing, then begins a mad dance in the same soft moonlight.

Earth has an eerie, telling simplicity Dovzhenko was not to match again in his later sound-films, made amid the growing insistence on Socialist Realism in the thirties.

Earth

CHAPTER FOUR

The Germans and Expressionism

Despite their differences and conflicts, the Russians were united in their attempt to extend and refine the expressive means of manipulating and re-constituting objective social reality into significant form. At the same time, German film-makers—particularly in the first half of the decade—were exploring another avenue of expressiveness. They sought to break from the literal imitation of surface reality to release the subjectivity—often intense and tormented—of the inner life. While the most extreme tendencies of German film Expressionism did not continue for long, they have exerted a continuing influence to the present day, and in the mid-twenties they shaped the distinct nature and style of a new movement toward Realism, *Die Neue Sachlichkeit* (The New Realism).

A FORM FOR THE INNER LIFE

The German film-makers' stylization of reality rested, not on the bedrock reassemblies of montage, but on the more amorphous creation of mood and revelation of emotion—in the typical and revealing term of the period, of ''soul''—through the use of setting, light, movement and composition within the shot, and movement of the camera in achieving the shot. While the development of complex studio methods of production influenced their approach and contributed the technical means by which to implement it, there are deeper, more important reasons.

Beyond Fact: The Subjective Emphasis

Their conception of dramatic content resulted most frequently (with important variations) in studies of individual crises within a small compass of action. The eventfulness of Russian films (and Griffith films) had made the fragmenting of space, time, and action through montage an appropriate instrument of expression. Whether working with situations of fantasy or commonplace life, the Germans sought not so much to manipulate space and time as to manipulate the planes of reality—dealing with the blurrings and confusions between reality and illusion, emotion and objective fact. They wanted the nuance and ambiguity, the suggestive interrelationship of man and things that the insistent precision of montage seemed, at least to them, to restrict. It is not, of course, an either-or matter. The Germans used montage effects, the Russians had used lighting, composition, and movement. It was, rather, a matter of emphasis and tone: To record the shadows of the soul, the Germans concentrated on the moving shadows of the film.

Influences

Much of this conception of content and the particular means used to express it were a clear result of developments in German art during the first decades of this century. In painting, in literature, in drama, in music, it was the Germans who had picked up the implications of the break with literal representation, carried it into the furthest reaches of Expressionism, and then maintained it as a vital movement into the twenties.

The work of Van Gogh's final period suggests most directly the direction in which German painters and sculptors were to take the innovations in non-objective, formalist painting. Color, form, and figure were to be the carriers of expression, a means for making an inner emotional state visible. Art was not to imitate the visible, but to make visible the ineffable, the feel of experience that was beyond or beneath surface perceptions. As Van Gogh had said, "For instead of trying to render exactly what I have before my eyes, I use color more arbitrarily in order to express myself powerfully . . . ." In German Expressionism, what was to be expressed was most characteristically an extreme state of feeling, whether ideally euphoric or, more frequently, deeply anguished. In an extremely representative work of Edvard Munch, "The Scream," the background is reduced and distorted into lines of force. These lines surround and threaten to engulf the central figure, but they also mirror in their form the scream of anguish into which the face has been wrenched. The work not only typifies the kind of alienation, futility, and despair that is pervasive in the German films of the twenties but exhibits as well the way in which they would mold the figure and its surroundings into a single, interacting mood.

In German poets such as Benn, Trakle, and Klages, we find much the same emphasis in content and the same use of sensory data for expressive purposes beyond fact itself.

The musical theater of Richard Wagner had set the example for the use of legendary material—the German "mythos," in Wagner's term, that is present in one group of Expressionist films; but whatever the subject matter, they show his emphasis on the total employment of stage space, setting, and lighting for the purpose of establishing mood, for placing the mind (as Wagner said) "in that dream-like state wherein it presently shall come to full clairvoyance and thus perceive a new coherence in the world's phenomena."

But the strongest influence of all was the German drama. Strongly expressionistic since the plays of Franz Wedekind, in the years after World War I it was in one of its peak periods—notably through the works and influence of von Unruh, Hasenclever, Kaiser, and Toller, among others. This drama generally focused on one of two themes: a deep emotional and spiritual crisis of an individual or a similarly intense crisis of man in the mass, in society. Both types, many of the basic themes and motifs of the stage dramas, and many of the staging devices of theatricalists like Max Reinhardt are found in the films of the twenties. Also present are techniques, derived from the earlier innovations of Strindberg's dream plays, to project the intangible, intense, subjective truths beyond surface phenomena through the expressive manipulation of these external phenomena.

Within the general cultural patterns, the content and tone of the German film took their distinct shapes from the intense and unresolved crises, the social chaos and consequent psychological tensions of German society in these years.

WEGENER, WIENE AND MAYER, LENI

*The
Cabinet
of
Dr.
Caligari*

While it was *The Cabinet of Dr. Caligari* (1920) that focused attention on the movement, earlier films—especially three by Paul Wegener—had foreshadowed what was to follow. On one level they were the result of the complex collaboration of writers, directors, designers, producers—so difficult to assess —that was to become typical of film. In content, they forged into new, more sophisticated areas of inner conflict and confusion. In manner, they followed the lead of Georges Méliès in using the devices of the cinema to make the fantastic credible, but they went beyond him in using the fantastic symbolically, to project the reality of the inner life. Awkward, even at times ludicrous, these earliest examples did not have the level of sophistication, imagination, or artistry of the later productions, despite their revelation of the nuclear psychological motif of the period—the precariousness of the normality and unity of the self in the face of both inner and outer stresses.

Caligari gives these disturbances a more consciously artistic form, in certain ways a too consciously artistic, too artificial form. Written by Hans Janowitz and Carl Mayer, who was to become one of the central creative forces of the movement, it was directed by Robert Wiene and designed by three Expressionist painters associated with the influential art magazine *Der Sturm*. It was Wiene who, paradoxically, gave the original script both a more realistic narrative frame and a bizarre expressionistic decor and style.

The film is a projection of psychotic hallucination within a rational framework. In this frame, Francis, the central figure, is seen telling his story to some others, but at the end they are all revealed as inmates of an asylum. What we have seen in the central portion of the film is his distorted view of the world and of Dr. Caligari, who is really trying to cure him. But the explanatory framework does not completely dissipate the fearful anxieties of the central "dream work," the exaggerated extreme of a world of unfocused fears and threats, a world turned upside down, in which figures of security and authority who might help can also destroy—a world not too unreal in its implications.

The "feel"—the emotional ambience and reality—of the hallucinatory world of Francis is projected through several key devices. Primary among these are the intentionally obvious painted settings. These create the grotesque terrain of the mind—distorted, twisted, tilted landscapes and blocks of houses; heavy, unnatural shadows; unexpected angles of light; converging or tilting lines and planes of floor and wall. These painted artifacts of the mind were alternated with literal backgrounds and juxtaposed with actual lighting and real artifacts (the props—chairs, tables, and so forth) and the

**The Cabinet
of Dr. Caligari**

actors. But even the props were transformed into distorted ornaments of consciousness. The stool of the threatening, unreasonable town official is six or seven feet high, the back of a chair in an attic looms like a wall, the constantly turning arm of an organ grinder at the fair blends with the wild turning of the merry-go-round. The actors' costuming, makeup, and acting are equally stylized and set in counterpoint against other elements of the compositions, such as actors moving in highly mannered ways, tilting even as they walk.

All is sinister, threatening, on the brink of chaos, but all is not exactly cinematic. For both the unique impact and the limitations of *Caligari* lie in its special combinations of artificiality. For one thing, much of its decor and movement is like a stage play, heightened by incidental cinematic devices: emphatic lighting, irising in and out, selection of angle, distance, and material of shot, some movement of the camera. Moreover, there is a basic confusion (not finally supportive of the confusions of the character) of the planes of reality of the film image. For in playing actual props and living figures against painted settings, the film does not take into account the paradoxical literalness of the camera, which turns the fantasy of literal real-life objects into a special kind of reality; but the painted settings, not real-life objects to begin with, remain painted settings, used as symbols. They are thus kept divorced from the characters, not fully integrated as projections of the consciousness of the characters, not part of the illusion and distortion in the same way as the real-life objects. *Caligari* shows the way in which a film can make anything a possible psychological reality, but it does not fully capitalize on this ability—as would the works, among others, of a Buñuel, a Pasolini, a Fellini—to turn the materials of the real world into the world of subjective fantasy and then back, newly and differently, into a deeper kind of reality.

Later in the same year in which *Caligari* was released, Wiene and Mayer collaborated on *Genuine*, which was anything but. Against exotic decor and settings—again blurring the literal and the painted—a slave girl revenges herself on her master and then on all the men she can find. More solidly anchored in human emotion was Wiene's *Raskolnikov* (1923), based on the Dostoevski novel, in which a highly mannered performance by the Moscow Art Players was placed against similar painted settings, with less unity of effect.

Others, however, were to continue further into the areas of Expressionist fantasy and myth. Wegener remade his 1915 *Golem* in 1920; F. W. Murnau did *Nosferatu* (1922), with a script by Henrik Galeen, who had worked with Wegener. While the latter is more strictly a horror film, vampire-conquered-by-courage-and-love variety, it is the most cinematically imaginative and artistic of all the versions of Dracula, at times a striking embodiment of nightmare images. Woods become a maze of white trees against a black sky, stop-motion gives a coach's journey a phantomlike quality, a spectral ship glides over hot, glowing waters, and, with the overlapping images of a cross-dissolve, the vampire is dissipated into the sunlight of morning. And in most cases Murnau does start with the physically literal and real as his raw material for fantasy.

Waxworks While clearly indebted to *Caligari*, Paul Leni's *Waxworks* (1924) in several instances effects a more successful integration of the painted and the literal in depicting the fears and violence of a nightmare world. Using the gaiety of a fair for the same ironic counterpoint as is used in *Caligari*, Leni sets up a frame story in which three waxworks—Haroun-el-Rashid, Ivan the Terrible, and Jack the Ripper—are brought to imaginative life by a formidable acting trio—Emil Jannings, Conrad Veidt, and Werner Krauss, respectively. In the more straightforward handling of the Ivan sequence, lighting and composition are often quite effective: the anguished face of a wife seen through iron bars watching the torture of her husband, followed by a close-up of the ring on Ivan's hand. In the Jack the Ripper episode the people from the frame story are pursued, in a literal dream, through the original fair-turned-into-Expressionist-nightmare landscape by a most effective integration of lighting, shadows, painted scenery, moving shapes, and camera and character movement. It is possibly the German film's best single integration of these elements into the visual correlative of unshakable nightmare fear.

In Arthur Robison's *Warning Shadows* (1922), unconscious fears and desires are given a more literal psychological structuring, within settings that are completely realistic. It is the behavior that is extreme, heightened further by lighting and camera angles. At the dinner party of a jealous count, a conjurer hypnotizes the guests, who then act out their unformed passions—the count forcing his courtiers to stab his wife, the courtiers then throwing the count out of the window. All are purged of their conflicts and hostilities by this session of magical therapy.

FRITZ LANG: EXPRESSIONIST EPIC AND EXPRESSIVE REALISM

Fritz Lang, the most important (with Murnau) of the directors who employed Expressionist techniques, contributed three films in which the ornamental manner of *Caligari* was extended to treat materials with the mythic scope and grandiosity of Wagnerian opera and with Wagnerian, if not Germanic, ponderousness carried to extremes that only the resources of the cinema could manage. In Lang's films, the sweep and simplification, the reduction to type of the epic are given a new tone and dimension by Expressionist fantasy and mood. While more complex in psychology than those of Mayer and Galeen, Lang's scripts, written chiefly by his wife Theo von Harbou with his constant close collaboration, dramatize the actions of typal figures, not individualized human beings. Though the result is more a mélange of ideas than a coherent development of an historical point of view, certain basic themes, mainly psychological, can be traced through these and other Lang films. The themes, representative of the period, focus on duality—the inner split in man between his emotions and intellect, body and spirit, aggressiveness and love. Often these dichotomies are correlated with conflicts in external society.

Destiny and Die Nibelungen

The three mythic epics—*Destiny* (1921) and *Die Nibelungen* (in two parts, 1924)—are an often amazing, often ludicrous mixing of artificial scenery and ornamental architecture (both two- and three-dimensional), magical tricks of camera and printing (including flying-carpet rides), exaggerated histrionics and posturings, prodigious adventures, emphatic and inventive visual symbolism, and consistently imaginative lighting. When the mixture works, the devices produce vivid images of great power. In *Destiny*, a giant wall erected by Fate-Death extends beyond the boundaries of three sides of the frame, dwarfing the human figures below. Shadowy silhouettes stagger drunkenly over a bridge at the height of a wild carnival. In *Die Nibelungen*, the tremendous task facing Siegfried is captured in the composition: He and his vassals, at the upper frame-line, are tiny figures on a bridge; below, a tremendous ravine threatens. Chained dwarfs are like stone figures bearing the giant treasure urn of their master. The pomp of a procession in Gunther's court is kept in long shot, followed through the framing device of the armor-clad legs of rows of sentinels. But overall, the excessive length of the films becomes an exercise in self-indulgence, an orgy of artifice and melodramatic over-simplification of meaning as great as the greed and power exhibited in the tales.

Metropolis: In *Metropolis* (1927), Lang's penchant for technological artifice and epic
Man gigantism found a more contemporary and, at least sporadically, more fruit-
vs. ful form. The form is that of the social type of Expressionist play—like
Technology Toller's *Man and the Masses* (1920), Kaiser's *Die Koralle* (1917) and *Gas* (1918), or Capek's *R.U.R.* (1921). Lang's inventiveness and cinematic re-sources allow him to build incisive visual metaphors for the genre's typical crisis in man's relationship to technological society, seen as an extension of traumatic tensions within man himself. But he blurs the metaphors with melodramatic plot complications, eclectic borrowing and psychologizing, and his usual excesses of detail. The result almost swamps the valuable aspects of the film. It also exacerbated the financial problems of the producers, the important UFA Studio, which had gone heavily into debt to finance the movie. Significantly, the major creditors were American film companies, whose varied interventions in German film matters not only brought many Germans to Hollywood but contributed to the dissipation of the momentum of the Expressionist movement.

Clearly indebted to H. G. Wells, among others, *Metropolis* projects to the year 2000 to envision the destructive results of greed fed by technological progress. On the social level, the bosses have subjugated the workers, made them one with their machines. But psychologically the conflicts are within men, even workers. Both sides have repressed natural emotionality—the one turned authoritarian and decadent, the other, spiritless and mechanical. In one personification, the split is shown in the heroine, who in her real self is pure and loving but in her mechanical double (à la Frankenstein) is a cruel harlot.

But the plot complications and psychological confusions are more Flash Gordon than Expressionist protest. It is the visual treatment of the material that works best. The symbolic and ornamental architecture is this time solid and substantial, exaggerated into horror, not glibly distorted. The geometric patterns of the machines, of the workers' houses (empty forms with black rectangles for windows), of the endless tunnels and stairs become oppressive forces. In details, men are the victims: One man is splayed on a giant re-volving disc, used as a clock; hundreds of men on platforms (in a scene that

Metropolis

Eugene O'Neill remarked upon and parallels in *The Hairy Ape*) are mere robot appendages to a giant wall of furnaces, belching patterns of smoke. The movement of the workers, individually or, more effectively, in groups that become mere formal arrangements, is robotlike, stylized into the embodiment of soulless masses. Carefully controlled design and lighting even raise a melodramatic chase sequence to symbolic significance: Maria, fleeing through the maze of tunnels, beset by threatening shadows, chased by the implacable force of an automated beam of light.

Dr. Mabuse and M

Among Lang's other films at this time, two are notable in suggesting a shift toward more literal, realistic rendering of these social and psychological themes. In *Dr. Mabuse* (1922), Lang created a thriller with a basis in literal contemporary life developed into extreme, fast-paced gangster melodrama and Expressionist symbolism. Even though the power-mad gambler, public enemy, hypnotist, chameleon Dr. Mabuse is finally driven mad himself by his archnemesis, Dr. Wenk, the ending is more cynical than affirmative. Wenk, although a public prosecutor, is equally unscrupulous and vicious. In its visual design, the film's rendering of the almost unending turns of the plot (in its original version it had to be shown in two parts) is a fascinating blend of the literal and expressionistic that makes of Mabuse a personification of the disordered evils of a rapacious society: A nightclub has distorted archi-

tecture and painted shadows; during a dance, sexual symbols are highlighted; dark streets are twisted, jagged shapes and threatening shadows; a
steel-girdered staircase menaces with the cruel efficiency of the world of
Metropolis.

While *M* is a later sound-film (released in 1931), it is useful to note it
here, for it represents one of the peak refinements of expressive devices that
create mood and reveal extreme inner states within an essentially realistic
treatment. Here the killer is no mad genius or technological wizard but a
tormented, pathetic young man, driven by his uncontrollable impulses to kill,
in much the same way that, from the onset, the stylized characters in the
earlier German films are driven by the devilish sides of their disoriented,
fragmented selves. The realistic treatment is correlated with a heavier
emphasis on editing, particularly effective in varying tempo and thus mood.
But the careful composition, movement, and lighting of shots still carry the
chief burden in rendering mood and emotional state. In one of the sharpest
series of juxtapositions, Lang intercuts between the parallel meetings of the
underworld and of the police—each working separately to catch the killer.
In a powerful single cut, a close-up of the anguished face of the killer, who
has been thrown to the floor during the kangaroo trial by the underworld, is
followed by a long shot capturing the massed force of the criminals, who

M

are surrounded by threatening shadows, one shaft of light from the rear illuminating the central judges and table. Shadows and shafts of light become a motif for the omnipresent threat of evil—by the killer, against the killer, within the killer. Objects assume symbolic import. In one image, the killer (Peter Lorre) is surrounded by reflections from the knives in the shop window through which he is looking and is photographed. Lang puts the new invention of sound in film to the same use—expressive heightening—as his visual devices. He does this in a number of ways—among them one of the most distinguished early uses: The whistled phrase of a Grieg melody becomes a motif for the killer and then the means of his recognition by a blind beggar—a much-imitated device in many later films, including John Ford's *The Informer* (1935). Lang is particularly strong in relating sound to visual images, as in the repeated cry of "Elise" by the lost girl's mother, while we see a series of brief shots that recapitulate the girl's fate: one of Lang's frightening geometric stairwells, an attic, an unused plate, a ball in high grass, a balloon caught in a telegraph wire.

TOWARD GREATER REALISM—AND PESSIMISM

M appeared some years after a general shift had begun in the German film toward greater Realism—but a Realism still distinctly flavored by Expressionist themes and approaches. It was a kind of film Realism that was again influenced by developments in other areas of German art, especially the above-mentioned New Realism or New Objectivity. In painting, in drama and literature, it was a Realism marked by passivity and despair, noticeably different from the more affirmative attitudes that underlay the Realism of the thirties in all countries. In drama, it was an equivocal Realism that still stressed the inner tensions of alienation and dislocation, that still was blended with the expressive use of representative types and of objects to reveal extreme states of those inner tensions and social distress.

The "Street" Films"

In the German film, it was associated with "street films," which dealt with commonplace lives and petty defeats. Conceived and acted in rather strident sentimental terms, Lupu Pick's *New Year's Eve* and Karl Grune's *The Street* (both 1923) were among the first to manifest a more literal approach to the disintegration of individual autonomy and happiness in the face of social pressures. *New Year's Eve*, written by Carl Mayer as part of a series of films of despair, ends in suicide; *The Street*, in abject capitulation to external pressures. Both films continue the Expressionist use of lighting, symbolic composition, and ritualistic acting; in both, for example, a dramatic oscillation of lighting suggests irrational disturbances, montages of objects suggest chaos, troubled yearnings, or fears—a line on the pavement turns wavy, the glowing eyes of an optician's sign suddenly loom. (Did F. Scott Fitzgerald see *The Street* before inserting the eyes of Dr. Eichelberger in *The Great Gatsby*?)

The
Last
Laugh
and
Variety

Of these depictions of collapse and despair (besides the more directly Realist films of Pabst), the two outstanding productions were E. A. Dupont's *Variety* (1925) and Murnau and Mayer's *The Last Laugh* (1924), both starring Emil Jannings as the victim of himself and society, although in the former he is allowed a second chance. *Variety* was the rather surprising high point of Dupont's otherwise mediocre career—in America and England as well as Germany. It clearly owed much to *The Last Laugh* and to recent developments of technique embodied in other films. More immediately striking, it is also more melodramatic, artificial, and mannered. A catalog of unusual camera angles, moving camera setups, lighting, multiple exposures, juxtapositions of editing, *Variety* does not really develop a probing, subjective penetration of the growing jealousy and eventual murder among a trio of circus acrobats. It uses devices for projecting inner reality without having much to show about that subjective reality beyond the reiterated motif of jealousy.

The Murnau-Mayer film (which, like *Variety*, had highly innovative and important camera work by Karl Freund) does probe deeper, does merge Expressionist and Realist approaches to reveal the fuller texture of a man's inner world. Fuller, but not yet complete. For it is still clearly one of Mayer's "instinct films," in Siegfried Kracauer's term. Beginning with the extreme distortions of *Caligari,* Mayer's films had been concerned with the overriding force of passions and impulses. While his portrait of "the doorman" (like many of Mayer's characters, without a name) in *The Last Laugh* is his most realistic creation—more intimate and introspective, less melodramatic—it is still not that of a fully rounded human being with passions and mind, with intellectualized consciousness, with intricate relations to other people and society. It is a rigorously limited vision: man in collapse, unable to control his life and his self-unity. All else is excluded. But while the scope may be limited, its texture is dense and subtly wrought.

The expressive techniques for rendering, for transmitting powerfully the subjective "feel" of the emotional world of a man in collapse are emphatic but not artificial. They rise organically from the materials. Mayer and Murnau had been concerned with developing cinematic methods to express subjective states of emotion; *The Last Laugh* is the peak of their work, separately or together, and significant in showing the modulation of Expressionist themes and techniques into a less distorted, more literal mode. Murnau was still to make a film—*Faust* (1926)—in the mythic fantasy mode, full of artifice and pyrotechnics and some of the most elaborately poetic use of lighting and shadow in the Expressionist period.

More quietly human, *The Last Laugh* is a subjective film, but not strictly a first-person film. While most of the techniques are directed toward expressing the point of view of the doorman—his perception and sense of his world—other points of view are interjected. Sometimes these are clearly the points of view of another character—the manager, a bystander in the street. But at times a more problematic shift occurs—one that to this day has not

Faust

been resolved to the point where one can bring to the screen the full flavor and texture of a first-person narration in print. When a character is photographed, the resulting shot can reflect his subjective experience of the action. But when the shot is from the director's point of view, it tends to comment on the action and experience, not merely reflect them. The result, where both kinds of shots are used, is a kind of alternation, which does occur in *The Last Laugh*. One shot of the doorman at work captures his sense of his prowess and power; but another, from a different angle, seems to mock his sense of himself. Even the lovely, haunting, climactic shot of the doorman in the lavatory is touched by this subtle problem: Does the exquisite combination of shot elements express *his* sense of his pathetic situation, or that of Mayer and Murnau, or that of the night watchman *toward* him?

This moot subtlety notwithstanding, the shot just referred to is indicative of the consummate level achieved in expressing emotional tones and moods. The aging doorman's sense of himself and of his relationship to his family and neighbors rests on his status as doorman at a fancy hotel. When he is demoted to attendant in the lavatory, his life collapses as a result of mocking pressures from without, but more important, from the vacuum within. Throughout the film, the objects of his surroundings—those by which he defines himself and his world—are captured in compositions that incarnate the emotional boundaries of his life: the repeated whirling of the revolving door of the hotel, rain or shine, the unstopping bustle and activity he relishes but that leads nowhere; the baggage that looms and threatens, that is there to be conquered, but finally initiates his defeat when he can no longer bear its weight; the contrast between the architecture of the luxurious hotel and the lower-class neighborhood; the heaving of the walls of the hotel, as though to topple on him after he has been demoted; even the mouths of the gossips, shot in huge, inhuman close-ups. There are many other examples, such as his ubiquitous grand uniform—his externalized self —which he must relinquish, but then is driven to steal from the darkened hotel; and, finally, the downstairs lavatory to which he has been demoted, to which inwardly he has sunk. Its entrance is like a dark and lonely cave, brightened only by the lantern of the night watchman, who comes, the only remaining glow of tenderness in the doorman's life, to look for him. Inside, in shadows at the further end of the room, huddled babylike on a stool the doorman is asleep. To our left, a gleaming line of ornate sinks, reflected in a mirror, point at him. They are illuminated; he is not. Through a window above him, an outside light casts the barlike shadows of a railing. Things, composition, shadows, and lighting keyed to the mood—the hallmarks of the German film—are here fully literal, yet ultimately expressive.

It is at this point that Mayer and Murnau insert the film's only title, promising a happy ending. The mocking good spirits of the epilogue—in

The Last Laugh

which, through happenstance, the doorman has become a millionaire—strangely enough seem only to add another dimension to the tones of defeat, as though to reiterate that wishing doesn't make it so. (Compare Vittorio De Sica's "impossible" happy ending to *Miracle in Milan,* 1950, as well as the parallel situation in *Umberto D,* 1952.)

In addition, *The Last Laugh* carries to fruition the earlier German experiments with a moving camera, not merely to follow movement or create emotion in the audience but to express the emotion and the subjective perspective of the character. The film's opening shot sets the rhythm (and illustrates as well the shifting of point of view). From a descending elevator, the camera takes in the vast lobby in a long shot, then crosses the lobby, sees the doorman through the whirling door, emerges into the street, and assumes his point of view as it pans and swings to take in the swirl of traffic about him. Most of the camera's significant movements are from the perspective of the doorman. It rushes across the street with him, turns and catches sight of the heaving walls. It meets the responses of the neighbors, whether admiring or derisive. It steals down a shadowy hall as he tries to regain his uniform. At a wedding, where he is desperately drunk, it swings and tilts in response to the playing of the band, whirls in dizzy frenzy, stops as the things of the room whirl around it. When the doorman fantasizes—the shots in blurred focus and double exposure—it moves with him as he faces and triumphs over an immense trunk; it stays with his perspective but includes him in the shot as, with one hand, he carries the trunk into the lobby and receives the throng's applause.

With moving or stationary camera, Murnau achieved his most salient effects with the shot rather than with editing. The way in which his camera remains open to the unfragmented flow of motion within the space of the shot remains an important development in the movement toward a more transparent Realism.

Sunrise and Tabu

Mayer and Murnau sought to repeat their expressive rendering of emotional states on a broader, more complex canvas in *Sunrise,* made in 1927 in America. While the film is successful in this respect, it is also more melodramatic and banal in content, more cluttered and excessive in technique. It has a wealth of invention but not the organic purity of *The Last Laugh.* In part, this is due to its dramatic content. In portraying the deep emotions and drives within a simple, natural farmer, it develops a primal triangle in excessively broad strokes: the simple farmer, an unbelievably good, true wife, and an unconvincingly evil city-woman seductress. Still, the situation develops well through the seduction, the inner conflict over the intention to murder the wife, the relinquishing of the plan, and subsequent remorse and reconciliation (although the last sequence, in a church, is cloyingly sentimental). But then melodramatic plot-turns mar the latter half of the film: the accidental temporary loss of the wife in the same lake water in which the husband had thought to drown her, his histrionic anguish, his turning on the seductress, and the return of the wife.

It is in the earlier stages that the myriad visual devices—physical symbolism, moving camera, overlapping dissolves, slow-motion, montages, flashbacks—are most impressive. Even here, however, they often seem intrusive rather than organic, carried on too long, with too much detail and artifice—overelaborating and exaggerating almost every emotion that rises. Much, however, is singularly effective. To some extent, even the insistently excessive heightening can be justified as the expression of the intensity of the husband, faced with unacceptable drives he cannot control. It is indicative, for example, that there is no touch of lightness or humor until the reconciliation has been completed and the tension in the man's way of experiencing his surroundings has eased. But, in balance, the fine rendition of limited subjectivity in visual terms is restricted by the psychological oversimplification of the conception.

In conjunction with Robert Flaherty, Murnau was to go on to complete (just before his death in an automobile accident) the lyrical but uneven *Tabu* (1931)—it, too, beset by a melodramatic plot and a final stylistic disunity. Mayer was to move through an increasingly sporadic, progressively unsatisfying series of collaborations and uncompleted projects, wandering (like one of his own driven, dispossessed characters) from loss to loss, country to country until his death more than a decade later.

CHAPTER FIVE

TOWARD
REALISM—
A GAMUT OF
APPROACHES

Paradoxically, the brief burst of Expressionism had made its own contribution to the screen's inevitable tendency toward a style of Realism. The Russian epic directors, although concerned with the historical veracity of their material, were insistent on manipulating it onto an abstract plane through expressive editing, separating the images from their real-life counterparts. The Expressionists, on the other hand, fostered a greater concern for the inner life—one aspect of the materials of Realism. Moreover, despite their heightening and distortion, their emphasis on the contents of individual shots gave a greater autonomy to the dramatic materials in those shots. This use of a flow of events that was unimpeded, though manipulated in other ways, fostered increased interest in achievement of an unbroken illusion of reality. The films under the influence of *Die Neue Sachlichkeit*, discussed in Chapter 4, were the first signs of this increased interest; in the last half of the decade, the current toward more objective, literal representation grew stronger in a number of countries. The works that resulted brought a greater correspondence between screen image and commonplace reality, less intrusion on the flow of the dramatic materials; but in a variety of ways, they still carried on many of the tendencies of the expressive style.

TOWARD OBJECTIVE REPRESENTATION: PABST

In content, The New Realism meant greater individualization of character, fuller development and explanation of motivation, increased concern for more lifelike situations. But all this was a matter of degree, not of a complete break. For even in G. W. Pabst—probably the most realistic of the directors of the period—the crises and emotions are still heightened to melodramatic extremes; the emotions, while given more detailed concreteness, are still essences of emotional states; the characters, to a great extent, still exhibit the dislocated passivity of the Expressionist type.

In style, the tendency gave a greater autonomy and credibility to the physical, plastic contents of the screen image. The films of G. W. Pabst again typify this development. For although he clearly continues the Expressionist emphasis on angle and lighting, on camera movement, on the symbolic use of objects, on functional editing, in each case he adapts the devices toward less and less stylization. He is less intrusive, less subjective, less visible. This more covert manipulation of materials balances on an important question of emphasis: Does a detail of the material or a device appear as an obvious expression of emotion or idea, standing out and functioning first as a means of expression, or does its expressiveness arise secondarily from its primary function as a credible part of a dramatic event? Pabst's work was to produce a tipping of the balance toward the latter, Realist pole, but not without a good deal of oscillation.

His approach was first evident in *The Joyless Street* (1925), although its place in the series of similar street films is also apparent in its melodramatic heightening: sentimentality, typical extreme contrasts between rich and poor, and excessive plot manipulations, including a compromise happy ending. But the arrangement of people in scenes and settings, their patterns and movements are allowed a greater degree of freedom to unfold before us. If anything, it is the lighting that retains the more discordant traces of Expressionist emphasis. Pabst's camera positions, for example, are expressive without distortions: a poor professor shot from above and at a distance, the rich dancers in a nightclub shot head-on at the waist, dramatically close. (The motif of shooting the cruel butcher from below becomes more obtrusive.) But these are molded too strongly by the conventional shadows and highlights. Even the famous use of the coats' physical detail is telegraphed by the surrounding shadow and a spotlight on them as Greta Garbo's hand reaches in and hangs a new fur coat next to her old, worn, plain coat. The shot, however, is not dwelled upon, is a normal part of the flow of event. Garbo's part, incidentally, was her first major role and led to her career in Hollywood.

Less interesting technically, *Secrets of a Soul* (1926) is significant in that it literally follows the course of a series of psychoanalytic therapy sessions, alternating dream shots (full of meaningful Freudian symbols), memory shots, and current shots—in contrast to the more fanciful treatment of psychoanalytical material in films like Arthur Robison's *Warning Shadows*, made four years earlier.

The Love of Jeanne Ney (1927) exhibits Pabst's continued development (and possibly the peak of that development) in the use of camera position and movement, physical objects, and editing in ways that were highly selective and expressive without intruding upon the literal reality of the images. Conceived on a broader social scale, this reality, however, is not without more than its share of dramatic sham and hokum. It places the tensions in the emotional life of a young woman within the parallel torments of political and economic disturbance in Europe, but the plot becomes an incredible porridge of communists, capitalists, spies, rogues, working-girls, flower-sellers, a blind girl, robbery, rape, and murder. The lapses of taste carry over into the style; there is a lingering, ornamental, artificial heightening of image that would be more consonant with Expressionist stylization than Pabst's intended literalness.

Still, the film abounds in individual instances of selection and compression of physical detail within the natural patterns of life to achieve subtly evocative images. It opens with a shot of the shoe tips of a reclining man, the camera gliding along his legs and beyond to scattered newspapers, dirty clothes, scattered records, dirty ashtrays, a hand selecting a stub, the face of the man, then on to the further dirty surroundings, replete with erotic art, of the scoundrel Khalibiev. Here is the full textural detail of the Realist

The Love of Jeanne Ney

style—palpable, concrete, yet expressive of character and mood. Similarly, information within a shot or scene takes on meaning within the flow of action. Khalibiev, preparing to rape Jeanne Ney, roughly forces open the knot of his tie. With more indirect and subtle composition, an iron washbasin undercuts the romance of the lovers' meeting place; a broken mirror, seen at the back of a room crowded with triumphant Bolsheviks, just over Jeanne's head for emphasis, reflects the personal upheavals that accompany abrupt social change.

While many shots of such details and action are of long duration, often with camera movement, Pabst does employ extensive cutting. For peak moments of the action, he does cut with the pronounced juxtapositions of the Russian style. For example, in *Crisis* (1928), his next film, he alternates close-ups of the bobbing heads and of the moving feet of dancers coming toward the camera. But his major contribution to the evolving Realist style was his concentration on a kind of editing that, even when intense or rapid, remains unobtrusive, even "invisible." Although he intrudes upon the development of action, he seeks to disguise that intrusion (to reinforce the realistic illusion) by concealing the cut rather than emphasizing it to produce the shock of "collision" editing. "Every cut," he stated (with some exaggeration, to be sure), "is made on some movement. At the end of one cut somebody is moving, at the beginning of the adjoining one the movement is continued. The eye is thus so occupied in following the movements that it misses the cuts." Since cutting on a movement makes the cut less evident to the audience, it tends, while still directing the audience's attention, to give more of an illusion of unimpeded flow to the dramatic action. Another way in which Pabst maintained the autonomy of the dramatic action was with cutting that followed not the literal physical action but rather the impetus inferred by the audience—from a character's glance, for example, or stated intention. Also, on occasion, reverse cuts followed the implications of a shift of speaker as characters conversed, reversing from one to the other and foreshadowing the fundamental dialogue-cutting of the sound-film.

In several subsequent films Pabst was to continue as in *The Love of Jeanne Ney* to explore the world through the emotional focus of a woman's torments, but in three later films early in the era of sound, he was to turn to the direct depiction of social and economic problems that was to become so central in the Realism of the thirties. In his version of Bertolt Brecht's *Threepenny Opera,* the ornamental detail and vivid atmosphere are touched with Expressionism, but the adaptation of the dramatic materials dulls Brecht's satire. In *Westfront 1918* (1930) and *Kameradschaft* (1931), he created two lasting works of Social Realism, still touched by a kind of lyrical heightening, especially in the lighting and pictorial artifice of some compositions. Unable to employ his previous rapid cutting because of early sound-production conditions, he achieved in both films further refinements in camera movement—especially in the use of camera movement that matched the action within the shot and in developing rhythm and emphasis with more static material.

In the subsequent turmoil of Nazism, Pabst seemed to lose his way, none of his later films ever reaching the social seriousness or artistic quality of his earlier ones.

NATURALISM: VON STROHEIM

Somewhat longer (1918–28), the creative period in the career of Vienna-born American director Erich von Stroheim revealed the influence of another variant of Realism, literary Naturalism. It also produced film Naturalism's most

Kameradschaft

impressive single work, its biggest production scandal, and its biggest box office failure—*Greed,* made from Frank Norris's novel *McTeague.*

Von Stroheim's entire career is built of such paradoxes. *Greed* itself, consistently rated by critics as among the world's best films, is not the film as it was directed by von Stroheim because the studio had eliminated three-quarters of the original version, estimated to have been about 40 reels. For all of his films, he was screen-writer, art director, and director (though often with collaboration), and yet all of his most important films are available only in versions markedly different from his original conception. *Foolish Wives* was cut from 20 to 12 reels. *Merry Go Round* was finished by others and cut. *The Merry Widow* was cut from 14 to 12 reels, *The Wedding March* from about 40 (in two parts) to 20 (the 10 reels of the second part never being released in the United States). Von Stroheim was fired from his last film of this period, *Queen Kelly,* ostensibly because of the arrival of sound. Hackwork editing and a new ending made its 8 reels (half remained to be shot) into the whole film. Finally, von Stroheim's comeback attempt, *Walking Down Broadway,* exists only as part of a film that was reshot by another director.

The record of these films shows the same kind of exaggeration of situation and extremes of bitter irony that were central in the conception of von Stroheim's films. Obviously, personality and business conflicts had much to do with his problems with the studios. But the original length of these films suggests at least a major part of the problem and, more importantly, the distinction and limitations of his own approach to film-making. It has often been remarked that the astonishing length of *Greed* (it would have taken more than 10 hours to view the original version) is due to von Stroheim's concern for "putting a novel *completely* [his italics] on the screen." This is true, in part. But it is indicative, for example, that von Stroheim planned about two and a half hours of film before reaching the first page of the novel, filling in details of background that even the novel only alludes to briefly. Similarly, he not only presents details of the novel conscientiously but expands upon them, repeats them, heightens them by the way they are reconstituted in sequences of shots. Furthermore, the time taken to experience a sequence of five, or ten, physical details, and thus the emphasis given to all of them, is far greater in a film than in the novel form. By this repetition and emphasis, extremes become even more extreme, exaggerations more exaggerated.

The problems inherent in literary Naturalism loom even larger when the approach is applied to the screen as von Stroheim intended. His avowed purpose was to bring the Naturalist art of Zola and Norris and Dreiser to the screen so that the "spectator will come to believe that what he is looking at is real. . . ." This illusion of reality, for the naturalistic writer, was to be created by a vast accumulation, a sprawling flood of detail, rather than by selection, condensation, compression. But the attitude toward reality of literary Naturalism was based on an extreme view of Darwinian determinism —one that not only placed man among the creatures of nature but particularly stressed the primitive impulses or uncontrollable external forces that drove him—usually to destruction. As a result, its followers had a predilection for dealing with extremes of social crisis or inner pathology, most frequently in sordid, low-life circumstances. It was, thus, on occasion a romanticized, heightened Realism, bordering on and overlapping the grotesque traumas of the inner and social world of the Expressionists.

With this viewpoint, von Stroheim created an idiosyncratic weighting (and in his case, blending) of the terms of the two equations introduced in Chapter 1: content—form, realistic imitation—expressiveness. The monumental length of his films reveals his major emphasis on the details of content as the autonomous producers of the illusion of reality. Obviously, in his view, more detail meant more reality. More meant more truth—whatever the overelaboration and repetition, whatever the exaggeration. Von Stroheim's films, then, are epics of detail—not of scope of action, or celebrated grandeur, or historical panorama. Thus, in extending the stories of individuals into epic length, structure and editing pattern meant less than the presentation of detail. Still, there is much of the Griffith epic style in von Stroheim—the repeated motifs (like McTeague and his bird in *Greed*), exaggerated expressions of emotion, parallel cutting—and these are often the weakest links in what remains. The parallel chase cross-cutting at the climax of *Greed,* while often praised, is actually inappropriate to the tone and rhythm of the film. The celebrated cross-cutting between the tender love scene and orgiastic party in *The Wedding March* is derivative and obvious—less successful than the kind of juxtapositions von Stroheim could achieve within a single scene or shot.

The glaring moments and blatant devices are exacerbated, to be sure, by the omission (in the released versions) of so much of the original balancing detail. They are, nonetheless, the result of von Stroheim's naturalistic conception of his material in terms of extremes of emotion and of his rendition of them in an exaggerated manner. His is a Realism of dense, accurate detail and of the harsh, sophisticated facts of life that others were not bringing to the screen. But, blended with exclamatory devices and compositions, it is a Realism that is heightened to an expressive symbolism of extremes. In *Greed,* for instance, the forced, often ludicrous way in which Tina (Zasu Pitts) deteriorates into the madness of her obsession with money is, like much in the film, difficult to assess. Part of the trouble is Norris's original conception and treatment in *McTeague;* part, the absence of tremendous amounts of material (from the original screen version) that would have shown the transition to her obsessive state while presenting a fuller portrait of the character. Still, the exaggerations of certain of the images that remain would not be mitigated by improved context; they are flawed by their nature as film symbols, whatever their original form in the novel: Tina, nude in bed, eyes bugging out, sensually aroused by the coins that surround her; close-ups of Tina's hands fondling the coins as they drop back into the pile through her fingers; another close-up of her face insanely distorted. And all repeated and repeated and lit with all the telegraphing found in the conventional use of shadow and focused light.

Nevertheless, it *is* the imagery that develops within the contents of a single shot or scene that is the source of the film's greatest artistry and power. Von Stroheim rises and falls on his details, and so, paradoxically again, the flagrant tampering with his films has not destroyed them as it would films with tighter editing patterns and structure. What remains are individual sequences of audacity and power, toned by a sardonic cynicism, that have survived all tampering and even von Stroheim's own disregard of the selectivity and suggestive compression that are found in tight structure.

Working as his own set-designer, von Stroheim builds his scenes into a complex pattern of details. Whether on sets or outside the studio on "location" (and he was one of the first to make such use of existing sites), he plays individuals against their surroundings, the physical or social world with which they interact. From this interaction within the shot, he achieves his meaning. The prime expression of his sardonic attitude toward his materials lies principally in ironic juxtapositions of elements within the shot but also between consecutive shots and sequences.

At the wedding of McTeague and Tina, the inner rooms are jammed with a grotesque assortment of relatives and friends, all their tawdriness manifest. The dismal details of the event within the room are juxtaposed, in a shot with amazing depth of focus for the time, with a view through the window of a funeral procession, complete with a crippled boy using a crutch.

The use of composition in depth for interplay between characters can be seen in the single shot that captures the developing tension between McTeague and Marcus. In a pub, McTeague is seen in the background, just over the shoulder of Marcus, who is in medium close-up. McTeague puffs heavily on his pipe; Marcus scowls, then begins to twirl a coin rapidly on the table, finally turns and shouts at McTeague.

Ironic interplay between people and objects is frequent: A courting scene between Mac and Tina has them sitting on the top of a sewer outlet, refuse draining behind them, a train belching heavy smoke. Dark, heavy rain interrupts the courtship scene and the proposal scene.

After they marry and begin to destroy each other and themselves with their uncontrollable animal impulses and obsession with the money Tina has won in a lottery, the surroundings of their apartment and then their run-down hut mirror their degradation—the neat, gaudy clutter of the bedroom becoming the filthy disorder of an animal pen, their own appearances equally debased, their formal wedding picture a ruin.

When McTeague, angry beyond rationality, comes to kill Tina—who has driven him out after ruining him—they are surrounded by the bedraggled remnants of Christmas decorations in the house she is cleaning. "MERRY CHRISTMAS" hangs over their heads as he first grabs her; they are in the foreground, in shadow, the decorations in light behind. Throughout this sequence, von Stroheim uses light for underplaying (rather unusual for him): They move in the shadows from room to room as McTeague chases her and finally kills her in the darkness.

Pursued by Marcus and his own inner demons, McTeague flees into the last sardonic context—the gray, burned-out wastes of Death Valley. Visual ironies abound. When Marcus catches Mac, they fight. Mac has Marcus down, Marcus's body being on the same plane at the middle of the shot with the money-laden mule, dead from exhaustion. Mac is on his knees, arm raised, beating Marcus with a pistol—all in dark forms against the bleached gray-white of the desert and sky. With Marcus dead, Mac tries to pull away but is bent back down by the handcuffs that link him to the dead body. He opens the cage of the bird he has kept with him; the bird too is too weak to fly and sits among the dead bodies and spilled coins on the sand. With the kind of last long shot that was later to become a basic convention for endings, von Stroheim then shoots Mac as a tiny dark form, surrounded by the endless white haze of desert and sky.

At first glance, this starkness and the tawdry reality of the whole film could not seem more different from the rest of von Stroheim's films, mainly

Greed

highly ornamental and artificial sexual melodramas of a kind popular in the twenties and peopled with decadent noblemen (played usually by von Stroheim) encountering innocent ladies—object: corruption. But von Stroheim's treatment of eroticism, opulence, and decadence was carried to such extremes of corruption, with such bold depictions of psychopathology, that these films become more than frippery. They expose the same deep, driving lusts, the same frail social hypocrisies as did *Greed;* but in them, the cynical juxtapositions of the details are frequently weakened by the romantic sentimentalism of the plots and happy endings. While goodness may triumph in his films, it is really evil that interests von Stroheim and impells his best arrangement of incongruous details. In *Foolish Wives* (1921) the seducer, Karamzin, and his prey are forced by a storm to stop in a beggar's hovel. The lecherous Karamzin must share a corner with a goat. We see Karamzin's lady given some dry clothes by an old hag, then Karamzin peeking with a pocket mirror. Following his glance, the camera pans slowly up the lady's body, but she now wears the bulky ragged garments of the beggar. In *Merry Go Round* (1922), Kallafati attempts to rape Mitzi among the wooden horses of the merry-go-round. In both *The Merry Widow* (1925) and *The Wedding*

Foolish Wives

March (1928), von Stroheim intercuts between a tender love scene and an orgiastic party. The latter film is probably the most important of his cynically romantic denunciations of rampant lust among the upper classes—tempered by large doses of sweet sentimentalism. It has two innocent heroines, both religious, one crippled, one injured in an accident. In the scenes of their seduction, crucifixes hang above them. One is almost raped among the carcasses in a butcher shop. Two men slobberingly drunk on the floor of a brothel arrange the marriage of the other; at the wedding she hobbles up the aisle of a church full of human and architectural opulence. In *Queen Kelly,* the innocent girl (along with a young prince) is victimized by an aging, possessive queen. Forced to marry a lecherous old cripple, she is wed in a brothel, in the bedroom of her dying aunt, surrounded by religious images and prostitutes.

There are many more ironies, both in the films and the career. The last was not to come until 1950, when it was played out in Billy Wilder's *Sunset Boulevard,* a film in which a possessive harridan of a movie queen (played by Gloria Swanson, who had played the young girl in *Queen Kelly*) dominates and finally destroys the life of a young man. Her butler, who had once been her lover and director but now has been completely forgotten, is played by Erich von Stroheim.

THE SPECTRUM OF MIXED STYLES

America

Among those who worked on the editing of von Stroheim's *The Wedding March* was Josef von Sternberg, whose career (not without its own ironies) through both the silent and sound eras embodied another variation on the blending of a greater realism with a heightened expressiveness. Indeed, as the era of sound progressed and the tendency toward Realism solidified, von Sternberg intensified his concern for the ornamental, his "search for abstraction not normally contained in presenting things as they are." Since von Sternberg's sound-films most completely illustrate the results of his search, we will postpone discussion of his work until Chapter 8.

The spectrum of mixed styles was well represented in American films of the twenties. The work of Maurice Tourneur, in such films as *Woman* (1918) and *Aloma of the South Seas* (1925), revealed significant advances in exotic, expressive mood and pictorial composition, blended with extreme plot sentimentality and an epic emptiness. The films of Rex Ingram continued developing the action epic; its form and style were taken further into realms of fantasy and high spirits in the many films of Douglas Fairbanks; its costume, pseudohistorical splendors soaked in sexual titillation in the very successful erotic ornamentation of Cecil B. DeMille. James Cruze's *The Covered Wagon* (1923) and John Ford's *The Iron Horse* (1924) capped, in both effectiveness and popularity, the developments in the romanticized epic Western.

All of these films were marked by a pace, a vitality of movement and editing structure that were markedly distinct from the slower, more intense moods of most European productions. In the works of directors moving more directly toward a fuller Realist style, however, the sober moods of the continental film were also apparent. Henry King, with *Tol'able David* (1921) and *Stella Dallas* (1925), among many others, essayed romantically emotional pieces with a greater concern for restraint and credibility. King Vidor, at the start of a long career, also produced films that were distinctly "blends": harsh realism of war and tear-jerking epic sentimentality in *The Big Parade* (1925); the somber, empty drift of the street films with fine details of social context and arch Griffith sentimentality in *The Crowd* (1928). After some comedies and action epics, Clarence Brown turned to romantic melodramas with strong touches of naturalistic detail and expressive Germanic heightening, especially in a series of Garbo films, *Flesh and the Devil* (1927), *A Woman of Affairs* (1929), and four others in the period of sound.

France, Italy, Scandinavia

On the Continent, the Italians vainly tried to repeat their earlier successes with the costume epic; Hans Richter applied expressionistic techniques to both abstract works and social documentaries; Luis Buñuel, in *Un Chien Andalou* (1928) and *L'Age d'Or* (1930), was beginning to forge his own distinctly Surrealist style.

In France, with the exception of epics like those of Abel Gance and the comic fantasies of René Clair, the chief development was the beginning of a kind of poetic Realism of mood and emotion that would continue to develop in the sound era. This variety of Realism was to partake more of the Germans' careful evocation of mood through composition of the shot than of the montage rhythms and juxtapositions of the Russians and Griffith, but with less of the expressive heightening and subjectivity of the major German works. Its naturalistic groundwork was set by the theories and films of Louis Delluc—*Fièvre* (1921), for example—the harsh content somewhat modulated and softened by a pictorial lyricism. Jacques Feyder's *Thérèse Racquin* (1928) mixed a Zolaesque sordidness with a meticulous craftsmanship of images, a touch of sentimentality, and some Germanic lighting and symbolism. After his earlier impressionistic works, Jean Epstein's *Finis Terrae* (1928) was a subdued, almost documentary treatment of life in a small fishing village (compare with films by Robert Flaherty and Luchino Visconti's *La Terra Trema*); yet it too shared the moody pictorialism, sometimes obvious and forced, of the French style, as did Alberto Cavalcanti's films of this period. Jean Renoir's silent films have marked ties to these approaches but already were developing the humane concern for people, the distinct blend of Naturalism and personal tone, the painterly involvement with composition that we will examine in Chapter 15.

Before turning to the most distinguished single film made in France during this period, Danish-born Carl Dreyer's *The Passion of Joan of Arc,* we can note the place in this blending of styles of the work of three other Scandinavian directors—Asta Nielsen, Victor Seastrom, and Mauritz Stiller. Before going on to make films in Germany, Nielsen, who is Danish, had already begun—in *Toward the Light* (1918)—to forge a style that emphasized expressive lighting and symbolism within the single shot.

Stiller and Seastrom began work in Sweden and then moved on to America. Stiller worked with a variety of approaches, never finding one that was wholly fulfilling. His *Erotikon* (1920) was the screen's earliest sophisticated sex comedy. His *The Atonement of Gosta Berling* (with Greta Garbo, 1924) was marked by the moodiness and use of natural settings that was particularly to be associated with the Scandinavian school. But his *Hotel Imperial* (1927), made in America, was strong in the provocative camera angles and moving camera of the German style.

Seastrom's career was also varied, eclectic, and uneven. His best work is marked by a seriousness of theme and expressive treatment of setting, conveying the moods and emotions of people pitted against the natural elements or the pressures of society. His evocative compositions of man in the context of his environment employ the Swedish landscape in *Thy Soul Shall Bear Witness* (or *Love's Crucible*, 1920); the American landscape in his two most important films made in the United States, *The Scarlet Letter* (1926) and *The Wind* (1928), both with Lillian Gish.

Dreyer:
The
Passion
of
Joan
of
Arc

In contrast, Carl Dreyer's *The Passion of Joan of Arc* (1928) is the work of a personal, unique style—suggested earlier by the intimacy, the slow unfolding of mind and heart, the careful selection of detail in his more conventional dramas, such as *Heart's Desire* (1924), *The Parson's Widow* (1925), and *The Master of the House* (1926). Yet distinct as it is, in many ways Dreyer's *Joan* culminates the blending of expressiveness and realism that marked the last half of the twenties.

While *Joan* is based on documents that had only been brought to public scrutiny in the twenties, it is a very special kind of historical documentary. While it does characterize Joan's inquisitors and suggest their personal motives as well as their theological arguments, it is not basically concerned with explanation or argument, or even with a psychological examination of Joan or her antagonists. It is more a devout, awed expression of the paradox of a God working through both Joan and her cruel persecutors, a paradox finally apotheosized by the transfiguration of the peasant girl's confusion into grandeur of spirit.

In its special way, it is an epic, a celebration of spirit in its paradoxical wonder and terror. But since it is an epic of the inner world, it scrupulously avoids the sweep and panorama of its surrounding history, which is only glimpsed in sketchy, suggestive detail. It is an intense, intimate epic in which the tremendous power of selection and compression achieves the heightening and enlarging of human affairs that the normal epic achieves by the sweep or vehemence of action or the intensity of montage.

Dreyer's film focuses on the last day of Joan's trial and on her execution, focuses so minutely and lingeringly that it bestows on its contents a sense of living reality—the shapes, the marks, the blotches, the lines, the dirt of humanity rendered with tangible, literal, even harsh concreteness. But the things, the objects of man's world and, most of all, the faces of man are there for more than themselves, for more than the accuracy of their literal representation; they are part of an expressive epic of faces, abstracted out of reality into revelation. Seen almost entirely in close-up, they become sculpted forms, often as immobile as stone sculpture. Held in shot for extremely long duration, viewed from unusual angles or by a moving camera, they are monumental, almost floating, in stylized idealization against the shadows and the dull white of the walls and sky.

The magnified details of the actors' faces and of their expressions, held before us often to the point of tension, do reveal character and the emotions of the dramatic situation in the normal dramatic sense. The pockmarks on the face of the actor playing Bishop Cauchon merge with his glances and the set and movement of his mouth to render his knowledge of the futility of his compassion. The heavy eyebrows of the Duke of Warwick dance his revenge. The roughened naturalness of Joan's skin, the dirt-clogged fingernails, the giant eyes make tangible her open innocence, record the accumulation within her of mystical power.

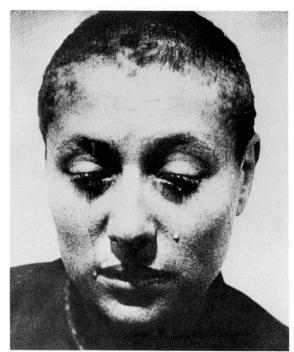

**The Passion
of Joan of Arc**

When the sympathetic priest informs Joan of her impending execution at the stake, his eyes carry his sorrow and resoluteness, hers first flood with fear and then shine wetly with more, with her sense of the glory of her martyrdom. In this scene—as in so many others—the lighting and the careful sculpting of the composition render more than character, expressing the strange spirit of her moment of doom and triumph. At the climax of Joan's interrogation, the horror of the metaphysical mystery of God in the world of men mounts with tighter and tighter close-ups of the inquisitors, finally of disembodied, dehumanized mouths filling the screen—against which the God-filled girl can only cower, covering her eyes, unable to control her tears. Yet, in contrast, her power, and that of this mystery, is rendered as well. In one amazing shot, for example, Joan's black-trousered legs, below the knee at the right of the frame, project down into the shot against the white-gray stone, the manacles between her ankles catching the light. Shadow surrounds the circle of light she stands in; into the frame from the left come the black back and shoulders of a priest, his collar and cuffs, his hands, the shaved top of his head white, as he bows before her chains, his face pressed against the stones in the circle of light.

The power of these shots and their strong, cumulative rhythm is, of course, interrupted by subtitles, which record the questions and answers of the dialogue. It might be said that it is appropriate to the visual abstraction of the style to have the words presented visually, in alternation with the silent tableaux that then render their inner meanings. There are moments when this seems true, when the form of the mythic images is best left unbroken by the sounds of words, which themselves would introduce a reality (or realism) that would play against the heightened expressiveness of the images. But it is also too often true that the subtitles intrude, break the rhythm, the emotion, the mood. As visual material, they are in no way comparable to the images and cannot sustain their impact. In this way, too, Dreyer's film sums up the development and limitations of the silent film—and the dilemmas it would face in incorporating sound—at the end of the decade.

CHAPTER SIX

COMEDY AND EXPRES- SIVENESS

Throughout the silent period (from 1915 through the twenties), comedy also developed ways of capitalizing on the expressiveness of movement and form. In the films of the American clowns, who made the deepest mark on early screen comedy, the direction was functional and not without adroit employment of angle and composition and cutting; but it is the physical, visual presence of the great comedians themselves that is the key to the heightening, the expressive stylization of their comic worlds. The core is their acting—movements and expressions broadly yet subtly stylized—and their actions—exaggerated almost surrealistically into the epitome of movement in a precarious world of objects, all gone wild yet related to the world of literal possibility.

The comedy of the clowns preceded the development of comic drama and then continued along with it. In this later development, the mad acceleration of actions and things is of course present, as it is to some degree in all comedy. But as directors solidified this comedy of character and situation—of actors instead of mythic clowns—they incorporated a greater use of camera and cinematic devices.

THE DIRECTORS

René
Clair

Of these directors, René Clair is closest to the efforts of the noncomic film-makers of the twenties in his use of a mixture of manipulation and observation, expressiveness and representation, fantasy and reality. Clair's social satire is always softened by sentimentality, but conversely, that same strong sentiment touches his wit and flights of fancy with a tenderness and humaneness, producing joyful good spirits in the face of comic plights or a hovering sadness.

His first two films satirize the conditions and institutions of contemporary life in his most abstracted, distant manner. In *The Crazy Ray* (*Paris Qui Dort,* 1923), the silliness and emptiness of Paris life are captured in the cinematic tricks of a fantasy: First, all are frozen, caught in the midst of actions by the effects of a paralyzing ray; when it is shut off, all actions are first speeded up to wildness, then reversed into slow motion. In *Entr'acte* (1924), there is a strong influence of surrealist images and free association—in one instance intercutting the artificiality of an amusement park with the trappings of a funeral, led by a camel, and disintegrating finally into a slapstick chase.

The Italian Straw Hat (1927) blends more sympathetic character delineation with the satire and fantasy, more drama with the cinematic devices. It is the high point of Clair's silent films. Again, he focuses on the absurdity of the ritual formalities of behavior in the bourgeoisie. In the expert highlighting of character foibles, visual touches enhance the characterization: the aggressively twitching mustache of the cavalry officer, the dogmatic old uncle with a wad of paper stuffed in his ear trumpet, the pretentious gentle-man whose tie keeps slipping. The structure combines an extended mocking of all the ceremonial formalities of a wedding day with a varied form of chase: A young bridegroom goes through all the rituals while trying to find a replacement for a hat his horse has eaten and while being chased by the angry officer who had been kissing a married woman when the hat (hers) was eaten.

Clair's camera not only focuses on significant, telling detail but moves in a manner that comments as well as captures. In one of his favorite devices, his camera moves up and away, accenting the pettiness of the scurrying action now seen in suddenly broader perspective. Again, he uses slow motion—when the officer furiously tears apart the apartment of the young man—and fast motion—when the boy is caught in the wedding dance, unable to continue with his search.

Similar sympathetic puncturing of social pretenses and personal peccadil-loes occurs in *Les Deux Timides* (1929)—with less drama and more cinematic tricks—and his first two sound-films, *Sous les Toits de Paris* (1930) and *Le Million* (1931). In the latter pair, Clair accommodates to sound by adapting it to his own stylization of fantasy: An offscreen voice com-ments on the action, voices counterpoint one another like a chorus, the dances and songs of the new screen musical suddenly and magically shift the perspective on events or give way to action, music sets up amusing contrasts to action, sound effects to objects (in *Le Million*, while we see an ornately decorated clock, complete with cupids blowing trumpets, we *hear* the trumpets).

In his third sound-film, *À Nous la Liberté* (1931), the social comment is touched by the severe economic crises of the time. The harshness of its world—beset by the tyranny of competition, machines, and money—is, how-ever, mitigated by Clair's sentimental trust in human joy. The ending is typical of both the conception and the imaginative approach: The greedy, driven factory magnate is defeated but escapes; the workers sing and dance with balletic freedom and fish in a stream; the machines operate themselves with equal balletic grace. Throughout, the artificiality of chases and the dances of fantasy both convey the satire and lighten it. While an old bureaucrat mouths platitudes concerning justice, etc., his audience of mag-nates and aristocrats—seen in part from above by the moving camera—scramble madly after bank notes floating through the air, the accompanying music an appropriate final touch of gentle mockery. While Clair's treatment of sound was to become more prosaic, his early sound-films were to in-fluence many other film-makers, especially in the more imaginative treat-ments of the musical form.

The "Lubitsch Touch"

In the comedies of Ernst Lubitsch, there is no merging into fantasy, no exaggeration beyond the possible, no overt manipulation through cinematic device. But there is, in what became known as "the Lubitsch touch," a bit

À Nous la Liberté

of all these. Of all the comedies of the twenties, his show the greatest sense of the look and feel of reality. On the surface, they do not violate literal probability; more deeply, they have a subtlety and discretion of acting, of expression and gesture that go beyond even the usual serious acting of the period; they have an equivalent controlled subtlety in the expository use of the camera. Yet the Lubitsch world is highly stylized, expressive of a tone, an attitude; it abstracts formal elements from the possibilities of its reality, unconcerned with accurate representation. (This is not to say that the formal artifice does not unfold a good deal of truth along the way, after all.)

But truth was not the intention or essence of Lubitsch's work. In his earlier German films, he had dabbled with a variety of approaches, even a street film, but most notably a series of successful historical epics in which strong camera work and touches of psychology and sex had brought him great success—and to Hollywood. After one more, but unsuccessful, attempt at an epic, he came upon the conception that was to be uniquely his (though much imitated). His is a comic world of sex and love intrigues, of manners and moods, sophisticated in its wit and its urbane attitude toward sensuality, but cloistered, cynically innocent in restricting its conflicts to those between the clods and the bothersome routines of life (whether husbands or revolutions) and the desires of those who know, or can learn to know, how to live and love well.

In staging this world, Lubitsch kept his sets light in tone, airy, with large, open areas, clean lines. In them his characters move gracefully among telling, revealing objects, followed with equal grace by a gliding camera: It is the German mobility of camera without the shadows of anguish. Moving or still, the camera is highly selective, subtle in its use of detail for understatement or suggestion of both character and plot event, witty in its use of detail for comic comment. In *Forbidden Paradise* (1924) along with *The Marriage Circle* (1924), the best of his silent films, the always suave Adolphe Menjou faces the angry, rebelling subjects of Catherine the Great's Russia and reaches into his pocket, not for a gun, but for a checkbook. It is a world in which the dialogue of the sound-film, used with equal discretion and wit, added the final, necessary touch, and so we will look at the work of Lubitsch further in the era of sound (see Chapter 12).

James
Cruze

One of the American directors who attempted comedies in the Lubitsch manner was James Cruze, whose uneven and inevitably unfulfilled versatility illustrates the many directions in which comedy was being developed in the twenties. Cruze has long been recognized for his epic Western *The Covered Wagon* (1923), but his many comedies have been lost sight of, critically and (most unfortunately) physically. He did innocent romantic comedies with the early idol Wallace Reid; slapstick comedies with Fatty Arbuckle; social comedies (one with Will Rogers), in which he employed sequences of Expressionist fantasy (*One Glorious Day, Hollywood, The Beggar on Horseback*); more conventional social comedies (such as *The Goose Hangs High* and *City Gone Wild*); and love comedies à la Lubitsch. But for all his films, or possibly because of them, he did not build a developing, unified body of work; thus, the degree of his achievement, with his films now mainly inaccessible, is difficult to assess.

THE CLOWNS

Cruze's haphazard career does, however, cast an indirect light on the kind of work that formed the core of comic achievement in American silent films—the work of the great clowns. In contrast to Cruze's dabbling, each of these was to develop a highly individualized persona and comedy; despite differences, all followed a direct line of development from the earlier short comedies, both European and American. The mode was characterized by frenetic movement within the shot, plainly photographed, of physical encounters between humans or humans and things, built into sequences of accelerating, proliferating events and momentum. Using the ability of the film to make anything at least temporarily possible and real, this central vein of silent comedy developed a zany heightening and magnifying of the physically literal into an expressiveness of action.

From the time of *The Birth of a Nation* on, it was Mack Sennett, for whom most American clowns worked at one time or another, who pushed furthest with the comedy of accelerated motion. It was Sennett who focused not only on speeding up movements but on *building* them—first into sequences of just one more gag, one more variation, one more physical explosion; then into a crescendo of such sequences, climaxed by the "rally," the chase, in which all overflowed in madcap catharsis. To the impact of speed itself was added the welter of confusion, compounded and accelerated, and the anarchy of things gone mad. With straightforward photography and with trickery, things—and especially mechanized things—rose in mischievous revolt against order and man. Cars roar through houses, beds race down highways, men chase objects, objects chase men; all things get recreated equal, somehow equally real, equally absurd. It is the kind of acceleration of fusion and confusion that Ionesco was later to put to much more metaphysical use in his comedy of the absurd.

It was a depersonalized slapstick comedy of mechanics and movement. In turn, it was the great individual comedians who refined the style by sharpening and deepening the human *response* to the action and thus the empathetic response of the audience, its involvement in a dramatic reality of sorts. To comic motion they joined comic and pathetic emotion, using their own bodies with expressive magnification, creating figures of silent speech depicting man's encounters with his world.

One of the earliest clowns who began to personalize comedy by creating a comic persona was the Frenchman Max Linder. Often an immaculate dandy of a ladies' man, tight mustached, alternating pursed lips and a pixie smile, he was still much like a Sennett comic, though a more restrained figure. He is in almost constant motion and has a playful impishness as he pulls his tricks, often acrobatic. While things fail him and he draws comedy from his modulated responses to what befalls him, many of his routines stress tricks he plays on others, which produce counterattacks but eventual success for Max. At his best, physical gags are touched with a wry invention: In jail, Max must scratch the back of a hulking tough, variations continuing through a courtroom scene until he gets *his* back scratched. In a Douglas Fairbanks parody, *The Three Must-get-theirs* (1922), he works some imaginative variations on confusion over the bald head of a cardinal. This was made while he was working in both Hollywood and France during a period of increasingly disturbing personal and professional troubles. In 1925 he took his life and that of his wife.

The rotund John Bunny and even rounder Fatty Arbuckle, with the contrasting runty Ben Turpin, were among the first American comedy-players to stand out as individualized characters, though their physical characteristics were still emphasized.

CHAPLIN

Everyman

Charlie Chaplin, who was open in expressing his debt to Linder, still relied on his own physical qualities—but with quantitative differences that became qualitative, a new comic essence. With Chaplin, the expressive comedy of accelerated movement and objects was given its fullest dramatic, and human, context.

Chaplin developed the approach through many shorts and a dozen or so longer films. His Little Tramp, and his comic (yet not-so-comic) conflicts, became inventive variations on a theme—always fresh, surprising, highly imaginative, yet rooted in a pattern of recurring motifs of character and situation. At the deepest level, the Little Tramp is an Everyman figure for the twentieth century, part clown, part homeless waif, wandering dispossessed through a world he never made, but that somebody made—and turned into chaos. Through the disorder he seeks a kind of temporary order, is often betrayed by the things and people of the world, often by himself, when he too becomes mechanized. But his resilience enables him to bounce back and up (both physically and emotionally), to wander off again, still lonely, but a survivor.

While Chaplin's tramp-clown wanders, Samuel Beckett's, in *Waiting for Godot*, wait—much more hopelessly and futilely—for order; but they too are bound up in physical (as well as metaphysical) disorder, constantly betrayed by their boots, hats, belts, ropes, food, and bodies.

The differences of skepticism and complexity in Beckett's use of Chaplin's materials cast a helpful light on the pattern—and in today's world, possibly the limitations—of Chaplin's comic world. Not only are Beckett's tramps themselves more flawed, but the evils of their surrounding world are more complex and ambiguous. In Chaplin's world, what was added in the humanizing of slapstick comedy still carried the simplifications and sentimentality of the early film world of Griffith's harassed waifs, the world of late nineteenth- early twentieth-century melodrama. To be sure, this quality can prevail longer in comedy, but even comedy can be limited by sentimentality.

The Gold Rush

Chaplin's comedy not only places much greater emphasis on the human response to the comic encounters but also makes *things* more expressive. Things become like other things and like humans; they become a part of a human world, more directly related to humans and their excesses—whether individual greed and selfishness or their more pointed manifestation in the compulsions of society. As in the Sennett comedies, comic tension is increased by building on and extending material already introduced. *The Gold Rush* (1925) probably represents the peak of Chaplin's use, often subtly, sometimes not, of the extended "topper." Typically, the orchestrated and accelerated material is used thematically as well as comically, the three main focuses being the wind, hunger, and love (the girl)—the natural and human forces in Chaplin's world of gold-prospecting. In a sequence early in *The Gold Rush*, Charlie enters from the right, practically blown onto the screen by the wind and snow. In the subsequent sequence, single shots and combinations of shots play a set of 13 different variations on people and things being blown by the wind. Later, at the film's climax of action, the wind is used as the cabin is blown onto the edge of a cliff. This introduces the

The Gold Rush

famous cabin-teetering sequence, with its own set of variations, which in 59 shots leads to the triumph—the discovery of gold.

More subtle in invention and inflection are the sequences that cluster around the theme of hunger and food. In the first, eating a chicken leg leads to Charlie's hand being bitten, some shooting, a pantomime over the mistaken belief that he's shot. In the second, the dog is threatened, Charlie eats a candle (with salt, the small touch), the dog seems to have been eaten, is not. In the third, the material is heightened, the inflections of Charlie's facial responses more varied and important; this is the famous sequence of eating the shoe, with small toppers such as the laces as spaghetti, the nails as chicken bones, a crooked one a wishbone. But the real topper is the subsequent lengthy fantasy sequence, in which Charlie is chased by Big Jim, whose hallucination of Charlie as a chicken is shared intermittently by the audience.

In the best of the sequences centering on the girl, the mood shifts between success and embarrassment. Sad and longing, Charlie is pleased to get to dance with Georgia. But his pants begin to fall (see Beckett's *Godot*). He first overcomes this by putting his trusty cane through one of his belt loops, then by grabbing a piece of rope. But the rope is attached to a dog, the dog joins the dance, then chases a cat. All end in a muddle—the last topper, the dog's rear in Charlie's face. But up he bounces and cuts the rope with a borrowed knife.

Immediately following, however, there is a sentimental touch: a close-up of Charlie wistfully picking up Georgia's dropped rose, followed by several related shots. In all of his feature films of this period, Chaplin attempted, with varying success, to integrate a fuller range of sentiment with the comedy, though most often in the form of stereotyped sentimentality. In the earlier *The Kid* (1921), the bathos dominates, replete with abandoned babes, the darling boy, social villains, threatened separation of child and tramp, and final happy ending. In *The Gold Rush,* the love-seeking, kept rather separate, does not reach the same level as the other segments. In the much undervalued *The Circus* (1928), a more touching integration is achieved.

The Circus and City Lights

Although not as directly concerned with social realities, this film's variation on the conventional circus clown is one of Chaplin's most revealing personal comments. The Tramp, chased into a circus by a policeman, becomes a successful star clown—using his natural behavior as the basis of his clowning. He falls in love with an aerial artist and loses her, despite his success. The comedy affects and reveals the film's attitude toward the sentiments. Charlie is a natural innocent; the aerialist, a trained performer, is worldly and artificial. Charlie's comedy is different from that of the other clowns as dramatized by many of the comic routines. In one telling highlight, after the broadness of the clowns' routine of William Tell and the apple—one takes a bite when the other turns around—Charlie plays his variation: He bites, responds facially in controlled shock, wiggles a finger to indicate the truth— a worm in the apple. Not only is it an apt symbol for Chaplin's own sense of the difference of his comedy, but it also captures in a comic moment the Tramp's recognition of the flaw in the apple of innocence, even of love, in the circus that is the world. Although not a high flyer, Charlie dares the tightrope. In the climactic scene, his safety belt betrays him, he teeters, is swarmed by monkeys, but survives. Yet he now knows his limits and what he must lose in a world that can use but not accommodate the innocence of his tenderness.

In *City Lights,* made in 1931, the Tramp must again lose all to the ways of the world. While the film has a more specific social background and makes a more direct critique of a world based on money values, it is again a fable of rejected sentiment. To help a blind girl, whom he loves, Charlie must enter the world of money—represented by a prize fight and a millionaire whom he saves from drowning and who almost drowns him. The erratic undependability of the millionaire is the basis of many fine gags but leads to a trite cause-and-effect plot, the film's weakest element. The millionaire gives Charlie money. Later, when he has been robbed, and suspicion falls on Charlie, he refuses to admit that he had given the money to Charlie, who is then taken to jail. Before he goes, Charlie gives the blind girl the money, which she uses for an operation that restores her sight. On his return from jail, she can see that he is but a tramp, and so he must lose her.

The girl's blindness, the plot machinations, her final rejection of the

Modern Times

Tramp are banal, without those touches of special invention at crucial points, contrivances to produce the teary pathos of the loss. It is a loss more inflicted, demanded, than inevitable. And yet Chaplin does somehow raise the last moments above the level to which their content, reasonably considered, might entitle them. There is a control to the manipulation—in the touching theme music, in the beautifully modulated expressions of both girl and Tramp, in the directness of the final close-ups—that releases an expression of the emotional core of the fable from the artifice of the plot.

Modern Times — In Chaplin's *Modern Times*, made in 1936, his social satire is harsher, more direct still; yet the sentimentality is more jaunty. The Tramp wins the girl, and together they leave the mess of society behind them. While the Tramp's final decision may stem from his experiences with the world of machines in the first half of the film, and while the second half (after he meets the girl) may be an intentional counterpoint of mood and style, there is still a disturbing separation between the two parts—and thus between the social satire and the sentimentality. The second part is more a series of lyrical arias, extended virtuoso performances in the old Chaplin style: Charlie diving into about six inches of water, yet retaining his dignity; Charlie skating blindfolded near the unprotected edge of a height; Charlie wonderfully out of place as a waiter in a crowded restaurant. In the first half, however, Charlie's gags and inflections of response are *in,* not tangential to, a world gone mad with machines and economic strife. His jauntiness is threatened, though it survives; the individual gags have significant echoes. The orchestration of "toppers" is part of a total fabric of social satire, not a series of separate routines.

In one of his best buildups of movement and expression, Charlie, overworked on a speeded-up assembly line, cannot stop his hands from repeating the turning motion he had been applying to bolts, even when he's in the street without his bolts or wrench. A woman approaches, buttons on her ample bosom just like his bolts; the hands move, the mustache twitches, we know the inevitable will occur. Yet this excellent routine is only one of several harsher ones that compose a larger indictment of the soulless mechanization of life: a fellow worker caught (albeit comically) in the rollers of a giant machine, Charlie gruesomely stuffed with food by a feeding machine, Charlie sent to a psychiatric ward for his rebellion. On his release, the basic pattern of comic confusion builds to another crescendo of social entrapment: to an unintended participation in a chaotic protest march, to jail, to unplanned heroism in a jailbreak. But with Charlie's pardon and meeting of the girl, the mood shifts. Excellent as the latter routines are, the Tramp's way out of the trap slights the social issues raised in the first half of the film.

While Chaplin imaginatively used some elements of sound (but not full dialogue) in *City Lights* and *Modern Times,* they are still one with his silent work, not only in their underlying sentimental tone but in the conservativeness of their basic technique. Chaplin's modulation of slapstick technique to smaller detail of action and greater nuance of response is integral to his basic sense of the expressive power of the film image, of the kind of exaggerations it produced. Yet his use of the film image stressed the contents of that image rather than formal elements of composition or juxtapositions or editing structures. That stress on the selection of detail in the content enhances the comic and dramatic realism of his work, involves the audience through matter rather than the effects of cinematic devices. But the same emphasis contributed to a deficiency in the plastic quality of the image of that detail and to a weaker sense of film movement and flow in the shots themselves. Chaplin's selection of angle, for example, could often be quite telling: As Charlie first longingly watches Georgia in *The Gold Rush,* a big miner casually leans on a stair rail in the left foreground, Georgia stands facing him in the center, and the Tramp looks on from the distant right, separated from them and also from the crowd at the rear right of the shot. Yet, often too, the angles are pedestrian, even dull, the camera static and unmoving through long bits of action. In cutting, he is again sometimes awkward, commonly precise, but mainly functional: the expected close-ups for emphasis, reverse shots as in the sequence in *The Gold Rush* when someone blown out of a door is seen first from the interior and then from the outside.

In one of Chaplin's earlier films, *The Woman of Paris* (1924), he used a somewhat more mannered style, a greater allusiveness, a more symbolic composition for the carefully selected details: A distraught boy, seated on his bed, is in a flood of white surrounded by blackness—quite unlike the usual Chaplin composition. The film was not a Tramp film; Chaplin did not appear. The difference suggests Chaplin's concern in the Tramp films for maintaining what he believed was a kind of purity and directness in his treatment of his persona. *The Woman of Paris* blends a maudlin sentimentality with a witty, sophisticated treatment of sexual themes in a manner highly original for its time. It preceded the first sophisticated comedy of Ernst Lubitsch and has often been said to have influenced Lubitsch. Actually, Lubitsch's approach to sexually tinged comedy and melodrama had already been established in parts of his costume epics, but certainly the release of Chaplin's film and its treatment of sex through innuendo had some effect. Whatever the connection, it was clearly to become the field and manner of Lubitsch, and others, quite distinct from the main development of Chaplin's career in both silents and sound.

LANGDON AND LLOYD

Of the other clowns of the period who established a distinct persona and consistent tone, only Laurel and Hardy continued (into the sound era) to maintain and develop their career as long as Chaplin did. Indeed, though their work in the twenties created, for the first time, their dual image of contrasting yet surprisingly similar characters, their chief feature work came later, when sound allowed for the verbal interchanges, in their wonderfully appropriate and expressive voices, that were the perfect complement for their physical comedy.

In contrast, the career of Harry Langdon was uneven—especially in the twenties, after he had moved on from Sennett two-reelers to features of his own—and cut short finally by personal problems and changes in fashion. Like the personas of each of the major comedians of the era, Langdon's was that of an innocent in a threatening world. But his innocence was the strangest of the lot. Pudgy and short in clothes that never fit, face painted white, he had the wistful, dreaming tenderness of a Pierrot and the emotional patterns and intellectual comprehension—the total self-absorption—of a baby verging on childhood and middle age at the same time. Bewildered and excruciatingly uncapable, he was a mass of modulated hesitations, apprehensions, and confusions, surviving more through luck and happenstance than through any effectual action of his own. Though more limited in persona and situation, he was instinctively inventive in developing variations on a narrow theme—leading up to the inevitable as he rubs his chest with limburger cheese in a crowded bus (thinking it a cold salve) or as he cycles in dangerously slower and slower circles, in rapt adoration of his beloved. Langdon improvised his own bits but usually in situations devised by and under the direction of others. His best films—*Tramp Tramp Tramp* and *The Strong Man* (both 1926) and *Long Pants* (1927)—were the first impor-

Safety Last

tant efforts of Frank Capra, who later refined a type of sentimental comedy based more on character and situation, but always with a touch of the physical and the visual inventiveness of the clowns' slapstick world.

If Langdon was always tremulously aflutter, never in control, Harold Lloyd was the innocent at the opposite pole. Brash and undaunted, he *knows* nothing is beyond his control. Even in his occasional timidity, the certainty is there, just behind the horn-rimmed glasses. Though at first (or for some time) he is always wrong, despite all the pitfalls of society and things and his own mistakes, he is right, he does control in the end. The go-getter who does succeed, but always likeable nonetheless, he has a whole gamut of toothy smiles to express the changing tones of the young man made better by his trials. There is a strong conventional morality—shaped in part by the Horatio Alger success of Lloyd's own life—underlying his films, which depend a good deal on the conventional manipulations of boy-next-door seeks girl or money or success (or all three at once). But their key comic ingredient is Lloyd surmounting situations of social embarrassment or physical danger in long sequences of inventive "toppers."

Most successful of all are the sequences that add to the humorous invention the new element of suspenseful thrills from extended danger. The finest (and longest) of these—both in inventiveness and the rhythmic control of variation and crescendo—is the climactic half-hour of *Safety Last* (1923). Substituting for a professional human fly (no need to wonder why), Lloyd manages to perform prodigious feats of acrobatics up the side of a building. In the process there are dozens of comic turns. In the long climax, the separate gags tend more and more to interlock: One success leads to the next problem. Escaping a dog, Lloyd hangs from a flagpole; when the flagpole breaks, he grabs the hand of a huge clock; hanging onto the hand, he pulls it precariously down to "VI." In a further variation, the buildup of one gag begins our expectations of the next. While he's trying to survive the clock—its whole face threatens to fall out—we know he's going to get his foot caught in the spring. As he plays a series of variations on almost getting hit, unknowingly, by a revolving wind gauge, he begins to get his foot entangled in a rope. When he's finally hit, the rope catches him, saves him, only to leave him dangling head down high above the street.

KEATON

Buster Keaton's version of the innocent was, like Lloyd's, closer to the young man down the street than were those of Charlie, Laurel and Hardy, Harry Langdon, and Fatty Arbuckle. And yet it had a more distinctive, more emotional, and finally touching, oddness—halfway between our block and the rootless world of the wandering waifs.

Restraint and Reserve

The face, of course, is the key. Although never so deeply moody or bleak, so craggy tough as latter-day commentators are prone to read it, the face of Buster in the twenties did play against its own surface innocence, its cool passivity, its protective, one-track-mind solemnity; it did somehow suggest in his manipulation of its youthful, smooth marble the presence of the truly tragic granite of the Keaton face of the later, lost years. In the twenties it is the face of an incurable optimist who knows better—touched by a distant melancholy, but even more by an obsessive zeal that betrays the need beneath the cool surface. Buster *must* control, protect himself in the midst of disorder, restrain his own emotionality. While he knows he can, he knows (more than Lloyd's persona) the risks and the severity of the threat. He is never surprised when the inevitable occurs and compounds itself. His dour face has already been prepared for the worst, and he is prepared, and able, to act against it. A clue to the dimension in Keaton that goes beyond Lloyd is the basic, recurrent metaphor of his face and carriage: maintaining poise and balance, stiffly upright, hat flat and straight, face set—order and dignity at any cost, and all precarious.

He plays against the reserve of his own face and with the restraint of his whole body plays against the madcap whirl of the world—even when his own zeal to keep things straight has added to the momentum. In Keaton's work—in contrast to that of Chaplin—the intangibles of the human spirit are not emphasized in the basic situations or focused on in shots of response. He does not directly deal with the sentiments; sentiment is as restrained as his facial expressions. Fully emotional human relationships or problems, social criticism are secondary. While Keaton as a director uses film more creatively, with greater visual resourcefulness, flow, excitement, even beauty, and while he is free of the Victorian sentimentalism and preachiness that lingers on in Chaplin, his films do not have the density, the fullness of texture, the broad range of emotions of Chaplin's. They are about less not only in terms of comment on man and society but in terms of a deeper resonance of human emotion and spirit. In some ways, they risk less.

In the construction of his films, Keaton, like Buster, maintains a straight-line purity. It is a purity of movement, perfect in execution, stylized into a kind of abstraction: a poetry of visual action and rhythm, but without the substance that turns Chaplin's visual images into a poetry of the spirit as well. Like Lloyd, Buster faces physical dangers, but these involve more intricately mechanical, man-made devices that have gotten out of hand. Still, there are other, more crucial differences beyond this emphasis on the mechanical and Keaton's ingenious technology. There is Keaton's sense of the comic life in things; they are not merely problems to work through. Like Chaplin, he sees the surprising relationships between things and between things and man, the unexpected connections and interchangeability, especially the ludicrousness of use outside of or beyond normal function. But he goes beyond Chaplin in his employment of the plastic, physical qualities of things, of sizes, shapes, and functions. This is particularly evident in his more integral use of settings, mechanical or natural. For Chaplin, Charlie's response and the small details of action are all-important; for Keaton, each piece—a face, an arm, a sword, a motor, an engine, a boat, a river, a bridge, a mountain—is visually, actively functioning in a total comic interaction.

Sherlock Junior   Keaton's *Sherlock Junior* (1924), one of his more unusual films, is full of gags derived from the unexpected connections or uses of objects: from the more prosaic oddities of billiard balls full of explosives jumping into coat pockets or of a train's water tank dousing first the hero and then the villains, to the more poetic use of a canvas car roof as a sail, when the body of the car is shot off and lands in the water. (Inevitably it sinks, but with Buster still in firm control as the ship goes down.)

The comic use of setting is particularly ingenious in *Sherlock Junior*, for it is a film that plays with the manipulations of space, time, and reality possible in moviemaking, the various unrealities made real. In it, a film projectionist falls asleep, and his dream-double is absorbed into the images projected on the screen. Through a series of quick cuts, he is kicked out of the screen, faces a locked door, stands in a garden, sits in a garden chair only to find himself in the midst of a street full of traffic, walks in the street as it becomes a precipice, wanders in a desert, is almost run over by a train (still in the desert!), is on an island, and dives into a sea that becomes an arctic snowdrift. Absorbed fully into the screen story, he ends finally in a climactic chase that is one of the peaks of Keaton's ingenuity and of his use of accelerating momentum: Early in his ride on the handlebars of a speeding (and driverless) motorcycle, he is rhythmically splattered with dirt from a line of ditchdiggers; as he moves along, things lose their normal functions, often to his benefit—a threatening gap in a bridge is suddenly filled by two roofs, the bridge helpfully collapses only as he zooms off its unfinished end. The last increase in velocity is captured in four brief shots that telescope the final topper: (1) Sherlock Junior approaching camera on cycle; (2) gangster hut on right, Sherlock Junior entering frame on left, hitting obstruction, flying through hut window; (3) inside, Sherlock Junior shooting across top of table into butler; (4) hut now on left, butler crashing through back wall (toward right) and out into field.

But the most expressionistic or surrealistic of his effects was achieved at the end of *Steamboat Bill Jr.* (also made in 1928), without any explanatory frame to justify the strangeness of it. In a town completely desolated by a great flood, Buster wanders through strange adventures (including a dive into the false water of a stage backdrop) that are capped by his viewing all the people of the town floating on the river, each on the distinctive possessions, the objects, of his life. It might well have been an image out of Fellini.

The Navigator

In *The Navigator* (1924), certain separate images display a surreal touch: the leering face of a portrait appearing and disappearing outside a porthole; all the doors on one side of the ship's cabin deck simultaneously slamming silently shut behind Buster (and repeating this each time he turns away); Buster, knife in hand, in a diving suit at the bottom of the sea, embroiled with an octopus; Buster in the diving suit, rising from the sea like a sea monster; Buster cutting the stomach of the diving suit, water pouring out like blood.

But in the main, *The Navigator*, in which the physical implications of a

Steamboat Bill Jr.

central situation are carried out, is one of Keaton's purest ballets of function, movement, and response. It has some of the best images of Buster's obsessiveness: refusing to be daunted by a folding deck chair, which he somehow resurrects from the shambles it has become only to have it collapse under him; leaning, pivoting, peering intently while investigating the darkened ship, blithely unaware of the fireworks shooting from the roman candle he has lit instead of a candle; rowing rapidly, towing a giant ship with his rowboat (a nicely timed cut to a long shot catching the ludicrousness of the big hull, the taut line, and the tiny rowboat straining away); then rowing even more furiously as the boat begins to sink; and rowing still when it's gone.

As Buster and his fiancée try to exist on the empty, drifting liner onto which they've stumbled, Keaton draws on the comic qualities inherent in things, building a rising line of challenge, threat, and success. He capitalizes on the reversible quality of objects. At first, all the devices and objects on the ship are too much for them—whether eggs, cans of soup, or bunk beds. After time has passed, the same things are seen conquered with zany inventiveness: Their beds have been placed cozily in the empty ship's boilers; they cook gracefully with a whole series of intricate contraptions put to use in odd ways. When they are then threatened by cannibals, much of the comedy is based on this kind of reversibility: The diving suit that almost kills Buster saves them from the natives and is even used as a boat for the girl (with Buster still in it, though it almost suffocates him). A toy cannon, its rope caught in his feet, chases him madly but shoots a cannibal as Buster ducks. Even a swordfish that attacks him under water is used in a successful duel with another swordfish.

The
General

Like *The Navigator, The General,* filmed in 1928, is almost all movement, balletlike, although it has a stronger plot premise in Buster's obsessive pursuit of his chance to help win the war and the girl, and (not necessarily least) to retrieve his beloved locomotive, "the General." Every piece of comic action develops the dramatic motivation. Through all the gags and toppers, the graceful, and often beautiful, image of Buster coolly and passionately seeking to salvage what he loves from the confusions of war is built. Obsessively Buster tries to master an errant axe and chop the needed firewood, while a whole army passes unnoticed behind him. A number of trains misbehave and interact in intricate maneuvers; a waterspout douses; cannons fire in the wrong direction. A sword doggedly fights Buster's equally relentless efforts to get it out of its scabbard, only to send its broken blade flying when he succeeds—impaling a sniper before he can shoot Buster. But nothing better illustrates the film's integration of gag and drama (and its union of all things, human and non-, in a single world verging on utter disorder) than one small moment on the train. After rejecting (and tossing out) their last piece of firewood because it had a knot, the girl offers a tiny chip as her choice and then proceeds to sweep out the last remaining pieces on the cab floor. Losing control for one brief moment, Buster turns and shakes her violently—then stops, kisses her quickly and lightly, and continues his work.

In eight years, Keaton created more than 20 shorts and 11 features. Although he would continue to appear sporadically in the sound era, he was never again given the artistic control or comic material to continue his work. Just before his death in 1966, he appeared in two unusual featurettes. In the Canadian-made *Railrodder* (1965), on a motorized handcar he crosses Canada—upright as an old tree, lonely and resolute as stone. Through almost all of Samuel Beckett's *Film* (1965), we are allowed to see only the amazingly eloquent silence of Keaton's back, until in one brief moment there are the ineffably sad, remembering eyes.

Does it only seem that the history of the film is—so much more than that of the purer arts—a history of broken promise, or of broken promises?

2

SOUND,

SOCIETY,

AND

THE

ESTABLISHMENT

OF

REALISM

CHAPTER SEVEN

CHANGING STRUCTURES FOR CHANGING FEELINGS

In earlier decades, defining and refining what it meant that movies had visual images that moved had led to a complex development of the obvious. In the thirties and forties, defining and refining what it meant that movie images moved *and* talked and were a palpably accurate imitation of real life resulted in a shift in style—not all at once, not total, not without exceptions and variations. So complete a shift is not likely in any of the arts, least of all in a mass art as subject to a variety of pressures and intentions as the movies. But there was a distinct shift of the point of balance, of consensus, as a result of which new tensions and mixtures would arise. The shift consolidated and established more centrally the tendencies toward Realism that had been present from the earliest work of Louis Lumière on.

REALISM'S NEW DOMINANCE

For many, the film had always been the inevitable final stage in the tradition of artistic, dramatic, and literary Realism that had been a central force since the mid-nineteenth century and that in the thirties—despite incursions and countermovements—was still the most popular set of esthetic conventions in drama and literature. As with any other, this tradition (with its slippery appellation *Realism*), because it embraces only one varying set of ways to penetrate, capture, and understand reality, suffers from certain limitations and exclusions. It is not necessarily more successful in its attempt than other styles and is clearly less so in its most conventionalized forms. Realism is one way of giving body and form to a way of seeing, one kind of structuring of feelings about life, society, the nature of reality, art itself.

The Realist View One of the most extreme advocates of this way of rendering reality in art, Émile Zola, suggests the essence of the approach in his metaphor of the three screens. Although he was of course not referring to the movie screen, his definitions are apropos in tracing the application of the theory to the film. For Zola, the classic screen, or filtering process of art (as in the epic style), enlarges; the romantic screen (as in the Expressionist style) is a prism and distorts. But "the realist screen is plain glass, very thin, very clear, which aspires to be so perfectly transparent that images may pass through it and remake themselves in all their reality."

This view, in turn, reflects certain ways of looking at what life, reality, is and at what art is, and should do. It stems, for one thing, from the distinctly nineteenth-century view of scientific truth, not truth from faith; it leads to an art that displays this truth, like scientific proof, with step by step accumulation of details—not by inspired revelation, suddenly and intuitively, of given essences. And it is a truth of scientific certainty (in contrast to contemporary scientific theories of uncertainty, indeterminacy, relativity), a relatively secure view of the world as something fixed and stable. One objective reality out there, patterned and patternable, knowable. And in man, a human consciousness capable of accurately recording it and then ordering it in neat, significant, and controllable patterns—as in Darwin's sweeping patterns for biological life, Marx's for social and economic life, and Freud's for even the intangible depths of man's unconscious.

Like the theories of Zola, this conception of reality leads to an emphasis in art on observation and imitation rather than on imagination and subjective expression; an emphasis on representation of what is clearly knowable, on the literal, accurate rendering of the surface manifestations of the patterns of reality. In dramatic art, this emphasis led especially to the attempt to maintain an unbroken illusion of reality for the stage or screen performance, to an immersion of the spectator in the dramatic action without the apparent intrusion of imaginative or artificial devices, to a transparent fourth wall or screen, to the use of devices that disguise the use of devices. In retrospect, however, devices contrived to allow the unhindered passage of reality have often proved hindering, restricting artifices, obstacles to the very sense of reality being sought.

While the old Realist tradition, along with the intrinsic capacity of the film image for accurate reproduction, had clearly influenced the development of the film all along, a new confluence of factors in and out of the film world now—at the time of its deep and far-reaching entrenchment in the early thirties—began to reshape the form of film Realism.

In literature, a variety of more or less Realist styles were still felt to be the foundation of the art. In America about 1930, the position of Ernest Hemingway in "serious" fiction and Dashiell Hammett in the detective story can stand as symptomatic. Both demanded a laconic, selective representation of surface detail, a restriction of obvious subjectivity in the careful, unobtrusive (though again often quite artificially and thus obtrusively unobtrusive) rendering of things, action, and dialogue.

In the drama, the movement in Germany toward The New Realism in the later twenties had been typical of the beginning of the decline of the flirtation with more expressive forms. By the thirties, the major forms of stage drama had reduced or eliminated the extremes and exaggerations of both naturalistic and melodramatic plays; they were in the main a careful rendering of the commonplace, whether in social or domestic crisis. The model was the Ibsen of the social plays—with careful orchestration of character and conflict in a social context. In America, even Eugene O'Neill ceased his extreme, eclectic experimentation of the twenties. Although his relative silence in the thirties served to indicate his continued separation from the conventional forms of Realism, he did in his later plays rebuild a subjective, individualized style on the foundations of Realism rather than on the kind of extremely theatrical devices he struggled with in the twenties. The theater of Social Realism became the dominant mode, exemplified in the productions of the Group Theater and in the works of Clifford Odets, Sidney Kingsley, Lillian Hellman, and S. N. Behrman.

SHAPING INFLUENCES

Social
Realism

The depiction and criticism of social problems was long associated with the Realist style. In the eighteenth century, the earliest Realist theorizing—of Diderot and Champfleury, and even of the painter Courbet—related the new needs for accuracy in art to the needs for social reform. In the thirties, earthquake social and economic crises in the world called forth, on both stage and screen, the full implementation of this strong earlier line of development. Subjects and motifs, patterns of character development are as much the constituents of a style as are attitudes and techniques. Realist drama traditionally makes a clear-cut distinction between illusion and reality, dream and fact; in its most characteristic form, it recounts an individual's movement toward a knowable position of truth. In the drama of Social Realism, individual illusions and dreams are given social definition, are part of and influenced by social illusions; the movement of a character toward the truth is also a movement toward the solution of the social problem.

The tradition of Social Realism that has evolved since the early thirties—especially in America—breaks in several important ways with the earlier tradition of Zola's literary Naturalism. For though it continues to emphasize materialistic surfaces of life and the strong deterministic pressures of society, it does not hold the extreme earlier view of man as enslaved by uncontrollable animality or as a passive victim of external pressures. This newer tradition—and even more so its screen versions—devises conflicts that dramatize both strong, shaping social forces and the possibilities of the assertion of individual conscious will. These conflicts postulate a dynamic interaction between man and society, with the individual allowed the possibility of recognition and efficacious action, or at least judged on the basis of this possibility. Thus from this Realist perspective, social problems can be understood, the alternatives clearly evaluated, the choices judged, and change implemented. *Doing something* about the problems gets transformed into a staple component of dramatic structure—often carried to the point of affirmative resolutions that are the weakest element of such works of Social Realism.

A prevailing attitude toward crisis in the social world, then, found a natural and appropriate tool in Realist representation—accurately placing individuals in a credible context. This conjunction of a social viewpoint and an esthetic mode was reinforced by events within the film world—making strange allies of deep, organic social crisis and of commercial developments in the film industry. The prosperity and growth of the industry and its consolidation into larger corporations had far-reaching, often contradictory effects. Growth and consolidation tended to encourage the entrenchment of techniques and, in this case, a style that could efficiently accomplish an accurate representation of the surface realities of life; yet, quite often, the surface accuracies were applied to dramatic situations that had little to do with what anyone could call reality. In the commercial film, the paradox of the Realist style takes its extreme form: There is no necessary connection between devices of realistic representation and the serious, honest representation of reality. The commercial compromise affected films of the period that attempted a more serious social rendering of reality as well, tending to soften and diffuse—even defuse—the thrust of protest found in stage drama. Some social problems, such as race, were ignored; others, and their solutions, were oversimplified, reduced to a tinkering with the easy edges of manageable issues. Critics whose most common basis of evaluation was social concern often managed to find sustenance in crumbs. Indeed, in one last twist of the paradox, the application of Realist techniques by those engaged in producing "pure entertainment" at times produced a more artistic result even more revealing of life than the efforts of those soberly pursuing an accredited version of Realist truth.

The complex organization and procedures of big-studio movie production—movies made by interlocking groups of people—favored the implementation of less personalized, more functional, efficient techniques. So did the increase in the number of films made and the cost of making them. Cuts on obvious movements or changes of situation or setting, for example, could be planned and thus more economically coordinated with the building of sets and the arranging of lighting.

In this business perspective, the product—the content—overswayed all, coinciding with the emphasis in serious Realist theory on content revealing itself through a transparent screen. This emphasis encouraged the development, on the one hand, of genres and stars, escapist pleasures; on the other, the serious depiction of social problems. But, as it turned out, both hands were tied by the demands of business.

In seeking the largest audience possible, film-makers sought to make response to content easy—technique put to use for ease of perception and enjoyment. Again, this coincided with the esthetic trend toward observation by the audience rather than control of the audience through such means as epic montage or Expressionist symbolism. Still, control and manipulation of the audience are obviously always present to some degree. But the difference in degree is significant as are the kind and purpose of control—especially in terms of the obtrusiveness of the devices used.

Refined
Techniques

Also favoring consolidation of the Realist style—in addition to the cultural context and the business demands of the industry—were developments in the refinement of film technique. These tended to carry further an earlier negative reaction to the Expressionist excesses of technique; not the extremes but the middle ground of a quieter, if possibly blander, excellence—a cinema of substance and clear, careful surface.

Sound

And overlapping all three areas—the Realist tradition and society, the industry, and refinements in technique—was sound. Jolson sang, and soon everything was "ALL-TALKING; ALL-SINGING; ALL-DANCING." Sound was novelty (and money), but even before the shock of novelty began to fade, exploration of the obvious fact that the movies now talked as well as moved began to have important effects on the development of technique and style. The most obvious of the immediate effects were mechanical—new limits on when and how cuts could be made, leading to less dynamic editing, but leading also to imaginative combinations of visual and aural elements. The dramatic economy of sound—presenting and explaining more dramatic material more quickly—lessened the need for visual expressiveness, for symbolic correlatives to lay open the inner life of characters. Words revealed. Words also allowed for greater dramatic complexity, more emphasis on plot and the dramatic mode. And words served to intensify the film's intrinsic bias toward Realism, to strengthen its immediate, tangible sense of close correspondence with life itself. With sound, the movies moved even closer to normal experience, appealing to both the major senses man uses in responding to life. This sense of greater commonplace normality also favored less heightening of materials, less distorting, less expressive separating (in Eisenstein's term) of images from the objects in reality that they reproduce.

MANIFESTATIONS IN TECHNIQUE

Not even the accommodation to sound, however, produced a monolithic shift of style. At the new point of balance of the sound era, the stylistic equations of technique-content and expressiveness-imitativeness came to emphasize the latter terms in both—"content" and "imitativeness"—but not without a continuing fruitfulness of balances struck with the other two terms, a variety of counterassertions against the prevailing consensus.

A style that seeks to present content with as strong an illusion of reality as possible will be a contextual style. Thus, the Realist film continued and even increased the film's use of objects and physical environment to place characters and their actions in fully textured, concrete, dramatic contexts. In the more conventional or even stereotyped film of this style, however, there is greater reliance on accuracy of imitation, less on extracting significance from the world of physical things.

Invisible
Editing
and
the
Long
Take

In the Realist style, the illusion of reality is further maintained by less asser- tive, more functional editing—"invisible" editing, which does not seek the shock effect of parallel and accelerating montage, of provocative individual juxtapositions, of symbolic associations or attractions, of dialectical conflict- collision montage. It does seek to implement psychological and dramatic de- velopment, and its clear antecedents are found particularly in G. W. Pabst's films—the twenties' films most akin to the Realist style. With less expressive flourishes than Pabst employed, the style cuts on physical movement or shifts of setting and on changes in a character's attention or intentions. Such cutting fulfills the expectation of the spectator, seemingly at the service of his observation though obviously still controlling that observation.

A corollary to invisible editing is a greater emphasis on the single shot by means of the long take—that is, holding a single shot within a scene for an extended duration. Again, this approach builds more on the tradition of the single image, (as in the German film of the twenties or in von Stroheim's) than on the tradition of juxtaposition of images through montage. In the more conventional films of the sound era, this revealing of the content of the shot employed less symbolic heightening of the image through lighting, selection, and composition and less expressive movement of the camera than the Ger- man film. The long take—with a changing flow of material in the shot—makes selection and emphasis less overt, though still controllable. Relationship is established between the components of a single image rather than between selected components of more than one image. The result can be a greater sense of simultaneity—things happen, are not abstracted into their parts— and a greater sense of spectator participation in observing and interpreting.

With the gradual perfection of deep-focus photography, the long take was to become a much more versatile instrument—whether in the more expressive style of Orson Welles or in the literal representationalism of William Wyler. In a discussion of deep focus in 1947, Wyler summed up the basis of his approach to the long take:

> Gregg Toland's remarkable [cinematographic] facility for handling background and foreground action has enabled me to develop a better technique of staging my scenes. I can have action and re- action in the same shot, without having to cut back and forth from individual cuts of the characters. This makes for smooth conti- nuity and an almost effortless flow of the scene, for more interest-

ing composition in each shot, and lets the spectator look from one to the other character at his own will, do his own cutting.

This approach to editing and the single shot produced a smooth, functional technique, but one that could become too blandly mechanical. The emphasis on fulfilling the shallowest expectations of the spectator by the least demanding means tended to reduce the style to a set of editing clichés —overly careful and pedestrian in building transitions without gaps and overly repetitious in normal patterns of sequences: from the long, establishing shot, to the medium two-shots, to the obligatory reverse close-up cutting for dialogue or the obvious close-up to follow the glance of a character.

Mise en Scène

Nevertheless, this approach also became the basis of a serious esthetic of the film, in intentional opposition to the esthetic of montage. In his writings after World War II, the French critic André Bazin recapitulated and synthesized the principles of this approach, present from the beginnings of film but often drowned out by the voices of the advocates of montage. In Bazin's words, the aim is to let "reality lay itself bare," to have "respect for the spatial unity of an event at the moment when to split it up would change it from something real into something imaginary." Central to the maintenance of this concrete objectivity, this authenticity and autonomy of the spatial image and the event is *mise en scène*. Among other things, this elusive term, often invoked magically and mysteriously by its exponents, calls for the careful composition of design and decor, the careful arrangement and orchestration of the elements of the shot in a structure and flow that reveal their essential truths. In this revelation, the camera must have an extreme concentration on events, a reticence that furthers its unity with the action. While this esthetic approach implements the film's ability to capture reality, in the long run it has also contributed to more subtle and sophisticated forms of expressiveness, serving to reveal not only the movements of events but, in the phrase of Alexandre Astruc, "the movements of the soul." With greater Realism eventually came more subtle forms of expressive manipulation.

Dramatic Structure and Characterization

Still, in the thirties the shift of stylistic balance brought greater solidification of the film's basic tendency toward Realism and, in turn, further substantiated it as a dramatic art. Obviously, epic celebration and structure, pure description, and episodic or fragmentary development continued. But with the introduction of sound, the tendency toward the dramatic, innate in film, was also consolidated, especially in concordance with the structure of Realist stage drama. Even epics became more dramatic.

Film drama of the thirties exhibited a greater flexibility in manipulation of space and time but nonetheless stood firmly on the foundations of the Realist mode. This convention of drama—having developed from the tradition of the well-made play—focuses on a specific, concrete problem, particularized in a clearly defined, initiating conflict. The structure of action that develops this conflict has a tight coherence; all individual scenes and complications contribute, step by step, to the development of the conflict and the rising tension between episodes. They are not, for example, separate illustrations or variations on a theme. Most indicative of all, the action follows a precise pattern of cause and effect, and is presented in rather full, concrete detail, developing within individual scenes clear stages of internal conflict worked out without gaps or ambiguities of motivation or influence. The straight-line explanatory connections of this causal sequence are further locked into place by careful methods of transition. Finally, the sequence produces a clear climax and well-defined resolution, conventionally affirmative or with implied affirmation, especially in terms of the possibility of growth of human will and awareness.

Dramatic characterization follows suit. It too is contextual, tends toward ease of audience empathy and identification. It generally provides a fully detailed psychological context in which the characters act, often with clear references (and even flashback dramatization) to past influence on current behavior and attitudes. While there is more applied psychology in terms of motives and patterns of behavior, there is less subjectivity, less probing or revealing of the kind of inner states that Expressionism attempts to externalize.

Characters in the Realist mode are more individualized, particularized, than in the melodramatic or epic films. While often still types—especially social types—they are delineated with more sophistication; they are less extreme and one-sided than a typical Griffith or melodramatic character. Acting, too, develops greater particularization, is more modulated and credible, built with small details of movement, voice, and expression rather than the broader, more exaggerated strokes of most silent acting.

Within this developing framework of greater sophistication in the delineation of character, the patterns of behavior are still precisely laid out, often too precisely—carefully guiding the audience's response while seemingly not. Although who the characters are, the kind of people they are, still tends to be too symmetrically typal, the Realist style does show a particular advance in establishing credibility of motivation and character change, with behavior more solidly prepared for, changes less sudden and extreme than in earlier films. But again, this very precision for the sake of literal credibility and ease of response becomes restrictive of both the kinds of truth and the kinds of response its own kind of manipulation allows. The same attempt to find and embody a securely ordered pattern of reality—and one that does not make too great a demand on the admission-paying audience—leads to one last effect: the unambiguous, neatly classified, sometimes compromised terms of the social and moral judgments of the conventional Realist film.

This outline of the consensus Realist position in the sound era makes clear that even the transparent screen creates its own kind of filtering of reality. Developments in the period produced a wide spectrum of individual filters, all of which struck new balances in the equations of technique and content, expressiveness and imitativeness, in the face of the basic consolidation of a greater screen Realism.

CHAPTER EIGHT

sound and style: expres-siveness

There had been much talk of films talking before films actually talked. There were forebodings of dire consequences, but in the main the issues that were to be central in the sound period were defined. Chief among these was a concern for the creative possibilities of sound as both a functional and expressive device. As we have seen, the direct appeal of sound used functionally as a dramatic element, without particular artistic manipulation, seemed to demand a greater realism, which stood in the way of assertive technique. But sound too, it was early recognized, could be used as part of an expressive technique that combined both aural and visual elements.

Some responses to the introduction of sound did little to unify and harmonize the two elements. At one extreme were films heavy with dialogue and careless with visual patterns. At the other were theories, and resulting films, showing that only by limiting and restricting dialogue could cinematic values be maintained. One of the eventual results of this position was the cult of the action film, which upheld films of physical action, usually violent, as the only true cinema. Between these and the talky dramas was the main body of creative effort of the period, which was based on the premise that what mattered was not the amount of sound but the manner and means of its use.

On this middle ground, most of the thirties' development was pointed toward adjusting the balance between image and sound within the Realist style. But the work of the Soviet directors, of Josef von Sternberg, and briefly of Jean Vigo continued the development of the expressive style as it was modified by the demands of sound and the prevailing Realist assumptions. Their work is a more pronounced indication of the undercurrent of expressiveness that continued to affect the forms of representationalism.

THE SOVIET APPROACH: SOUND AND IDEOLOGY

As might be expected, the approach of the Soviet directors of the montage school was the most determined and theoretically complex attempt to maintain a high degree of heightened expressiveness. Although their theories of montage-editing underwent some alteration, the Russians insisted that sound too could be treated as a formal element of manipulated montage. In particular, it could be used disjunctively—separated from its normal correspondence to real-life words and noises in the same way that a visual image was separated and raised from natural representation to a formal element of expressiveness. In practice, however, it proved too difficult to use disjunctive sound as basically or extensively as visual montage for any extended duration in a film with a continuous narrative.

But the introduction of sound was only half of a double-barreled force that influenced the montage directors. The other barrel was political. By the thirties, Socialist Realism had become the Soviet Union's official approach to art; as such, it shaped not only the general run of conventional films but also the sound epics of Eisenstein, Pudovkin, and Dovzhenko. Socialist Realism can be seen as the extreme limits of the tradition of Social Realism, made even more rigid and extreme by being carried out through the bureaucracy of the state. In the thirties its tenets demanded the utter exclusion of personal and "arty" expressive techniques in art; excessive artifice was decadent, unsocialist. As in the earlier epic theories, the social substance was of central importance in a work but more narrowly defined. Simple, empathic stories were to carry the message. Though these stories may show personal situations in a social context, their characters are basically types, representing aspects of society, their problems equally typical and representative. The whole programmatic drama was shaped, finally, by officially sanctioned interpretations of the problems dramatized and their solutions.

Eisenstein
The thirties of sound and Socialist Realism was a troubled time for Eisenstein. Nine years went by between release of his *Old and New* and his first completed sound film, *Alexander Nevsky*, in 1938. In the meantime, many projects were shelved; two films were interrupted in the course of actual shooting. One of these, *Que Viva Mexico,* was financed in the United States and shot in Mexico in 1931. It was to be a six-part epic of Mexican life and culture, fully integrating sound in what was to be Eisenstein's most complex use of montage. With one section still to be shot (and some 40 hours of unedited film already shot), Upton Sinclair, who controlled all rights, took the film out of Eisenstein's hands. Parts of it have been edited by others and released at various times, but none with any further work by Eisenstein. In 1947, when he saw some of the excerpts for the first time, he found the results of their misediting "heartbreaking."

In Russia in 1935 and 1936, Eisenstein began shooting an epic of rural progress, *Bezhin Meadow* (with a script by Isaac Babel, who later died in a Soviet prison camp). In 1937 Soviet authorities stopped the production midway, claiming arbitrary artiness was destroying its Socialist efficacy. Eisenstein, it was officially proclaimed, had "detached his work from reality." In a piece called "The Mistakes of *Bezhin Meadow,*" Eisenstein publicly recanted, apologizing for the subjective stylization and abstraction that had resulted in "mythologically stylized figures and associations," promising that his new work would be "popular in its style."

In truth, *Alexander Nevsky* was still expressively stylized, but it shows a clear and successful accommodation to the demands of sound and Realism, with a corresponding dramatic structure. Epic still, in its intention to arouse and stir a people and to give meaning to their history, it develops more empathy and identification with the central figure of Nevsky (and other characters) and uses many scenes of dramatic give-and-take. Its overall structure, however, is still carefully composed on the basis of more than plot sequence: There is a careful alternation and acceleration of emotional moods through

Alexander Nevsky

both visual and aural structuring. The opening section alternates the peaceful life of Nevsky's province—lovely, lyrical shots of men fishing with nets in shallow water—with the attack by the Germans. Nevsky accepts leadership of the resisting forces, and the sheltered, illusory peacefulness of his province is shattered. In the second section, there is the rush and tension of organizing an army, shifting in the next section to a slow, heroic buildup to the clash with the German Knights on the ice, and then the frenzy of the battle. The final section, in the tragic aftermath of the battle, has the longest lyrical sequence in Eisenstein's work. In its slow-moving camera, slow dissolves, and plaintive soprano aria, it is like a medieval tapestry. The section closes with the excitement and affirmation of victory.

There is, in general, more lyrical heightening to epic grandeur and less shock-cutting, which abstracts fragments from the action. Certainly the basis is still editing: In one typical sequence of the first section, after the initial conquests of the Germans, only 2 of a sequence of 35 shots in the village of Pskov are longer than 15 feet, or roughly 7 seconds. Sound becomes an integral part of the total composite of sensation, particularly in the use of the music track and natural noises; dialogue is basically functional. However, instead of stressing a disjunctive counterpoint of sound and image, the film attempts to fuse the two, so that the effect on the involved senses is one of similarity rather than juxtaposition.

The action sequence of the battle on the ice is the most emphatic illustration of expressive heightening that still maintains a functional sense of depicting the event. Careful, heroic compositions—for example, the Russian leaders on the top of a round hill, shot from below against the sky, with long lines of soldiers against the horizon—build to a point of tension. Typical of Eisenstein's gradual modulations is his placement of a head in a foreground corner of the frame in a medium shot of the troops before shifting to several tight close-ups. At the same time, the musical score (by Prokofiev) is carefully matched not only for general mood but for specifics of sensation. Rising camera movement is paralleled by rising musical phrases, a close-up by a heavy chord. The crescendo of the battle builds with ever faster cross-cutting. Especially powerful is the depiction of what Eisenstein called the "leaping wedge" of the German cavalry and its destruction by the Russians, with consonant visual and aural disruption of the image patterns.

Stylization of sound—bells, chants, footsteps, music—and repeated use of musical motifs (as in the poisoning theme) are also part of the sensory complex of *Ivan the Terrible,* but they, like the theme and conflict of the movie, are overwhelmed by the staggering impact of the visual imagery. Two parts of the proposed three-part epic were completed by 1946, but the second part was condemned and locked away by Soviet authorities, not to be seen until 1958. Even Nikolai Cherkassov, the actor who played both Nevsky and Ivan, joined in denouncing the film. Criticized for esthetic excess, it was also attacked for emphasizing the inner torment of Ivan to the detriment of the ideological point of the cementing of a nation's unity through victorious war.

It is, indeed, a film of excess. Though it focuses on a central hero and develops dramatic conflict, it is nonetheless Eisenstein's most formal, ornamental film. Movement is but a part of décor and design, which build through a monumental accumulation of detail—brooding, shadowed, baroque, grotesque. Always exquisitely patterned, molded like statuary, the details become a ceremonial, allegorical figuration of a period and of the mood of a man tormented by inner conflicts and by forces that seek to block his destiny and the nation's. There is a strong sense of *mise en scène,* as opposed to empathic editing (though the editing is still Eisensteinian), but it is a *mise en scène* balanced with movement and event.

Acting is broad and stylized, captured in formal, frozen attitudes: A pan over the attendant mixture of faces, friends and foes, at the wedding of Ivan holds on the embrace of Ivan and his wife, figures in a medieval painting. Again and again, Eisenstein returns to brooding close-ups of faces—especially Ivan's—that have typal, operatic expressions. Often the faces or body attitudes combined with images of movement make up a formal pattern. As Ivan, at a low point, ponders his next move, a procession of the people is caught in distant shots, their massed patterns building the forcefulness of their demands, the need of the nation. These are intercut with close-ups of Ivan, but there is also a repeated composition in which both elements appear —Ivan's troubled face in profile in the foreground (as he looks out through

Ivan the Terrible

an arch) and the moving procession in the distance. The patterns are expressive yet also reductive in their insistent and static repetition.

Though still oppressively dense and repetitious in their images, the final sequences of Part 2 are a striking high point of Eisenstein's attempt to render dramatic conflict and inner complexities with formal patterns of expressiveness. In these sequences, Eisenstein, somewhat imperfectly, uses color for the first time. Although heavy-handed, his use of tonal emphasis, rather than literal representation, captures the emotional coloration of the final tensions. Still indecisive, Ivan must ally himself with the Oprinchniks, whom Eisenstein wants to suggest are the imperfect clay out of which political action must be molded. Their possible undependability, their wildness and cruelty, mixed good spirits and power are captured in the busy, frenzied clutter of the dancing, toned bloody red and gold, and the mock coronation of the traitorous Prince Vladimir. In contrast, Vladimir's defeat and the moment of his death are a slow, abstracted ballet, toned blue. The emergence, during the religious ceremony, of Ivan's final resolve builds with somber patterns of black, gray, and white, moving curves and masses of the black-robed Oprinchniks, and Ivan in black. In a final scene (color-toned again), Ivan, in a brighter robe, is seen formally announcing, "We will not let Russia be abused," while the swords of the Oprinchniks catch and reflect the light of the candles.

Pudovkin

While Eisenstein seemed to move toward and then pull back from an accommodation with the new point of balance of greater realism, Pudovkin's career in the sound era moved toward a more conventional, though carefully constructed, representation of content. He continued to place an individual instance within a historical social context. With increasingly greater use of conventional plotting and nonobtrusive technique, he made a series of historical epics focusing on Russian heroism in the past and present. Most successful in its application of his earlier theories of expressive sound was his first film to be fully conceived as a sound-film—*Deserter*, which was released in 1933.

In *Deserter*, Pudovkin sought to combine a personal story with an account of mass social conflict, building a didactic theme by "constructive editing," which used aural images for the same expressive purposes as visual images. Though contributing to the development of a dramatic plot, the complexes of imagery mainly succeed as separate and separable sequences of montage. The plot focuses on the return to Germany of a German Communist and draws a parallel between the decisions that lead to his action in the streets of Hamburg and the stirring to action of the masses. In theory, the montage effects are aimed at forming a link between the individual life and the social forces.

In bringing sound into montage, Pudovkin worked both with dialogue and nondialogue sound. In the use of both types, he was primarily concerned with the relationship between synchronized and disjunctive sound and with controlling the rhythms of elements of sound in much the same way that the flow of visual images is controlled—accelerating, decelerating, fragmenting for emotional effects. Even music sometimes assumes a disjunctive function. In the sequence of the street uprising in Hamburg, the visual images are of varying moods—a peaceful gathering, police aggressiveness, workers' defeatism, workers' stirring, violent and tragic action; in contrast, however, the music builds from the beginning a mood of heroic militancy, sometimes matching the visual images, sometimes set against them. In a sequence in which three debating leaders address a crowd, words (as dialogue or abstracted into nonverbal sound) are used both synchronically and nonsynchronically with the visual elements to build the mood of conflict, rising tension, and crescendo of the crowd's spirit. Sounds originating in the visual images of one shot often overlap onto the next; both aural and visual images accelerate toward the crescendo with increasingly shorter duration, more frequent overlap, more abstraction. For the triumphant May Day celebration, even more involved complexes are built, mixing the sounds of the crowd, band music, singing, accordion playing, automobiles, radio noises, and passing airplanes with equally fragmented visual imagery.

The film was said to contain some 3,000 separate shots, far beyond the fragmentation of most films or even of Pudovkin's own silent films. It was sharply criticized for excessive intellectualism, and Pudovkin subsequently moved to a greater accommodation with the prevailing tenets of Socialist Realism.

Dovzhenko   Made about the same time, Dovzhenko's *Ivan* (1931) and *Aerograd* (1935)—also known as *Frontier*—and Vertov's documentary *Three Songs of Lenin* (1934) involve even more poetic blending of sight and sound in montage. *Aerograd* stylized the actions and tones of the two conflicting factions in the Soviet struggle to replace regionalism with national unity, exaggerating the older regionalists into practitioners of barbaric ritual, and Communist youth into idealized bearers of life's energies. Its value resides, again, in separate lyrical sequences that survive the oversimplifications of its didactic themes. But it was the direct representation (with unobtrusive techniques) of these themes of nationalism and heroism that held sway in the bulk of Soviet films from this point on.

Sergei and Georgy Vassiliev's *Chapayev* (1934) set the fashion for the historical epic of social propaganda and surface credibility. Officially lauded, it was followed by such films as *We Are from Kronstadt* (1936), *Baltic Deputy* (1935), *Lenin in October* (1938), and Mark Donskoy's trilogy on the life of Maxim Gorki (1938–40).

VON STERNBERG: SOUND AND STYLIZATION

If the works of Eisenstein, Pudovkin, and Dovzhenko represent an attempt—though truncated—to carry forward the principles of epic montage into the sound era, those of Josef von Sternberg can be seen as an extension of the German Expressionists' approach of the twenties. Von Sternberg's efforts, however, were distinct extensions of cinematic expressiveness, colored by his own personality and by the demands for surface literalness of the realism at which he scoffed.

The ground of von Sternberg's expressive style is marked initially by his rejections. As he pointed out in a letter of 1946, he "always avoided emotionalizing [his] films." He rejected "selling emotions" or "easily digestible formulas," yet his forte is really a more subtle form of emotionalism. He opposed the emotionalist manipulations of Griffith's editing or the ideological manipulations of Eisenstein's. He dissented from the serious social comment of the Social Realists. He opposed, too, the distortions, the depth psychologizing through external symbols of the Germans, though it is to their expressive use of object and light and pattern, as in the moody composition of a shot, that he is closest.

What is left is a special ground, too narrow for significant human exploration yet, when von Sternberg is at his best, not without its consistent terrain of meaning. The key is emotionalism. Suspicious of emotion, even his own, von Sternberg handled it with a mixture of cynicism and romanticism, assertiveness and surrender that underlies much of the exotic ornamentation of the style. On the surface literalness of the commercial film (pushed to limits that, if not probable, were still always possible) and in the artificiality of exotic situations, he created a lyrical surface poetry—formal, abstracted from life, sensual and evocative, often empty or merely affected. Life and the emotions are stylized, distanced, not expressed directly by the rococo artifice.

Thus, always full of feeling, von Sternberg's films are not especially moving. The resonances he sought by carefully harmonizing all the elements of the film build a fascinating ambience of the passions—the fatal lures, stern lessons, rare fruits, and frequent losses—but they do not escape the emptiness of the literal package. Von Sternberg's deepening rejection of overt content ultimately limited his exploration and evocation of human emotions (see, in contrast, Max Ophuls's *Lola Montes,* Chapter 15) and the development of his work.

Although in his silent films von Sternberg had dealt with the materials of the developing Realist tendency, he had already begun to apply to them his stylizing control of lighting and composition, rhythm, tone. In the late twenties, his *Underworld* and *Dragnet,* for example, and the early sound-film *Thunderbolt* presage the rise of the low-life gangster genre yet are characterized by a heightening pictorialism that differs from the main tendencies of the genre. In *The Salvation Hunters* (1925) and *The Docks of New York* (1928), poverty, slums, degradation, and defeat—staples of The New Realism in Germany—are treated with the rich chiaroscuro of contrasting tones, the artful, moody composition, the long-held shots of his later films, but with a sober, soulful kind of symbolism that he would later reject for more playfully baroque imagery. But even here in these more conventional serious films, in the space before the camera, it is the sensuous feel of surfaces that dominates—the presence of bodies and faces, mists and dredging scoops, anchor chains and tawdry furniture.

The Blue Angel With his first major sound-film, *The Blue Angel* (1930), he achieved the fullest, most harmonious (and revealing) blending of his increasingly ornamental style with a straightforward, seriously developed depiction of his obsessive fascination with the dangerous fruits of desire. Here sounds and the tangible surfaces of things are more directly expressive of states of being than in subsequent films. As a result, *The Blue Angel* is the most openly affecting and moving of von Sternberg's films. Made in Germany (in both German and English), it is von Sternberg's closest paralleling of the later style of German Expressionism, especially the work of Murnau and Lang, and in some ways the epitome of the themes and means of the style.

In it, the German school's favorite shipwrecked victim of life and inner flaws, Emil Jannings, portrays a rigidly authoritarian, sadistic high-school teacher, unable to exorcise the inner demons he has repressed. It is noteworthy that in the original novel's satire of German bureaucracy, the professor rises in social rank after succumbing to the femme fatale, while in von Sternberg's revision, he is progressively and unalterably destroyed. Von Sternberg also enlarges the role of the temptress to equal that of Jannings. The decadence of a time and society is still palpable in the décor and mood, but its embodiment of destructive inner desire is the point of intense, burning focus. The controls of society—embodied in the repeated motif of the town clock's chiming of "virtue and sincerity to the grave"—are no match

The Blue Angel

for the husky-voiced animality of Lola Lola's insolent, coolly provocative songs, in turn, the perfect aural correlative to her overpowering legs. Von Sternberg's images of Marlene Dietrich's legs (sexual and suggestive beyond the more explicit display of female flesh of later films) are perfect examples of his intricate and meaningful use of the stimuli of physical surface. On a small, tawdry, cluttered stage—closely hemmed in by fat, beer-drinking hostesses and a vulgar backdrop with ugly, fat cherubs—Dietrich's legs insist on a physical frankness beyond their decadently artificial surroundings. Spread, planted strong as tree trunks as she stands, bent up to reveal the broad undersides of the thighs as she sits on a barrel, they are encased in gleaming silk but live most fully in the white gap, smooth and marmoreal, between the stockings and the dark, frilly lingerie.

Similarly, both aural and visual images make tangible the descent of Jannings into irrationality and death. His harsh, professorial bark turns into the cock-a-doodle-doo of a crowing rooster, first when in drunken disarray he tries to amuse his new show business companions, later when dressed in a clown suit (a large white collar surrounding the destruction seen on his face) he is forced to perform his cock crow on stage as part of the show. Finally, he emits the wild bellowing of an animal as he tries to strangle Lola, the body his degraded body cannot control.

Throughout, the general décor, specific objects, and human forms and voices are merged, equal in value, giving body to the inner torment. Drunk and debased, Jannings stumbles offstage after a performance into the narrow darkness of a passage, frantically clawing his way through a maze of enveloping fishnets hanging backstage. In some of the film's most effective uses of motifs, his relation to the furnishings of his schoolroom mark the stages of his defeat: his blackboard, defaced by chalk cartoons of himself, fat cherubs, and a leg; the crowded roomful of boys in taunting aural and visual confusion; his last moments in the empty schoolroom, a long traveling shot taking in his sad farewell to the life of control he is driven to forsake; his final return to the same emptied furniture, embracing all that he has lost, his arms around his desk as he dies.

Such intricate compositions and blendings of human and nonhuman forms, lovingly bathed in romantic lighting, will continue through all his films, with increasingly bizarre décor, yet with a distinct difference. The difference is suggested by the transformation of Dietrich, who appears in half a dozen subsequent von Sternberg films, but not as the same coarse, bluntly physical beer hall tart of *The Blue Angel,* more instinctive animal than sensual woman. The sleek and mysterious Dietrich of the later films still exudes the sexual mystery that lies beyond the cool impassivity under her elaborate gowns. But she has become aware, the true initiate of grace, the love goddess maintaining the precious life of sensuality in a hostile world. The crisis, the inner turmoil of desire has been distanced into artificial plot situations; the female incarnation of sexuality, with all its ambiguous power, has been transformed into idealized myth. Dietrich glides through the often ambiguous trappings of the sensual world untouched—both figuratively and literally, for there is actually little literal sexual action in these films. The surface, ornamental trappings are severed from their connections with the depths of emotion to which they still abstractly allude, becoming a kind of free-floating symbolism of sensuality. Emotionalism is now a controlling style, but not without cost.

Morocco   In *Morocco* (1930), the trappings are of a romanticized North Africa of nightclub and Foreign Legion where, in the midst of decadence, the two initiates of grace—Dietrich, the singer, and Gary Cooper, the Legionnaire—do their jobs, love as they can, and part. The final parting is more heroically sentimental than inevitable, yet it does arise to some degree from what the characters have cynically-heroically had to become. It is captured neatly in a scene that illustrates von Sternberg's fusing of sound and sight. After Cooper and Dietrich have agreed to go away together, she goes on stage one last time. He wanders around her dressing room, the things of her world, while we hear her performance in that world. Among other things, he sees a necklace her rich fiancé has given her, then goes on to other things, even puts on (in a fine touch) her black top hat. Then, after writing on her mirror that he has changed his mind, he leaves; on stage, Dietrich is still singing.

Earlier in the film, the scene of Dietrich's engagement weaves a more complex aural-visual texture. At the start, the conversation is busy and gay; Dietrich's new necklace glistens. Outside, drumbeats and then drum and bugles together signal the return of the Legion and Cooper. Both the fiancé and Dietrich become distracted as the conversation slows and the Legion sounds increase. She rises suddenly to go outside and catches her necklace on the back of the chair, breaking it. Outside she scans the night for Cooper; inside the fiancé is completely distracted as the talk drifts dully and then finally collapses.

The subsequent von Sternberg-Dietrich films play out the same motif of grace in passion in a variety of equally exotic, equally ornamental settings, laced with hangings and trappings of many textures, touched by shadows of unfocused and unfaced emotion, rhythmic with the kind of artificial grace that is always capped by the lush close-up portraits of Dietrich herself: *Dishonored* (1931), *Shanghai Express* and *Blonde Venus* (both 1932), *The Scarlet Empress* (1934), *The Devil Is a Woman* (1935).

Of these, *The Scarlet Empress* reveals von Sternberg at his flamboyant, romantically rococo best. Almost kaleidoscopic in the swirl of its elaborate images, the film pushes further than ever beyond the probable, stretching the literalness of surface image into greater exaggeration and distortion, a playfully grotesque Expressionism, not quite either real or fantastic. Its blatantly operatic plot (the screenplay, as in many of his films, by von Sternberg) is merely a vehicle for the visual and aural images that unfold the ambiguous expression of his insistent theme. Maturing, blooming from innocence into full, complex, mysterious womanhood, Dietrich as Catherine of Russia, and as sensual life force, triumphs over excess ambition, greed, ruthlessness, murder, and madness. And with her triumph, the nation is saved as well. Yet she herself uses and becomes part of the swamp of lust, immerses herself in the destructive element. The power of her womanhood is threatening and ruinous; but despite history and the impetus of the plot-action, she rises purified from the morass.

This film, more than any other by von Sternberg, mixes and makes equal images of the human and the nonhuman. Objects assume life and motion under the camera's eye, people are caught immobile in statuesque postures. The palace of the mad Czar Peter becomes a physical emanation of the warps of emotionality. Its ubiquitous statues and icons, more grotesque than their Byzantine counterparts, intimidate the humans who are always near them, under them, over them, the postures and attitudes of both carefully juxtaposed. Stairs and halls are endless, shadowed, confusing; doors are elaborately decorated giants, towering over human figures. Paintings in the palace seem to live on the same plane of reality as the images of the people. In one startling shot, the point of a drill comes through the eye of a painted saint—and, in a sense, through the screen—as behind it, Peter drills a hole to spy on his wife. At the wedding feast, the camera first traverses the long table, encountering a crammed chaos of hideously diverse objects—almost a Cubist abstraction of areas of black and white. When it returns from the end of its traverse, its view becomes wider, including now the guests and, further, the icon-gargoyles they sit among, all silent, living-dead, except for a violin playing a gypsy tune.

Throughout, sound is integral to the expressiveness, as is silence broken

The Scarlet Empress

by slight sounds—a breath, a turning lock, a rustling skirt. Music stops and starts, brings circus tunes or waltzes to play against the images. At the dreamlike exuberant finale, the thunderous triumph of Tchaikovsky's *1812 Overture*, its pealing bells and cannonades stressed and repeated, joins a joyful whirl of montage images: a horde of black and white horses, stamping with equal thunder through the palace and up the stairs to the throne; bells in cross-dissolves; bells and faces; Catherine, finally, smiling and excited, her smile in slow cross-dissolves with bells; Catherine dressed in white, surrounded by bright flags and banners, the lovely head of her white stallion, the white fluttering of doves of peace transcending the blackness and shadows of the destructive element. These images have all the insistent over-ripeness of a dream work in which the dream strives to surmount the tensions that give it impetus and energy.

Beyond the Dietrich films, von Sternberg's work seems erratic, uncertain, often even desultory. Several serious projects—*An American Tragedy* (1931) and *Crime and Punishment* (1936)—are disappointingly directed. Most projects are increasingly unworthy, unevenly executed under commercial pressures and domination, yet never commercially successful. The best of these is probably *The Shanghai Gesture* (1941), a re-mining of the Dietrich vein, with Gene Tierney and Ona Munson as a double-imaged Dietrich.

But then, in 1953, there is a last unusual return to the creative sources. Directly and poetically, *The Saga of Anatahan* deals again with the lure and fear of passion and woman. Made in Japan with Japanese dialogue and an English narration by von Sternberg himself, the film incorporates an Oriental musical score. Using a true story, the film raises this realistic basis to the level of formal abstraction by the intentional—on occasion excessive—artificiality of décor (the lushest of sound-stage jungles), lighting, pattern, and movement. Its island in the Pacific becomes an island of nowhere but the trap of the emotions. On it, in it, men are driven to kill themselves over the one woman who lures and obsesses them. But her domination, unintentional, is life-giving as well as life-destroying. With her, they are led to destruction; but when she has gone, they are nothing. It is a valuable last statement, amazingly frank and revealing in the intricate, evasive lacework of its artifice.

VIGO: SOUND AND THE INTERIOR LIFE

More directly personal, more subjectively expressive of the Surrealist dimensions of fantasy and dream—yet also shaped by the demands of Realism—are the two masterpieces of the French director Jean Vigo, tragically cut down by tuberculosis at the age of 29. These two films—*Zéro de Conduite* and *L'Atalante*—provide another illustration of the kinds of expressiveness possible in the sound-film. Still somewhat spare and austere in their use of sound, the films combine emphatic editing and camera and printing devices with carefully balanced and dramatically functional apt compositions in the single image. Their blending of Realist and Expressionist styles is particularly effective in asserting the congruence of literal, surface reality and inner consciousness.

Zéro de Conduite   After two short documentaries (the satiric À *Propos de Nice* and *Taris*), Vigo created *Zéro de Conduite* in 1932. The 40-minute film expresses a kind of group subjectivism—beyond objective, realistic logic—showing the disordered experiencing of a world of adult authority by a group of schoolboys. Briefly, the repressed wild freedom of the boys explodes in a macabre revolt, then subsides. From the opening, the images, chiefly visual, suggest the world as the boys see and feel it. In the enclosing smoke of a railroad car, two boys see on one bench the legs of one passenger, the upper body of another. This fragmenting of the logic of external reality leads to fantasizing play in which literal objects from their pockets are wrenched out of their commonplace functions and connections and merged with the fantasizing of the boys.

Zéro de Conduite

In the smoky haze of the car, their faces and some hovering balloons seem to float as equals. The balloons still floating magically about them, they disembark and confront the sign "No Smoking"—signifying "no dreaming allowed." They are back in the adult-controlled world of the boarding school.

With slow-motion, partially slowed motion, naturalistic action, elongation of time, expressive imagery, this world is unfolded. Its authorities are a shrieking midget, a shuffling, skinny, peeping spy, a flushed-face toady tiptoeing about in the severe suit of an undertaker. Its setting is stripped barren and shadowed. The agonizing durations of its boredom and its punishments are captured in a clever manipulation of long-held shots that suggest endlessness in an actually short span of time.

The climactic revolt is in slow-motion, with the boys moving through a strange nightmare light—nightshirts and sheets and the gracefully wild snow of pillow feathers released, like their spirits, into the air, almost floating against the background shadows. Through the drifting feathers they carry the headmaster, trussed as if for crucifixion. It is a triumph that can only be momentary.

L'Atalante   In Vigo's next and last film, *L'Atalante* (first released, but only in a mutilated form, in 1934), he depicts only a standoff with social pressures—a precarious resolution but possibly more lasting than that in *Zéro*. More directly in the line of developing Realism, this full-length film constructs its characters and their social context much more fully, much more within the Realist dramatic pattern. Yet its plot is not conventionally tight, its characters' responses left more oblique and ambiguous. It does not have the experimental devices of *Zéro;* rather, its images (with camera work by Boris Kaufman, his first feature film in a long and notable career) raise the objects of the surface world to an expressive level, produce a poetic realism of mood and suggestion beyond the patness of one-to-one symbolism. Movement, as well as object and pattern, is raised to this level. On her wedding night, the emotional confusion of the sensually unawakened bride is captured by the opposed movements of the girl and the barge (*L'Atalante*), which is to be her home; as the latter progresses slowly along the canal to the right, she walks to the left on its deck, her wedding gown and veil, white against the darkness, blown back to the right. Earlier, set against the mocking clutter and tawdriness of the wedding procession to the barge, the young couple walk slowly and silently, separate from each other and from the procession, symbol of the environment that constrains them.

The girl, awakened confusedly to emotions and sensuality, lured by the seductions of the world on shore, breaks off the marriage. A reunion is effected with the help of the gross, jack-of-all-trades bargeman (wonderfully played by Michel Simon), who is an ambiguous character contrasted with the possibilities of growth in the couple. Helpful, lovable, he is a man of the senses, yet reduced in humanity, almost premental, animal in his unthinking consciousness. His sensuality is not a freedom from things. The objects that clutter his cabin dominate him, trigger his responses, make him one with them. When he shows the girl his treasures, the shots keep the scene fragmented, unpatterned—thing after thing seen from confusing angles, with no unifying human control of object or response. A mechanical doll marches and emits musical sounds, momentarily the equal of its owner, who nonetheless maintains a deep reservoir of natural humanity. The path to the emotional life is a precarious one, beset on all sides.

The constant and poetic use of objects in *L'Atalante* is less artificial and abstract than the more extreme ornamental tendencies of von Sternberg's films. Objects affect people, reflect them. If, as in the case of the doll, objects are seen as having a correspondence to a person, the relation between them keeps the distinctions clear; they are not equal formal elements of a décor that comprises human and nonhuman forms. The expressiveness arises from the maintenance of a surface of realistic literalness, not from the transformation of a literal surface into expressive ornamentation.

It is Vigo's approach, modulated even further into a greater transparency for the images of plot action and a greater accommodation to the literalness of sound, that becomes the dominant French style of the thirties and forties.

CHAPTER NINE

SOUND AND STYLE: VARIETIES OF REALISM

Accommodation to sound and to developments within the industry produced in the thirties and forties a variety of substyles that, whatever their differences, are all clearly of the Realist school. The work of the French and American directors examined below constitutes a spectrum of those substyles; indeed, the works of the French cinema of this period can, alone, compose such a spectrum.

THE FRENCH APPROACH

The paradox of the French style might be summed up by the term most frequently applied to it—poetic Realism—for it is a combination of a subdued artifice and a toned transparency. Its seeking of Zola's "transparent screen" of Realism leads to an emphasis on *mise en scène*—rather than obtrusive editing—with careful design of décor and setting and the individuals within it, with meaningful camera angles and lighting. It often has a static quality—broken by occasional sequences of action—images serving emphatic, theatrical dialogue, or sometimes balanced more with the sound. Its central subject is commonplace life, mainly urban, ranging from the merely poor to the hopelessly poverty-stricken, the desperately outlawed.

Poetic Realism is a style of strong moods, and it is this pervasive moodiness that is the bridge to its moderate, expressive stylizing. Thus its works tend to extremes of emotion—whether an occasional comic exuberance or a gloomy despair. The despair, however, seems the shaping attitude—even for the works that play against it comically—for the style is one of tragic romanticism, a fatalistic emotionalism of drift and defeat, which tends to sentimentalize the harsh facts of the realistic contents. One can hear in it interesting echoes of the decade of social drift and decay that led to abrupt collapse before the German Panzers and to the moral ambiguities of the Vichy government.

The romantic coloration is reflected in techniques that blend with the Realist tendency but do not obtrude upon it: precise details of interior and exterior surface reality reproduced in studio sets; lighting and tones tending toward oppressive, brooding shadows and patterns of black and gray; artful composition of static images, suggestive of mood rather than productive of exact symbolic correspondences; heightened "poetic" dialogue; abstracted characters that become both thematic instruments and vehicles for the vivid screen personalities of the "stars."

Duvivier The career of Julien Duvivier illustrates one combination of these qualities, one that in itself embraces the gamut from realism to romance. Duvivier's early sound-works were among the first to call attention to the new Realist style in France. In 1932, *Poil de Carotte* traced the destructive impact of

125

society on the emotional health of a young boy with a rhythmic lyricism that expresses the subjective responses and encroaching mental breakdown of the boy. In contrast, *La Belle Équipe* (1935) provides one of the period's most objective French works of Social Realism. Without the usual moody tones it depicts an unsuccessful attempt at social action by five unemployed workers.

But by 1937, Duvivier had turned from this direction for good. His *Pépé Le Moko* was an adroit action melodrama. (Duvivier's films in general had more striking action sequences than most French films of the period.) Its polished, romanticized version of the doomed gangster, so popular in both France and America, was one of many similar vehicles for the rugged, electric personality of Jean Gabin. Duvivier's *Un Carnet de Bal* was a nostalgic spectacular, a series of vignettes for stars, loosely tied by a central plot device. It was a vein he was to mine in a number of subsequent films in both France and America, including *Flesh and Fantasy* (1943), with its highly stylized supernaturalism.

Late in his career, in the postwar *Pot-Bouille* (1957), Duvivier built one of the most effective amalgams of his typical materials: a spectacle of stars, a lavish but precise reproduction of a historical period, a romping Zolaesque satire on middle-class crassness and animality. Earlier, *Panique* (1946) had revealed what had become of the now commercialized style of poetic Realism, how far Duvivier had come from the quietly tragic *Poil de Carotte*. Stunning visually, with all the mood photography of the school and Duvivier's more intensive editing, it is exaggerated psychological hokum, its more serious thematic overtones jarringly discordant with the forced melodrama.

Carné   In the thirties, the peak of the style and the most lyrical Realist poems of defeat were represented in the works of the youthful Marcel Carné. Although Carné's work is the epitome of this style, his career, too, shifted its basic ground and then, in the postwar period, continued with little fruitful development or unity.

In his best films, Carné worked with the screenwriter Jacques Prévert. Their collaborations reflect a Gallic fatalism that fluctuates between cold determinism and romantic despair. These moods are in turn affected by two other balances in their work: between image and dialogue, and between Realism and stylization.

The French critic Jean Mitry has authoritatively outlined how in their first two films together, the initial and shaping control was Carné's. From Carné's fully detailed continuity script, Prévert worked out the dialogue. The major emphasis was on the images, which build out from, extend with greater resonance the content of the speeches. At the same time the romantic stylizing remains more a surrounding aura for the Realist core. But even when rooted in the sordid details of everyday life, the films take on an emotional coloration that reflects beyond the literal surface.

Quai des Brumes (Port of Shadows, 1938) and *Le Jour Se Lève* (Daybreak,

1939) give full expression to the characteristics of this style. In the first, Jean Gabin, a rootless deserter from the army, briefly finds love (Michele Morgan) in the midst of squalor, gets involved in a murder, starts to flee, returns to his love, and is shot in the streets. In the second, even more enervated by the industrial and waterfront environment, Gabin awaits his death, and remembers his life, behind the shadowed windows of a dingy hotel room.

The sentimentalized fatalism—less melodramatic in plot in *Le Jour Se Lève* —flows through the interplay between the laconically tragic notes of the dialogue and the statically beautiful images. In *Le Jour Se Lève*, the images are given a more intricate setting by a masterful use of "narratage," the slowly accumulating, suspended reconstruction of the past through flashbacks, the

Le Jour Se Lève

juxtapositions of which add a further dimension of lyricism to the compositions. Examples of these moments sculpted out of time abound. Thus, in *Le Jour Se Lève*, Gabin awaiting his death: Dressed in black he stands behind a narrow window, a vertical member of its heavy frame—in the left center of the image—also black except for a reflection of light at the base; light reflects strongly off the strip of curtained glass to the left, plays erratically on Gabin in the right frame within a frame. Or, in *Quai des Brumes*, Gabin and Morgan behind a dusty double window framed in worn wood, she in one half, he in the other, his subdivided by two crossbars, his face in the top segment. And, in the same film, Gabin at left center at his death: on a narrow cobblestone street grayly reflecting light, passers-by in black rushing by, a narrower street receding and descending behind him, goods hanging like bodies from one storefront, another with a sign "Style Moderne"; at right foreground, the black canvas top of a convertible, from it the smoke from the fatal pistol rising, blurring into the gray light.

In the next two films of Carné and Prévert, made during the German occupation, there is a shift in style and tone. Mitry has pointed out that for these films Prévert first conceived and wrote a fully elaborated screenplay from which Carné then directed. Both still present a sentimentally fatalistic view of love beset and lost, but they take place not in the contemporary world but in days gone by. They are thus more openly romantic, heightened in characterization and emotionality; the romantic beauty of the images, the poetry, is now given a foundation in the literal, realistic re-creation of a period and way of life, the acting pushed just a bit further into open theatricality. Dialogue is more elaborate, rhetorical, witty, directly philosophic; at the same time, the lengthy dialogues are immersed in much greater surrounding action and spectacle, visually rich and imaginative yet often supplementary to, not equal partners with, the text.

This imbalance is more true of the first of the pair, *Les Visiteurs du Soir* (*The Devil's Envoys*, 1942). Set in beautifully evoked images of the mysteries of the Middle Ages, its characters expound on and, with a slow, stylized formality, act out an allegory of love and inevitable evil. More balanced—despite its heavy and heady verbalizing—is *Les Enfants du Paradis* (*The Children of Paradise*, 1944). Its better balance is a wonderfully precarious one. All is magnified to an overly ripe romantic essence. Yet, whenever the film seems to be taking itself and its philosophizing too intensely, whenever its sentiments creak and wheeze, whenever its spectacle seems too lush, too operatic, its confrontations too melodramatic, it is kept from tipping over into banality by the good taste of its elegant visual formality, by the elaborately concrete rendering of its nineteenth-century milieu of low life, high life, and actors' life, by the unobtrusive transparency (ornate but never interposing) of its visual patterns, by its fine acting, by the wit and irony of its language. In other words, *Les Enfants* is *knowingly* a film about romance—with the realism that implies—as well as a romantic film.

This combination of tones in its attitudes toward romance (and, on another level, toward art) is embodied in the life styles of its four central men who seek, ambiguously possess, but lose Garance (played with enigmatic allure by Arletty) and the fulfillments of love. Its wistful mime (Jean-Louis Barrault, magnificently pure in his clown's greasepaint, more forced when he plays the man behind the mime) has the lyric simplicity of direct and innocent sentiment. Its grandiloquent Shakespearean declaimer, more rococo and artificial, is emotionally rich, complex. Its cynically violent criminal, driven to excesses, understands them. Its hard aristocrat, coldly disciplined, is a prisoner of his passions. And at the center, Garance—elusive, unknowable, no less caught in a life she cannot finally control.

The film carries the essence of this period's French film—the sentimentally depicted tragic inability to control life's course—to its epitome of intertwined artifice and reality. In its eloquent final imagery, the mime Deburau decides too late to forsake his wife and child and pursues Garance through the streets jammed with the crowds of Carnival. The screen overflows with images of the celebrants, who, the very lifeblood of the characters' livelihood, now block Deburau's path. In close-ups and medium shots we alternate between the blocked Deburau, pushing his way through the nightmare torrent of the crowd, and Garance, edging further and further away within the trap of her carriage; finally, in long shot, Deburau is lost in the mob, the carriage and Garance forever going out of reach.

Grémillon and Pagnol   In contrast to the self-aware nostalgia of these two films, two unusual and little known films of the Occupation period present a strikingly different development of the style of poetic Realism. They are the work of Jean Grémillon, whose prewar work never reached artistic fulfillment and whose postwar career found its fullest expression in a series of superb documentaries. Influenced particularly by Renoir's *La Règle du Jeu* (*The Rules of the Game*, 1939), his wartime films foreshadow the freer expressive Realism of the postwar style. The first, *Lumière d'Été* (1942), was written by Prévert; the second, *Le Ciel Est à Vous* (1944), was written by Charles Spaak, who did screenplays for Renoir, Duvivier, and Carné. Both focus on the destructive patterns and objects in the lives of the rich. While never going beyond the literal and the concrete, the complex dramatic materials and unexpected juxtapositions of the vivid imagery develop a harsh, satiric expressiveness that condemns a whole society. Typical of Grémillon's ability to extract significance from details while not obtruding upon their literal flow is a wild auto ride from a fancy dress ball in *Lumière d'Été*, climaxed by the forceful image of a wrecked car, a limp body, and in the foreground, two of the rich in their costumes of medieval courtier and lady of the court.

Of the French directors of this time, Marcel Pagnol goes furthest in stressing the spoken word. Pagnol came to film-directing from the theater—first writing the screenplays for and then directing the last of his successful Marseilles trilogy, *Marius* (1931), *Fanny* (1932), and *César* (1934). These films set the pattern for his work of the thirties, which he too was not able to equal or extend in subsequent years. They focus on the relatively down-and-out on waterfronts or in farm communities, but Pagnol's optimistic attitude toward the material is in sharp contrast to that of his contemporaries. From the restrictions and crises of these lives, he draws good-natured humor. His characters may not control fate, but they stand up to it with the animal innocence of the poor—especially, the men and women of the soil. His fullest portrait of the gusto of innocent natures—tender, affectionate, often sentimentalized to a smug cuteness—is probably *Regain* (*Harvest*, 1937), from the regional novel of Jean Giono. His most successful comic farces were *The Baker's Wife* (1938) and *The Well-Digger's Daughter* (1940).

Pagnol created vivid and concrete settings in which to place his characters, using more actual locations than his contemporaries. But his chief concern was to provide an unobtrusive visual vehicle for the dialogue, comic action, and lusty character portrayals of the vivid screen personalities he regularly gathered for his films—Raimu, Fernandel, Harry Baur. In his phrase, he saw the sound-cinema as "canned theater."

THE AMERICAN APPROACH

Mamoulian Meanwhile, in America another man of the theater, Rouben Mamoulian, was to attempt a different balance between words and images, stylization and Realist transparency, art and commerce. Mamoulian set himself an interesting but impossible task of synthesis—films that would maintain a verve, an expressive stylization and freedom, talk, and, moreover, retain an ease of perception and understanding that would appeal to the mass commercial audience. However erratic and incomplete his results, they served to continue the creative possibilities of film technique in the crucial early years of the sound period. In his musicals Mamoulian was able to blend his virtuoso devices with a free play of fantasy. In his dramas he tended to apply the devices of the German and Russian film-makers to conventional melodramatic material. But the expressive devices that he used did not consistently embody a point of view or develop a personal attitude or theme; rather than growing out of the material, they were arbitrary embellishments on its simplified literal surfaces.

In the fantasy of *Dr. Jekyll and Mr. Hyde* (1932), the visual and aural flourishes did have a greater organic consistency with the material. His use of a freely moving camera is particularly effective in the first section of the film in maintaining the first-person viewpoint of Dr. Jekyll and introducing the subjective, supernatural nature of his experience. Later, the ingenious transformations to Mr. Hyde are accompanied by an expressive mélange of sounds: magnified heartbeats, music, distorted bells and gongs. In one of Mamoulian's most effective displays of disjunctive sound, Hyde has forced the music hall girl to sing, pushing her down out of the frame while she continues to sing, following her out of the frame while the camera records a love goddess carved on the bedpost; the singing continues, then stops abruptly.

Dr. Jekyll and Mr. Hyde

Mamoulian had begun his attempts to free the sound-bound camera and sound itself in *Applause* (1929), a sentimentally realistic tale of the degradation and suicide of a faded burlesque queen. He embellishes the sordid, low-life details with striking touches, derived mainly from a moving camera, visual symbolism and allusions, and disjunctive sound. When the woman's lover insultingly decries her lost beauty, the camera is first on her face and then pans to a photo of her as a young beauty. Later, a montage of neon lights and the sounds and sights of the glamorous night world that has destroyed her mark a harsh counterpoint to her death. In the following gangster melodrama, *City Streets* (1931), the "touches" seem more imposed and erratic but are often individually impressive: a montage of delicate china figurines during a violent verbal clash; a confused replay of remembered conversation accompanying a close-up of the weeping Sylvia Sidney in jail.

Following *Dr. Jekyll* were a series of vehicles for women stars—Dietrich, Garbo, Anna Sten. The finale of Garbo's *Queen Christiana* (1933) reveals Mamoulian at his realist-expressive best: A series of slow dissolves—ships' sails, faces, silent action—flows rhythmically into the last shot of Garbo, on the prow of a ship, seen first from a distance and then, with the camera moving in an unbroken shot, in enigmatic final close-up.

With *Becky Sharp* (1935), Mamoulian became the first to take advantage of advances in color film and processing both to achieve more accurate reproductions of natural color and express emotionality with color tones. While the color plan of the film—worked out by New York stage-designer Robert Edmund Jones—adjusts dominant tones to match certain emotional moods, it does not develop distortions that break with the literal nor does it use subjective dislocations as reflections of the point of view of a character. There is, rather, an attempt at a generalized heightening through emphasized color tonalities on top of the realistic base, with occasional grand flourishes such as the climax of the ballroom scene before the battle of Waterloo. As the sounds of cannons increase, the emphasized color changes from pastel blues to yellows, orange, and red, and finally to the scarlet red of the swirling capes of the officers as they rush out into the night. In contrast, many of the less dramatic changes in tone seem extraneous to the film's many talky scenes of dialogue and large scenes of spectacle.

In *Blood and Sand* (1942), Mamoulian achieves an integration of color and drama that is both more organic and more exciting. The carefully developed color patterns of whole scenes and individual details reproduce vividly the concrete surfaces of the settings, but they also heighten mood and express theme. Thus, they both intensify emotion and give a literal substantiation to the account of the temptations of a young Spanish bullfighter (Tyrone Power): the broad canvas of an ornate church, altar artifacts toned a greenish-bronze to capture the ritual feel of the bullfighter's prayer before the *corrida;* the misted filtering of the bright colors of an exciting, dangerous dance by Rita Hayworth and Anthony Quinn in a smoky club; the precise detail of Hayworth's scarlet fingernails, first against her guitar, then against the black hair of Power's head as she seduces him; or, the symbolic detail of a wineskin bursting and pouring purple wine on a white napkin at the moment of the bull's slaughter.

Mamoulian's work is representative of this widespread kind of highly polished Realism—at its best when the flair and flourishes arise naturally from the representational level of the dramatic material. By heightening without openly obtruding, by vividly but accurately rendering surfaces, this tendency of the Realistic style, commercial branch, is able to lend credibility to any dramatic materials—however slight their actual relationship to reality.

Flaherty   In his documentaries of the silent and sound periods, Robert Flaherty followed an esthetics that made him influential in the development of a Realism that would be more transparent than that of a director like Mamoulian. Though Flaherty used the sensory realism of the film image to order and interpret actuality, not fictional drama, he did reconstitute and re-create that actuality in ways that bring his work to the border between fictional and documentary films. All but one of his documentaries built a narrative line, a quietly modulated plot that reached a dramatic climax. But the simple, vignette patterns of his plots were strikingly different from the elaborately devised cause-and-effect constructions of the twenties and thirties; they were foreshadowings of the looser, postwar structures but did not individualize, analyze, and reveal the personality of characters within the narrative. For in reordering the raw materials of actuality in his narratives, Flaherty focused on types, representative individuals, or small groups. Following them on the course of their everyday affairs, Flaherty would capitalize on fortuitous events, later selecting and shaping material to fill out his patterns—though they were flexibly developed in response to the material shot. (Flaherty did stage some "typical" events and situations, reenacting prior occurrences or actually creating new ones.)

The impression of actuality in this re-creation of the essential features of a way of life is strengthened by Flaherty's visual style. Although toward the end of his career he did move toward more intensive editing, he approached both editing and the single shot in terms of what they might reveal of reality, not add to it. From the twenties on, his shots, like those of Murnau and von Stroheim, stay with the materials within the shot as they develop rather than fragment their space and time with different camera setups and reedited continuity. But unlike the expressive subjective heightening of Murnau's shots and the radical juxtaposed ironies and hyperbolic actions of von Stroheim's, Flaherty's remain unobtrusive in observing and representing the literal details of surface reality.

Unobtrusive, but *not* objective. Despite Zola's claim, even the transparent screen of Realism is toned. Certainly Flaherty's was by his interpretation of the essences revealed by the surface data he recorded. In contrast to the main trends of the Realist movement, Flaherty's chief concerns are not the city and the contemporary but the primitive, the out of the way, the timeless. Indeed, his Realist technique has a romantic basis, idealizing the simple, natural life. Flaherty's sympathetic response to his subjects produces images that are acutely sensitive to the "feel" of the life depicted and transmit this impression to the spectator. But the images also transmit the reductive sentimentality of his Rousseauian idealizing of the noble savage. As in all applications of the Realist esthetic, his technique—the faithful and beautiful recording of concrete detail—is shaped by his conception of the content.

The first result of his approach was *Nanook of the North* (1922). After an earlier surveying expedition, he returned to northern Canada in 1920 to become acquainted with the present life of the Eskimos and then to re-create on film a sense of the essential traditions of their culture in a blending of past and present. It was a procedure he followed in subsequent films as well. *Nanook* is an admiring portrayal of the goodness and joy found in a life of constant struggle with nature on a primitive level of existence. Flaherty was untrained and relatively unpracticed in film at the time, and *Nanook* has the least studied artfulness of any of his work.

The film was popular, and Flaherty was sent by Paramount to do the same thing in the South Seas, but hopefully with a little more of the love and romance that that area suggested. For two years Flaherty lived and worked on Samoa and then produced *Moana* (1926). Not only did the film not have the romance Paramount had wanted, but it lacked the adventures of *Nanook* as well. For Flaherty had discovered a way of life with little conflict, even between man and nature, and he had filmed this idyllic life as it serenely unfolded, jarred only by the occasional ceremonial pains embodied in some of the rituals. Typically, he refused as well to include the changes that encounters with Western civilization had produced in the islanders. Appropriately, the compositions are much more carefully modeled, the lighting more dramatic—a greater lyricism in tune with the lovely lushness that was so in contrast to the stark *Nanook.*

On a return trip to the South Seas, he and F. W. Murnau began and then broke off a collaboration on *Tabu* (1931), a strange conglomeration of Murnau's expressionistic artifice and mystery, Flaherty's direct, quiet lyricism, and a plot that doomed them both.

Working next in England, Flaherty chose one of the rugged, primitive Aran Isles, off the coast of Ireland, where he filmed *Man of Aran* (1934). His simple narrative follows a small group of islanders, principally a single family, through representative, selected, but crucial rounds of their everyday life: combatting the changing sea, bringing in and repairing a damaged boat, creating a potato patch out of rock and seaweed, battling a school of sharks, and catching one. (Actually, this central crisis of *Man of Aran,* the battle with the sharks, was no longer a part of life on the island, and had to be simulated.) With these materials, he builds his finest epic celebration of dignity and courage in man's struggle for life. The compositions, the sharp tonal contrasts within and between shots, the relationship of shots—all pointedly dramatic and awesome—still respect the natural flow of the action. He regularly shoots the black-clad islanders against the strong contrasts of the harsh, rocky terrain, or the surging sea, or poised on precarious horizons against the limitless sky. In the sequence of the father breaking rocks for the potato patch, Flaherty moves toward more intensive editing, with greater fragmentation and repetition, and juxtaposition against sound.

In England, Flaherty's insistence on blending past and present and on dealing with timeless, primitively innocent problems aroused bitter controversy. John Grierson and others in the young documentary movement there criticized Flaherty's approach as politically evasive and reactionary and his use of the representative story line as ineffective in articulating complex social processes. As it developed, the British movement did forsake Flaherty's approach for an emphasis on social themes and on the more intensively edited cross section or panorama. For all its concern for the social responsibility of the film-maker, however, it was not a movement of protest; rather, it was largely supportive of the establishment and meliorist.

Still in England, Flaherty attempted a collaboration with the leading commercial producer, Alexander Korda, but the result, *Elephant Boy* (1937), was mainly a syrupy commercial film, starring Sabu, with touches of Flaherty documentary. But even in those touches there is a troubling escapist quaintness in the depiction of India.

Flaherty finally did turn to contemporary problems in *The Land,* completed just before United States entry into the war in 1941. He had been invited by

Man of Aran

Pare Lorentz, head of the short-lived United States Film Service, to film a study of farm poverty and the depletion of the land. But by the time the film was edited and a commentary by Flaherty added, World War II was on; *The Land* was deemed too pessimistic at a time when morale on the home front was considered critical. Flaherty's only documentary of strong social criticism was not to be shown publicly. A panoramic cross section, rather than a microcosm, *The Land* mixes Flaherty's direct humaneness with a much greater emphasis on manipulation and reconstitution through editing. The subject matter clearly prompted this new approach, but so did Flaherty's new association with Helen van Dongen, who had previously edited for Joris Ivens and other documentarists. In a sequence that shows the new mixture, we have a rapid intercutting of machine and men that dramatizes how they are being cut down like the corn. This is followed by a slower, quiet observation of displaced farm-workers, like refuse at the side of a country road, and then of the dullness and pain in the eyes of a starving woman.

Van Dongen was also editor of Flaherty's last film, *Louisiana Story* (1948). Although again a narrative, even smaller in scope than earlier films, *Louisiana Story* is far more emphatically and complexly edited than Flaherty's earlier films and owes more of its effects to a meticulously worked out mosaic of reconstruction. Throughout, it maintains the careful rhythmic and emotional development of its lovely opening scene: seven carefully patterned and modulated detail shots of creatures and growth in the swamp, and then a long shot held longer than the first seven together. In that scene the camera, slowly tracking in contrast to the earlier cuts, finds, then loses among the trees, then finds again, a boy paddling a boat in the distance. The film is the swamp boy's view of the wonders and mysteries of his bayou world, but its insistent innocence becomes disturbing—incomplete and artificial—when it reduces the invasion of the swampland by oil-drilling equipment to the same level of easy, idyllic harmony. As a document, *Louisiana Story* does not reflect the full contemporary impact on land and people of industry and technology.

Wyler Although William Wyler did not seek Flaherty's romantic lyricism, he did apply Flaherty's kind of transparency to the psychosocial material of the commercial narrative film. Wyler's devoted deference to this material was betrayed by the simplifications and sentimentalities of the political and social fashions it served; his technique was more important than the content. But it is one of the ironies of current criticism that the distinctive refinement of his techniques of transparency has led to deprecation of his "stylelessness," of his lack of a personal signature—despite such voices as André Bazin's pointing up his importance in the consolidation of the Realist tradition.

Wyler's approach emphasizes maintaining the integrity of the space, action, and sound of the filmic image, intruding only subtly upon the illusion of reality that such ostensibly unmanipulated images render. But of course there is manipulation still in this kind of structuring of the feel of reality. Wyler's consists in the careful composition of fixed or moving shots and in precise editing, decisive but not emphatic. In part, it pursues the Pabstian line of invisible editing, following character movement or intention, shifting point of view with shifts in dialogue or action, matching patterns from shot to shot. But to this Wyler has added more distinctive features aimed at maintaining an orientation to material, such as returning to an established guiding shot in the midst of cutting to new elements or, while alternating between fixed camera setups, changing their impact subtly (by moving slightly closer, for example).

Depending on the dramatic material, Wyler's composition can invoke either mood or symbolic overtones; but from the early thirties on he has been more concerned with giving precise visual form to conventional (often contrived) dramatic structure by the use of patterned movement and dialogue that reveal character and especially character interaction. Wyler carefully arranges characters within a scene, then maps out their movements, groupings, and regroupings to create, within the held shot, shifting visual patterns and spatial relationships that parallel and fulfill the dramatic development of the scene. While this often involves a moving camera—though not in the subjective manner of the expressive style—his particular signature is the fixed shot. From the early thirties on, often working with cameraman Gregg Toland, he has made important contributions in the structuring of continuously unfolding dramatic action. (Toland's contribution—not only to Wyler's films, but to film technique in general—should not be underestimated; yet it is important to note how the tones and total effects achieved by his cinematography vary with the differing styles of directors under whom he worked—men like Wyler, John Ford, and Orson Welles. His innovations in high-key lighting, precisely controlled overall illumination, and strong contrast and intense shadows are more functional with Wyler, more poetic with Ford, expressively distorted with Welles. His refinement of deep-focus photography—in which the foreground and background are simultaneously in focus—is used with striking within-shot juxtapositions and extreme camera angles with Ford and Welles. With Wyler, it is the key instrument in the orchestration of action and interaction within the single shot.)

Wyler's carefully unobtrusive composition based on character interaction was honed through the years on his many adaptations of plays and novels. In other hands such adaptations have often been either statically uncinematic or fruitlessly distorted to include cinematic movement and visuality. At his best, Wyler has managed to be both faithful and filmic, even when the original material has given his cool, ascetic patterns a shallow foundation.

Wyler's best work was done in the 20-year period between the early thirties and early fifties—when his tone and style seemed most consonant with the mood and style of the times. Most of these films were social-thesis works that varied in their balancing of psychological and social conflicts and concerns but in one way or another embedded the character in a detailed social context whose conflicts shaped his own, whose conflicts he represented. Typical of the central ground of Social Realism, these tended to be tightly plotted, well-made plays, whose patterns of give-and-take interaction and tension were admirably given visual form in Wyler's compositions.

His *Counsellor-at-Law* (1933), based on an Elmer Rice play, is a precise rendering of the conflicts of a ghetto-born lawyer, with signs of the beginnings of Wyler's approach to composition. By *These Three* (1936), Lillian Hellman's *The Children's Hour*, his formal integration of spatial pattern with the meaning of a dramatic moment not only proves effective, but saves the film from the plot compromise demanded by producer Sam Goldwyn and the Hays Office. Though the script (by Miss Hellman) has turned the original psychological ambiguities of latent lesbianism into a plain love triangle, its members unfairly assailed by social bigotry, Wyler's patterns play against these changes: capturing the two girls in shots whose relationships convey more than the dialogue, shooting Miriam Hopkins from the back in a way that undercuts her confession of love to Joel McCrea, and, in the final scenes, varying the pattern among the three although they are always grouped as a unit set against the hostile townspeople.

After popular adaptations of Sinclair Lewis's *Dodsworth* (1936) and Sidney

Kingsley's *Dead End* (1937)—the latter with a screenplay by Hellman and Kingsley, and with Humphrey Bogart in his second tough-guy role—Wyler filmed another Hellman play, *The Little Foxes* (1941), one of the era's most polished and representative thesis plays. In it the social comment is embodied in the personalities and personal conflicts within a Southern family that is more representative of warping by greed in capitalist society than of anything particularly or solely Southern. The family wars of the film, centering on the ruthlessly driving Regina Gidden (Bette Davis), develop a higher level of emotional intensity than in Wyler's other thesis films, and in consequence his staging employs more tonal contrasts and shadowing, more striking angles. In one of his most famous shots, Wyler uses deep focus to make even more striking a staging pattern taken from the original play. Regina, refusing to help her dying husband, is in the foreground in large, unmoving close-up, while deep in the background her husband, in the midst of a heart attack, struggles futilely to climb the stairs. But there is something about the film that does not capitalize on the intensity. Wyler and Davis feuded over her performance, which he felt relied on mannerisms of neurotic viciousness without fully rounding out the passionate nature of the warped woman. Yet there would seem to be, too, something in the cool precision of Wyler's patterns and direction that does not give echo to the passions.

Theses, with sentimentality but no passion, are clearly the wartime order of the day in *Mrs. Miniver* (1942) and in the postwar *The Best Years of Our Lives* (1946). The latter, one of the most awarded and praised films of its period, is the epitome of the dilemma of Social Realism's thesis works. Wyler and Toland reached skillful heights in giving grace and form to inferior dramatic material that they (and everybody else) apparently believed in but that crumbles into platitude, indeed almost hypocrisy, under objective examination and the passage of time.

Felt in its time to be probing and forthright, the script (by the noted Robert E. Sherwood) is timidly evasive and shallow; its central figures are glossy surfaces, representational types of the Social Realist movement, with none of the rough edges of character and situation needed to give them a living presence. Its height of protest is the ex-sergeant—bank vice-president (Fredric March) drunkenly telling off his fellow bankers and then going ahead and giving that veteran a loan even if he doesn't have collateral!

Yet even its checkerboard dramatic moves are given a sense of grace and rhythm, of dramatic feeling by the compositions of Wyler and Toland. In the early homecoming sequence, the impermanent camaraderie of three disparate returning servicemen is captured in alternating shots, looking out through a plane's window, then inside, close, the three forced together. Later, the despair of the out-of-work former Air Force captain (Dana Andrews) is caught (more than in any of the plot or dialogue) by a wandering camera following him aimlessly through a field of obsolete bombers, peering at him, still distant, as he sits behind the dimming plastic of a gunner's bubble.

The reunion of the armless sailor with his girl blends arrangement and editing to produce the perfect emotional tone for the scene. The sailor's back

**The Best Years of
Our Lives**

is to us, between his mother and father, and in long shot the girl appears in front of her house in the upper-right background. In medium shot she starts to run toward him. In medium shot from behind the veteran she gets closer, then stops just beyond his head, her eyes bright, his arms down, his hooks in view at the bottom of the screen. As she embraces him, still behind him, the camera moves in close. Her arms are around his neck, her happy and excited face seen over his shoulder, even closer. Then, for the first time, Wyler cuts to a reverse shot, a close-up of the veteran's face—tight, sad, and worried. In contrast, the patterns for the first meeting of the banker and his daughter and wife are distinctly different, equally appropriate and effective.

Wyler's technique of building around a basic guiding shot and then orchestrating beyond it is beautifully exemplified in the final wedding scene, in which the armless veteran marries his girl and the captain and the banker's daughter (Theresa Wright) are reunited. The guiding shot is from the minister's point of view initially, with the bride and groom in the center foreground, Andrews at the left foreground in profile. In the background, seen between him and the couple, is Theresa Wright, and behind her a crowd including her mother and father. As Wyler alternates telling closer shots, he always returns to a shot from behind Andrews, now clearly his point of view, until finally the bride and groom embrace and walk out of the shot to the right. Andrews turns more fully toward Theresa Wright, still beyond him in the same position. The crowd moves out of the frame, and then her mother and father. The shot is still held as Andrews moves toward her, but then, as they meet and embrace, Wyler cuts to a closer shot and finally a close-up of her smiling face.

In *Detective Story* (1951), from the Kingsley play, there is less pure grace and formal loveliness (Toland died in 1948) but an equal visual rightness for the dramatic flow, an even more intricate handling of the orchestration of two-person and group interrelationships during dialogue. Moreover, there is a better balance between material and means in what is probably the best of Wyler's social films. The play from which it is taken is a more solid piece of work than those of earlier films; its social themes of duty and justice are submerged in the fuller development of the inner torment of a detective shaped and destroyed by the rules to which he has given himself.

There are many examples in it of the way the held shot both allows the unimpeded flow of dramatic action and dialogue and gives form to the meaning of that action. In one, a young man who has stolen from his employer stands in the right foreground, framed in the doorway that leads to the crowded detective room in the background. The employer walks forward to the left side of the doorway to reconsider his complaint, the girl who loves the boy seen between them in the middle distance. Then she walks forward to stand between them, adding her pleas to the boy's. But in the gap still left in the doorway we see, beyond them, the detective, the threat to the arrangements being made. While they come to an agreement, we see him talking with typical firmness on the telephone. Just as they happily agree, he comes forward to dominate the grouping and reject the agreement.

The Wyler films that ventured beyond contemporary social situations tended to have more visual flair. These included a pair of artfully mounted Westerns—*The Westerner* (1940) and *The Big Country* (1958)—two Bette Davis melodramas, and two of Laurence Olivier's best screen vehicles. Davis's flamboyant *Jezebel* (1938) reveals a more ornate Wyler, without the weight of serious social message (as does a more subdued mood piece, *The Heiress*, 1949, full of shadows and the interplay of physical forms). In one of *Jezebel's* fine moments, the perverse Southern belle has come to an antebellum ball in a red instead of the conventional white dress. When she is rebuked, the camera travels with her down an aisle of white hoops that mockingly part to let her by, then moves in to focus on her chagrin as her lover forces her to stay, then pulls back to catch the swirl of their dancing out her shame. In *The Letter* (1940), with camerawork by Tony Gaudio, Wyler makes great use of exotic Malaysian décor. The murder-producing emotional trap in which Davis's bored and errant plantation wife futilely writhes is given a tenor that transcends its artificiality by the intense Germanic patterns of extreme black and white tones, shadows, and high-keyed lighting. Throughout, Wyler employs a varied motif of barlike lines—whether in a lace shawl, a railing, window blinds and shutters with light filtered through them casting strong geometric patterns of light and shadow, or even in the fabric on a sofa.

In the last sequence, the distraught Davis goes to accept the retribution of the Malay woman whose husband she killed. She opens a black door, and

The Letter

a pattern of light widens to balance, then overbalance, the rectangle of the opened door. Her own shadow is caught moving out onto a moonlit porch in shots edged by the geometrics of shutters and a railing. Outside, the moon passes behind a cloud, darkening all, then emerges, is concealed again. The moment of her murder is in darkness; then the moon casts light again, the camera moves, in recapitulation, back past poles and lines of lattice, past the shuttered windows into the house, to one last contrast shot: the lower left screen in shadow and, highlighted above an abrupt dividing diagonal, Davis's lace shawl over a chair. The gothic quality is one that Wyler recaptured in the color patterns and contrasts of *The Collector* (1965).

Wuthering Heights (1939) and *Carrie* (1952) embody not only some of Wyler's best screen moments but also Olivier's. Still there is something forced, overreaching, out of balance in his strenuous attempt to find visual form for the gothic horror and passionate romance of the Brontë novel, the unrelenting despair of the Dreiser. Beyond the problem of the compromises in the scripts, there are depths of emotion, of passion in the materials that are beyond the reach of Wyler's careful precision of flow and pattern. The result is a pastiche of Realist styles—Wyler's lucid, cool transparency, the imposed flourishes of a Mamoulian, the lyricism of Flaherty, the heightening moodiness of the French—but all without Carné's bedrock of truly felt experience. As it turns out, somewhere among all the possibilities offered by these four tendencies, the bulk of the works of the Realist style find their balances —or imbalances—of content and technique, imitativeness and expressiveness.

CHAPTER TEN

SOCIAL PROBLEMS AND REALISM

The discussion (Chapter 9) of the work of William Wyler indicated the close connection between social content and the techniques of the Realist style. From the thirties on, this content—especially in terms of specifically, and often simplistically, defined social problems—was one of the strongest forces in shaping the form and style of films, most of all in America, where the social-problem film was most common. And, somewhat paradoxically, in most cases the response to the requirements of this content coalesced rather than clashed with the response to the demands of commercial success. For both sets of requirements led to an approach to the audience that emphasized a technique of unobtrusiveness that would facilitate basic and easy identification and empathy, emotional immersion in the dramatic materials. Simplicity of content matched that of technique, so that there would be a clear understanding of the materials: Zola's transparent screen. Unfortunately, box-office demands also led to vitiation of the social content.

The treatment of social problems had long been part of the Realist tradition in literature and drama. The manner of dealing with social problems in other styles—as in the earlier, agonized, desperate protests of German social Expressionism—reflected attitudes not predominant in the thirties, when, despite the severity of the worldwide depression and acceleration of the pressures leading to war, the cultural context in which films were made did not encourage this kind of futility and desperation. For the political currents of the time seemed to join with the beliefs of the producers in encouraging idealism and optimism—a belief that social problems could be readily defined, exposed, and solved. Even the intellectuals of the left shared the prevalent assumptions of easy, almost painless change, as typified by the attitudes animating the Popular Front coalitions of the latter half of the decade. Whatever the combination of influences, the net result was a sense of certainty (in understanding and explaining the dramatic materials) that matched that of earlier Realist theorists like Zola and an often naive affirmation of man's ability to control and shape social reality.

The transparent screen, however, is not without distortion, for any screen —being a set of shared views about what is real—structures and thus limits. When such a structuring becomes conventional, habitual, unquestioned, merely fashionable, the limitations, evasions, and softenings become more pronounced. Thus, Realist simplicity—whether commercial, liberal, or radical in orientation—can produce its own sentimentalities of content and mannerisms of form, even while rejecting those of an earlier era. This process presents a critical problem in a period of strong emphasis on social content, and most films of the period under discussion are cases in point: With the passage of time, their social and psychological content has not retained its original validity—the Realism of one era has become the romance of another. As a result, it has become fashionable when evaluating works of the thirties to celebrate films that feature embellishments of technique at the expense of those that attempt a meaningful depiction of human life but do not fit current conventions for structuring reality, underestimating the centrality of the interaction of content and technique in the development of film as an art. This interaction can be traced in many films of the thirties and forties that directly depict specific social problems or that imply them.

WAR AND ANTIWAR

Among the directors whose best work was concerned with social themes, Lewis Milestone furnishes a valuable starting point. His films span the period and reflect its variations and trends in both content and approach. This can be seen particularly in his war films.

In the same year, 1930, that G. W. Pabst's *Westfront* marked a new but short-lived directness in the treatment of basic social issues in the German film, Milestone's own antiwar film, *All Quiet on the Western Front*, signaled a similar but lasting development in the American film. Milestone's film displays the combination of qualities that became typical of his work. The film, based on the novel of the same name by Erich Maria Remarque, takes a strong, simplified social stand on its subject yet is careful and convincing in its individualized details of character. Its humanness, in fact, outweighs the

All Quiet on the Western Front

significance of its specific thesis. It blends its realistic treatment with lyrical cinematic effects of mood, movement, and rhythm that are sometimes appropriately heightening, sometimes artificially obtrusive. It shows a special concern for the place and possibilities of dialogue.

The dialogue (based on that in the novel) is by the playwright Maxwell Anderson, and its poetic qualities are intentionally employed by Milestone to add resonance to the Realism of the details. Too often, however, they, and the mannered touches of the acting, seem more cloying than resonant. A similar artificiality also intrudes upon the carefully composed settings and lighting, the repeated motifs of visual pattern. But on the whole the vividness of visual form has a moving eloquence that gives added dimension to the realistic core: an alternating cutting pattern, back and forth between shots of running soldiers shot down in a field (the futility intensified by movements of the camera) and static shots of the machine gunners—all blended with the sound of the guns; insistent but rhythmic close-ups of the faces of a number of the young soldiers on the eve of battle, meaningfully repetitious; a pattern of shots of objects and faces that captures the mixed emotions felt in the appropriation of the boots of a dead soldier; an artfully selected final composition—the hand of a young soldier (the central character, played by Lew Ayres) reaching to capture a butterfly and then falling limp when he is shot.

The film is also typical of Milestone's approach in that its pacifist view of war is placed in a wider social context—not only by alternating sequences of the war front and German home front, but also by stressing the connections between broader social patterns and the specific evils of the war.

Most interesting of the other antiwar films of the period is Howard Hawks's *The Road to Glory* (1936), with a script, in part, by William Faulkner. Hawks's approach—typical of his style—is less mannered visually, more efficiently direct, faster-paced, much in the manner of the commercial melodramas of the time. Similarly, it builds more conventional patterns of emotional crescendo—the terror of a platoon when sappers are placing explosives under their bunker, the acceleration of the nightmare-driven collapse of the tormented company commander. While its depiction of the ravaging, useless grind of war has a harsh bluntness that Milestone's lyricisms tend to mute in *All Quiet, Road to Glory* has no broader social implications. The dirty war is there, and—as in Hawks's more romanticized *Dawn Patrol* (1930), the patriotic World War II *Air Force* (1944), or other films of his with different milieus—the film's emphasis is on the men who struggle to do their jobs, dirty as they may be, and maintain their comradeship.

The Hawks film appeared at a pivotal point in development of the film. After 1936, political attitudes and the world situation dictated a new approach to war that was embodied in many films—from the spate of glowing service academy films of the late thirties (Dick Powell, in one, singing "Shipmates Stand Forever") that stressed the comradeship and duty but left out the dirt, to the myriad patriotic visions of battle during the war years of the forties. In 1938, the Walter Wanger–William Dieterle *Blockade*, with script by John Howard Lawson, was unique in its attempt to deal with the threat and horrors of Fascism as manifest in the Spanish Civil War; yet it awkwardly mixes large amounts of commercial softening and sentimentalizing with small doses of political significance. Like so many films that followed, it portrays a version of an historical event through the complications of a story of individuals—this time a spy story. More visually arresting than many of the type, it manipulates its emotional and propagandistic climax (the siege of a city) by an effective application of Eisensteinian epic-style editing.

The pattern was applied to a variety of wartime situations and battlegrounds. One of the strangest products is the Warner Brothers—Michael Curtiz *Mission to Moscow* (1943), in which, in a paean to a wartime ally, a bravura combination of convincing realistic visual surface and manipulative editing are applied to incredibly sanguine simplifications concerning Stalin's Soviet Russia.

The home front fight against Fascism also received ample treatment. Three examples can provide a sampling of the approaches. In *Meet John Doe* (1943), a celebration of the common man in battle against an insidious Fascist conspiracy, Frank Capra adds—to the usual combination of business-like plot elaboration and bravura mass-scene and climax-editing—his own particular flavor, with human touches of characterization within the morality play manipulations. In *The Watch on the Rhine* (1943), directed by Herman Shumlin from Lillian Hellman's adaptation of her own play, the tight dramatic plotting and careful, straight-line motivational and emotional development are given the unobtrusive treatment of the conventional Social Realist play. The world situation is portrayed through the events of a small-compassed domestic drama, the representative, message-bearing characters given the trappings of realistic detail within the precise geometry of the film's specific political thesis: that though the decision be difficult, it is necessary to stand up and fight authoritarianism. In contrast, the David O. Selznick—John Cromwell *Since You Went Away* (1944), its screenplay by Selznick, has a message no more specific than America the Beautiful (which is sung in the course of the film) facing war, its good folk troubled but undaunted. It is a paradoxical wedding of social content and commercialism. Its banal dilution of social reality is actually lent a degree of credibility by the expertise of its commercial technicians, who, evoking a detailed physical context of an era's sights and sounds, mount deftly developed vignettes—especially the last dance before departure for the war—that do have the ambience of at least a part of the truth of a time.

During World War II, the films of Lewis Milestone underwent this same shift of attitude. But representative as they are of the more romantic view of war, they still reveal his individuality. *North Star* (1943), with a script by Hellman that was much altered in production, romanticizes the courage of the people of rural Russia in the face of German occupation. While Milestone's tendencies to beautify often only further bloat the platitudes of the script, his excellence with filmic rhythm and mood often surmount them. Similarly, his *Edge of Darkness* (1943), with script by Robert Rossen, has carefully wrought sequences of image and emotion and a rendering of individualized characters that rise above the expected routines of its story—the Nazi occupation of Norway. The more blatant *The Purple Heart* (1944), which deals with brutality in a Japanese prison camp, nonetheless has a contextual detail and power, a hard-edged intensity that render some sense of the Japanese enemy far beyond anything else achieved in the many superpatriotic productions of the war years.

At the war's end, Milestone and Rossen did *A Walk in the Sun* (1946), which, with William Wellman's *The Story of G.I. Joe* (1945), provides the most valuable rendering of the life of the frontline soldier to come out of the war. Both employ the device of the platoon or squad composed of a cross section of American types, one that had become standard in battle films. But rather than engage in the conventional meretricious heroics or crusades against Fascist evil, both stay with the small-scale commonplaces, the ordinary everyday killing and being killed, not quite antiwar or anti-Fascist, but sensitive to the pains and the dignities of courage and endurance. Together, they make an interesting contrast in the ways in which films of the period struck balances between accuracy of realistic representation and sentimentality, either commercial or idealogical, or both. Wellman's adaptation of the writings of Ernie Pyle—the war correspondent who focused on the common soldier—is more patently an attempt at transparency. In the main, it is laconic in dialogue, eschews plot complications, and maintains a documentary casualness, a freedom of little touches and vignettes of impression and character interaction. Yet it *is* carefully controlled, more mannered in its character types and representative small actions than it wants to admit, more openly sentimental in its big speeches and attitudes than it can justify or earn with its lucid surface quietness. The platitudes stick out like awkward elbows. Milestone's *Walk* does not escape its romancing either. But it approaches its similar materials quite differently. Milestone more openly imposes a heightening, formal perspective on the quiet, careful realities of the action. It celebrates its commonplace heroes more openly, and in so doing maintains a greater unity between its sentiments and its documentary recording. The tone is set by a ballad—an excellent choice—by Earl Robinson, which is carried throughout the film in an attempt at poetic heightening of the dialogue and visual images. The film's verbal and visual poetry falls short of true excellence, but it is, yet, a unique specimen of lyrical Realism.

Wartime Documentary

During the war, the documentary film had begun to reach a wider audience. The government had turned, especially for its large-scale films, mainly to Hollywood film-makers, although, on a smaller scale, the overseas branch of the Office of War Information did employ such non-Hollywood documentarists as Willard Van Dyke and Irving Lerner.

In the first years of the war, the major effort directed at servicemen was the series of compilation films supervised by Frank Capra—the *Why We*

Fight series. Researching and editing vast amounts of stock footage, Capra's group shaped a perspective on the course of Nazi advances until America's entry into the war that was lucid, reasonable, and emotionally stirring, though oversimplified. As the war progressed, Hollywood was reporting the triumphs of battle to the home front, as were British commercial film-makers in such works as *Desert Victory* (1943). Some of the films were broadly focused, such as the joint British-American *The True Glory* (1945) and Louis de Rochemont's *The Fighting Lady* (1945). Others followed more closely a smaller element of the fighting, as in William Wyler's *Memphis Belle* and John Ford's *The Battle of Midway* (both 1944). Unique among these was John Huston's *The Battle of San Pietro* (1944), much more personally felt and artistically shaped in depicting the tragedy of battle along with the glory.

POVERTY, INJUSTICE, OPPRESSION

Milestone

Beyond his war films, Lewis Milestone's other work was also illustrative of social trends and the new demands of sound. *The Front Page* (1931), with script by Charles MacArthur and the ubiquitous Ben Hecht, had been among the first to blend a commercial sheen and pace with a sense of the harsher realities of big-city life. In it, Milestone was particularly effective in finding editing patterns to match the rapid-fire cynicism of the Hecht-MacArthur wisecracks. *Hallelujah, I'm a Bum* (1933) was a strange and unsuccessful attempt at social comment on the depression through the musical form, with some rhyming dialogue in addition to the usual songs and dances. A more successful merging and heightening of conventional forms was *The General Died at Dawn* (1936). From an exotic plot of spy intrigue and military power struggles in China, Milestone and Clifford Odets drew meaningful implications about individuals buffeted by the oppressive forces of society. While meaning and credibility of character are hobbled by the tortuosities of the plot, free rein is given to the lyrical dialogue of Odets (whose plays, for better or worse, had set the tone for most movie attempts at a folk poetry) and the visual inventiveness of Milestone. Milestone's honest adaptation of John Steinbeck's *Of Mice and Men* (1940) is a moving balancing of the emotional pathos of the imbecile Lennie and the harsh surrounding realities of the itinerant poor. And in 1946, out of the fashion of the darkly shadowed tough-guy, night-life films of that era, Milestone and Rossen (who wrote the original screenplay) again drew a greater realism and social significance in *The Strange Loves of Martha Ivers*. It is full of virtuoso visual touches and literate dialogue that effectuate the emotional brutality of its situation. Despite melodramatic pointing and dated mannerisms, it keeps its developments within the limits of credibility. In it, the desperate, clawing viciousness of Martha Ivers (Barbara Stanwyck at her best) is seen as the pathological extreme—mirrored in other forms by other characters—of obsessive drives for power and wealth, alluringly false symbols of identity of a warped culture.

Milestone, of course—like the other most active directors of the period—made numerous films that were not concerned, even indirectly, with social problems or issues. But his social films are clearly the most important phase of his work. Although they never fully solved the problem, so typical of the period, of fusing disparate elements—such as accuracy of representation, concern for social statement, an artful (and arty) personal style, and the demands of the commercial genres—they do constitute a body of work that had significant cinematic and social goals, which were generally achieved.

Curtiz   A contrasting case is that of Michael Curtiz, whose social films form only a small and less successful portion of his vast and varied output, in which purely commercial adventures and melodramas dominate. Yet they are like his other films in their eclecticism of approach and technique, lit with brilliant flourishes that seem more a mark of cynicism toward the materials assigned him by the studio than an attempt to give them significant form. His *The Strange Love of Molly Louain* (1932) blends the cynical-newspaper-man motif with harsh details of slum life (reminiscent of German street films) but establishes no consistent point of view toward the material. He did his prison picture in *20,000 Years in Sing Sing* (1933) and touched on the plight of oppressed sharecroppers in *Cabin in the Cotton* (1932), where typically he was at his best in depicting the erotic viciousness of the rich girl (Bette Davis). His *Black Fury* (1935) dealt ambivalently with the violence in a strike promoted by an antilabor provocateur, yet his sentimentalization of violence by deprived slum youth (the "Dead End" kids) in *Angels with Dirty Faces* (1938–39) was typical of the period. In *Four Daughters* (1938) and *Daughters Courageous* (1939), he worked, with the then fashionable image of the tough-tender John Garfield rebel up from the slums, in domestic melodramas that displayed a typically equivocal attitude toward Garfield's rebelliousness and the solid middle-class virtues of the family of the Lane sisters (Rosemary, Priscilla, and Lola).

In the war years his taut development of Robert Rossen's script of Jack London's *The Sea Wolf* (1941) had strong admonitory overtones concerning the need to stand up to Fascism, while the aforementioned *Mission to Moscow* found him applying his gaudiest craftsmanship to promotion of the short-lived, wartime friendship with the Russians. Less gaudy was the worldly and sentimental *Casablanca* (1943), which transformed the timely issues of war into a timeless romance of lost second chances and disciplined emotional resilience: Rick's Place, the epitome of Hollywood havens for the world-weary in a rootless world, its bar full of Frenchmen drowning out the Nazis with the "Marseillaise"; Dooley Wilson playing it ("As Time Goes By") again; Bogart and Bergman sharing glances and memories; Bogart and Claude Rains walking off into the fog in shared defeat and acceptance of the way of the world.

Le Roy   Mervyn Le Roy was another director whose work indicated the tight, fast pace, the harsh low-life details, the prolific alternation of social themes and commercial genres that were the mark of the Warner Brothers organization. (That studio and its assembly-line economics produced more films of social content than any other, yet its head, Jack L. Warner, was among the first in the postwar period to denounce the alleged, but never substantiated, Communist subversion of the movie industry and to fire many of his key employees for political reasons.)

More like Milestone than Curtiz, Le Roy did his best work in movies with social themes and approached them from a consistent stylistic and political stance. His *Little Caesar* (1931) was the first of three gangster films that early in the sound era set the pattern for the genre and established its connections to social themes. It also set the pattern for Le Roy's efficient, audience-immersion Realism: taut scripting; short, intense scenes; rapid pace of plot and editing; settings evocative of society's grubby underbelly; occasional excellence of composition and lighting for dramatic and thematic heightening. In one example of the last, as Caesar (Edward G. Robinson) shoots a rival, he is framed by the pattern of a stairwell from which he has just emerged at the right. He fires offscreen to the left; and we see his victim only as a shadow crumpling on the wall above the stairway.

In several subsequent films, Le Roy was to employ the approach in more direct social commentary (in the midst of a host of mediocre "entertainment" films, which came to occupy wholly his career as director and producer). *Five-Star Final* (1931) turned the fashionable tough-newspaperman plot into a strongly moral attack on the irresponsibility of big-business journalism. *Two Seconds* (1932) used the condemned-criminal format to build a bleak and credible picture of human and social decay with a picture-long flashback (beginning at the moment of his death) of the life of a criminal. In *I Am a Fugitive from a Chain Gang* (1932), he completely overturned the commercial prison-genre film with a combination of intense melodrama and episodic, documentarylike realism of situation and detail. As the film follows the plight of fugitive Paul Muni, it indicts not only the harshness of the prison system, but the society that first imprisons an innocent man, then—to the picture's end—pursues him. Its finale—in which Muni, with resigned hatred, says he will steal to live—is one of the most uncompromising, in its social implications, of any gangster film. In the highly different milieu of a primitive China, Le Roy's *Oil for the Lamps of China* (1935) sporadically criticizes the ethics of big business in its impact on the individual, in this case a dedicated employee (Pat O'Brien), ruthlessly sidelined after long service. However, it undercuts its own protests, particularly in its flagrantly happy ending.

The last and possibly the best of this series was *They Won't Forget* (1937), with script by Rossen and Aben Kandel, which examines with unmitigated anger the injustices in the administration of justice and the passions of the mob. On the one hand, it is naive and overexplicit; on the other, it has vigor in a cynical toughness of social detail accented with visual flourishes. A Black janitor in a Southern town, who finds the body of a schoolgirl (Lana Turner, in her first role), is promptly taken to be the murderer. But the cor-

I Am a Fugitive from a
Chain Gang

ruption of justice is compounded when the politically ambitious prosecutor
seeks more politically fruitful prey in a white Northern interloper: Anybody
could convict the janitor. Despite much plot attention to the lynch mob, the
final emphasis is on the callousness of public leaders, the prosecutor (Claude
Rains) remaining, to the end, unconcerned about the guilt or innocence of
the accused. Typical of the visual excitement is the kidnapping and lynching sequence. As the victim is dragged from a train, another comes by, brutal in its violent force, its roar drowning out the victim's screams. At the
moment of lynching nearby, Le Roy cuts to another train shrieking by, its
steel hook catching up a mail sack and bearing it, dangling like a body,
down the track.

Lang   A year before Le Roy's examination of the subject, Fritz Lang's first American film, *Fury*, had also dealt with lynch-mob violence; yet, like Lang's two
subsequent social films, it had the imprint of a much more individualized
cinematic personality (though one not free of commercial studio demands).
Lang brought to these three films the kind of heightened, expressive Realism
he had developed in *M*, but modified toward the less obtrusive Realism of
the American style—with *M* standing at midpoint between his American work
and his earlier Expressionist films in Germany. Similarly, he used the established genre—as he was later to do in conventional melodrama—as a spring-

board for a more personal interpretation of the paradoxical relationship between the law and lawbreakers, tensions that arise (as he had also shown in his German films) from dislocations within society and within man himself.

Fury is the most audacious of the three in examining the complexities of the justice theme, though Lang, and Bartley Cormack, who strongly adapted the original Norman Krasna story, could not work out a satisfactory ending. For the fury is seen as present on all sides: in the authorities, who wrongly accuse and jail Joe Wilson (in a typically complex shot, the sheriff questions Joe while a moronic cellmate snatches at flies); in the mob that burns the jail and attempts to lynch Joe (with such biting details as a boy chanting "I'm Popeye the sailor man," another munching a hot dog, a woman holding a child aloft for a better view); and in Joe himself, for when he escapes, and members of the lynch mob are indicted for his murder, he does nothing to prevent their execution. Thus, Lang's point that all men are potential lynchers as well as brothers. But the terms of the ending soften the ironies into a generalized sympathy that dissipates responsibility: Joe (Spencer Tracy) is convinced by his girl (Sylvia Sidney) that the people had no power to act as individuals once they had become a mob.

Despite the ending, the treatment of man the lyncher is harsh and exciting throughout the film. All is literal, yet all is heightened to an angry excitement by patterns of composition and lighting, juxtapositions of editing, expressive use of sound. In extending the analogy that each is trapped in his own prison, the shots within the jail are followed by a shot of the mob seen through, and as if behind, the heavy bars. At the trial the righteousness of the townspeople is juxtaposed with newsreel shots of them during the lynch attempt. In an earlier shot, gossiping, babbling women had been juxtaposed with a shot of cackling hens. As Joe becomes more and more fanatical, he is caught more and more in separating, isolating close-ups.

The literal surfaces of the Realist style are similarly heightened in *You Only Live Once* (1937), one of the period's finest cinematic realizations of conventionally simplified material. In it, Eddie and Joan (modeled on the actual hoodlums Bonnie and Clyde Barrow) are innocent victims of the depression and of vindictive, persecuting authority, which will not allow them, in Joan's phrase, their "right to live." A three-time loser (though presented as no fault of his), Eddie is kept from working, convicted of a murder he didn't commit, and seemingly forced (though there is a touch here of the greater complexity of the demons within, as in *Fury*) to murder a priest when he makes his escape. On the run, he and Joan are accused of other major crimes of which they are innocent, commit only minor ones to live, are eventually shot to death.

The special pleading is given vibrantly successful form. Surrounding contextual details and lighting embed plot actions in convincing, deepening mood: rain during a holdup; fog during the confusion of the jailbreak; an idyllic, evening love scene tinged with the ominous croaking of frogs, fore-

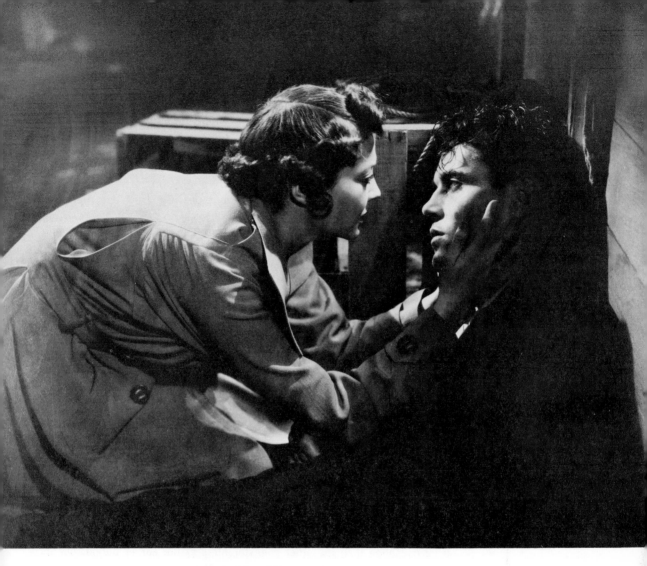

You Only Live Once

shadowing the muddy slime of the embankment on which the two are finally killed. Nondialogue sounds play an expressive role throughout, most successfully in sequences depicting the imaginings of the protagonists. Juxtapositions are ironic: Joan (Sylvia Sidney) steeling herself against the hour of Eddie's execution, accidentally striking a piano's keys, the jangle intruding on the silence, as Eddie (Henry Fonda) is seen beginning his escape; press reports of their supposed exploits followed by shots of Joan giving birth in a shack in a hobo jungle, Eddie bringing her a bunch of wildflowers.

Again, the ending—obviously studio-imposed—jars. It is an extreme example of the destructive compromises that pock the social films of the era:

As a heavenly choir sings, the dead priest welcomes Eddie to heaven, telling him that he's free. It could almost be irony, but it isn't.

You and Me (1938), the last of the three, is related in theme, but less successful. In it, Lang unsuccessfully attempts to mix differing narrative approaches—a poetic moodiness in the love scenes, a harsh documentary brutality in the prison scenes, a framework of montage images and poetic narration to summarize themes. He also tries for a kind of existential-deterministic mix: The ex-convict is represented as a victim of social bias and, yet, as responsible for embracing bankrupt values. But Lang does not work out a plot to develop this validly, as witness the hero's reason for reverting to a life of crime: his discovery that his love, his chance for a new life (Sylvia Sidney again), is also an ex-convict!

Lang's two crime films mark an important turning point in the film treatment of the subject during the thirties. The gangster—tough-guy films of the first half of the decade, which established a lasting genre that also influenced the visual and verbal styles of other kinds of films, had dealt with powerful, vicious criminals in gangland settings. But their treatment of the gangster phenomenon had had no consistent social implications, had seemingly indicted crime yet glorified the winning, powerful personalities of its gangland barons. But by 1937—as in Lang's two films—a more conscious, consistent social point was being made. Now the commonest approach was to examine and indict the social causes of crime. Though not always as pure as Lang's protagonists, the criminals began to be seen largely as victims of forces beyond their control.

Wellman   In one way or another, the problems of the economic system became one of the leading motifs in social films, whether indirectly in terms of the pressures of greed or the relation of poverty to crime, or more directly in studies of specific sectors of economic drought.

William Wellman's *The Public Enemy* (1931) attempted to suggest more social causation than the other gangster films of the earlier period, but its social points were mainly intermissions in the excitement of the exploits, doomed but vivacious, of Jimmy Cagney. With *Wild Boys of the Road* (1933), Wellman, using an adaptation of a Russian film, dealt in more direct terms with the plight of homeless youth driven by economic deprivation into antisocial behavior. In *The President Vanishes* (1935), he used a fanciful intrigue melodrama for pointed comments about the dangers of dictatorship by the lords of high finance.

Lachman,   One of the most unusual treatments of the evils inherent in a passion for
Murphy,   wealth was *Dante's Inferno* (1925), directed by Harry Lachman, with excep-
Vidor,   tional photography by Rudolph Maté. It is part realistic melodrama, part
Ford   symbolic fantasy—the only American film of the period to make a serious attempt to blend a literal surface with the distorted, subjective projections

of Expressionist symbolism, to blur the line between reality and the truths of fantasy. In it, a ruthless ex-seaman (Spencer Tracy) takes over a failing sideshow (which, ironically, had been intended to show the vanity of temporal wealth and power) and uses it as a means to gain control of a carnival combine, capitalizing on the public's fascination with the horrors of hell, putting hell, as he says, "on a paying basis." In the first part of the picture, Lachman and Maté use the exotic details of the carnival and of the gigantic fun house of horror "Dante's Inferno" to build provocative moods and overtones on literal events. In a coma after his palace of hell collapses (as a result of shoddy construction) and his gambling ship burns, Tracy has a climactic dream. In it the literal fun house Inferno is turned into a fantastic and frightening dream of hell, based on illustrations of the Dante poem—a nightmare whose allegory purges Tracy of his destructive greed.

Three films dealing with the impoverished provide a cross section of the more direct ways films commented on the economic crisis. Ralph Murphy's *Golden Harvest* (1937) is a direct-protest film on a minor scale, emphasizing obvious plot actions and crises to depict the economic squeeze on poor farmers and their final stand against seizure of their lands. King Vidor's *Our Daily Bread* (1934) was a more personal effort, yet a disjointed one. Written and financed by Vidor, it poses a sentimental solution to unemployment and poverty through nonprofit cooperative and small collective farms— a back-to-the-soil answer at a time when the small farmer was the worst casualty of a deteriorating economy. Its means are diffuse: well-handled but talky, informative discussions of the issues; the usual melodramatic crises from government and business interference and opposition; heightening visual sequences, such as the finale, which, with Eisenstein-like montage-editing, excitingly though rather artificially builds the rhythm of the triumphant opening of the farm's irrigation channel. In contrast, in his adaptation (with Nunnally Johnson) of John Steinbeck's *The Grapes of Wrath* (1940), John Ford took similar material beyond pointed protest and thesis into an epic evocation of the dignity of people in the face of travail. Ford did not escape the simplifications and sentimentalities of the problem film, so strongly tied to the conventional perspectives of its period, nor his own calculated efforts to achieve something more. Yet on the whole the film stands distinctly above the era's other depictions of social injustice and is one of Ford's best mixtures of a credible, literal Realism and a poeticized folk epic.

In 1938, Vidor's *The Citadel* (from the A. J. Cronin novel) was his most successful effort in imbuing a social theme—as Ford could—with a sense of the felt life of a people. His depiction of the Welsh mining community (influenced by earlier British documentary treatment of similar materials) has a warmth and humanity, a sensitive vividness that earlier he had not been able to draw from Elmer Rice's play about American slum life, *Street Scene*. Yet even in *The Citadel*, the evocation of a milieu is left behind by the plot

The Grapes of Wrath

complications aimed at dramatizing the evils of the system of medical care
and the crusade of the progressive young doctor (Robert Donat). And in
The Informer (1935), Ford's depiction of the dilemmas of political conscience and action, the emotional intensity is marred by the overinsistent
thrust of social theme and by plot and dialogue banality that are echoed in
the obviousness of his "poetic" effects. Ford's *Young Mr. Lincoln* (1939)
is a quiet, restrained example of the popular historical-biography, nicely
capturing the spirit of its time without undue drawing of contemporary political lessons.

HISTORICAL-BIOGRAPHICAL

Dieterle   By the late thirties, especially in Warner Brothers' productions, the commercially successful historical-biographical genre of *Young Mr. Lincoln* was
frequently shaped to provide lessons in social and political matters—the
nature of justice, business, democracy, freedom. The chief exponent of this
approach in Hollywood was William Dieterle, who was adroit and workman-

like in juggling the typical elements of politically oriented scripts (several by John Huston): the credible contexts of details of the historical period; the literate, informative discussions of the issues; the individualized development of the basic plot centering on the crusade of a progressive hero against the forces of reaction. In *The Story of Louis Pasteur* (1936), *The Life of Émile Zola* (1937), and *Juarez* (1939), Dieterle used Paul Muni, who had left his tough-guy image behind. In *Dr. Ehrlich's Magic Bullet* (1940) and *Reuter's* (1941), the hero was Edward G. Robinson, who was still to return to that role on occasion. In Italy, a broader sweep of spectacle was joined with political themes in Allesandro Blasetti's excellent biography of Garibaldi, *1860* (1933).

A later Dieterle effort in this field, *The Searching Wind* (1946), marks an advance in both dramatic and political sophistication in the use of the historical materials but created little notice. Adapted by Lillian Hellman from her own play, it places a fictional character at the center of the major events of the twenties and thirties. Intelligently intertwining the events of his personal life and the public events (though it attempts to encompass too many of the latter), it draws a parallel between his growing ability to face and act on political facts and a similar development with respect to the realities of his personal life. Civilized and thoughtful as it was, it seems out of its time, too late—or even too early. It was also Dieterle's last job of work in the social film.

EUROPE

Although these and hundreds of other social films were a major aspect of American film production in the thirties and early forties, the social film did not play as large a role in the film-making of other countries, with of course the obvious exception of Soviet Russia, where it played the only role. In Germany, the influence of the important early sound-film efforts of G. W. Pabst's *Westfront, The Beggar's Opera, Kameradschaft;* of Bertolt Brecht's *Kuhle Wampe* (1932); and of Leontine Sagen's *Maedchen in Uniform* (1931) was cut short by the rise of the Nazis.

In England, the documentary film had paid steady attention to man in society, though not in terms of protest. In the commercial film, however, social comment was less central until the patriotic social-message films of World War II.

Anthony Asquith, with *Tell England* (1930), and John Baxter, with *Doss House* (1932), had touched on the impact of the depression, but it was not until the end of the thirties that the major works with this theme were produced. Typically, Baxter's depiction of the effects of unemployment on domestic life, *Love on the Dole,* was held up by censorship problems until 1941. In 1937, Michael Powell's *The Edge of the World* had been obliquely concerned with poverty in its artful, semidocumentary view of life in remote seashore villages. But the most significant direct view of economic conflicts was Carol Reed's *The Stars Look Down* (1939). Both honest and emotionally intense, it is a film of careful composition and solid mood, without flourish or exaggeration. Its visual exactness is matched by its sound treatment of the plot material, centering on the strife between workers and owners in a Welsh mining town. Its evocation of the sturdy, traditional life of the people is not extraneous but integral to the plot, used to give a fully rounded sense of the situation. For unlike most films on the subject, it does not present an either-or simplification. It shows workers in conflict among themselves as well as with the owners, dramatizes the necessary but complex impact of unionism upon the traditional patterns of their life. It stands unique as well in the development of Reed's career.

During the war, Reed's major contribution, *The Way Ahead* (1944), was typical of British films of this kind in applying the lessons of documentary to the fiction film, and typical of both British and American films in focusing on a cross section of service types. Yet it stood out in its balancing of home and war front and its greater emphasis on the war's implications for the postwar period.

Among the wartime films, the David Lean–Noel Coward *In Which We Serve* (1942) and *This Happy Breed* (1944) were the most polished and commercial, blending realistic materials with sentimental patriotism. More matter-of-fact in building personal stories in the midst of documentarylike reportage were Baxter's *One of Our Aircraft Is Missing* (1942), Charles Frend's *The Foreman Went to France* (1942), Asquith's *We Dive at Dawn* (1943), and Frank Launder and Sidney Gilliat's *Millions Like Us* (1943)—although none escaped sentimentalism in the messages drawn from the material. Less commonplace was Thorold Dickinson's *Next of Kin* (1942), a fictionalized re-creation of an actual case of espionage that resulted from loose talk. The film was used both in the armed services and commercial theaters.

In 1943, the important documentary film-maker Harry Watt combined actual war-front footage and studio re-creations in a sober and honest fictional film of the desert war, *Nine Men*. Like the American *Story of G.I. Joe* and *A Walk in the Sun*, it sought a sense of the feel of the common soldier's life but intruded less on the lifelike flow of its material. At the close of the war, Watt pioneered in placing a fictional plot amidst a strongly documentary evocation of natural locations in Australia, in the *Overlanders* (1946), but there was no development of the approach in subsequent work.

In France, the German occupation precluded any extensive development of the war theme, with the major exception of the surprising *La Bataille du Rail*. Made in 1944 by René Clément, it is an exciting depiction of the French railwaymen's resistance against the Nazis, combining the newsreellike spontaneity of Roberto Rossellini's *Open City* (made the same year but not seen by Clément) with a more tightly structured plot.

In the prewar period, André Malraux's production of his novel, *L'Espoir*

(1939), had dealt with the political complexities of the Spanish Civil War, and Jean Renoir's *Grand Illusion* (1937) had provided one of the screen's most humane and artful of all protests against war. In fact, the major social films of the prewar period in France were the work of Renoir—*La Vie Est à Nous* (1936), *La Marseillaise* (1937), *La Bête Humaine* (1938), *La Règle du Jeu (The Rules of the Game,* 1939). But these are works that are best appraised within the context of Renoir's personal *oeuvre,* (Chapter 14), for like all of his best work, they go beyond the shaping limits of social message, beyond the demands of the social film as a conventional genre.

CHAPTER ELEVEN

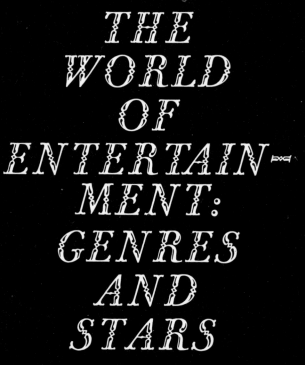

THE WORLD OF ENTERTAIN- MENT: GENRES AND STARS

The development of the social film in the thirties was but one reflection of the tendency in commercial film production to categorize films on the basis of content. This categorization helped in the tailoring of films to serve a specific function, to reach and satisfy certain specific expectations—indeed, to cultivate such an expectation in the audience and maintain it through constant repetition. Salable categories of films had, of course, existed earlier. The continued growth of the audience, the spread of the major production organizations, and the introduction of sound now accentuated the commercial value of shaping product to match expectations already instilled in the audience. The drive to establish and exploit these genres became the most obvious influence on the vast bulk of commercial film production. Hollywood became the chief shaper of the patterns, its products the chief supply to meet the new demands.

Although the social film differed from the purely commercial, "entertainment" genres, it shared many characteristics with them. While the social film was a broader category than such genres as the musical or Western, all had their subtypes or subgenres and did develop variations and changes as fashions and interests changed. While not so totally commercially oriented, the social film also tended to flow in the direction of those forms that seemed to draw the largest audiences. As a result, it was often blended with some of the more commercial genres, as in the gangster films, in the kind of overlapping of category types that was prevalent in the entertainment genres too. The desire to please and be understood by the largest audience contributed in both types to content simplification and to the use of unobtrusive styles that could maintain a semblance of the illusion of reality for any materials and provide easy patterns of identification and response. And for both kinds of films—social and entertainment—one of the strongest forces in both luring audiences and shaping and fulfilling audience expectation and identification was the development and repeated exhibition of the personality images of the major stars, often in conjunction with certain regular and familiar genre patterns.

GANGSTER FILMS

One of the frequent vehicles of social comment in the movies has been the gangster or crime film. Probably, along with the Western, the most deep-rooted of the genres, this type of film, even when not purposely used to reflect social issues, has developed in ways that do mirror changing social attitudes. Taken literally, the term "gangster" denotes only a subtype—criminals who operate in gangs—that is too narrow, although it has the connotation of a tough substratum of society, an underworld, that is necessary in delimiting the genre. On the other hand, "crime film" is too broadly denotative, allowing the inclusion of other treatments of crime not here intended, especially those involving intricacies of plot in order to develop suspense. For suspense and plot complexity, while they can be present, are not the essence of this genre. That essence is a tone, an ambience of toughness and violence, whose chief embodiments are the *events* of crime. It may be that "tough-guy films" is the most useful designation.

Crime and criminals had always been a staple of film production, but not until the late twenties, with Prohibition's stimulus to organized crime, did films begin to evoke the tone and pace of the underworld with any artfulness or social point. The strongest silent contributions at this time were Lewis Milestone's *The Racket* (1928) and two films by Josef von Sternberg— *Underworld* (1927), with original screen story by Ben Hecht, and *Dragnet* (1928). *Thunderbolt* (1930), also by von Sternberg and properly part of this group, had sound. The latter two had scenarios by Jules Furthman. Von Sternberg embellished and softened the toughness with the sensual atmosphere of shadows and textures—his usual style, although this kind of pictorial heightening, used with more restraint, did become part of the approach to the genre. Milestone's film, as would be expected, had a much stronger social point, establishing a connection between the criminal and official corruption.

In the early thirties, the depression and the continued expansion of gangland activities were joined by the advent of sound to give further impetus to the genre. For sound was the necessary completion of the illusion of the material's reality—the sounds of cities that bred the criminals, the sounds of their nightclubs and honky-tonks, the sounds of their tools of the trade, from screeching tires to machine guns, the sounds of their romantic argot. Sound in the tough-guy film could always be balanced by action enough.

The Early Thirties Phase
George Hill's *The Secret Six* and *The Big House,* and Rowland Brown's excellent *Quick Millions, Hell's Highway,* and *Blood Money* were typical of the early thirties phase, but three other films were its peak and epitome: William Wellman's *The Public Enemy* (1931), Mervyn Le Roy's *Little Caesar* (1931), and Howard Hawks's *Scarface* (1932). All three joined an almost operatic pictorial atmosphere to the abruptness, the frantic, nervy pace of the plot; they established the heightened folk poetry of the romantically cynical tough-guy; they displayed the typically contradictory attitude of criticism mixed with romanticized awe of the panache, of the vibrance of the life style, of the powerful personalities the inevitably doomed protagonists exhibited.

Of the three, *The Public Enemy* was the most socially oriented, in structure at least, designed to show the shaping of the criminal by society. But in effect the film was carried by the jaunty movements and bullet-quick tongue of Jimmy Cagney, in the first of many depictions of the feisty, nervous go-getter, up from the streets. Paul Muni in *Scarface* and Edward G. Robinson (who established the image for the type) in *Little Caesar* had a

Scarface

more brooding force, impelled more from within than by the streets, but finally caught and doomed by those city streets, whatever their own power and dreams: Muni lying dead in a gutter, above him a neon light blinking, in ironic counterpoint to his dreams of glory, "The World is Yours"; Robinson, riddled with bullets in the shadows of a sleazy hotel room, muttering, "Mother of God, is this the end of Rico?" For all its high points, *Little Caesar* is overshadowed by *Scarface*, with its script by Hecht setting the pace with poetic gab and adding an intricacy of character relationship, and its photography by Lee Garmes and Hawks accentuating the cynicism with visual ironies and gauzing it in romanticized, moody tragedy. It is probably the most visually intricate and ornamental—almost Germanically decadent—of all Hawks's films, beginning with the opening sequence: debris and streamers left over from a wild party (a device used earlier by von Sternberg, with whom Garmes had made four pictures), wilting flowers, and a cleaner, sniffing the flowers, unaware of the shadowy killer, whistling softly as he shoots the party's guest of honor.

With the demise of Prohibition and some official complaint about the violence, the early phase ebbed in the mid-thirties—the Cagney image to continue with greater and greater social emphasis, the Robinson image to hold on but decline, often depicted as a peripheral force, a gangland pressure on the central character.

Shifting
Image
of
the
Tough
Guy

The above-mentioned shift in emphasis to the criminal as victim (Chapter 10) is marked not only by Fritz Lang's two films but also by William Wyler's *Dead End* (1937), based closely on the Sidney Kingsley play, which melodramatizes the new social emphasis. For in it, "Baby Face" Martin (Humphrey Bogart) is seen as the earlier product of the slums now influencing the new generation (the "Dead End" kids). The counterforces are the innocent hero and heroine (respectively, Joel McCrea and, as almost always at this point, Sylvia Sidney), themselves barely escaping victimization by the slums. But the Bogart character (first seen on the screen in *The Petrified Forest* a year earlier) marks a shift as well. In his laconic, wisecracking cynicism and mask of distance there is a lingering sense of the inner man, a sensitivity under the toughness that is to solidify in subsequent appearances. Sometimes the Bogart character is poised against the total callousness of a Cagney, as in Curtiz's *Angels with Dirty Faces* (1938); sometimes, tragically doomed (ultimately holding off the whole state militia from a lone crag), even when he wants to go straight, as in Raoul Walsh's *High Sierra* (1941). Gradually he shifts to the toughened, resolute idealist in a vicious world, on the side of justice but outside the corrupt law, as in *The Maltese Falcon* (1941), *Casablanca* (1943), *To Have and Have Not* (1944), *The Big Sleep* (1946), *Dark Passage* (1947), and *Key Largo* (1948).

A further shift is reflected in the John Garfield image—the tough-guy now fully sympathetic, more clearly sensitive. Still yearning for something more, he is victimized by society, often legally guilty but still morally innocent, caught by dilemmas (so often expressed by the honest, blunt timbres of his voice in offscreen narration) and by bullets he has not made and cannot control. Garfield first appears as a mocking, Socialist rebel in Curtiz's *Four Daughters* but assumes his full depression-driven persona in *They Made Me a Criminal* (1939) and *Dust Be My Destiny* (1939), imitated in several other films including *He Ran All the Way* and, with variations on a theme, in the different contexts of *The Sea Wolf* (1941), *The Pride of the Marines* (1945), *The Postman Always Rings Twice* and *Humoresque* (both 1946) and *Gentleman's Agreement* (1947). In the two best versions of the hero grappling with the pressures of a money-oriented society, gangsters are a pervasive force that Garfield as boxer finally surmounts, though not without losses (*Body and Soul*, 1947) and, as shyster lawyer, succumbs to (*Force of Evil*, 1948). *Body and Soul* was directed by Robert Rossen, who had done two earlier Garfield screenplays, and written by Abraham Polonsky. Polonsky both wrote and directed *Force of Evil*. In one last variation, Michael Curtiz's quietly excellent *The Breaking Point* (1950), laid in a Florida fishing village, it is money and its corruption of integrity that destroy Garfield. This version hews far closer to Hemingway's *To Have and Have Not* than does the above-mentioned one by Hawks made in 1944.

Another transformation may be seen in the Alan Ladd image of such films as *This Gun for Hire* and *The Glass Key* (both 1942) and *The Blue Dahlia*

(1946), where there is a greater emptiness of self, a hollowing out of emotion in a viciously toughened world. Though coincident in time with the Bogart-Garfield phase (along with the Boulting Brothers' *Brighton Rock*, 1946, in England), the Ladd films mark also a turn to greater cruelty, brutality, and violence in the tough-guy films, both in the central character—even though often a gritty private detective—and his surrounding antagonists. In *White Heat* (1948), Cagney has become a psychopathic sadist; in *Kiss of Death* (1947), Richard Widmark, giggling joyfully, pushes a crippled old lady down a flight of stairs. On the side of the law, of sorts, the brutalities mount from Dick Powell films such as *Murder My Sweet* (1944) and *Cornered* (1945) to Robert Aldrich's Mickey Spillanish sadism in *Kiss Me, Deadly* (1955). While cynically eschewing the political simplicities of earlier tough-guy films, the latter trend nonetheless reflects social attitudes—those of a world that was beginning to accept violence on all levels as a day-to-day, year-after-year commonplace.

MYSTERY AND DETECTION

A related, yet differing, genre is the mystery film, in which suspense, generally related to a crime, is the central determiner of structure. The mystery has always been popular, yet without the mythmaking impact, the developing continuity of the tough-guy film (although with some overlapping of the two, of course, and with the exception of the unique world of Alfred Hitchcock). For with the mystery, there seems to be involvement of the audience on a different and less durable level of emotion, involvement that is without depth of identification with character and with the image of the star, without connection, if even indirect or unconscious, to the everyday world or to fundamental psychological needs and desires. One exception to this was a popular series of mystery films in the thirties that developed an additional dimension of humor and sophistication and an identification with the characters and actors comparable only to a television series. These films were *The Thin Man* (1934) and its two sequels, starring the embodiment of the suave, cool, married lovers, William Powell and Myrna Loy (as well as the dog Asta), directed by the deftly efficient W. S. Van Dyke. Van Dyke was particularly attuned to exploiting the potential for developing an image, which a series offered. His were the Tarzan series, beginning with *Tarzan, the Ape Man* (with Johnny Weissmuller) in 1932; the Nelson Eddy—Jeanette MacDonald series, beginning with *Naughty Marietta* in 1935; and the Andy Hardy series, starring Mickey Rooney and begun by George Seitz, who directed a dozen of them.

Michael Curtiz had first used William Powell's persona of cool imperturbability in one film of Warner Brothers' earlier Philo Vance series, *The Kennel Murder Case* (1933). In this, and in a Perry Mason series film, *The Case of the Curious Bride* (1935), Curtiz played with surprising images of décor (a recurrent food motif in the latter, for example), with camera movements and optical printing tricks, and an inventive array of transition devices. The result is an unusual and cynical counterpoint to the surface blandness of the mystery-solving.

In England in the late thirties, the visual modishness of Carol Reed's *Night Train* (1939), much in the Hitchcock manner, gave that exercise in suspense a cumulative emotionality beyond most in its field.

In the forties two developments gave a greater sophistication, realism, and emotional resonance to the mystery genre. One is best exemplified by Otto Preminger's *Laura* (1944), in which a routine suspense plot involving a limited, interrelated set of murder suspects is developed with a high sophistication of mood and dialogue and of interaction among the characters. The mood, enveloping the objects of the world of New York high taste with a growing presence of emotional wretchedness, ties *Laura* to the *film noir* of the late forties—the cynical, shadowed films, such as Robert Siodmak's *Cry of the City* or Billy Wilder's *Double Indemnity,* that charge suspense plots with a bitter emotionality that makes them more than mysteries (Chapter 13).

The other development that contributed greater sophistication and dimensionality to the mystery film was the liberating forties' trend toward exciting, big-city location-shooting, as exemplified by the careful documentary illusion of a spy film like Louis de Rochemont's *The House on 92nd Street* (1945); or a police-blotter film like *Boomerang* (1947), produced by de Rochemont and directed, with surprising quietness, by Elia Kazan; and by the more vigorous camera and editing fireworks of Jules Dassin's *The Naked City* (1948), racing through the cinematic décor of the streets of New York on the trail of the killer.

HORROR FANTASY

A genre with interesting relationships to crime and mystery is horror fantasy. (The term will have to serve although there are fantasy films without horror and horror films devoid of fantasy.) It is a genre that builds and fulfills audience expectation by reshuffling and reinventing specifics within set general structures in ways that combine some of the elements of the tough-guy and mystery films yet add a dimension. Its conventional structure involves (or at least assumes and implies) the cruelty, brutality, and violence, often of cataclysmic proportions, that is part of the pattern of expectation of the tough-guy film. At the same time its structure stresses the suspense excitement of the mystery film. But in both cases the pattern is carried beyond, to the supernatural, the grotesque, the outrageous, to produce the shock effect of horror, the thrill of fright and the even greater thrill of fearful expectation erupting into actuality (or, in one of many variations, the subtle evasion of that eruption).

With the arrival of sound and because of the demands of the enlarged commercial production system, the haunting moodiness and thematic mysticism of the silent fantasies gave way to new emphases. The German fantasies of the twenties were still particularly influential in a major carry-over of subjects and motifs, mood photography, and, to some degree, thematic implications. But all of this was reshaped to emphasize shock effect, the buildup and explosion of fearful tension, partly through tighter plotting, partly through heightened illusion of reality. As in the gangster film, the addition of sound seemed to be necessary to complete the genre in its most compelling form, bringing it that much closer to everyday life.

The
Monstrous

In the thirties, the central vein of the horror lode was struck, with monsters made shockingly real, individual, and anthropomorphic—of a piece with those from the traditional literature of gothic horror. Much like the figure of the gangster, the monster seemed to bring, along with his thrills, echoes of real evils—social to some extent, but even more from deep within the psyche.

The first to reappear from the depths was the vampire figure of traditional legend and many silent films. In 1931 Tod Browning's *Dracula* introduced Bela Lugosi in the role that he was to repeat in many sequels and in turn be imitated and supplanted in. For later audiences, its dialogue inhibits rather than facilitates immersion in its mysteries, and its climaxes seem often forced or muted. But Karl Freund's photography, in its misty, shadowy evocation of the nightmare world of threatening death and strange lusts made palpable, is still a disturbing standard.

Browning had made several silent fantasies, including Lon Chaney's *London at Midnight* (1927), and routinely turned out several more in the thirties. But among these is the most unusual of all grotesqueries—*Freaks* (1932). More unnerving in immediacy and deeply disturbing in the long run because it is *not* a fantasy, it created a great furor. Long suppressed—unofficially and haphazardly—it is still shown only infrequently. In *Freaks*, all the dreads and twistings of repulsion and yearning that are usually embodied—and thus to some degree distanced—in supernatural monsters are embodied in the real-life deformities of the freaks and midgets of a seedy circus. But the disturbance goes deeper, for through much of the film these repulsively deformed humans win our affection as their characters are played off against the viciousness of the two physically "normal" people of the circus—the aerialist Cleopatra and the strong man. The latter plot to have Cleopatra seduce, marry, and poison one of the midgets in order to inherit his money. At the wedding dinner, the truth comes out through a beautifully modulated sequence of emotion and action. Cleopatra then brazenly shames her new husband by carrying him on her shoulders. With the horror mounting (given depth by the shift of emotion involved), the freaks revenge themselves in a scene that is a nightmare welter of rain and mud, formless masses of grotesque, crawling, hopping bodies, and flashing weapons. In a horrifying epilogue, on a later sunny day the camera probes the mystery of a small enclosed pit to find what appears to be the remains of Cleopatra, a strange lump, almost limbless, groveling in the dirt, covered with chicken feathers—a circus "geek."

In another variation on the disturbing emotions latent in human deformity, the period saw several versions of *The Hunchback of Notre Dame* and of *The Phantom of the Opera,* and three versions of *Dr. Jekyll and Mr. Hyde* (Mamoulian's probably the best), in which twisted lusts are manifested in form and action.

King Kong

One of the most pervasive patterns of projecting human evil in supernatural forms centers on the aberrations of science gone out of control, sometimes in the hands of the now stereotyped mad scientists. Of the many variations, the most telling through the years has been the Frankenstein motif, and, of films using it, the first sound *Frankenstein* (1931) remains the most memorable. Directed by James Whale, it does not strive merely to shock with monstrous behavior; rather, with the wonderfully mimed performance of Boris Karloff, it builds our sympathy for this driven, uncomprehending creature, the result of man's violation of nature's mysteries. Typical of its telling mixtures of feelings is the sequence in which the monster, full of rage, encounters a small girl. Our fears are dissipated as she soothes him and they gently throw flowers onto the lake, watching them float. But then, in all innocence, thinking she too will float, he throws her in and she drowns, and we sympathize with the agony of his remorse.

One of Whale's other films, *The Invisible Man* (1937), using cool, macabre suspense, rather than horror, builds on one of the most common variations on the science motif, the experiment that has unexpected but not necessarily monstrous results. Another example is Frank Ernest Schoedsack's *Dr. Cyclops* (1940), in which humans are reduced to six-inch miniatures. Films such as these lead into the science fiction realm, more thoroughly exploited in films of the fifties.

Schoedsack's most famous film, the first of the supernatural animal films, is *King Kong* (1933), which Schoedsack later imitated in *Mighty Joe Young* (1947). Unlike so many of its successors (such as *Godzilla*), it does not merely pile destruction on destruction. Despite crudities and banalities, it successfully engages our sympathy, as in *Frankenstein,* for the goodness buried in the power that, at the same time, engenders fear. And who can ever forget that wonderful image of the gap between desire and consummation—Fay Wray perched, protected yet in peril, in the giant palm of the fond Kong?

The Credible and Explainable

There were three other noteworthy trends in the forties. One was the development of a tamer brand of fantasy, which gave greater credibility to the ghostly, the supernatural, the fantastic—either divested of menacing forces or with dangers less monstrous, though still eerie or bizarre. From England, Alexander Korda's *The Thief of Bagdad* (1940), which had three directors, set the style for dealing more lightly with the marvels and Arabian Nights dangers of a fairy tale world. In another vein, Frank Capra's *It's a Wonderful Life* (1947) merges heaven and small-town America in a morality tale, and William Dieterle's ornamental *Portrait of Jennie* (1949) gives touching form to the wish fulfillment of an artist captivated by a girl who exists outside of time. Designed more for subdued and sophisticated thrills were such multistory films as Julien Duvivier's *Flesh and Fantasy* (1943) and Michael Balcon's *Dead of Night* (1945), produced at Ealing, in England, with four directors. In the latter, the last story, directed by Cavalcanti, mixes the supernatural with a powerful depiction of emotional collapse in the tale of a ventriloquist (Michael Redgrave) possessed by his dummy.

The second trend was the development of films of terror in which the menace bordered on the fantastic and monstrous but was kept within the bounds of human credibility. Robert Siodmak built this kind of terror in films with fuller emotional content. His *The Spiral Staircase* (1945) sets the pattern for the pure tale of suspenseful danger, in which, amidst unusual circumstances, a mysterious, but explainable danger threatens—in this case, threatens a deaf-and-dumb girl in an out-of-the-way old house.

While many of the familiar monsters and their newer cousins were being reduced to tasteless second-feature horrors, producer Val Lewton at Radio-Keith-Orpheum (R.K.O.) studios produced a series of second-generation monster films that transcended their small budgets and hurried schedules and introduced new creatures to the conventional stable. The Lewton productions are marked by a carefulness and economy of means; their moods are sustained with psychological honesty and without glaring or cloying excesses, their climaxes built and executed by underplaying and indirection, a tasteful if possibly overrefined reworking of basic structures. Jacques Tourneur directed several of the films—the best, the quietly developed *The Cat People* (1943) and the poetically composed (despite its title) *I Walked with a Zombie* (1943). Robert Wise did *The Body Snatcher* (1945) and Mark Robson *The Seventh Victim* (1943) and *Isle of the Dead* (1945), in which things that are literally explainable are raised to intense levels of terror, as in the climactic opening of a coffin and the emergence of a woman, now insane, who had been trapped in it.

Of the conventional monster variations of the time, only George Waggner's *The Wolf Man* (1941) and Robert Florey's *The Beast with Five Fingers* (1947) are the equal of those produced by Lewton, who died in 1951 after beginning to explore other genres.

THE WESTERN

Established even earlier in the silent period than the horror film, the Western has proved the hardiest of all the genres, whether or not it is, in the phrase of a typically laudatory French critic, J. L. Rieupeyrout, "le cinéma Américain par excellence." Yet, strangely enough, the development of the Western was dormant for almost the first decade of the sound era.

At the very opening of the sound era, there were attempts in several major Westerns to adapt the established patterns of the silent Western to the sound mode; and despite their limitations, these films did have themes and motifs that later were to become central. The earliest, Victor Fleming's *The Virginian* (1929), which loosely followed the famed Owen Wister novel, was stagy and talky. It did not have the balance and flow between drama and action that is the rhythm of the Western at its best; but it did deal with the themes of the individual (a very young Gary Cooper) doggedly pursuing a personal code of justice and of two cultures clashing; and it did capture the look of the endless plains. In 1930, the more routine *The Big Trail* (directed by Raoul Walsh) picked up on the movement across the plains of such earlier films as *The Covered Wagon* (1923) and *The Iron Horse* (1924). In the same year, King Vidor's *Billy the Kid*, with Johnny Mack Brown, was a surprisingly harsh depiction of the gunfighter, with the mixture of cynicism and romanticizing found in the early gangster films, romantic grandiosity, unfortunately, winning out. It was the most consciously artful attempt of its day to put the barrenness of landscape into some relationship with mood and characterization. In 1931, Cecil B. De Mille added sound to his earlier *The Squaw Man*, and Wesley Ruggles, with *Cimarron* (based on the Edna Ferber novel), worked with the historical themes of the clash between the lone lawman and the frontiermen over the establishment of law and order in the towns—the film being awkwardly split between its gunfighting action and talky plot.

But from then until the *annus mirabilis* of Western films—1939—major works were few. Westerns and cowboys, to be sure, were plentiful, but in second-feature, second-class form—quickies with the barest semblance of plot or development and plenty of loosely patterned riding and shooting, films with a whole panoply of Saturday-matinee idols: Tom Mix, Ken Maynard, Hoot Gibson (still riding from the silent days), Buck Jones, Johnny Mack Brown, Gene Autry, even Randolph Scott and John Wayne. These films did maintain the surface situation and action structures of the Western genre— the expected chases and shootouts—but they had little of the rhythm of action and use of setting, little of the sense and significance of history, however sentimentalized, little extraction of social and psychological themes, of the resonance of the epic celebration, little of the structures of emotion and mythic essence that, in the mature form, play against the structures of physical action.

It should be stressed that in the silent period, the Western had rarely risen much above the shoot-em-up level. The thirties' fare represented, then, a continuation and proliferation of this tendency, not a decline. Sound, of course, was used—hoofbeats, gunshots, Indian war whoops, and, unfortunately, words—but major efforts with the imaginative use of sound and the merging of sound and image were reserved for other subjects and genres. The events and mood of the depression era, and the production executives' assessment of these, tended to make the wide-open spaces seem an anachronism. The credibility sought by the Realist mode was, for a time at least, more applied in mounting gaudy, historical costume-epics than Westerns, although even *action* costume extravaganzas were slow to develop until after the Michael Curtiz–Errol Flynn *Captain Blood*, late in 1935.

In these interim years, the chief Westerns were approached from the perspective of the costume, period film, though with differing results. Vidor's *The Texas Rangers* (1937) has vivid action, Frank Lloyd's *Wells Fargo* (1937) stiff, historical tableaux; De Mille's elaborate *The Plainsman* (1936)—with Gary Cooper as Wild Bill Hickock and Jean Arthur as Calamity Jane—was one of a series of De Millean epics with varied settings. But all three did presage a breakthrough for Western action onto a higher plane than that trod by Buck Jones and Ginger.

The best Western of this phase *was* a historical film—*Viva Villa* (1934), begun by Howard Hawks and finished by Jack Conway. With the bandits of Pancho Villa battling the Mexican Army, the film has the ingredients of the full-blooded Western: the violent gusto, the rhythmic pace, the evocative imagery (cavalry charging out of clouds of dust), and particularly the crucial sense of harmonizing the form of physical action and setting with the personality dimensions of the central figure—in this case, the mercurial extravagances of Wallace Beery's blustering, roistering Villa, part psychology, part history, part caricature and hokum.

In important ways, the shaping imprint of personality had much to do with the development and popularity of the Western in its major phase from 1939 to 1950—whether the personality of the director and his understanding of the materials, or of the stars, or of the heroes and villains, often historical, whom they depicted with much the same mixture as in the case of Villa.

The
Beginning
of
Maturity

Early in 1939, John Ford's *Stagecoach* cleared the way, but not without its own excess baggage. It eliminated the historical sweep and pageantry, taking it for granted, condensing and purifying its structure down to essentials. Yet to the straight-line action it added the interaction of character, even delaying the main explosion of action until the empathy with characters could be established and so give it added resonance. And, with camerawork by Bert Glennon, Ford revealed character, action, and setting with the photographic zest of a man savoring his materials: artful combinations, balances, juxtapositions, emphases that heightened, yet maintained purity and efficiency. For all of its importance, however, *Stagecoach* is weaker than is often admitted. Its clean line is flawed by hokum. There is a humor and deftness of characterization in developing the set of characters thrown together to make the dangerous ride through Injun territory (script by Nunnally Johnson), but the naive stereotyping jars: the ruined drunk, the cowardly cad, the good-hearted whore, the tragic mother giving birth. The same mechanical obviousness mars the often brilliant and lovely pattern of images. Too many repeat shots: of stupid Indians riding alongside the coach, somehow unable to *do* anything. Too many "surprise" shots: Donald Meek giving a toast and falling forward with an arrow in his chest; the cad putting his gun against someone's head and, at the sound of a shot, falling dead out of the frame; cutting from the final showdown in progress to the villain walking into the bar as though he'd won, then falling dead. Too many darting eyes and sudden glances: three men at a bar turning in unison to look at a door through which Thomas Mitchell then enters.

But in perspective these are more than balanced by excellences. The impressive use of the rock formations of Monument Mountain in patterns with the people; John Wayne's hat filling the frame and then moving out to reveal two men lurking behind him; after a series of two-shots establishing the tension over the whore (Claire Trevor), a long shot of the interplay of the whole group as Wayne supports her against all of them; a close-up on the first intimate exchange between Trevor and Wayne interrupted by a longer shot in which the sheriff comes in from right, Wayne stays with him, and Trevor walks off into the night. But most of all, the idealization giving its expected pleasures, yet nicely undercut by Wayne's abrupt jauntiness and Ford's good-humored sense of what he is doing with his nostalgia.

A jaunty mockery and humor is carried even further in the surprising *Destry Rides Again* of the same year, directed by George Marshall. Here Marlene Dietrich's ironic attitudes toward her charms are played nicely against Jimmy Stewart's naive Destry, a pattern used for Dietrich in four subsequent films with varying action locales. But the other main films of that year were unalloyed in their idealization of the materials of the West and of the nation's attitudes toward the Indian and his lands. Each established or reestablished a major subterritory of the genre, each colored by the personalities of director and central stars. De Mille's railroad epic *Union Pacific* continued the motif of civilization's movement through the wilderness, keyed by Joel McCrea's boyish, forthright social energies. Michael Curtiz and Errol Flynn joined some of the swashbuckling verve of their costume productions to the crusading-D.A. formula of big-city films, with Flynn bringing law and order to the frontier in *Dodge City*. In *Jesse James*, the reticent, bedrock straightness of Henry Fonda and Randolph Scott, whatever their crimes, set the distinguishing tone for Henry King's otherwise undistinguished approach to the central lode of badmen of the plains with hearts of gold.

The idealization continued through the wartime years with Flynn doing several more in the same vein, the best probably Curtiz's *The Santa Fe Trail* (1940). Fonda was Frank James again in *The Return of Frank James* (1940), an erratic piece by Fritz Lang, with some excellent sequences capturing the relation of men and soil or the atmosphere of a nighttime train robbery, and with an interesting thematic connection to Lang's earlier work—the relative innocent pursued by the forces of an unjust state and indifferent fate. Some later noteworthy specimens of the genre saw Randolph Scott in *Western Union* (also 1940) and Joel McCrea in *Buffalo Bill* (1944) and another *Virginian* (1946).

Counteridealization   William Wellman's *Buffalo Bill* touched cynically and briefly on that character's decline to performer in a second-rate sideshow, but it was his *Ox-Bow Incident* two years earlier that was the period's strongest counterthrust to the idealization of the West. Based on the novel by Walter Van Tilburg Clark, it reduces the scale of the Western setting in order to make its social comment. Its value lies less in its message about lynching than in its exposure of the emotional undercurrents of mobs, their leaders and the led. It is developed through a somewhat arch but nonetheless expressive intermeshing of dialogue and emotional lighting and camera angles, with nicely revealing interaction between characters.

William Wyler's contribution stands out among the many others of these years in its attempt to give the legendary materials precision and grace. His *The Westerner* (1940), made with cinematographer Gregg Toland, is a thirties morality play—Gary Cooper and the people versus the selfish perversion of law by Walter Brennan (Judge Roy Bean) and the cattlemen. But the film has a consistent leavening of humor and the artful composition that one would expect of a Wyler-Toland film: for example, the final showdown in an empty theater (itself reflecting character—Brennan wants the singer in exclusive performance), filmed with a judicious blending of angles, shadows, cutting, and moving camera.

Character and Relationship

But it was to be the films of John Ford, beginning in 1946, and of Howard Hawks, in 1947, that established the basic tone of artistry, the right controlled resonance of epic simplicity to cap this period of idealization. These were Ford's *My Darling Clementine, Fort Apache, She Wore a Yellow Ribbon, Wagonmaster,* and *Rio Grande,* and Hawks's *Red River.* They were works—more in the Ford than the Hawks—consciously developed within a tradition, sounding the clear tones of its simplicities in form and rhythm yet building a fuller, more realistic texture of character and relationship. They do not break with the pattern of idealization but lead toward greater toying with and playing against structures of the genre, a trend that emerged fully in the fifties with such films as *Broken Arrow, The Gunfighter, High Noon,* and *Winchester 73.*

In Hawks's *Red River,* more than in many Ford films, there is an abrasive density of characterization rather awkwardly joined to an array of conventional types and the personas of the stars. A swaggering, domineering, cattle-driver John Wayne, and his sullen, rebellious stepson Montgomery Clift (with the tangential, threatening presence of a black-garbed, brooding John Ireland) provide an unusual tone to the clash of personality at the center of the action. Their psychological combat is nicely articulated into a physical showdown: They fight, but not to the point of the formerly inevitable gun duel. Much of the action is still rather boyishly magnified, replete with the expected heroic close-ups and camera angles; much of the byplay of camaraderie too routinely cute. But overall, the human dimensions are enlarged to give a new total shape to the sweep of the cattle drive across the prairies and the truly felt and rendered wonders of their vastness.

Red River

THE HISTORICAL FILM

The Western has a unique, deeply engrained, archetypal structure that is not only especially satisfying of audience expectations, but seems to offer a particularly fertile field for the sowing of mythic implications. Unfortunately, its myths often obscured understanding of the nation's past and promoted racial stereotypes. For all its distortions, however, the Western is one type of historical film, not very different in its stereotyping from the general simplistic patterns of other movie histories. While always popular, historical films have never developed the special patterns and meanings, the mystique, of the Western. In the thirties, with the addition of sound, and later, color, the historical film was given renewed prominence. In it, the ability of the film to create an illusion of reality was turned to making credible, though highly simplified and romanticized, historical tales and, occasionally, more rounded, plausible versions of the past. In a like manner, the developing careful, efficient style of shooting and editing was applied to manipulating emotions as unobtrusively as possible, to balancing immense pageantry with the events of dramatic plot.

In the thirties and forties the subjects and purposes of historical costume films ranged widely. Some, as we have noted, were used to carry contemporary implications; most were not.

One of the most influential films early in the period was Alexander Korda's production of *The Private Life of Henry VIII* (1933), with Charles Laughton. The first British film to be successful in America, it set a pattern for sophisticated, often gossipy portrayals of the private lives of the greats in films made both in Britain and America—*Catherine the Great* (1934), *Rembrandt* (1936), and *Lady Hamilton* (1943) among them. The British also established their equivalent of the Western in such successful Empire films as *The Four Feathers* (1936), with its counterparts in American production, such as Curtiz's *The Charge of the Light Brigade* (1936) and George Stevens's *Gunga Din* (1939). More serious British subtypes included the transcription of plays, such as Laurence Olivier's *King Henry V* (1944) and Gabriel Pascal's *Caesar and Cleopatra* (1945), and of period novels, such as David Lean's fine adaptations of *Great Expectations* (1946) and *Oliver Twist* (1947).

American production also featured transcriptions of plays and novels, such as Ford's *Mary of Scotland* (1936), George Cukor's *David Copperfield* (1935), Jack Conway's *A Tale of Two Cities* (1935), *Romeo and Juliet* (1936), and *Camille* (1937), Mervyn Le Roy's *Anthony Adverse* (1936), Sidney Franklin's *The Good Earth* (1937), and Henry King's *Song of Bernadette* (1943). One variation was the more intimate, often sober, almost gothic period piece, such as Sam Woods's *Kings Row* (1941) and Robert Stevenson's *Jane Eyre* (1941).

The biographical, or "biopic," film became a staple, especially from the late thirties on, ranging from Norman Taurog's *Young Tom Edison* (1940) to those dealing with authors, as in *The Loves of Edgar Allan Poe*, *The Adventures of Mark Twain*, *Jack London*, and political figures, including Daryl Zanuck's period spectacle *Wilson* (1944), directed by Henry King.

Spectacles touched all ports, whether in the South Seas (Ford's *Hurricane*, 1937) or Africa (William Cowan's *Kongo*, 1932). And no producer ranged more widely in space and time—nor flourished more pomp, circumstance, and sex—than Cecil B. De Mille in films such as *The Sign of the Cross* (1932), *Cleopatra* (1934), *The Crusades* (1935), *The Buccaneer* (1938), *Northwest Mounted Police* (1940), and *Reap the Wild Wind* (1942).

With *Captain Blood* (1935), Michael Curtiz and Errol Flynn gave the usual action inherent in the spectacle an added swashbuckling fillip, reducing the pageantry, increasing the physical action, and bringing to bear the Westerns' emphasis on the lone gun—in this case, the lone sword. Flynn leaped, lunged home, and smiled his way through many years and films, his *Robin Hood* (1938) an especially exuberant display. He was challenged in 1940 by Tyrone Power (whose first entry was *The Mark of Zorro)*, as well as by such other worthies as Douglas Fairbanks, Jr., and Cornell Wilde.

Throughout the period, the quality purveyor of the illusion of historical reality, of sorts, was producer David O. Selznick. In *Gone with the Wind* (1939) and *Duel in the Sun* (1946), he gave the era of the period piece its twin monuments. (This almost single-handedly, although, with his control

Gone with the Wind

over so many other hands, it becomes difficult to determine who did what.) Directed mainly, it would seem, by Victor Fleming, *Gone with the Wind* is most careful in its re-creation and sumptuously (even grandiosely) ornate in its sweep and tone—the epitome of the genre's strange blending of fairy tale and reality. Magnificently acted in slick professional style, it reveals romantic character types with a density of detail that makes its grand hokum less susceptible to the cynical ravages of time than many a serious, sober attempt at Social Realism. *Duel in the Sun,* directed by King Vidor and three or four others, is a rougher monument, florid, operatic, flamingly overheated in its attempt to give form to grandiose passions among the tumbleweeds. Convincingly mounted and detailed, it is more openly flamboyant in its flourishes, a romantic version of the expressive epic, never quite admitting it is not Realism. Topping all is the Wagnerian finale of Jennifer Jones's doomed march across the desert, accompanied only by a wordless chorus and the burning sun, and the monumental close-ups of her Love-Death shootout with Gregory Peck on a barren hill.

THE MUSICAL

There is an open indulgence in sentiment here not usually found outside the musical, which of all the genres was most obviously a product of the introduction of sound. After the first flurry of attempts to capitalize quickly on

Dames

the new element, the first major type took its durable shape in a series of 1933 productions. In these, the musical numbers—the fantasy—were kept separate from the dramatic plot, deriving relatively realistically from it as alleged production numbers within a show-business plot, but exceeding in scope any kind of production that would be literally possible. These back-stage-life plots frequently embellished romantic love stories with a more realistic veneer of fast-paced, cynical wisecracks, while the production numbers themselves were infinitely romantic and expressive in form. Typical early examples were Mervyn Le Roy's *Gold Diggers of 1933;* Lloyd Bacon's *42nd Street, Footlight Parade* (both 1933), and *Wonder Bar* (1934); Archie Mayo's *Go into Your Dance* (1935), and Roy Del Ruth's *Broadway Melody of 1936 and 1938* (Al Jolson, Dick Powell, Ruby Keeler, Ned Sparks, Ginger Rogers, and Frank McHugh among the regulars).

Berkeley:
The
Production
Number

The epitome of the "production numbers" created in these films was the work of Busby Berkeley. With complex camera and editing procedures, he turned armies of leggy chorines into kaleidoscopic abstract forms, blending humans and props in Surrealist patterns, creating almost Expressionistic story vignettes. (Two such are the long dream sequence with tragic ending in

42nd Street and the "Shanghai Lil" sequence, with Jimmy Cagney, in *Footlight Parade*.) Of the musicals that Berkeley went on to direct in their entirety, his Mickey Rooney–Judy Garland films *Strike up the Band* (1940) and *Babes on Broadway* (1942) were more subdued, but *The Gang's All Here* (1943), with Alice Faye, provided one last explosion of his favorite fireworks.

Blending
Music
and
Drama

As early as 1932, Rouben Mamoulian's *Love Me Tonight* had more integrally blended music and drama with a touch of René Clair-like fantasy, as did early films in the stage operetta tradition—like Ernst Lubitsch's *The Merry Widow* (1934)—many with Maurice Chevalier and Jeanette MacDonald.

By late 1933, Fred Astaire and Ginger Rogers had begun their extensive series of musicals as a team, with *Flying Down to Rio*. But it wasn't until several films later—*Top Hat* (1935), *Swing Time* (1936), *Shall We Dance* (1937)—that their films fully established a better blend of song-and-dance

Swing Time

numbers with drama. Although most of their films were still backstage stories, with some production numbers still "on stage," they also used musical routines that flowed, with no discernible break, from plot action and developed in the dances the emotions of the plot situation. Both types of number, however, had a greater harmony of tone with the drama, so that the films developed a distinct style. Keyed to quiet, cool sophistication—the focus and emphasis of Astaire's acting and dancing—they had a lighter, drawing-room-comedy touch in plotting, more imaginative variations in large and small dance numbers, a greater intimacy in love-song dances. Less flamboyant than Berkeley's films, they made highly flexible and expressive use of the camera for the dances—especially in numbers directed by Astaire.

The Everyday-life Musical

For all their greater blending of the real and the expressive, the Astaire-Rogers musicals still did not attempt to translate what anyone might call everyday life and people into expressive musical terms. This next development—a romantic Realism—was the chief contribution of the varied and prolific output of musicals in the forties. Backstage plots were still the favorite vehicle, but even these involved a greater flair in using nostalgic period settings, as in *Hello, Frisco, Hello* (1943), or romantic settings, as in *Springtime in the Rockies* (1942) and *Down Argentine Way* (1940). These films often used popular big bands such as those of Glenn Miller and Harry James and usually featured Betty Grable or Alice Faye. One of the most imaginative was Charles Vidor's *Cover Girl* (1944), with Rita Hayworth and Gene Kelly, highlighted by two exuberant numbers that start in an interior shot, then break free into the streets of New York.

This free flow into ordinary surroundings, joined to a lighthearted gusto and an innocent pleasure in the orchestration of real-life situation into musical fantasy, was central to the development of the everyday-life musicals. Some, such as *State Fair* (1943), were romantic views of the past; others, such as *Anchors Aweigh* (1945), romantic views of the present. But in both categories the peak works were those produced by Arthur Freed at Metro-Goldwyn-Mayer (M.G.M.). Notable were Vincente Minelli's *Meet Me in St. Louis* (1944), with Judy Garland singing "The Trolley Song" (on a trolley), and the Stanley Donen–Gene Kelly work *On the Town* (1949)—still the epitome of the effervescent spirit of the type, despite such later famous successes as the Freed-Minelli-Kelly *American in Paris* (1951) and the Freed-Donen-Kelly *Singing in the Rain* (1952) and *It's Always Fair Weather* (1954).

At the same time, there were several attempts to dramatize an entire film musically, in works by Minelli and Kelly, and to combine classical music and fantasy with a realistic base, as in the British productions *Stairway to Heaven* (1946), *Red Shoes* (1948), and *The Tales of Hoffman* (1951). But by the sixties, a turn had been solidified, even ossified, into the solemn, stolid staging of proven stage hits—as in Robert Wise's monumentally profitable *The*

Sound of Music (1965)—with occasional flashes of dramatic and visual vitality, such as Wise's *West Side Story* (1960), Jacques Demy's dreamy film opera *The Umbrellas of Cherbourg* (1964), and Bob Fosse's *Cabaret* (1972). What had been lost along the way, what had given the period of flair and exuberance its tonic note, what the conventional form could no longer maintain, was an airy innocence. For all its romance, the musical imagination has been most buoyant and free when touched with the lightness of comedy.

CHAPTER TWELVE

*comedy
and
sound—
smooth
and
wild*

The comic potential of the screen's visual image had been discovered early. One of Louis Lumière's first (1896) exercises in representing the movement of reality on film, *Watering the Gardener*, described in Chapter 1, was essentially comic. By the twenties, comedy had arguably become the most popular and creative genre of the silent film. While there were comedy dramas and comedies of manners—such as those of Ernst Lubitsch—the epitome of silent-film comedy were the hectic ballets of the great clowns, the comic personas in visual battle with the things (and men) of the physical world.

In the thirties, the introduction of sound and a new concern with society wrought changes both obvious and complex. In many musicals, comedy became the means of keeping things lively between musical numbers but also tinged the whole with an aura of verve and caprice. In the big extravaganzas—the *Big Broadcast* series, for example—musical numbers and comic routines, in artificial alternation, shared equal billing. In many comedies, even those of the Marx Brothers, musical numbers were methodically inserted at intervals because of a persistent notion of mutual dependency.

Great comic personas endured. But their madcap visual world was adjusted to the more complex world of words and society, was often given more plausible, if not exactly realistic, structures of conventional life to play against.

The biggest change was in the proliferation of a varied breed of comedy dramas, and directors and writers of comedy drama. In these films, the greater comic complexity of witty dialogue was joined with a greater concern for the detailed delineation of the manners and mores, the paraphernalia and attitudes of social class and type. In them, actors—quite distinct from the personas of the great clowns—played relatively plausible, conventional characters, tightly structured in plotted dramas that, to one degree or another, attempted to represent and maintain a comically mitigated illusion of reality.

SOUND AND THE CLOWNS

Laurel and Hardy

Of the great clowns of the thirties and forties, Stan Laurel and Oliver Hardy remained the purest, the most innocent representatives of comic screen ballet. Their world, barely touched by the nuances of literal social reality, was still a world of comic essences; yet in the hyperbole of their accelerated interaction with the threatening universe of man and things (and with each other), there was a newer complexity of characterization, a closer reflection of the emotional foibles of men in everyday life. This shift is indicated in the relation of sound and image in their films. While physical action still carries the most laughs, sound provides the fuller expression of personality, the context that enhances audience empathy, that gives the laughs of these films their essential flavor, their greater density of tender and foolish humanness. The sound of their voices—their timbres, tones, and inflections—is as important as, if not more important than, the content of the dialogue in building the fuller dimensions of their screen personalities and of the clashes between them. An element of these clashes—that it occurs as an interaction between equals—is also part of their distinctive and influential quality.

In their silent movies and sound-films, whether shorts or features, their visual comedy is a comedy of routines, of orchestration, of acceleration and accumulation and variation of a core physical gag. But the routines are also an orchestration, as well as a result, of personality. In them, human frailty subverts its own cause in its struggle against an inexorably antagonistic physical world yet somehow manages to survive. The stand of the individual against the nature of things is complicated by the contrast and conflict of their personalities, which nevertheless have an underlying similarity. The thin, plaintive Laurel is timid and kind, with a desire to be helpful that culminates in a destructiveness matched by his bumbling in carrying out his good intentions. The rotund, eternally exasperated Hardy is pompous and rude, with an aggressiveness that courts ruin, a mammoth and fastidious grace that is highly likely to deteriorate into its own bumbling and botching, especially when provoked by Laurel.

The routines that result are rituals of physical destruction, infinitely varied, but with a number of basic motifs: One is the collaboration of things and personalities in a stubbornness that makes all work treacherous and finally futile, whether painting a wall, building a boat, fixing a car, carrying a piano upstairs—as in the perfect elaboration of gags in the short *The Music Box* (1932). Another deals with the pitfalls and shortcomings of helping friends and neighbors. And the motif of inevitable escalation of retaliation, tit for tat, in encounters between man and man is based on the two distinct and psychologically persuasive Laurel and Hardy features of allowance (indeed encouragement) and proliferation. Thus, if they are opposing others (or each other, on those occasions when Laurel can be provoked to strike back), each side allows the other its turn, as the demolishing of rooms, possessions, autos, clothing escalates. Whenever bystanders are present, they too inevitably succumb, and the mayhem proliferates, as in the wonderful *You're Darn Tootin'*, when the two-pronged allowance ritual of Hardy punching Laurel in the stomach and Laurel kicking Hardy in the shins (with its resultant stooping, hopping, and trouser-ripping) spreads until a whole streetful of people are in the same strange tribal dance.

While in the short films the routines may make more rounded wholes, in the features they are burdened by the weakness and overextension of plot situation. Yet, in these longer films, the routines do gain from the fuller contexts of personality and situation that they allow, and especially from the greater possibilities of extending, toying with, returning to gags and motifs, paralleling, modulating, reprising them. Among the best examples of this are *Way Out West* (1937) and *Blockheads* (1938). But overall the comedy of Laurel and Hardy is one of great moments, not great feature films. Rather than mining more deeply, they seem to have made too many films too quickly, with a too commercial repetitiveness, using too many assembly-line collaborators—demonstrating, like one of their motifs, the perils of acceleration, when men and things get going and escalate to chaos.

Chaplin As for Charlie Chaplin, he did not repeat himself, did mine more deeply as the sound period progressed. Still probing more, risking more in terms of content, he showed a developing use of sound that paralleled a developing complexity of theme, while maintaining on the whole the functional—sometimes pedestrian, sometimes pure—visual approach of his earlier films.

In *City Lights*, music and sound gags had been sporadically applied to what was still basically a silent film. In *Modern Times*, sound was treated more conventionally and realistically (but still not as an equal to the silent images) as the social content became more literal, the satire more critical of industrial society. Charlie the Tramp still did not speak, nor was he ever to do so.

In *The Great Dictator* (1940), Chaplin speaks, in three voices, each different in tone, none exactly that of the Tramp. All, though, had been a part of that figure whose world has passed, as his persona has been fragmented and distorted. Chaplin speaks as Hynkel, the Führer, in whom the brashness of the Tramp in response to the intransigence of the world is carried to extremes of hysterical paranoic destructiveness. He speaks as the Jew, in whom the passivity and goodness of the Tramp become the weakness of the victim. The relation of dictator and victim is drawn with particular poignancy when, at one point, Chaplin the Jew masquerades as Chaplin the Führer. At the end, Chaplin speaks directly to the audience as Chaplin.

This last speech is probably an indication that Chaplin himself sensed the difficulty of dealing with so vast and monstrous a subject in terms of farcical satire. Certainly his film does not solve that problem, the farce often too facile, the message often too obvious. The end speech, is, however, a means of catching us up in our easy laughter, of reminding us, however uncinematically, of the dangers of heedlessly going along with the gag. The Tramp had known that and simply opted out; *The Great Dictator* demands a more active response.

At the end of *Monsieur Verdoux* (1947), Chaplin speaks directly to the audience again. This time it is within his characterization of Verdoux, and it makes a much more effectively integrated Brechtian dislocation of the audience's perspective on the comic drama. For now the Chaplin persona is deeply embedded within a complex dramatic structure, whose mixture of tones and of comedy and message has an appropriately cold and bitter unity. In this bleak forerunner of cinematic black comedy, even the moments of farce and slapstick are carefully timed and placed, modulated in pace and

Monsieur Verdoux

tone, invested with the emotion and meaning of the surrounding situation. The farce is the touch of the Tramp still left in this new and bleaker Chaplin world, just as the lingering charm and insouciance is evidence of the whimsy still alive within the meticulous ruthlessness of Verdoux. Typical is the unsuccessful attempt in the rowboat to drown the rich widow (Martha Raye). The scene's camera angles are more varied, its editing rhythm faster than in earlier films. The opposite actor, Raye, is given the broader movements and responses; Chaplin's, while ruffling his stainless-steel impeccability, are more restrained, with delicate nuances of gesture, voice, and expression. As in all the scenes of broader humor, we are drawn to Verdoux—to the Tramp in him—for he too can make mistakes, is human. Throughout, the farcical scenes have this effect, enlarging our sympathetic response to the humanness of the complexly drawn character, while the basic overall tone of irony —in the plotting, in the visual and verbal wit—distances us from the cool terror of his principles and actions.

The effect is unsettling, and Verdoux's speech to the court after he has been sentenced to death makes the point of these jarring, mixed responses clear. The speech (as do many of the speeches) includes many tenuously related or extraneous issues—the presence of both good and evil in men, for example, and the abuses of journalism. But its main thrust is that Verdoux is one of us: We as a society do what he does but try to disown and deny the tie. He too is shaped by the principles of the society that sentences him (in an echo of the courtroom scene in Dreiser's *American*

Tragedy, to which the rowboat scene is also a reference). He merely carries out the logic of those principles in a way that incenses us, while their more outrageous application in war or business is condoned.

A bank teller dismissed after the stock market crash of 1929, Verdoux conceives a good cause, and then proceeds to defend that cause by any means necessary. He will protect his wife and child from the economic ravages of the time by killing rich women for their fortunes. The crucial irony is depicted in the results of his perverted ethic. The carefully furnished insulation of the family home has become a prison for Verdoux's child and invalid wife and offers no relief from his own loneliness. In the scenes of his short visits home, there is a pervasive, draining sadness, counterpointed by the sharp wittiness of the moments when he is at his "trade" (as lady-killer) in the business world. His cause has become hollow, emptied. There is a gaiety in the scenes of Verdoux plying his trade, for the means have really become the source of energy. And yet, in the sardonic turns of plot and in the fastidiousness and primness of mannerism in Chaplin's finely articulated performance, the melancholy emptiness, the desperate strain under the slick veneer are sensed. The momentum of the action is all that is really left.

After his wife and child die, Verdoux meets again the young woman who, much like himself, offers a possibility of an emotional life. But with only the surface glitter of the aged charmer left, he tells her, in a voice of weakened, weary, but still coldly, obstinately clipped charm, "Go on about your business." Soon after, he allows himself to be captured, for the game was not worth the winning. Like the Tramp, Verdoux in the last shot walks away from the camera, not down the road this time, but to the guillotine. Yet, still there, though embedded in the prim, stiff, righteous elegance of his businessman's gait, is a vestige of the winning warm touch of the Tramp.

Limelight (1952) is another farewell to the lost Tramp's unquenchable innocence, more nostalgic and bittersweet, more personal. While not Chaplin's last work, it is in all likelihood his last significant film. Fittingly, it is a reprise on the silent *The Circus* and its use of the world of clowns as a metaphor for human struggle and loss. Its clowns are aging (Buster Keaton makes a touching appearance), and love and life have defeated them. Unlike the early Tramp, they can no longer bounce back with undaunted resiliency; his antics appear only on stage. Resigned to the loss of the dream of a clown's and tramp's world, they still, like jugglers, keep it afloat, until death intervenes. In this mainly successful balance between sentimentality and harshness, humor and sadness, the film, while stumbling occasionally over self-pity, is a moving and insightful backward glance at the basic elements of Chaplin's attitudes and art.

W. C. Fields   The chief comic personas of the sound era were a new breed, brash but not innocent, irrepressible, surviving all shambles, even the chaotic clutter of many of their own movies. In their verbal wit, added to the action and things of their visual comedy, was the signature of their aggressive invulnerability.

Seedy and tarnished himself, odorously disrespectable, armored by that all-knowing, unblinking slow rasp of his cynical drawl, W. C. Fields knows that anything can happen and always will. He knows the world threatens him, knows he must be sharp-witted, nimble of tongue and limb in the face of that constant threat. And in Fields's world *everything* is the enemy, justice and injustice alike, things and people alike, babies and women, hats, light bulbs, or cigars. Thus prepared, he endures.

The records of this endurance—defiantly unstructured in the films he wrote himself—are often an apt combination of orchestrated and accelerated physical routines balanced against the pithy terseness of his epigrammatic complaints and insults. In the early *The Old-Fashioned Way* (1934), based on his stage success *Poppy,* as he battles an intruding elk for an upper berth in a Pullman car, he complains as he would to wife, child, salesman, or minister, "If you're an elk, get into the cattle car." In the midst of the wild mayhem of *Never Give a Sucker an Even Break* (1941), he refuses a helping offer of a Bromo with a curt, "Couldn't stand the noise." When he is terse, mumbling to himself or griping at others, he is on the defense, counter-punching; when he is floridly sweet-talking or persuasive, he is conning in a con man's world, punching before they do.

But, in the compromises that his pictures had to be, the balance is not always kept. In *Sucker,* for one, bowing to commercial necessity, he had to allow the dreary, drippy musical numbers featuring baby-faced Gloria Jean but countered by rendering the whole plot an aimless, incredible mess. Carried too far, overplotting (or self-indulgent plotlessness) and commercial compromises were sometimes to get the better of the unfailing verbal wit.

In battling the humans of the threatening world, his wit always wins him at least a standoff: whether cheating at cards or cozying up to Mae West in *My Little Chickadee* (1940), kissing her fingers and muttering, "What symmetrical digits." In situations where he is the aggressor, the preemptive con man—as in *The Old-Fashioned Way; Million Dollar Legs* (1932), written by Joseph L. Mankiewicz; *You Can't Cheat an Honest Man* (1939); *Sucker;* and *Chickadee*—his encounters with the world of things are usually successful, the chaos of the prop routines often at his own instigation. But in the films where his snarling misanthropy is trapped in the form of a woman- and world-beset bumbler—most notably in *It's a Gift* (1934) and *The Bank Dick* (1940), which are arguably his best films—his wit is needed to even the score somehow. In these temporarily unsuccessful encounters are many of his best gag sequences—whether in highly elaborate orchestrations or in small-scale improbabilities like the sequence in *The Bank Dick,* where he collaborates in his failure as a detective by donning a series of obviously ineffective disguises, topped by a mere piece of string running from the bridge of his nose to behind his ear.

In *It's a Gift* things and people conspire to harass the henpecked Bissonette in a fine collection of routines: While shaving, he is pushed out of the way by

My Little Chickadee

his daughter, has to hang a small mirror from a string in the middle of the bathroom. The mirror twirls, and, forced to circle with it, he almost slits his throat with his straight razor. When he tries to sit on the back of a wooden chair to get closer to the mirror, the chair rocks and he falls onto its seat. We cut to wife, daughter, and son marching toward the bathroom through the hall. When we cut back, he is lolling on his back on two chairs, blithely shaving in temporary triumph, the mirror lowered and now stationary above his face. Now the family towers above him, and a bit of repartee holds them off for a moment. But on the way to breakfast, he slips on a roller skate; at breakfast, he lights a flower instead of his cigar and later stubs out a cigar in his coffee instead of an ashtray.

In another sequence, he is driven by his wife's nagging to try sleeping on a couch on a sun porch, only to be beset in turn by various noises— human and inanimate. At his store, a baby sets loose a flood of molasses, and in a typically Fieldian touch, an old man with failing vision knocks over giant piles of neatly stacked glassware and electric light bulbs and can't be stopped because he is also virtually deaf. Wit eventually serves here too, but in this kind of a world, a man needs all the defensive armor that he can muster.

The
Marx
Brothers

While for Fields, the threat of losing to the hostile world is a constant irritation, the Marx Brothers are beyond loss, unconcerned about hostility, insensitive to the threats they know are there but accept as naturally as the air. Free spirits, they blithely wreak their own chaos, rendering all defenses, patterns, and rules of the game—all habits, assumptions, and inhibitions—helpless before their irrepressible assault.

This assault often took the form of satire of the formal in society: the stuffy and the pretentious; the ritual words, manners, and actions of various professions, social classes, and institutions; and the types—of places, of modes of entertainment, of public figures. But it was, underneath all of this, an assault on accepted patterns of literal reality itself. Its satire is touched with the zaniest of comic accelerations of actions, words, and things, a zigzagging of non sequiturs with a logic all their own, a changing and turning, a twisting of chains of association that confounds and confuses expectations. It plays the freedom and flexibility of the film medium against its realism, using its power to make anything acceptable as real, to jiggle and unsettle conventionally neat and easy expectations about reality.

There is, in the carefree Marxian wildness, a logic of illogic, a sense of the limitations of logic itself to grasp what is real, a sense of the truth of subjective, imaginative realms of consciousness, of something that lies beyond the surfaces. In this exuberant blurring of the fantastic and the real, there is a lighthearted lingering—the strongest of the thirties and a link to the later comedy of the absurd—of the insights and approaches of Expressionism. Far less serious, far from tormented, their version nonetheless not only reflects Expressionism's attempts to expose the limits of objective, surface truth and to disclose the less tangible dimensions of the inner life, but also Expressionism's basic device of confounding the literal and the figurative, turning the figurative back into the literal, finding connections that loosen and amuse, while they free convention-bound patterns of perception and understanding.

In this approach, their strongly verbal humor does not lead to the greater commonplace literalness and credibility, the fuller dramatic structure so typical of comedy in the sound era, even in Chaplin. Rather, like their visual humor, it toys with literalness, plays jokes on the accepted symbols of language as a producer and guarantor of meaning and truth. Whether in separate sequences or mixed, the verbal humor and the visual have a similar basis in finding unexpected, impossible connections and carrying them as far as they will go.

In a typical mixture, their takeoff on legal jargon in the contract sequence in *A Night at the Opera* (1935) first has Groucho and Chico exposing cliché by extending meanings verbally: Chico wants to hear only the first part about the party of the first part; Groucho wants to talk about the wild time he had at that first party. Then they advance to the visual, taking out offending clauses by literally ripping them out of the contract. While many of the inevitable musical numbers in their films were mere interruptions based on commercial prescription of the thirties, a few provide some of the best verbal wit, (or mixtures with visual wit) in their work—the utter chaos of the opera finale in *Opera*, for example, or the more pointed satire on jingoism in *Duck Soup* (1933). A welter of clichéd musical forms, including the revivalist "All God's Chillun Got Guns," the *Duck Soup* number is capped by Harpo's pantomime of a woman-crazy Paul Revere, who deserts his bugle for a blonde, hides in her bathtub, is sat on by her unsuspecting husband, and rises blowing a dampened call to arms. The dissection of war and the military in *Duck Soup* uses both visual and verbal gags: Groucho telling a general who asks for help in resisting a gas attack to take a teaspoonful of bicarbonate of soda; Groucho appearing in every new sequence with a different uniform.

Using sight and sound to blur distinctions between the figurative and real is interestingly connected to the particular role each of the three brothers—Groucho, Chico, and Harpo (Zeppo's role was never really integrated)—plays in their multiperson comic persona. Groucho is the closest to the conventional world, his knowing aggressions open exaggerations of those that are hypocritically masked in that world. He, of course, is the most verbal—his puns, digressions, associations never more fruitful than in *Monkey Business* (1931) and *Horse Feathers* (1932), on both of which S. J. Perelman collaborated. Whether in exchanges of clichés (in *Duck Soup,* a government minister says he washes his hands of the whole thing, and Groucho tells him not to forget to wash his neck) or in the inventive escalations of his monologues, he extracts from language the team's most pointed satire of social dogmas and hypocrisies.

But in turn, it is Groucho's literalness (most frequently when he is taking some social or artificial role) that is exposed by Chico's shifting to the figurative. Often this involves outrageous punning, as in the classic "real-estate con" in *The Coconuts* (1929). In this, a whole series of confusions (when Groucho says there are levees along the river, Chico says he didn't know any Jewish people lived there) is climaxed by many turns on the substitution of viaduct and "Why-a-duck?" for each other, with digressions into "Why-a-Ford?" (when Groucho mentions fording a river) and "Why-a-fence?" (when Groucho talks about a wire fence). Chico is the middle term of the team. Still a conniver, he is less conventionally oriented, less knowing than Groucho. Groucho is bourgeois, Chico working-class, more ordinary, plodding, but also more loyal. He can interpret Harpo to Groucho and the world, but he too gets caught up in Harpo's transformations to the figurative.

Harpo's transformations turn the abstractions of words into more basic things and actions, as befits his role as the most natural, unsocialized, spontaneous member of the trio. In his mute, nutty tenderness, his untrammeled lasciviousness, his ethereal spirituality when he plays the harp, his infantile openness, his ready, guiltless violence, he is the freest of the Marxes. He is the epitome of the unshaped inner self, the irrepressible id acting against the ego of Groucho (or Chico to a lesser extent) or the superego of society. In a primeval state of noble savagery, he is beyond, or before, conscious rebellion. When Chico says "Cut the cards," Harpo does it with an axe. When Groucho says he can't burn the candle at both ends, Harpo produces from within his incredibly capacious trench coat a candle burning at both ends. Chico often joins him. When Groucho, as a college president in *Horse Feathers,* tells them to bring in the college seal, they oblige with the creature itself. When he says his students will bear him out, they carry him out into the hall.

All three take part in the visual gags that assault both social conventions and rational perspectives. One of their most delicious routines is the "mirror" sequence in *Duck Soup* that provocatively toys with the perception of images of reality. Groucho in nightshirt, cap, and cigar encounters Chico, who, spying, is made up and dressed identically. Through a series of precise imitations of Groucho's movements (the precision marred by some intentional lapses), Chico pretends to be Groucho's image in a nonexistent mirror, only to have Harpo appear at his side—a third identical image.

But it is Harpo who goes furthest in visual humor. While the verbal wit of Groucho and Chico toys with conventional reality, his visual antics explode it, whether in whimsy or outrageous violence. In the lesser *At the Circus* (1939), his whimsical free association interrupts the calculated artifice of their detective work. While attempting to outfox a sleeping strong man, Chico slashes open a pillow, and Harpo accidentally turns on a fan. In the feathery snowstorm that results, Harpo, stomach stuffed with a pillow, is suddenly a street-corner Santa Claus ringing a large bell, threatening their enterprise and shifting to a new level of fantasy truth. In the customs sequence of *Monkey Business,* Chico and Groucho unsuccessfully try to dupe the establishment and sneak through customs by singing like Maurice Chevalier, whose passport they have stolen. Topping them, Harpo mimes a Chevalier song played on a phonograph strapped to his back. When it winds down and his deception is revealed, Harpo turns from guile to explosion. Stomping up and down the length of the long customs table, he scatters the copious paper work of the official world.

The brothers themselves, however, were part of the commercial world of the motion picture after all. Their fourth and fifth pictures—caricatures of college life in *Horse Feathers* and of government and war in *Duck Soup*— were their sharpest satire and most freewheeling vehicles of untrammeled exuberance. When they moved to MGM, under the aegis of Irving Thalberg, his careful control set a pattern for all their subsequent movies. Plot was more tightly structured, with some pretense at credibility. Romance and music were more carefully interlaced with the comic routines. The approach produced greater financial success in *A Night at the Opera,* probably their best combination of overall form and madcap antics. Following this, *A Day at the Races* (1937), after Thalberg's death, used the same formula and was even more successful financially, but less Marxian. In their subsequent six films, until *Love Happy* (1949), the formula was applied to a variety of situations with a steady weakening of the earlier flavor. Despite unconquer-

Horse Feathers

able bits and moments, the material and the constant retracing of the same patterns produced inevitable decay. Harpo seemed least restricted by the material, contributing some of his finest soaring solos in the lesser films. By the last film, *Love Happy* (for which he wrote the original story), he is at the center of the film, possibly at his finest, touched with new dimensions by age, as the production's imagination sags around him. In one of his last images, he turns the commercial artificiality of giant electrical signboards into a final imaginative liberation, putting a hand over the great yawning boy's mouth in a Goodyear "Time to Retire" ad, hiding in the open beak of a smoke-blowing Kool's penguin, soaring skyward on the back of the Mobil winged horse.

Other comedy teams followed in the trail of the Marxes—the Ritz Brothers, Abbott and Costello, Martin and Lewis—but the only film of the period that was to equal the Marxian Expressionist explosion of the norms of reality was the uniquely maniacal *Hellzapoppin* (1942), translated from the stage production with great cinematic flair by Olson and Johnson, under the nominal direction of H. C. Potter.

TOWARD PLAUSIBILITY

Lubitsch For the main thrust of sound-comedy was toward a fuller dramatic structure and texture: more orderly, containing, with a measure of plausibility, the exaggerations of comedy. This greater concern for dramatic structure and plausibility was sometimes allied with an attempt to deal accurately and honestly with real-life materials. But it was often at the service as well of the repeated patterns and motifs of commercial success—the realistic surfaces and observational camera style, the fuller character development merely a mask for evasions of reality.

The sound comedies of Ernst Lubitsch reveal an interesting mixture of these impulses. Beginning with the fanciful romantic operettas of the Maurice Chevalier–Jeanette MacDonald team—*The Merry Widow* (1934), the best in its satirical play against the material—he moved to an Americanized, somewhat more earthbound version of his earlier silent world of sophisticated lovers and graceful livers, then briefly bumped that world against politics. Later, he even dabbled more with the life style of the common man, as in the broader—and more sentimentally treated—mixture of social classes in *The Shop Around the Corner* (1940) and *Cluny Brown* (1946). In his sound-films, he continued his fluid camera and cutting techniques, but with less obtrusiveness than in the silent films and with a more skillful exploitation of the dialogue. Working with a variety of screenwriters, he maintained a worldly, elegantly arch tone and a comic structure that emphasized ironic contrasts and elaborately extended repetitions of motifs.

Trouble in Paradise (1932) and *Design for Living* (1934) seem the best of the mid-thirties sophisticated romances, pitting his people of grace against flat-footed intrusions of the mundane world. In *Trouble*, an opening panning shot (accompanied by a lovely "O Sole Mio") displays the beauties of the Venetian canals and closes on the wry disclosure that the singer is poling a garbage barge. The tone is set for the amoral machinations of Herbert Marshall and Miriam Hopkins, urbanely scheming to pry money loose from those who don't really know how to enjoy it—Edward Everett Horton, their chief foil. The climax of the gag motif of Horton trying to remember where he's seen Marshall before is a fine example of Lubitsch technique: With a mockingly Wagnerian climax on the sound track, Horton, too late, remembers, and the mobile camera follows his response—jumping up, sitting down, scurrying about the room.

The opening of *Design for Living* (script by Ben Hecht from the Noel Coward play) is an excellent set of close-ups that not only build to a gag but set up the film's central premise. In a train compartment, we see in sequence the mouth of a sleeping man, his feet on the facing seat, his face, a woman across from him, then a wider shot of the face of the first man and of another, side by side and sleeping. The woman props her legs between the extended legs of the two men. We then see the hand of the first man, his face, his hand resting on the woman's leg, the two men's faces, the hand on the leg again, the two men's faces, the first man's expression changing. The girl, Miriam Hopkins, falls in love with the two men, Frederic March and Gary Cooper, and they with her, much to the discomfort of the stuffy conventional world, again personified by Edward Everett Horton. The double love affair is given a comic structure that features juxtaposed parallels: each in turn kissing her and saying he loves her, each in turn lectured by Edward Everett Horton. In the most elaborate parallels, Cooper and Hopkins are in Paris, March in London for the opening of his play. In Paris, the couple pace the apartment nervously, vowing to be fair to March. But then in a typical reversal (action belying words just spoken), Hopkins throws herself on the daybed, saying, "I know we made a gentleman's agreement but I'm

Ninotchka

no gentleman." On the cut to London, we see March proud and happy, going through the excitement of his opening. After Horton tells him about the other two, he repeats the same sequence of successful-playwright actions, but now takes no pleasure in them.

In the two Lubitsch comedies that touch directly on international politics, there is an interesting shift in that a central character grows into a typical Lubitsch carrier-of-grace through the course of the movie. In *Ninotchka* (1939), the eminently svelte Greta Garbo, as a prim, clumsy, glum Soviet commissar, is transformed into a graceful swan by Parisian love and champagne. In this film, the inhibiting, flatfooted enemy is pointedly governmental ideology and bureaucracy. The script by Charles Brackett and Billy Wilder is heavier on direct verbal satire and lighter on the usual Lubitsch elaborations.

In contrast, Lubitsch's other venture into topical satire, *To Be or Not to Be* (1942)—script by Edwin Justus Mayer—has one of his most elaborate, cumulative, incremental structures. Its artificiality is played against the all-too-real terrors of the Nazi occupation of Poland. The resulting mixture is not really a serious anti-Nazi or political satire but an arrogantly black zaniness, appropriately and knowingly applied to the blurring of illusion and reality, of artifice and seriousness. In the story, Jack Benny's boorish actor Joseph Tura finds himself developing a personal character that matches the style of the characters he impersonates in dealing with both the Nazis and his wife (Carole Lombard in her last role).

In the elaborate pattern, hardly any plot, character, or dialogue essential is not picked up and reprised, often with mounting effect. Early, Benny's "to be or not to be" soliloquy is interrupted three times because, unknown to him, it is the signal to the young, infatuated airman to visit Benny's wife in her dressing room. At the very end, once again his speech is interrupted. All the developments of the theatrical situation—most especially the troupe's preparation of a play about Nazis but also the particular roles portrayed by the actors in the play within the play—are then applied to the daring plot to fool the real Nazis. Typical of the multilevel action that develops is the scene in which Benny goes to the hotel room of a Nazi professor who has just been killed and whom Benny is impersonating. His wife is there on some pretext, and Benny finds her in the company of a Nazi general. While Benny passes himself off to the general as the professor, he talks to his wife about himself, Joseph Tura, and about her trysts with the young flyer—information that he obtained while, in the role of a Gestapo officer, he interviewed the real professor.

The longest and most complicated running gag is built on Benny's dual impersonation of Gestapo officer and Nazi professor. The things he says as officer while talking to the professor are then used when he plays the professor in his dialogue with the real officer (Sig Ruman). Repeated throughout these sequences, with a cumulatively comic effect, is the line: "So they call me Concentration Camp Ehrhart, do they?"—uttered first by Benny, then by Ruman. Another Ruman motif, which is carried to a black-humor conclusion is his outraged, "Schultz!" reiterated at each of the many mistakes of his assistant. The last such "Schultz!" is followed immediately by Ruman's suicide. It is typical of the film's thrust that this is prompted by Ruman's mistaken belief that he has interrupted a love tryst of the Führer, which in reality is only another masquerade by one of the actors.

Cukor   In 1932, George Cukor directed *One Night with You,* which had a thorough Lubitsch plan. For decades he continued, in the midst of dramas and musicals, to turn out comedies typical of the sophisticated mold developed in the American film. Like Lubitsch's films, Cukor's comedies favored grace and style in a plodding world, but they were generally less naughty and cynical, generally sought a fuller dramatic verisimilitude. In Cukor's work, there was less intricate elaboration, less camera movement, with long takes frequent in order to permit uninterrupted concentration on character and dialogue. His comedies moved from the more aristocratic atmosphere of *Dinner at Eight* (1933), *The Women* (1939), and *The Philadelphia Story* (1940) to the brasher, knockabout (but still well heeled) world of Katherine Hepburn and Spencer Tracy in *Adam's Rib* (1949) and *Pat and Mike* (1952), and to more direct political satire in *Born Yesterday* (1950). While still replete with visual humor, the films of this type stress an articulate verbal wit, touching on social issues—free speech in the case of Elliott Nugent's deft satire of academia, *The Male Animal* (1942)—and reaching the peak of embellishment in Joseph L. Mankiewicz's *All about Eve* (1950).

Action-film
Directors:
Hawks
and
Others

While also stressing verbal wit, the comedies of Howard Hawks illustrate a staple type in American comedy that is one step further removed from the Lubitsch style. These have a harder tone, a more pointed, direct kind of satire, a faster, often frenetic pace in both action and dialogue. The best of Hawks's fast-paced, crackling "crazy" comedies of the late thirties and forties were *Bringing Up Baby* (1938), with Katherine Hepburn as the sleekly impudent society girl relentlessly chasing Cary Grant, a flustered but still cool paleontologist; *His Girl Friday* (1941), with Rosalind Russell and Cary Grant as fast-talking and predatory newspaper equals; and *Ball of Fire* (1941), with Barbara Stanwyck after Gary Cooper. Of these, *His Gal Friday* possibly holds the record for speed and volume of dialogue, with sharp editing and camera angles to match the ricochets of its repartee. Even in such Hawks mystery melodramas as *To Have and Have Not* (1944) and *The Big Sleep* (1946), with the strongest hand on the script that of the redoubtable old pro Jules Furthman, it is the hard-nosed verve of the repartee, especially between Humphrey Bogart and Lauren Bacall, that gives the lasting flavor of the films.

Bringing Up Baby

Another director of action films who also applied his sense of pace to rapid-fire satirical comedy was William Wellman, whose *Nothing Sacred* (1937), with a script by Ben Hecht, and *Roxie Hart* (1942), written by Nunnally Johnson, mixed sentimentality with buckshot satire of American manners and institutions.

One of the most cynical comedies of the type was Jack Conway's *Too Hot to Handle* (1938), featuring Clark Gable as a newsreel reporter who will do anything for a scoop, including setting off an air raid in the Sino-Japanese War and ruining the reputation of Myrna Loy, who eventually falls for and wins him.

Capra
The bulk of dramatic comedies of the period did not deal directly with specific social and political problems, despite the prevalent peppering of material with wisecracking satirical barbs. More direct than most in their treatment of current problems were *Mr. Deeds Goes to Town* (1936) and *Mr. Smith Goes to Washington* (1939) by Frank Capra, whose comedies of the period attempted to convey a greater verisimilitude, a greater identification with the world of the average man. In *It Happened One Night* (1934), his appealing hitchhikers, Clark Gable and Claudette Colbert, have the easy smoothness, the quick wit of typical comedy characters but share more of the hominess and troubles of the average man's depression world. Capra's satire and his expert editing for both comical and emotional point are softened by rosy sentimentality and a cracker-barrel populist political naiveté. In *Mr. Deeds*, the evils of the system are personified by well-off big-city intellectuals, and it is a group of farmers who make millionaire Deeds (James Stewart) forgo his disillusioned retreat and take responsible action to do something about the depression. In *Mr. Smith*, Stewart brings the virtues of small-town America into play against corrupt politicians. In 1941, Capra returned to the theme with a melodrama, *Meet John Doe*, delivered with skillful cinematic flourishes, and in 1949, he approached it comically again in *State of the Union*, with Spencer Tracy and Katherine Hepburn standing up to a stronger, more biting array of corrupt bigwigs than in the original stage version.

The sentimental side of Capra's comic mixture can be seen in such common-folk comedies as Leo McCarey's *Going My Way* (1944) and *The Bells of St. Mary's* (1945), with Bing Crosby in priest's garb as the sweet, good man of the people against some rather toothless forms of big-city venality.

Sturges
Quite the opposite was the irreverent cynicism in the comedies of Preston Sturges. In seven films from 1940 to 1945, he established himself as the most individual of the period's Hollywood comic directors, but his sporadic subsequent films failed to maintain this imaginative momentum. The confounding reversal is somehow typical of Sturges and his work. Iconoclastic as they were, his films were nonetheless part of a style and method of studio movie-making that Sturges had picked up while working as screenwriter

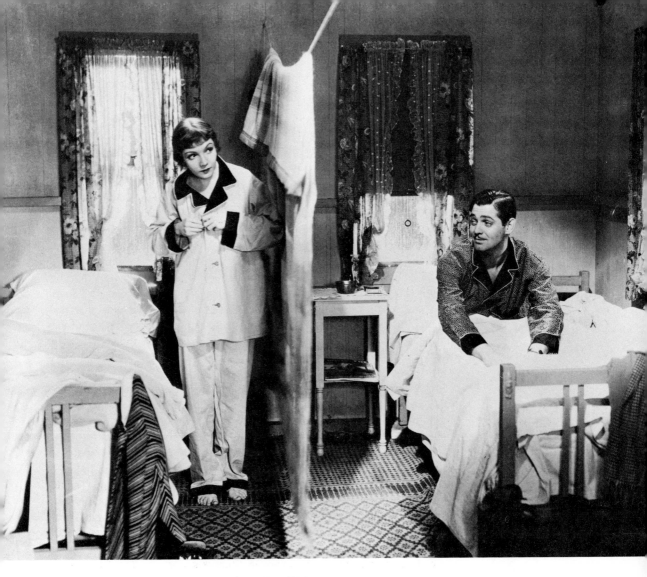

It Happened One Night

and director. Although the range of his satire was broader than other Hollywood film-makers', Sturges nonetheless stopped short of developing the satirical material fully or consistently, never building it to meaning. At his best, his films balanced some of the screen's most clever verbal wit with the wild accelerations of props and actions of silent-film comedy, and a degree of Realism with the most extravagant comic distortions. Yet too often the balance (as well as any deepening and fulfilling of the satire or clear sense of Sturges's attitude toward his material) was sacrificed to his emphasis on laughs—in a whirling proliferation of verbal and visual gags, an obsession with the frenetic acceleration of pace.

As a screenwriter, Sturges had worked skillfully in a number of genres.

His first original screenplay—*The Power and the Glory* (1933)—had a complicated flashback structure that toyed with chronology more extensively than did *Citizen Kane* (1941) and, like *Kane*, started with the death of a tycoon and then traced the inner failure of his life. Unlike *Kane*, however, neither its characters nor its visual form bring it to life.

In 1940, Sturges managed to get his first assignment as a director on *The Great McGinty*—one of the first movies in Hollywood to be directed by the man who wrote it. It is a crafty blend of mildly tough social satire and conventional Realist melodrama. Its lovable rogue (Brian Donlevy) is elevated through happenstance to political prominence, which he retains as long as he is more or less as corrupt as the rest of the politicians. When he reforms, he is broken; from here on, sentimentality wins out. His next film, *Christmas in July* (1940), is more farcical but still makes an effort at literal credibility. It toys directly with the cherished virtues of monetary success in more elaborated patterns of satire than other films of the time. Its hopeful young couple, Dick Powell and Ellen Drew, are buffeted by a typical combination of Sturges forces: plain luck, both good and bad; unnecessary cruelty and meddling; the venality of businessmen. Finally, in an irony that is too easy—again typical of Sturges's material—their entry in a slogan contest is named winner because it is so bad.

In *The Lady Eve* (1941) and *Palm Beach Story* (1942), he leaves social reality behind for his version of the Lubitsch world of the smooth life, which has its own distinctive stress: the virtue of those who are open and honest about going after what they want—money or a mate or both—and the bankruptcy of most other so-called virtues. In *The Lady Eve*, Sturges modulates the momentum of the comedy with appropriate visual means—long takes of characters interacting for the verbal humor, cutting and changing angles for madcap action. In it, rich, gullible Henry Fonda is first conned then pursued and captured by the charmingly unscrupulous Barbara Stanwyck—both at the peak of the comic sides of their star personas. The early stages of the action, on shipboard, are the most expertly sustained juggling of cynical wit, plot turns, and physical foolery in Sturges's work. In *The Palm Beach Story*, the love- and money-seekers form a complicated quartet: At one point, Joe E. Brown serenades Claudette Colbert while, unknown to him, she is being seduced by Joel McCrea—who is supposed to be in love with Mary Astor. The dialogue is as rapid-fire as in Hawks's *His Girl Friday* but doesn't hold its own with the slapstick acceleration of props, action, and plot.

Between these two, Sturges made *Sullivan's Travels* (1941), a strangely ambivalent swipe at Hollywood and himself. In it, Sullivan (McCrea), a filmmaker who thinks he ought to make more serious movies, gets caught in the vicious but very funny predatory shenanigans of the movie moguls and publicists, and ends on the road with the poor. He becomes tangled in a murder plot, and the film gets more earnest, but its view of the world of the downtrodden is suprisingly soft, except for one harrowing sequence in which a money-crazed derelict is run over by a train. At the conclusion, Sullivan, in

The Lady Eve

a prison work camp, witnesses how laughter at a Mickey Mouse cartoon alleviates the grimness of the inmates' lives—and, the significance of his work reaffirmed, he goes back to Hollywood to make comedies.

Sturges's next two comedies did not ignore society; in fact, they took on all the sacred cows of small-town, small-minded morality, manners, patriotism, and beliefs. In them, Sturges tried to incorporate the frantic geometric progressions of silent-film comedy with the greater sophistication of his satire and dialogue. They are his most daring attempt to expand the limits of his comedy, but the pattern and logic of the satire are buried under the desperate pace of the gags, the congestion of comic ideas. In a subsequent film, *Mad Wednesday* (1946), he tried to extend as far as possible the frenzy and precariousness of Harold Lloyd's surface visual comedy only, but the attempt was hollow and forced.

In the first of the two madcap satires, *The Miracle of Morgan's Creek* (1944), Sturges's scathing vision of the inanities of the common man's world is mitigated by the extravagance of the central plot device—Betty Hutton, pregnant out of wedlock, gets town bumbler Eddie Bracken to marry her and then gives birth to sextuplets. The extravagance is played against a credibility that is maintained in some scenes and characterizations, all in the midst of unrelenting sarcastic thrusts at every convention of mind and manners in sight. The pattern is much the same in *Hail the Conquering Hero* (also 1944), with false greatness this time thrust on Bracken because he is mistaken for a returning war hero. The tone is harsher than in *Miracle,* and the cast of characters even quirkier, including a ferociously intense real war hero with a dangerously absolute veneration of "Mom." But the satirical points are not pursued to their logical conclusions; typically, the climactic irony softens rather than intensifies: Having grown in stature, Bracken confesses his masquerade; when this wins the crowd's sympathy, he becomes useful to the politicians, who then get him elected mayor. The result is both happy-ending romanticism and a vague, displaced irony without a real point. Nonetheless, despite all that he undercut or failed to exploit or develop, Sturges built an imposing body of work, somehow both distinct from and closely tied to its time.

EUROPE

The flexibility of Sturges's comic structure and his freedom in moving in and out of varying degrees of Realism, fantasy, and satire were much influenced by the films of René Clair. After *À Nous la Liberté* (1932), Clair's work declined, although his films made in other countries, such as *The Ghost Goes West* (1935), in England, and *I Married a Witch* (1942), in America, did retain many high comic moments. Of his later work, once more in France, the high points in reworking his own special blend of fantasy and Realism are his free translation of the legend of Faust, *La Beauté du Diable* (1949), and *Les Belles de Nuit* (1952)—a charming set of variations on the interplay between a romantic young man's dreams and his waking life, climaxed by an ingenious comic chase through time, back to the present from the Stone Age in which he had landed.

Of the French comedians of the period, Fernandel and Noel-Noel had the strongest presence but never built an autonomy or continuity of comic persona in the random farces and dramas in which they appeared. On the whole, French comedy tended to be more a part of dramas, romances, spectaculars —as in the films of Marcel Pagnol, Julien Duvivier, or those of Jean Renoir. In the thirties, the most successful example of a disciplined, farcical comedy embedded in a fabric of realistic credibility was Jacques Feyder's *Carnival in Flanders* (*La Kermesse Héroique*), made in 1935. The script, by Charles Spaak, traces the collapse, under the nocturnal assault of the amorous ladies of Flanders, of an occupying sixteenth-century Spanish regiment. It is a deft development of the nuances of suggestive sexual comedy with a foundation of sharp characterization.

In England, the postwar forties brought a stunning increase in the production of top-level comedies, mainly those mining a rich vein of gentle satire of the quirks and foibles of British manners and character. The wartime *The Life and Death of Colonel Blimp* (1943) had touched on peripheral social issues, but in the main, the postwar comedies were concerned more with peccadillos than major issues. They ranged from the relatively plausible dramas based on the stories of W. Somerset Maugham—*Quartet* (1948), *Trio* (1950), and *Encore* (1951)—to the more fanciful exaggerations of *Passport to Pimlico* and *Tight Little Island* (both 1949). More acid was the satire in the excellent string of Alec Guinness vehicles—*Kind Hearts and Coronets* (1949), *The Lavender Hill Mob* (1950), *The Man in the White Suit* (1951), *The Promoter* (1952), all surpassed by the wonderful ensemble work in the absurdly sinister *The Ladykillers* (1956). With this abundant output, the British challenged American domination of the comedy field.

CHAPTER THIRTEEN

Genres,
Realism,
and
the
Personal
Style

The men who worked within the commercial production and distribution system worked also within the perimeter of Realist convention. In the great majority of cases, the Realist techniques (along with expressive embellishments) were applied to routine dramatic materials that stayed safely within the field of expectations of the standard entertainment genres. A number of directors, however, managed to strike a more distinctive balance among conflicting pressures. Accommodating commercial demands, they managed still to express personal attitudes toward a recognizable reality; they managed to shape a personal style, though, in some cases, only intermittently or erratically. In other cases, it was maintained only temporarily, then dissipated or, at least, vitiated. In rarer cases, the style was both maintained and refined through a long career; we will examine five representative cases of the studio style. We have touched on some others in other chapters, but the long careers of these five directors—all consolidated in the thirties and forties—make them especially revealing of the spectrum of fulfillment and unfulfillment of potential within the commercial genres. Both John Huston and Carol Reed built to a distinctive period of work, but then, in differing ways, lost momentum. David Lean's early emphatic editing style turned ostentatious with the elaborate sweep and décor of his later commercial epics. Alfred Hitchcock and John Ford found their basic genres and manners early and both mined and refined them through many years of film-making.

JOHN HUSTON

While it might be said that John Huston is a director who had a style and then lost it, there is a certain consistency of approach to film-making underlying both the early unity of his work and the later wandering. He has always worked clearly within the context of the transparent screen. He has said he believes in "letting the material have complete freedom and imposing myself only where necessary," and has sought "to say as much as possible with a minimum of means," rendering the subject by unobtrusive means, adapting the means to the subject. But, while this approach has remained consistent, it has not always been brought into the burning focus of style in the fullest sense—as the embodiment in form of a clear and strong attitude toward the materials. The adaptability of the means to the content has produced an effacing style but also all but effaced the style.

Huston has taken on an interesting catholicity of materials—possibly more daring than the straight-line continuity of a Hitchcock or Ford—but without an inner impetus that would make them ring with his own conviction of what to do or say with them.

205

The
Forties:
Tough-guy
Cynicism

With Dashiel Hammett's *The Maltese Falcon* (1941), Huston found an attitude and tone that were to be the core of his unified forties' work. Earlier, his screenwriting work in the thirties had been a part of the more soberly earnest, conventional, social-problem genre: *Dr. Ehrlich's Magic Bullet, Juarez, Jezebel, Sergeant York*. With the Hammett work, he was able to express a harder-edged Realism, socially aware but not earnest and preachy, with a sardonic bite that mixed humor and drama, a tough attitude for a hard world, and an economic naturalness of technique that was particularly apt for his continued emphasis on character and dialogue. The film crystallizes the emergent tough-guy crime genre at a high level of cynical wit, deepens (in the role of Sam Spade) the emotion and range of Humphrey Bogart's persona as the paragon of the genre, surrounds him with a mixture of grainy Realist details, heightened character types (Sydney Greenstreet and Peter Lorre), and some touch of contrivance. It was to be a typical Huston mixture. In *The Maltese Falcon,* he often magnifies the amoral greed of the characters to the point of comedy yet retains their disturbing harshness, constructs an entertainment that remains honest to its cynicism toward the world. Its visual pattern is abrupt, aggressive, dark, full of close-ups and tight shots of characters caught against each other and their seedy, cluttered surroundings. Huston often shoots past one to another who is speaking, though without the insistent rhythm and regular return he used later in *The Asphalt Jungle.* For a decade (interrupted by two early, quick,

The Maltese Falcon

impersonal films and by wartime service), Huston maintained this attitude, and its visual tone, through four more films. In each, however, the hard-edged transparent style underwent appropriate changes.

The Treasure of Sierra Madre (1948), from the B. Traven novel, probes more deeply into personality and is arguably Huston's best work. With echoes of von Stroheim's *Greed,* it draws more implications from the deadening viciousness, the destroying greed of the tough-guy world. Bogart's Fred C. Dobbs ("Nobody touches *my* goods!") is part Spade, part those whom Spade combatted, the pathological amplification of obsessive self-interest. He and his two partners are the have-nots—worsened rather than purified by deprivation—and gold is their means to become haves. The film first sharply delineates their rough-and-ready world in the seedy byways of Mexico, then sets them in an impersonally barren, coldly lit nature as they battle among themselves and against nature, intruders, and Mexican bandits, who win out over them but lose the slippery gold.

Huston observes their defeat and Dobbs's disintegration with a sardonic, but understatingly implacable camera, staying often in middle distance as they interact. In one beautiful example of this controlled naturalness (something on the order of William Wyler's patterns but not as elaborate or extended), the intruder whom the trio had been about to kill has been shot by the bandits. With the body in the foreground, Bogart, behind, stands with his foot cocked too jauntily on a rock, revealing more tensions than he thinks. Tim Holt walks into the frame, stands over the body, naively uncomprehending, hands clasped as though at church. Walter Huston then passes behind Holt, kneels, quietly goes about the practical business of rifling the dead man's pockets—all three now in the frame. Throughout, this passive observation of business that reveals character works better than the more pointed symbolic images—the bandits scurrying like children down the bank of a dry riverbed as they close in on Dobbs, as opposed to the final blowing away of the gold dust (leaked from a saddlebag) and Walter Huston's last knowing laugh at the loss.

In the same year, Huston extensively reworked Maxwell Anderson's *Key Largo* to give the underworld material more social point (although the producers eliminated some of the most direct comparisons). Here, as in the original play, there is a more idealistic counterthrust to the cynicism, as the weak and cynical finally stand up to the gangster-entrepreneurs. Edward G. Robinson, in a decadent, rococo extension of his mobster persona, is first seen, cigar in hand, naked in a bathtub to fight the heat; this time Bogart is the emptied cynic who makes a final stand. The film has a hothouse quality, sweltering, sticky with greed. In the confines of the hotel in which almost all of the action takes place, Huston's camera is this time more mobile, imposing as well as observing meaningful movement and gesture, relationship.

We Were Strangers (1949) also mixes a cynicism about individual action with a more affirmative political idealism. The plans of a small group that plots to overthrow a Cuban dictatorship in the thirties go awry: Most are killed, but in the end a general revolt does occur. While the plot emphasizes the suspense of the conflict between the conspirators and the secret police, the immediacy of Huston's patient camera does well with the painstaking details of their preparations and the interpersonal tensions that develop. The implications of the plot conflict are captured in an excellent visual motif: the alternation between the tight shadowy scene of the rebels in the tunnel they are digging and the bright lights and ornate settings of the ruling powers above.

The Asphalt Jungle (1950) is full of bitter, witty ironies of both structure and detail. It is the most artfully composed and skillfully edited Huston film, and the relentless reversals and juxtapositions of its visual and verbal patterns are a wonderfully apt vehicle for the reversals of human dreams with which it deals. In the typical Huston pattern, its conspirators (in a bank robbery) gain and then lose "their goods"—and the dreams ancillary to them—through accident and weakness. This time they are a rather likeable, if pathetic, group, each with an illusion that contributes to its own shattering. The impeccable lawyer, in love with a young beauty (Marilyn Monroe), is caught up by his own cleverness and by his infatuation. His last confrontation with the girl (when she gives testimony against him) is shown in long takes from his point of view that follow her into the room, past and above him, and back out of the room. The workaday crook wants money for a better life for his family. In an artful juxtaposition, two efficient detectives cautiously close in on his apartment. Inside, the camera pans to view a child, some old women mourning, a tormented wife, and then the foot of the coffin of the man they are stalking. The brains of the outfit wants one more bundle so that, free from prison at last, he can enjoy the sensual pleasures of life; he lingers too long to savor the spectacle of a young girl dancing in a bar and is caught. The central figure (Sterling Hayden) is a down-and-outer who wants money to set up a horse farm. Wounded and bleeding, he obsessively insists on driving back to Kentucky to his beloved horses. His flight is intercut with police reports about the mad-dog killer on the loose. In a series of shots of modulated distance—long into close-up and then back to long—he lies dying at the feet of the horses, one nuzzling his body, and then is hardly visible in a last long shot of the surrounding open fields of grazing horses.

Throughout, in dialogue sequences, Huston uses a tightly patterned set of reverse shots, capturing the interacting selfishness that finally destroys their dreams—shooting past one head (in profile or semi–rear shot) to the other and then reversing the angle with a similar pattern.

Post-Forties: Diversity, Wandering
Except for a late reprise in *Fat City* (1972), Huston went no further with the tone and manner of tough-guy cynicism. From the fifties on, he was to turn to a surprisingly diverse array of subjects, apparently with the aim of making commercially palatable a "Great Books" shelf of literary or arty materials.

It is indicative of the turn in his work that Huston's earlier mixtures of humor and seriousness now tend to get split, with the humorous works the more successful. In *The African Queen* (1952), the freewheeling, quirky by-play between Bogart and Katherine Hepburn gives the pedestrian adventure genre a winning comic dimension. In *Beat the Devil* (1954), he and Truman Capote set out more intentionally to produce a spoof on the crime-conspiracy plot (using Bogart and Lorre with Robert Morley instead of Greenstreet). The whole has a leisurely playfulness that many of his later works could well have used, even in small measure. In it, he obtains a delightfully comic performance from Jennifer Jones.

In Huston's serious efforts, the adaptable style still accommodates itself to the content and spirit of the material, but the style is no longer a reflection of a controlling attitude toward the material. The adaptation of Tennessee Williams's *The Night of the Iguana* (1964), for example, does have the intimacy of character interplay of Huston's earlier work, but, after unsuccessfully adding action at the opening, he effaces himself before the material, leaving no signature on the long dialogue scenes. Works of a larger scale have more embellishment, many excellent moments, but fail to jell in one way or another. *The Red Badge of Courage* (1951) mixes naturalness and monumental solemnity, gets tangled in a defeating web of reediting maneuvers, and strangely misses the novel's Impressionism. *Moulin Rouge* (1953) accurately (though ostentatiously) projects tones of the life of Toulouse-Lautrec but is never sure of its own attitude toward its materials. *Moby Dick* (1952)—straining for seriousness, yet omitting the central speeches—is an uneven attempt to capture the grandeur of Melville's conception. *The Misfits* (1961), for all its symbolic reachings, is a touching mounting of Arthur Miller's romanticism about the last frontiers of romanticism of love and free spirits in the modern West. *Freud* (1962) is a return to the earnest solemnity of the thirties' "discovery" films, with Expressionist touches for dream and memory sequences. *The Bible* (1966) is the epitome of reaching for too much —possibly because unsure of *what* to reach for—and yet not without coming up with a good deal.

But for all the wandering and the testing and stretching of genres of these later films, there is nothing that drives through them, nothing that shows Huston as impelled to build, consolidate, or deepen a personal vision and shaping style.

CAROL REED

In England, through the same decades, the careers of two major directors also reveal the interaction between the restraints of commercial production and the art of the film-maker.

Carol Reed's series of six differing but unified films (made in the first decade after World War II) shows, as in Huston, the emergence of a consistent viewpoint that controlled the arc of style from film to film. But, also as in Huston's case, that controlling attitude seemed to reach a dead end and, in subsequent films, he could do no more with it. Limited by the stock of commercial projects available to him and by his own inability to conceive or nurture others, he also wandered an erratic and unsatisfying course, with the best of his later films also a comedy.

Pre–World War II

Reed's two best films before World War II had established separately the two prime elements he was to combine in the work of his peak period—careful and sympathetic characterization in *The Stars Look Down* (1939) and a heightening of visual imagery in *Night Train to Munich* (1940).

The Stars Look Down was one of the few British films of the thirties to deal with contemporary social issues. In it a new labor union rises to challenge the traditional way of doing things. But Reed makes no abstract preachment about labor unions or working conditions in the Welsh mines. Rather, he evokes a palpable sense of the cruel work in the mines and—for his major emphasis—delineates with strong credibility the tensions provoked in individuals and in the community at this moment of social crisis. Although the characters represent various attitudes toward the union, and its effect on the community, these attitudes are an integral part of a convincingly developed personality. The film's indecisive idealist (Michael Redgrave)—inevitably defeated by the town, by himself, even by those who love him—is a masterful fulfillment of the Social Realist aim to capture the interaction between an individual and his environment.

In the entertaining thriller *Night Train to Munich,* Reed showed his interest in using the physical properties of place in creating atmosphere and developing plot. In this lighter film, he begins to give greater play to his bent for the dramatic camera angles and sound images and symbolic patterns of composition that were to become the keynote of his style.

Postwar: Man Apart

In the postwar films, Reed was not to deal directly with social issues. Using mainly suspense material, he invested the characters with Realist credibility and heightened the material to an abstract symbolic suggestiveness. Of the films of this kind, *Odd Man Out* (1947) is the most overt and ornate extension of the realistic base into symbolism, and *Outcast of the Islands* (1951), the purest realistic development of the human and dramatic material. Both have the theme that underlies Reed's best films—a man set apart, inwardly driven and torn, outwardly isolated or fugitive; and the impossibility of bridging the gaps, both within and without.

Odd Man Out is bravura cinema, yet it maintains Realist credibility and empathy to a strong degree—despite some reliance on portentous symbolic types. The film follows a dying man (James Mason as an IRA man wounded in a robbery) through a darkened, nightmarish city. Searching for a last touch of sympathy and charity, a final connection, he encounters people who both hinder and help—even the latter out of their needs, not his. The opening robbery is handled with a documentary matter-of-factness that is

Odd Man Out

nonetheless electric in its building and exploding of tension: playing, for example, a whole sequence of natural sounds (of mill machinery, a clock, footsteps, whistling, an office) against the silent actions of the robbers; shooting from the moving car as one of the IRA men falls in the street, panning to hold him in frame as the car leaves him behind and he is separated from the group. As he begins to run, then staggers and falls, sound again heightens and comments: the barking of a dog receding into the distance; the man's shoes crunching on broken glass, his breathing shifting from heavy panting to slow, labored breaths; the last continuing sound of the alarm bell, very distant.

While he searches, the manhunt for him intensifies. The camera maintains his point of view as he grows weak and feverish. Angles of perspective grow more striking and distorted, images more grotesque—as though, dying, he has become aware of the monstrous in the ordinary.

This amplification within the Realist approach and this same uncovering of the monstrous is found in *The Third Man* (1949) and *The Man Between* (1953). Especially in the first of these suspense adventures, a visual and aural excitement complements the plot excitement, bringing out its fullest dimensions of emotion and implication. In this film, Reed collaborated with Graham Greene and the film's star, Orson Welles. The world of *The Third Man* is rotting with corruption. Each of its characters has his price, but for the biggest price, Harry Lime (Welles), disturbingly engaging in his cool amorality, will go the furthest—trafficking in ineffective vaccines that are potentially lethal to the user. Its seeker after truth, Joseph Cotten, who fancied himself a cynic, finds the price of his loss of final innocence too high. Like so many of Reed's (and Greene's) figures, he finds there is nowhere to go from here.

The film is full of the shadows that fall across the illusory surfaces of the physical world of postwar Vienna, which seems to share in the corruption: The ruins and overstuffed rooms, ornate building façades and dark alleys, statues in broken streets, crowded squares, an empty carnival—all take on expressive connotations. With the shadows, with extreme (Wellesian) camera angles, with incongruities and ironies within images, Reed builds his symbolic interplay of men and the corrupted things of their world—while maintaining credible characterization and suspense within the adventure plot. It all ends fittingly—and on all levels simultaneously—in the final chase through the filth of the sewers beneath the city, shadows and angles misleading, sounds echoing chaotically, men stripped of pretense, breathing like animals.

Less ostentatious in technique—almost austere—*Outcast of the Islands* has a quiet aptness of camera angle and imagery that again turns place—the cold extremity of brightness of sea and sky, the lush fog and rain and tropical growth—into a metaphor of the tragic separateness of human beings. Based on the Joseph Conrad novel, the film has a fuller development of character than other Reed films. It traces Reed's recurrent motif of self-destruction—here through selfishness and, then, love; but it juxtaposes the loner's plight (wonderfully articulated by Trevor Howard) with the often comic emptiness of the conventional family life of his chief antagonist (Robert Morley). *The Fallen Idol* (1948), made before *Outcast,* was even more spare and laconic. In its world of dominating grays and blacks, Reed dealt with the isolation of the child and the painful beginnings of comprehension of human frailty by stressing camera angles that carried the boy's point of view throughout the film.

In *A Kid for Two Farthings* (1955), Reed uses the poetic vernacular of Wolf Mankowitz's East End (of London) characters and his own sense of the poetry of place to blur the boundary between fantasy and reality. It is a more optimistic film than the others discussed, a gentle tale of a boy who, seeking a unicorn, finds only a sick goat with one horn, but, unlike Reed's other seekers, manages to find the miraculous anyway. The film was not a commercial success, and Reed did not pursue its new dimensions of fantasy. Nor did the optimism seem to mark any real opening in the insistent deadening of disillusion; he did not pursue its thematic implications further. In subsequent years, he turned to random projects in the commercial genres.

These offered little impetus for further development of his stylistic heightening of realistic characterization, save for the comic excellence of *Our Man in Havana* (1959), which was also a collaboration with Graham Greene.

DAVID LEAN: REALISM TO GRANDIOSITY

In contrast, the career of David Lean does show a consolidation of a newer yet related later style after an earlier period of straightforward Realism; however, it is not a consolidation that proved to offer a greater fulfillment of potential. With a strong emphasis on patterns of editing, Lean has always been strong in achieving effects; in the later stage of his career, he has turned to making these effects more grandiose—heightened but less substantial.

Lean's wartime *In Which We Serve* (1942) and *This Happy Breed* (1944) and postwar *Breaking the Sound Barrier* (1951) exhibit a tightknit surface Realism, a disciplined but sentimental application of the British documentary style to patriotic themes. More valuable are the controlled, carefully wrought structures of the muted love stories *Brief Encounter* (1946) and *The Passionate Friends* (1948). Typical of Lean's precision in structuring the development of an underplayed climax is the confrontation scene in the latter. The husband has discovered his wife's affair and is toying with the lovers. First with the wife, then with her lover, he talks with pointed irony about other matters until finally the wife confesses at the end of the scene. As he does so, the shots are first long, then closer as he probes with barbed innuendo, and finally in close-up as she realizes that he knows. Then as he begins the same treatment of the lover the camera returns to a long shot. In his dialogue with his wife, the camera moves with him as he guides her ostentatiously to a seat. She sits stiffly as he goes on talking, his hands seen mixing drinks behind her. As the close-ups start and the cutting accelerates, she sees (as does the audience) the theater program, which he has left on the table (and which signals his knowledge of the affair). Her hands start to take a cigarette, then stop; her face registers her knowledge; he bends over her into the frame and says, "Ice?"

An unconsummated affair is at the center of Noel Coward's *Brief Encounter,* which is a perfect embodiment of a limited mood—of loss and regret. The film, which presents repressive middle-class solidity as both defect and virtue, is structured as a flashback and captures the inevitable, wistful futility of the affair. Its intricacy of both aural and visual counterpoint allows for a constant play of ironies between the dull but good marriage and the memories of the affair. At the opening of the film, as the wife (Celia Johnson) begins to remember, her husband is doing a crossword puzzle. He asks her about the title of a poem, "Romance," which he says fits with "delusion." She is listening to a Rachmaninoff piano concerto, and, from this point on, its passionate strains overlap the present and the flashback past, heightening the romantic scenes, yet mocking the lovers' failure to consummate their passion.

Ironies are also developed within the flashback segments, with certain materials reused so that they build in meaning: When the lovers meet in the railway station restaurant, a playful flirtation is going on at the counter; later a reprise of the flirting plays against their despair. The intrusive chatter of some lady passengers is used in the same way. Within the patterns of cumulative repetition, her memory of their final parting is played through twice. She first envisions some of the details of the latter part of the sequence; it is only when she then goes back to the conversation that preceded what we have been shown that we discover he is leaving for good. Thus, minor matters that seemed unimportant the first time through assume a poignant irony the second time: While they sit with a jabbering lady, the lover (Trevor Howard) quietly says, "I must go," and gets up. In a nicely appropriate last image of their blocked attempt at passion, there is a shot of his hand briefly touching her shoulder and then he is gone, and the talk goes on.

Lean's two Dickens adaptations—*Great Expectations* (1946) and *Oliver Twist* (1948)—use editing in a more flamboyant manner, as befits the material. They also begin to make use of elaborate décor and setting in a way that suggests the later direction of Lean's development. *Oliver Twist* gets closer to the grotesqueness of the Dickensian world, and the famous opening

Great Expectations

sequence of *Great Expectations* has one of the most effectively built jolts in the screen's history of creating and exploding suspense through editing. With wind howling and branches creaking, Pip walks, terrified, through a graveyard, the camera kept at his height to intensify the experience from his point of view. He kneels at a grave, sees a nightmarish tree in the distance, then a more distorted tree up close. He starts to run, and the camera pans with him, slightly ahead of him. Suddenly it stops, so that, continuing, he is running toward the camera. As he seems to run into it, a figure steps into the frame and they collide. The shot, held only a moment, is followed by a cut to a close-up of Pip screaming, then back for the first clear shot of the face of the man (a convict) he has run into.

In a later love story, *Summertime* (1955), a shifting of approach is apparent. This brief and defeated encounter in Venice, with Katherine Hepburn, is given a sumptuous and ornamental visual form, but the visual panoramas and images do not coincide with the emotions of the story, leaving a gap between the dramatic material—credible though commercialized—and the glossy effects.

The gap continued as Lean found his genre in the intelligent, grandiose, realistic romance—the huge epics he has turned out to great profit ever since. In each, there is an intelligent, interesting core of characterization and idea, but it tends to be dwarfed, even lost, in the mass of historical details and in the epic sweep of scene and increasingly sentimental display of scenery.

In the first of these, *The Bridge on the River Kwai* (1957), the drama and spectacle keep a rough balance, the ironic futilities of war nicely, though too neatly, poised among the representative characters. In *Lawrence of Arabia* (1962)—the first of three collaborations with playwright Robert Bolt —the intelligent attempt to probe the enigma of Lawrence and the authenticity of related historical events are lost in endless seas of desert. In *Doctor Zhivago* (1966), the core of characterization is hollow, the historical events swirl confusingly, the décor is called upon to carry the tone and feel. Its last image is a rainbow in the sky over the dam where Zhivago's lost daughter is working. Admittedly weaker than the rest, this image foretells the next stage in Lean's evolution. For in *Ryan's Daughter* (1970), such poetic nature images abound, bloated and arbitrary correlatives of a banal core of dramatization that, amid disjointed snippets of history, fails to provide a ground in reality from which to launch Lean's progressively more decorative style.

HITCHCOCK: THE EVERYDAY NIGHTMARE

Alfred Hitchcock found his commercial genre early and, with much variation and some intermissions, has pursued it since. He has taken a version of the suspense melodrama, the thriller, and developed it distinctively, opening it to include more diversity of materials, more motifs and themes, more combinations of emotion, and imprinting on it a personal style, toning it with his personality and attitudes. Paradoxical juxtapositions are his forte, and it is one of these that this director who has always done, in his words, "the commercial thing" should so strikingly indicate how style is more a matter of personal attitude than the repetition of general approaches to technique or particular devices.

Techniques
and
Themes

Not that Hitchcock has not developed a consistent technical manner. Beneath all the variations—the long, moving camera takes of *Rope* or the rapid montages of *The Birds*—the technical approach has been a reflection of personality and attitude. The result is an amalgam of the Expressionist and Realist styles, a Realism of expressive entertainment. On the one side, he has sought to control and compel the emotional responses of the audience with overt, extreme manipulations of space, time, and action. Montage effects (the clash of images in sequence, the reconstitution of the materials through emphatic editing) have been the key to his technique. Five forms of montage are typical: (1) *The slow buildup of physical detail,* as in the murder scene in *Sabotage* (sometimes called *A Woman Alone,* 1936)—the emphasis on images of eating, and especially the knife, as Sylvia Sidney decides to kill her husband; the shift to her grasping the knife; his recognition of her intention, captured in his lunge for the knife; their hands locked, his cry, his fall. (2) *The acceleration of shock on shock in climactic sequences,* as in the murder in the shower in *Psycho* (1960)—sensual images of Janet Leigh's body, her wet hair; a shadow of an old woman through the shower curtain, the curtain opened, a knife striking and striking and striking; blood going down the drain with the shower water, slumped body, dead eye. (3) *The sudden shift to shock,* as in *The Birds* (1963)—the townspeople waiting in a shuttered room, the sound of the birds outside, a shutter blowing open, a boy reaching to close it, and a sudden close-up of gulls biting his hand and drawing blood. (4) *Intercutting,* as in *Strangers on a Train* (1951)—Guy hurrying to finish a tennis match, Bruno miles away hurrying to retrieve the incriminating lighter from a drain. (5) *The surprising, incongruous image* (investing the inanimate with human significance), as in *Shadow of a Doubt* (1943)—the flare of anger at a dinner table remark revealed in a cut to a knife puncturing a boiled egg, spreading the yolk like blood.

Often these montage effects involve interplay of sound and image, Hitchcock being, from the early thirties, one of the most audacious in using sound expressively: the scream in *The Thirty-nine Steps* (1935) merging with the locomotive's shriek; in *Secret Agent* (1936), the continuing high peal of an organ note heard throughout the search for a man whose body, slumped on the keyboard, is its cause; in *Sabotage,* Silvia Sidney, plotting retaliation for her brother's death, wandering into a movie house, hearing the refrain of "Who Killed Cock Robin?" and joining impulsively in the audience's laughter at the animated cartoon that it accompanies.

But in his total application of film devices, Hitchcock has made equally overt and extreme use of camera movement and angle: the surprising open-ing of *Strangers on a Train,* shot at ankle level and following the differing shoes and walks of the two protagonists; in *Rear Window* (1954), the shot held and kept at the same angle, behind James Stewart, emphasizing his helplessness in a wheelchair as Raymond Burr enters to kill him, and Stew-art's firing of his flashbulbs—his only weapon—creating a kind of artificial editing of the shot by the resulting intermittent illumination; the varied movements that merge with character and emotional situation in *The Para-dine Case* (1947), the last painfully slow and long tracking shot as Mrs. Paradine is left, doomed, in the courtroom.

The open extravagance of Hitchcock's manipulations paradoxically blends with, rather than destroys, the contrasting Realism, a kind of abstract credi-bility that he also seeks to create. To compel the immersion and empathy of the audience. To force a suspension of disbelief, no matter how extravagant the situation or treatment, by making the characters seem credible within the artificial, abstract pattern in which he places them. Hitchcock is at his best when his blend of the plausible and the outrageous is most successful, when he can render believable the figures in his complicated plot patterns—through use of underplaying, mannerism, careful psychological development of char-acter, and the personas of his actors.

This audacious blend of technique reveals a wry, sophisticated cynicism, mocking life, characters, and audiences, yet always urbanely engaging. The Hitchcock world is one that demolishes habitual patterns of good and evil, normal and abnormal, even as it titillates our own lusts and perversities. And it permits us a reaction not of moral judgment or outrage, but of cynical amusement at each new combination of human frailties. A melodrama of counterpoint arises from this rearranging of bedrock materials. The terrors, the evils, the dangers, the aberrations are approached on the oblique: humor juxtaposed with horror and suspense; menace with the ordinary, even the dully habitual; the unexpected with the expected; treatment with subject. Ordinary people are swept up in conspiracies and plottings; ordinary locales —museums and music halls, dinner parties and charity balls, statues and monuments, funerals and merry-go-rounds—become the scenes of intrigues, struggles, and terrors. In the more serious Hitchcock, the seemingly ordinary person reveals that evil is not always in the external conspiracy but within the self.

In recent years, French critics especially have worked out the ethics and metaphysics that supposedly underlie Hitchcock's entertainments—with talk of motifs of transference of guilt, confession, integration and identity, and the like, generally traced to his early Jesuit training. However far one cares to take these, there certainly are recurrences of motif and situation in his work that reveal a consistent structuring of material: Surface incongruities expose deeper incongruities, emotional and moral. And, while the surface is finally ordered by explanation of the mystery, the exposed underground is not so easily resolved; its final pattern of unity is more provocative and disturbing. In the course of Hitchcock's career, the emphasis has steadily shifted to the underground, more and more sexual, more and more bizarre in its manifestations of psychological disturbance.

From Conspiracy to the Abnormal

Often considered Hitchcock's best silent work, *The Lodger* (1926), dealing with the sexual psychopathy of Jack the Ripper, is clothed in the moodiness of German Expressionism but concerns itself very little with inner tensions. But the sound-films of the thirties and early forties that established his reputation are in the main interested more in conspiracies than abnormalities, with murders and chases that take place in ordinary surroundings, involving and implicating ordinary people. Occasional aberrations and brutalities do spice the normal run of classical, genteel adventures. In the first, and still one of the best of these, *The Man Who Knew Too Much* (1934), Peter Lorre's criminal chief provides a bizarre, fussing homosexual presence; a scene in a dentist's office carries realistic seediness to nightmare. But the big flourishes are the straight ones: the famous assassination at the Albert Hall concert, with cross-cutting of disparate elements leading to the gunshot timed to the crash of the cymbals. Humor and the commonplace are played against the conspiracies in *The Thirty-nine Steps* and *The Lady Vanishes* (1938); greater emotionality is mixed into *Sabotage* and the cynical murders of *Secret Agent; Foreign Correspondent* (1940) and *Saboteur* (1942), made early in his American career, are further extensions of the international-conspiracy pattern, the former with some of his most cleverly developed sequences, the latter with some of his most forced repetitions.

The work of the first decade of his adjustment to the Hollywood system is erratic. *Shadow of a Doubt* is the best of the attempts to break with the international-chase pattern. It is the most realistically handled and quietly developed of all his films that center on inner rather than external conflict. Into the normality of small-town life—bitingly mocked by Hitchcock—steps the hidden abnormality, Uncle Charley, who, outwardly charming, kills women for their money. Hitchcock develops the subtle confrontation of normality and abnormality with humor and modulated suspense, especially deftly in the case of the frightening but affectionate relationship of Uncle Charley and his niece, the other side of himself, also called Charley. In this period, *Spellbound* (1945) shows a forced, artificial dabbling with psychological drives (surrealistic dream décor by Dali); *Rope* (1948) stays claustrophobically within the apartment of two homosexual Leopold-and-Loeb-like killers, with the camera always on the move, and each "take" a whole reel, or 10 minutes long. The technique does convey the relentless pressure of the psychological trap, but Hitchcock is forced into many awkward and dead moments by the commitment to long, continuous shots.

Strangers on a Train, which marks a reconsolidation on Hitchcock's part, is a glittering, acidly witty exposure of the common ground of abnormality that links its psychopathic killer—again with homosexual touches—and its normal nice-guy. The film is full of camera and sound flourishes (fittingly

Strangers on a Train

climaxed by a showdown on a merry-go-round gone mad) that are kept in expert balance with the film's cruel wit—of dialogue, of stance toward the material, of ruthless exposure of the "nice" people who surround the mad killer, fascinatingly played by Robert Walker. In *Rear Window* (1954), the exposure of the grotesque personalities who masquerade as the normal tenants of an apartment house has a slicker, genteel tone—one that matches the personas of its stars, James Stewart and Grace Kelly. A caustic undercurrent, however, cuts against the glossy veneer, for the invalid photographer who does the exposing—and the camera fascinatingly holds to his point of view—exposes himself (as well as Hitchcock and the audience) as a voyeur. Thus Hitchcock toys with his preoccupation with hidden aberrations, turning it back upon itself. In *The Trouble with Harry* (1956), exposure of personality quirks usually covered by social veneer—set off by discovery of Harry's body—is given a comic treatment in one of Hitchcock's more affectionate exposures of human foibles.

North by Northwest (1959), a return to the conspiratorial chase, is clever but forced. But *Vertigo* (1958), *Psycho*, *The Birds*, and *Marnie* (1964) strike out on new, wilder terrain. All four expose the chaos beneath the surface of self-control. The first three are his most openly perverse, gothically bizarre, cinematically extravagant blendings of suspense and portrayals of emotional disturbance. They assault the audience in a manner almost surrealistic and not unlike Antonin Artaud's prescription for a theater of extreme emotion and violence that would purge the emotions of the audience. Playfully terrifying while dealing with extreme states of feeling, Hitchcock makes the spectator aware of the ties between his own life and irrationality and chaos. Yet, unlike the radical excursions of Surrealism, these films also have a disciplined form, a matter-of-fact plausibility, an incongruous, harmonizing neatness—

chaos in neat packages, the Hitchcock blend of the plausible, the normal, and the outrageous.

In *Vertigo,* the key is the literal dizziness—with shots down stairwells, steep San Francisco streets, towers—that Hitchcock induces in the spectator to match that of the protagonist (Stewart). This shared perspective strengthens identification with this private detective as he tries to untangle an elaborate mystery and is swept into passion, betrayed, and delivered to obsession and guilt. As he loses control of his inner life, the physical dizziness becomes the external form of inner chaos. Thinking that a woman he had fallen in love with has been killed—in part through his own vertigo—he becomes obsessed with investing another woman, who looks like her (both are Kim Novak), with her identity. Possessed by his seeming delusion, he makes her change the details of her appearance and, in an eerie, sexual, green light, kisses her, while the camera makes a full circle around them relentlessly, haltingly. When he discovers that the two women *are* one and that he has been used in the killing of another, he forces her to an accidental, but punitive, death and is left standing, maddened, at the top of the vertigo-inducing tower of his unfathomed needs.

In *Psycho,* the shocks are primed and detonated with precision and gusto: the lonely motel and the stabbing, the gothic mansion, its mummy, and the final transvestite merging of the young man with his dead mother's image. At the start, the unusual structure shapes identification with the seeming protagonist, the ''normal'' victim (Janet Leigh); yet there is something troubling about her thievery, her cold, unsatisfying love scene. Before we can understand her, she is killed. Our empathy shifts to the pursuers, but also to the shy young motelkeeper (Tony Perkins). Moreover, we have watched the love scene, we have peeked at her, as he has, in the shower. When the plot twists expose his tormented wildness, the thrills released and the horrors imaged produce a disturbing resonance in the viewer.

In *The Birds,* the movement is slower as Hitchcock builds our empathy with the life and frictions of the small town before releasing the terror that even the smallest of creatures can evoke. Again manipulating our identification with the characters, he forces into consciousness our own fear of all that breaks the pattern of controlled expectation, of something threatening in life even beyond the inner anarchy of man.

In *Marnie,* that anarchy is largely repressed, although it smolders and occasionally slips to the surface. Here the treatment is more realistic and expository in a more conventional suspense melodrama about the same subjects. Its terms of tension are calmer, its occasional moments of shock somewhat forced. Its final explanation is weak and reductive. (A sexual assault and killing at the root of Marnie's self-destructiveness are acted out in flashback.) *Marnie* is at its best in its slow unraveling of the defenses and disguises of the cool woman who is driven to steal and lie. The film suggests, too, something irrational and driven under the surface of the man who marries her to help her, but it fails to develop that complexity.

Commercial neatness battled with buried complexities in *Marnie*; in several subsequent productions, it won out. But in 1972, with *Frenzy*, Hitchcock returned to England and returned also, with undiminished verve and wit, to mocking the illusory surface neatness of the conventions of society as well as of the commercial film, even as he deployed them masterfully.

JOHN FORD: REALISTIC EPIC

No two temperaments or attitudes, or resulting styles, could be more different than those of Alfred Hitchcock and John Ford, yet their careers trace a similar pattern: work through many decades from the silent film on, consolidation and unique development of a commercial genre, stylistic integrity within the commercial-studio system, growing and deepening of statement and style through the passing years. Ford's chief form has been the epic—mainly but not only in the Western genre. His chief contribution has been the development of a realistic epic style, adding the epic poetry of myth to Realism. His approach gives a base of credibility and character to the expressive sweep and celebration of the epic form, more sophisticated and complex than in Griffith, more dramatic and human than in Eisenstein. This interpretation of his work must, of course, be an oversimplification of the career of a man who made more than 100 features of many types and subjects over more than half a century—one of his best, *Cheyenne Autumn*, when he was 69.

In most of these—certainly in the best of them—there is an underlying attitude of genuine sympathy and respect, of praise for what he admires. This holds true even for the best of his comedies—in the lusty Irishness of *The Quiet Man* (1952), the small-town goodness of *Steamboat 'Round the Bend* (1935) and *The Sun Shines Bright* (1953). To a point, Ford can admit and show flaws, weaknesses, and limitations; but he insists on seeing and finding a form to show the exceptional in the flawed commonplace. He is at his best in mining the lyrical gold in defeat.

In two critical successes early in the major phase of his career, Ford sought to poeticize Social Realist materials, to elevate them to epic stature—in *The Informer* (1935) and, in a manner more integral and less artificial, in *The Grapes of Wrath* (1940). *The Informer*—the seventh of fourteen collaborations with screenwriter Dudley Nichols—has a tightly organized cause-and-effect dramatic structure of the traditional Realist type. Gypo Nolan's desperate desires lead him to inform, and his informing in turn leads the organization (in the Irish rebellion) to seek the informer, who, then, makes a further sequence of mistakes. Both lines of action lead to his trial, escape, and murder. The heightened dialogue and posturing, the artful compositions, the repeated symbolic motifs—the travel poster, the "Wanted" poster, the drinking, the echoing cane of the blind man—sometimes effect the desired eloquence, often intrude on the emotion and meaning that the action itself can engender. Typically, in a last scene, the dying Gypo enters the church, where he finds the mother of the rebel slain as a result of his informing. When he asks her forgiveness, the mood is strikingly captured: Gypo, seen from behind, his drab bulk filling the empty, shadowed church. But when he gets her forgiveness, the natural eloquence of the scene is marred by an attempt to elevate: a cut to a shot from above and behind the altar, Gypo in an artificially focused cone of light from a window, his arms out to the side like the Christ's, looking up to heaven and crying, while the operatic music gushes, "Frankie, Frankie, your mother forgives me!" In contrast, the trial scene is full of excellent camera angles and shadows, the dialogue natural, partially improvised. And the human dilemmas shine through.

In *The Grapes of Wrath*—scripted by Nunnally Johnson, from the John Steinbeck novel—Ford finds a form for eloquence, despite the pseudoelegance of some of the dialogue, the forced uplift that distorts the harsh condemnation in the novel. With photographer Gregg Toland, he begins to evolve here a pictorial form that gives to the naturalistic starkness an aptness of selected detail and a heightening poetry of quiet but artfully careful compositions, movement, and editing in a blend of Realism and expressive idealization. The Joads' old truck, moving through empty and impassive plains, becomes one of many of Ford's hauntingly right evocations of man against the vastness of natural and social forces, man dark against the lighter space and shapes of prairies, skies, mountains and cliffs, man small and dwarfed yet dignified in the eloquence of the compositions. In the night scenes of threat and intimidation, the shadows are excellently used, though never intrusive. The dance at the migrant workers' camp is brightly lit but surrounded by darkness—out of which come the troublemakers, and into which Tom Joad must flee. The camp itself is too perfect, too neat an answer —like so many of the thirties' solutions—to the social problems. But the bright release of the dance is the first of many similar oases in Ford's work, appropriately light and free in the midst of darker pressures. In *My Darling Clementine* (1946), for example, the troubled lonely lawman Wyatt Earp (Henry Fonda) is seen in isolated profile along the storefronts of the emptied town streets, then led by the woman he is falling in love with to the outdoor dance. The camera moves with them as they arrive, then as they dance, the sky bright behind them—Earp first hesitant, then exuberant for all his awkwardness.

In his three films of 1939, Ford had found the best subject for his eloquence—the past. In their situations and traditions, his characters can be given the simplicity and the pure essence of the epic, yet develop more realistically. In *Stagecoach*, he humanizes the Western, giving it humor, reducing it to its essential purity of form (though not without jars of contrivance). In *Drums along the Mohawk*, he uses the terrain, costumes, and details of American history to project a resonant feel of place. In *Young Mr. Lincoln*, he evokes a restrained, yet still idealized version of the legendary dignity of Lincoln, though not without a sentimentality that was always to threaten his work. In many ways, his conception of Lincoln becomes the archetype for the character of many of his mythic heroes. In 1943, Ford approached the dying traditions of a Welsh mining community, in *How Green Was My Valley,* with the same sense of enlargement of a luminous, lost past, again not unmarred by a sentimentality that evades some of the harsher areas of the subject—in this case, the underlying economic issues.

The Old West: Nostalgia

In Ford's most important postwar films, America's Old West becomes his most fertile ground for blending Realism and epic stylization. Though admiring and nostalgic, and dogmatically old fashioned, his point of view develops interesting variations in the balance of glory and defeat, especially in his later films. In *My Darling Clementine,* the planting of a civilization in the wilderness is turned into romantic legend, with its own sense of loss, epitomized in the life of the lawman—solitary and short. Its simplification of its personae—Wyatt Earp, Doc Holliday—into sentimental myth is, however, done with a vivid exactness, and the mood evoked carries a greater sense of truth than the characterizations might otherwise warrant: a slain man lying in mud and rain, photographed past the black brims of his brothers' hats; the flimsy beginnings of the town against the empty prairies and skies; Earp alone in the town street; the airiness of the town dance at the site of the just-begun church. Camera angles and editing intensify the rhythm of the dramatic structure (as does one of Ford's many uses of folk song on the sound track): the camera behind Earp for Holliday's long first walk toward him across the barroom, cutting to a close-up just as Holliday knocks off a gambler's hat; Earp and the new schoolteacher always in bashful two-shot when together; the growing closeness of Earp and Holliday standing at a bar, first in medium shots, then in two-shots, then in alternating close-ups as they defend the harassed Shakespearean actor from the Clantons; at the end, Earp riding off to tell his father of the death of his brothers, seen first from the position of the schoolteacher, then both characters in long shot against the prairie from the position of the town he has helped build.

The movement of masses of men through the prairies provides the tempo and visual motif of Ford's cavalry trilogy, which again deals with bringing civilization at the price of death, but with a fuller range of characterization and motivation than in *Clementine. Fort Apache* (1948) interestingly pits legend against fact: After showing the weaknesses that led the arrogant colonel (Fonda) to lead his men into a massacre, Ford defends the newspaper legends (even the survivors help create them) that arise after it as valuable to a larger cause. Typical of Ford's use of groups in movement are the grand march at the fort (stately, formal, shot in disciplined lines, a part of the army and the society it is bringing) and the buildup of the heroism of the troops in an Eisenstein-like montage: the lines of the cavalry, heroic close-ups from below of leaders on horseback; repetition of key shots in the sequence as they prepare for an Indian attack; alternation of half a dozen different shots of Indians rushing the stationary cavalry line, then alternation of the Indians with the cavalry line; finally a shot from close behind

John Wayne at the center of the troops as the Indians close in. In *She Wore a Yellow Ribbon* (1949), Ford models his colors and movements on the mythmaking works of Frederick Remington, early painter of the Western scene, and poses abstract public patterns against the troubled emotions of an aging officer (Wayne) facing an imposed retirement. In *Rio Grande* (1950), the disintegration of a family in the battles of the Civil War is balanced against the necessary battles of consolidation against the Apaches and the final reuniting of an officer with his wife and son.

Wagonmaster (1950) marks the high point in Ford's nostalgic belief in the nobility of the pioneer spirit of the West. It is a more serious and a larger-scaled version of *Stagecoach:* a group of diverse people interacting, revealing the best, and some of the worst, within themselves as they face and surmount the travails of a trek westward.

**The
Old
West:
A
New
Look**

Wayne's cavalry captain in *Rio Grande* had had traces of more intense and complex inner disturbance, but this was lost within the conventional patterns of purification through righteous battle. When, after six years, Ford made his next Western—*The Searchers* (1956)—the traces had become a fuller reconsideration of the nature of heroic action. From this point on, Ford's major Westerns—excluding the routine *The Horse Soldiers* (1959) and *Two Rode Together* (1961)—have a new inner tension, a deepening, elegiac tone. They make a thoughtful and subdued reappraisal of the myth of the West.

In *The Searchers,* passages of old-fashioned derring-do and conventional patterns of moralism and heroism are played against an ironic ambivalence, but the two thrusts do not fuse. The central paradox is more suggested than fulfilled. Even the touches of comedy sometimes sharpen the irony, sometimes dissipate it. The ambivalence centers on John Wayne's hero and his act of righteous revenge. Wayne's Ethan is a loner who arrives, the war over, still wearing his Confederate cloak and sword, too driven and too obstinate to have roots in home and community, or even love. What Ford has always admired in the individualist of the West is here seen for the first time with its warts showing. And so is Ethan's long and courageous enterprise to revenge a seemingly gratuitous Indian slaughter of his brother's family and abduction of his niece. At the close, it is not Ethan who finds the girl and kills the Indian leader. Ethan's fury over the murder of his brother's wife is tangled with the pain of a love lost between them, a loss to which he himself contributed. Ethan's righteousness is obsessive, tinged with deeper needs than he can fathom. He goes on longer and further in his revenge than the community can comprehend or condone. In some of the action, Ford loses the tension of the contradictions of principle, but a number of touches delineate its ragged edges. For example, Ethan destroys a white gang that could have been dealt with without killing. He slaughters buffalo to starve the Indians—any Indians—in the vicinity. But this act is counterpointed with the brutal massacre of an innocent Indian village by cavalry troops acting for the society that has ostensibly turned away from Ethan's extremism. Thus,

The Searchers

righteousness carried to violence is finally found in all—Ethan, American society, the Indians—and even the opening massacre takes on a different meaning within this more complex perspective. When Ethan learns that his niece has accepted cohabitation with the red man, he considers killing her, and, in another demonstration of the identity of his vengefulness and the needs and desires of the community, Laurie Jorgenson, standing in her white bridal gown, urges him to yield to his impulse.

The resolutions, however, soften the strong theme. Blood wins out, and Ethan takes his niece in his arms; whiteness wins out and she returns to the bosom of the community. All are reconciled except Ethan, who walks away into the wilderness and is last seen framed in the open door of the house he cannot come home to. He is Ford's most troubled and troubling character; neither society nor Ford know quite what to think of him or do with him.

Although less complex, *Sgt. Rutledge* (1960) also takes a new look at old materials. This time the dignity and troubling alienation of the inner-directed individual are brought to focus in the tragically proud Black cavalryman (Woody Strode) and the young lieutenant who defends him against false charges of rape and murder. The pattern has shifted, but the treatment does not probe deeply. It remained for *The Man Who Shot Liberty Valance* (1962) and *Cheyenne Autumn* (1964) to carry Ford's reappraisal of the myths of the West to its fullest expression.

Liberty Valance is comic but rueful, and it is not quite clear what its bittersweet lament—or the mixture of feelings that propel it and result from it—is actually bitter about. It is a reprise of much of the earlier legendary material, appropriately in a flashback narrated by Tom Stoddard (Jimmy Stewart). Now a senator, Stoddard has returned to Shinbone for the funeral of Doniphon (John Wayne). He and the town have succeeded with society by law, yet the town is still the same mixed bag of human goods it was. In the flashbacks, Stoddard's legalism and the primitive self-serving legalism of the town and state ratification convention are consistently satirized. In the flashback, the law (Andy Devine is the stomach-stuffing, skin-saving sheriff) has not been able to cope with the bullying evil of Liberty Valance. The ineffectual Stoddard is finally driven to shoot it out with Valance, but it is Doniphon who kills Valance. Doniphon lets Stoddard take the credit (and the girl), creating a legend on the basis of which Stoddard has risen to political power. Doniphon (a softened Ethan) had never found a place in the town, save that of town character, and died an unrespected relic. Stoddard, sensing something lost, finally tells the truth, but only privately. As Stoddard and his wife cross the prairies, they see from their train window that even the landscape has been tamed. But it is too late to do anything about it, as it is too late for the rekindled love for Doniphon that the wife feels. Change has come—whether progressively or not is open to question. "When the legend becomes fact," says the newspaper editor, "print the legend."

The reexamination of what it means to print (or in Ford's case, film) the legend is complex, possibly more so than Ford intended. For on the surface, he does undercut the legendary West, its heroes and the brand of civilization brought to it. The legend proved useful, but was not without drawbacks nor without loss—of something rugged and fascinatingly unmanageable in the primitive spirit of the plains. Yet, at the same time, Ford also resurrects the original heroic Wayne—the individualist, the man whose clear values and manly skill and action do the job, but who has no place in the messy mixture that is society. His time had passed; but might it not be only legend that it had ever existed?

Almost as if to make amends for earlier reductiveness in the treatment of Indians, the dispossession and destruction of something wildly noble that did indeed exist is given the dimensions and tone of epic tragedy in *Cheyenne Autumn*, Ford's last Western and the longest of his films. In it, he records the experiences of a group of Cheyenne making an 1,800-mile trek from the prison of their barren reservation to their old homelands in Colorado. He captures the impact of the impossible physical test, savors the feel of nature and the land (with some of his most magnificent shots of man in the wilderness), even as that same nature contributes to Cheyenne misery. Contrasted with their pilgrimage are the bureaucracy and callousness of the government, the viciousness of settlers they encounter, the false, drunken courage of the now civilized towns. Halfway through the film, the sequence in Dodge City makes a satiric counterpoint to the dignity of the trek, horses banging around in the genteel furnishings of the new homes, drunken new Westerners out to pick up a scalp but quickly frightened off.

Central to the whole, tragically pitted against each other, are the Indians and the pursuing cavalry, both on the land, both doing—with a mixture of motives and personalities—what they have to. Many sequences parallel their experiences in similar shots that nonetheless capture the differences: In the winter snow, the Indians form a black diagonal line, the color punctuated by an occasional white horse and by their colored blankets, the neatness of the line broken by men trudging wearily on foot; in the same snow, the cavalry form an unbroken diagonal line of black, all cloaked uniformly, all riding relentlessly forward. The film is a last long elegy of the Indian and the indefinable purity that Ford associated with the untamed land and the ways of natural men upon it. Ironically, the film suffered more studio interference than did most of his films (especially any he felt strongly about)—in cast selection, in editing and cutting, and in musical score (a particularly blatant one being inserted by the studio).

Still, it remains a fitting autumnal recapitulation of the kind of personally felt work—stylized yet realistic—that Ford could achieve within the commercial-studio structure. For all of its simplifications, it is a body of work in which (as Orson Welles has remarked) "you feel that the movie has lived and breathed in a real world. . . . He has told the American saga in human terms and made it come alive."

CHAPTER FOURTEEN

Welles
and
Renoir–
The
Personal
Vision
and
Voice

Appearing at the end of the first decade of sound, neither Jean Renoir's *The Rules of the Game* (1939) nor Orson Welles's *Citizen Kane* (1941) fit into or achieved success in the commercial production and distribution system of the period. Yet both not only recapitulated the progress of film technique to that point but prefigured and influenced the paths of its development in subsequent decades. The fifteenth film of Renoir and the first of Welles, the two works illustrate the comparable but differing ways in which Renoir and Welles forged an independent path and personal style to match their visions. The inclination of the Realist style is to let the world on film happen before our eyes, and Renoir pushed that inclination further and with more purity than conventionalized patterns of editing and emphasis usually allowed. Welles freed those patterns to produce a subjective stylization that built upon the Realist base.

Each film reveals its director's use of deep focus (in which back- and foreground may be in simultaneous focus), the long take, and a balancing of the visual openness to the flow of the scene of the single shot and the richness and impact of complex editing. Yet their differences also emerge—Welles's shots and editing being more obtrusive and flamboyant, a stylization of reality; Renoir's, a refinement of the concept of the transparent screen with its aim of conveying the free flow of the reality—yet never without a shaping form.

Well within the Realist tradition, Renoir uses deep focus to develop dramatic scenes without interruption and fragmentation. Welles does, too, but in a more expressively stylized way. In *Citizen Kane*, he employs cinematographer Gregg Toland's advances with deep-focus photography for baroque, ornamental heightening. (William Wyler had employed Toland's techniques for realistic dramatic purposes similar to those of Renoir and his cinematographers, including his nephew Pierre Renoir.) In addition, *Kane*'s stylistic bravado impressively incorporates a host of expressive techniques that were not to be used by others for basically realistic material for many years: intricate plot and time structure; overt visual and aural symbolism; elaborate montage sequences; striking camera angles and relationships of foreground and background; obtrusive but lyrical camera movement; abrupt cutting and transitions; stunning contrasts of stillness and violence, of light and shadow; complex interaction of sound and image; expressive use of natural sound; and Expressionist exaggeration, condensation, and distortion.

WELLES

While Welles's technical bravura seems a likely extension of his obsessive showmanship and idiosyncratic independence, it is nonetheless (in *Kane*, as in his later films) an appropriate vehicle for his dramatic materials and the significance he draws from them. The world of his typical dramatic materials is a bizarre one of paradox and complication, beset by time and change, corrupted by the contradictory and obsessive drives of men who want and seek too much—men much like himself. It is a world of excess and a world artificially abstracted by Welles into paradigm. While a world of moral complexity, it is coldly so; though the autocratic insistence of Welles's style gives that world its unique and peculiar tone, it does compound the coldness, the sense of manipulation and objectification, of obsession. Welles and his style deny easy judgment of his characters, even the most villainous, but they also seem to deny the warmth of sympathetic response, the kind of breathing humanity that Welles himself admired in Ford's work, that Renoir let flow in his.

Citizen Kane For some, *Kane* was the high point in Welles's career. It is less debatable and more meaningful to say that while it combined elements in a way not duplicated in Welles's later work, many other and separate elements in these works might surpass the achievements in *Kane*. Most particularly, it provided, for all its surface intricacy, a tightly organized, tidy, workmanlike script, based solidly on well-known and volatile personal and social realities; against it, Welles could display his mercurial flamboyance. For its solid topicalities had an extremity and satirical bite that made his exuberant theatrical approach appropriate.

The script was the work of Herman J. Mankiewicz, one of the earliest of the long-time pros in Hollywood writers' departments. A former newspaperman personally acquainted with William Randolph Hearst (the putative subject of *Kane*), he was temperamentally and creatively disposed to mine from Hearst's life its choicest materials for waspish satirical barbs. Earlier, Mankiewicz's best work had been in fast-talking, cynically witty thirties' comedy—some originals, some adaptations of Broadway successes, and some behind-the-scenes play-doctoring and supervising (as with several Marx Brothers comedies). Later, his only successes were in syrupy commercial products, strangely sentimental, such as *The Pride of the Yankees* (1942) and *The Enchanted Cottage* (1944). It is not enough to say that Welles provided him with the opportunity to do his true work. (A never produced later exposé of Aimée Semple McPherson, for example, shows little of the amazing verve and aptness of the touches in *Kane*.) Rather, it was the interaction with Welles (and with John Houseman) and, most importantly, with what Welles did with the basically realistic original materials that wrought the unique excellences of the film, took it far beyond anything Mankiewicz had done or was to do.

Despite the many masterful jobs of cinematography turned in by Toland in his career, he too found Welles's arrival in Hollywood, with the unprecedented free hand allowed him by RKO's George Schaeffer, an opportunity for unique accomplishment. Earlier he had dabbled once, somewhat erratically, with German Expressionist approaches in an unusual and flawed film, *Mad*

Love (1935), directed by Karl Freund, who had been the cinematographer on *The Cabinet of Dr. Caligari* (on which *Mad Love* was based) and other German films of the twenties. But working with Welles, Toland brought the expertise and suggestions that spurred Welles's imagination and his own to regenerate the static, derivative moodiness of the devices into witty flourishes, foreshadowing the lighter, defter expressiveness of later decades. The result was an approach and a style that were to shape Welles's later materials and his treatment of them—the baroque, magnified ornamentation of plot, character, acting, and visual devices.

Paradoxically, and typically for Welles, the free hand proved not so free. There were overwhelmingly laudatory reviews; but legal threats, pressure, and attempted intimidation by the Hearst press, and manipulation by frightened studio bosses restricted the film's distribution and set in motion the industry's distrust of Welles that was to give his subsequent career its strangely hobbled and harassed independence, a perpetual precariousness and undermining to which he too contributed—seemed, indeed, to need. But with the passage of time, it is not the literal and daring exposé of the powerful Hearst that continues to give the film its excitement. It survives the loss of its topicality—thrives on it—as it survives its simplistic Freudianism (the single, traumatic childhood episode), a favorite from *The Public Enemy* on, and its plot device—still favored—of the newspaperman investigating the mystery of a dead man's life. And it does so because its treatment of these conventions surmounts them. The childhood, briefly glimpsed, is patterned in masterful shots that leave echoes of truth beyond their plot specifics: in deep-focus shot, the boy in the distance through a closed window, playing with his sled in the snow while his parents and a lawyer settle on the plans to send East the newly wealthy "poor little rich boy" (as John Dos Passos titled his vignette on Hearst in *USA*); the boy then angrily hitting the lawyer with his sled when the adults come outside to tell him; then, disconsolate between the lawyer and mother, behind him his father powerless to prevent his uprooting; finally, the boy alone with his sled in the snow, as he will be alone all his life. The revelation of the facile central "Rosebud" mystery (the name of Kane's lost sled) is at least partially saved by its treatment, deepened by the composition of the shot in which it is shown: the sled being destroyed, burning furiously and brightly, in a deep, surrounding darkness, isolated like all the lost, wasted, futile *things* of Kane's life, seen in previous shots, piled endlessly in the cavernous, warehouselike rooms of his palatial home, Xanadu. An effort to make Rosebud less than the whole answer, suggested by a line of dialogue (to the effect that it is only one piece of the puzzle), is dramatized by the last shots, reprising in reverse the camera's first entrance into Xanadu, following the dark smoke up into the heavy clouds, pulling back outside the heavy fence and the "No Trespassing" sign that the film has violated but gives the final word to. It is a suggestion of ambiguity that the film only sporadically maintains, yet it shows a direction in the treatment of character that later films would capitalize on more fully.

Kane's structure breaks the mold of conventional narrative progression (multiple flashbacks had been used earlier but not with such vigor) in a way that was to open new directions in the manipulation of time and permit a new economy of narrative and emphasis on dramatic highlights, without the need for low-intensity expository scenes; most of all, it allowed the innovative visual and aural transitions that are among the film's most impressive effects. It does not, however, carry out fully the implications of subjective narrative viewpoint that it suggests. While there is some slight overlapping of time periods, in the main the flashback of each of the five narrators deals with a part of the story that follows chronologically that dealt with by the preceding narrator. While each flashback does emphasize the aspect of Kane's life related to the narrator's role in it, the episodes are taken at objective, face value and do not stress the character and subjective biases of the narrators.

What *are* carried to fulfillment are the opportunities for obtrusively expressive technique that the structure provides: the lawyer, Thatcher, saying a cold "Merry Christmas" to the boy Kane and finishing with a colder "Happy New Year" 25 years later in a letter he is dictating; the photograph of the *Chronicle* staff dissolving to them sitting for a new photograph six years later, when Kane's *Enquirer* has bought them en masse; the collapse of Kane's marriage in the elliptical diminution of breakfast-table conversation between Kane and his wife, depicted through the years as if in a single conversation, with alternating separate shots and dialogue statements of the two, finally cutting to a side shot of the two across a wide, silent expanse of table, conversation and love at an end; Kane applauding when Susan Alexander first sings to him in her apartment, merging into sporadic clapping at his first political rally (foreshadowing the disastrous impact of their affair on his later political campaign), his normal voice then merging into his voice blaring from a loudspeaker as the scene shifts to the crowd and a giant photo of Kane at a rally; the two montages of Susan's operatic career, with shots of painful confusion and ineptness building to a climax of flashing shots that capture her fear, and a final shot of a spotlight, the filament fading as her inadequate voice peters out; the delayed juxtaposition of the disturbing scream of a woman at a Xanadu beach party and the screech of a parakeet, the first while Kane argues with Susan, the latter at her final departure in a later scene.

But it is especially the harmonizing of these mosaics of editing with the patterns and lighting of long-held, deep-focus single shots that marks the film's style. Earlier, the single shots are basically realistic, though heightening: Kane, in middle distance, exposing the shallowness of his principles at the party for the *Chronicle* men, the reporters at the table that stretches into the distance, the troubled Jed Leland and Bernstein (Kane's closest colleagues and friends) in the foreground, the whole framed by two transparent ice sculptures seemingly laughing in mockery. Later, at Xanadu, as Kane's need for ownership of people and things gets more disastrously obsessive,

Citizen Kane

the compositions have more gothic, Expressionist import: past the balding, pasty face of the aging Kane, framed as though protruding from the back of a carved chair, past his giant fireplace and a statue of a nude male at Kane's end, to Susan across the vast room, working a crossword puzzle, Kane's voice echoing; Kane in a dark suit, the only blemish on the whiteness of Susan's room as she prepares to leave him; then a shot past Kane, shadowy, as Susan stands in the light and then walks out, the shot held, through a series of doors, then juxtaposed immediately with her in the darkness of a roadhouse, her escape not liberating after all; Kane and the camera careening around Susan's room as he tears it apart, the mad frenzy magnified by being shot from below; Kane shot from the side as he walks alone in a hall of mirrors, endlessly reflected on himself, the last imprisonment of the driven ego.

The Magnificent Ambersons Despite controversy over *Kane,* it was finished and left in the edited form desired by Welles; partly as a result of *Kane,* however, Welles's next film, *The Magnificent Ambersons* (1942), was extensively cut and reedited by the studio (RKO). Certain omissions are obvious, such as some details of the industrialization of the town to counterpoint the decline of the older way of life represented by the Ambersons (footage Welles had shot). But the material is again mainly developed in a series of separate vignettes arcing through

**The Magnificent
Ambersons**

the passage of time (this time not so intricately interlaced as in *Kane* but held together by an interpretive voice-over narration by Welles). The impact of the separate sequences is still powerful, their implications still clear.

Still echoing the social orientation of films of the thirties, and the success with social context in *Kane*, *Ambersons* again places its characters in the full social context that they represent. For the last time in Welles's films, the traits and significance of characters are grounded in carefully selected and reconstructed details of social reality; in subsequent films, there is a movement toward greater abstraction, the implications of the characters arising from artificial, fantastic, or literary material, elliptical and generalized environments.

In fact, there is more emphasis on the social context in *Ambersons* than in *Kane* and less probing of the psyche. As a consequence, though the techniques are still striking—heavy contrasts of shadow and light, much deep-focus composition, long-held takes, overlapping and elliptical speech—they are kept more naturalistic. They reflect mood, true to the tone of the Booth Tarkington novel, rather than reveal and project the inner life through subjective distortions. The tone is generally more mellow, nostalgic about a bygone way of life; encounters between characters are held for strikingly long times, and overlapping dissolves capture the slow flow of memory. The arrogant, destructive George Minafer (Tim Holt) is revealed as much in scenes with little dramatic action as in the major plot events: the details of his personal manner, down to the way he eats a cake during an encounter with his aunt; his talk, against a sequence of vivid details of the town, as he and his girl Lucy pass through the streets.

The Lady from Shanghai

In the next several years, two studio projects—*Journey into Fear* (1943), which Welles haphazardly produced and dabbled in, and *The Stranger* (1946), which he desultorily directed—displayed minor Wellesian touches. But in 1948 he turned a routine studio assignment, *The Lady from Shanghai* (a suspense tale that he suggested, he claims, without reading it), into a bravura allegory, full of visual excitement and moral metaphor. Ten years later, in *Touch of Evil,* he was to do the same—playing against the melodramatic plots and types with lush techniques that amplified the materials to larger-than-life, abstracted truths. In both, the key Welles theme of driven, destructive overreaching is developed; in both, the ambience of a corrupt, chaotic, fragmenting world is given gothically potent visual form.

In *The Lady from Shanghai,* Welles, as O'Hara, surprisingly, is an innocent —duped, threatened, finally extricating himself from the ruins. Everett Sloane, one of the last of Welles's Mercury Theater group to appear in a Welles production, is the lawyer Bannister, twisting justice to his own murderous purposes. The beautiful lure is Rita Hayworth (then Welles's wife),

The Lady from Shanghai

unable to break with her own corruption despite her spasmodic impulses to do so. The maze of deceit is set bizarrely against a variety of backgrounds, which produces a meaningful cumulative imagery: the looming, giant tanks of fish in an aquarium, bright behind the lovers as they talk, a metaphor of the human trap that thwarts them; the exotic confusions of a Chinese theater, the mocking grotesqueries of a fun house, the splintering chaos of the desperate shootout in a hall of mirrors—all in fireworks displays of images and editing, camera angles and lighting. In the satirical courtroom sequence, the angles and editing maintain an intense and witty interplay between characters that mocks the pretense at justice of the proceedings. Using setups that shoot past one character to others and to telling details, Welles returns in rhythmic patterns to the same previously established setups or holds a vivid angle through movement of both camera and actors: In one long-held shot, a close-up of Bannister's face gets larger as he walks toward the camera; when he turns, he is in profile and the camera moves with him as he passes behind the close-up broad neck of the district attorney; when the D.A. surprises Bannister by calling Mrs. Bannister to the witness stand, Bannister turns suddenly in surprise, his face close to the camera, Mrs. Bannister now seen past the face.

Touch of Evil   Justice turned grotesque in a world of the grotesque is again the theme drawn from the mystery plot of *Touch of Evil,* with Welles as the bloated cop Quinlan, driven to violation, but only one among many violators. From the petty, confusing plot materials, Welles draws a nightmare vision of decay and menace—as in his rapid cutting mixed with the flashing illumination from a neon sign at the scene of murder in a shabby hotel room. Yet it is a nightmare not without sympathy for its moral grotesques—the overstuffed ugliness of the brothel still a haven for lost hopes and kept illusions. Quinlan himself is pitiable, trapped—his last confession confusingly split between his own speaking and the pickup of his voice on a police radio, the paraphernalia of a construction site looming in disorder, oil pumps relentlessly driving on, filthy water thick in the murky shadows.

The Shakespeare Productions   In some ways, these two big-studio productions (*The Lady* and *Evil*) resulted in a greater unity of effect than the independent productions that Welles worked on through the years, the latter affected by economic problems that marred them technically and by Welles's own idiosyncrasies and compulsion to spread his talents too widely over too many trivial projects of others.

Welles's Shakespeare productions are free adaptations in which he used the literary materials for his own purposes. *Macbeth* (1948) was made rapidly (in 23 days) and reflects its production pressures. Yet, with Welles's conception of his characters as barbarians, rough, ragged-edged, driven in a misty, shadowed, primitive universe, the raggedness of the production details contributes a cumulative power; even Welles's own strangely mumbled, ferociously lunging, and jagged performance as Macbeth is both almost ludicrous, almost amazing. His *Othello* (1952) was made intermittently over a four-year period, with resulting gaps, lapses, and looseness, faulty dubbing, distracting shots to cover the gaps. Yet parts of it may be the most deeply felt and realized visually of all his films—stylized in composition and lighting, and in performance; magnified almost to excess; idiosyncratic and poetic. Its unique Wellesian conception is of a complicity in obsessiveness (part zeal, part compulsion), Iago and Othello sensing their membership in the brotherhood of the somehow powerless powerful, the brotherhood that links most of Welles's central figures.

In his *Falstaff* (or *Chimes at Midnight*, 1967), a reworking of materials from several of Shakespeare's plays, the mood is more mellow, elegiac. This time, the power whose extremity betrays is the power of naive goodness itself, a joyousness of life that cannot adapt and is left behind, must die out, yet even in its losses casts new light on the actions of public men of power. It is a lyrical film, quiet in its editing, full of faces, silhouettes against setting used as pattern, abstracted from the details of place, though with contrasting moments such as the battle scene fought in the mud, the mud-covered soldiers elephantine and inhuman, the music a cold counterpoint of defeat and death.

Mr. Arkadin and The Trial

In *Mr. Arkadin* (or *Confidential Report*, 1955), Welles attempted an original and monumental version of the mystery man of overreaching power. But here the abstraction seems too great, too solemnly portentous, without the saving touch of wit or disciplining counterpoint of contrasting materials. Welles's intention to embody the mystery of the legendary Arkadin in a framework of intricate flashbacks was frustrated by studio interference, but it is unlikely that it would have altered the basic hollowness of the allegory.

The case of *The Trial* (1963) is more complex. Both in response to the problems of shoestring production and out of his basic conception of Kafka's allegory, Welles filmed the tale of Joseph K. (played by Tony Perkins) in a variety of styles: the matter-of-fact detailing of the bizarre in the manner of Kafka himself (as in the police interrogations); the raising of the possible to the grotesque through angle, patterning, and lighting contrasts (as in the light-slanted attack by the children in the attic); Expressionist abstracting (as in the mechanized mass of workers in the huge office or the figures posed as statues in the field); the macabre black humor of gag and vignette (as in Tony Perkins's conversation about free will with the old woman who, for reasons inexplicable but blandly accepted, is dragging a mysterious trunk across a field to a bus stop); the final allegorical story and montage, which, though forced, do bring to a climax Welles's intent to build toward greater and greater abstraction through the course of the movie.

RENOIR

The later films of Jean Renoir, especially those of the fifties, showed in Renoir, too, a tendency toward greater abstraction, toward greater ornamentation and stylization. Yet even his theatrical allegories of the fifties maintain the strong touch of commonplace sensory reality, the tactile and emotional Impressionism that was the chief characteristic of his earlier style. Midway in his long career, *The Rules of the Game* had struck the finest balance between these two tendencies of his filmmaking—the unobtrusive rendering of personal and social reality and the expressive artifice of wit and form. For Renoir, the director's camera should be like the valuable individual he described in a 1962 interview: "I believe in the individual if he knows how to *absorb*. [Italics added.] It's imagination that we ought to be afraid of." Still, his greatest work has reflected the alliance of a sensitive, disciplined imagination and an openness to absorb without intruding or distorting.

Early
Work

Renoir's early work—silent films in the twenties, sound in the first half of the thirties—shows a greater emphasis on the naturalistic tendency, the camera placed before a reenactment of everyday life that seems to exist beyond its function as material for the camera. It is a style that does not overconcentrate, overrefine; yet the sensitivity and sympathy of Renoir's response to the materials before his camera—the telling interplay, for example, of character and setting—bring dimensions beyond those usually associated with the flat accuracy of representationalism.

Among the works of poetic Realism of the French cinema of the thirties, Renoir's were the least forced or imposed. These films place a strong emphasis on social influences and conflicts. *Nana* (1926) and *Madame Bovary* (1934) mark the polar boundaries of this approach—the Naturalist Social Realism of Zola, the subjective, Impressionist personal Realism of Flaubert, the individual still strongly shaped both by social pressures and by the impact of natural environment. In *Madame Bovary*, the quietly vivid sense of the icy chill of the country sky darkening with rain interacts with the emotions of the characters as much as the details of social scenes such as the town fair or the opera.

Renoir began and remained open to the look, feel, and significance of the physical things, large and small, among which human beings move; but his use of setting is casual, lingering, and matter of fact, rather than pointedly symbolic. In filming both nature and man, he early developed unobtrusive, natural camera angles, long takes, deep-focus shots, and responsive rather than aggressive movements of the camera in panning and tracking. Yet, so often, these calm renderings capture mood and meaning as well as fact. In the touching shorter film *A Day in the Country* (*Une Partie de Campagne*, 1936), the camera moves quietly and steadily across a field, through trees, along a shadowed riverbank, recording natural detail, building the romantic mood that leads to the seduction of the young bourgeois girl; afterwards, a shot of the wounded hope in her eyes. The sense of spontaneous emotion evoked by the country surroundings is set against the deadening of emotionality of her world—the texture of her class caught in dialogue, actions, details of dress and mannerism. In *The Crime of Monsieur Lange* (1935), Renoir deals with the desire of a group of working-class people to create the sense and actions of solidarity. Renoir's camera follows them around a courtyard and the square of buildings that encloses it and their lives. In long takes, he sets up relationships between characters and the setting—building overall the physical sense of their interaction within a restricted world as they struggle to build a cooperative. At the climax, the camera movements become more obtrusive, but appropriately so, for they mirror the tragic acceleration in the zeal of Monsieur Lange, wildly pursuing his class enemy Batala and trying to shoot him. The chase—which prefigures several others in later works—covers two floors of the building and a staircase, all details previously used. At its climax, the camera, in a movement more mannered than was typical of Renoir at this point, continues around the courtyard, re-turning to where Lange has now shot and killed Batala, thus suggesting the ambiguous but powerful influence of the place and its inhabitants on Lange's act.

Somber as are the dénouements of most of these films, they are never without their balancing touch of humor—a humor that plays a more central role in the affirmations of individual freedom and joy in life of *Boudu Saved from Drowning* (1932). In an exposition of one of the themes central to Renoir's work, the irrepressible naturalness of the shaggy dog of a man, Boudu (Michel Simon), grapples with and survives an encounter with middle-class life, which though limiting, is not depicted as obliterating human feeling in its members. The sympathetic appraisal of both sides is typical of Renoir's generous and affectionate humanism. The film is a loose and leisurely patterned series of anecdotes. For all its openness to what seems to just happen along for recording, it has a shaping comic structure of paral-lels and contrasts: Boudu's carelessness and sloppiness versus the ordered routine of the household; his strange postures and positions—for example, jamming his huge frame into sitting positions in doorways—as against the normally proper deportment of the household; the parallel seduction plots—Boudu and the wife, the husband and the maid—finally merging for the plot climax. The parallel structure is ordered by the framing shots at beginning and end: Boudu is first seen, accidentally, casually, in a panning shot through the telescope of the husband, who is watching girls' legs and sees Boudu in the river; at the end, idling along on the same river in the wedding boat (he is to marry the maid), Boudu reaches for a flower, falls out of the boat and drifts away, accidentally, casually—the camera panning with him as he reaches the shore and falls into a sleep on the grass, then panning further to survey the sunny flow of river that reflects the naturalness of Boudu's life.

La Grande Illusion

Five years later, *La Grande Illusion* (1937)—generally considered, with *The Rules of the Game,* a peak of Renoir's career—marked a summing up and a refining of the contents and approach of the films of this early period. It shared with them their social perception and conscience, their emphasis on the influence of class and status, yet countered this pressure with a more complex and dignified version of the personal indomitability of Boudu, with a more idealistic vision of a human unity that bridged the gaps of background, class, nationality, and war. In approach, it shared with the earlier films the basic seriousness and classic economy, the sympathetic response to the full humanity of all its characters. Its camera lingers in long takes and pans while action unfolds uninterrupted, but it is more tightly patterned and intricate in its balances and parallels, more selective and pointedly symbolic in its use of things and settings. It is—more than an antiwar film—a pro-peace film, a film about the nurturing of ties with others that enrich and deepen the individual, that can, ideally, surmount nationalism and war. Three kinds of ties are intricately patterned—of class, of nationality, of humanity. While the ties of class have their dignity and honor, these "rules of the game" (in the phrase of Boeldieu, the French aristocrat) are ironically viewed as finally self-defeating, at the service of the destructiveness of a war that has made them obsolete. Boeldieu and the aristocratic commandant of the German prison, Rauffenstein, find a comradeship that transcends nationality; yet their own code leads Rauffenstein to shoot Boeldieu, despite his own recognition of the war's triumph over his own values. Boeldieu has, in turn, sacrificed himself for the sake of his lower-class countrymen, but it is finally their growing sense of their common humanity with the Germans— first with a German soldier, most fully with the German woman who shelters them after their escape—that is given the final transcendent value.

In the first third of the film (scripted by Renoir and Charles Spaak), the class conflict among the French prisoners and their coexistent national solidarity are developed in the plans for escape from the first prison. In the stark isolation of the prison in the middle third, the paradoxical and doomed communion of aristocrats is developed. In the last third, the new freedom and greater humanity of the escapees is developed amid the spread of fields and hills that contrast sharply with the earlier setting of the prison atop a rocky peak.

Typically, Renoir (with cinematography by his nephew Claude Renoir) uses pans, rather than editing, to unfold these relationships. In a sequence of panning shots, the transition from old to new is dramatized visually: In an unbroken moving shot (after a close-up of the dying Boeldieu's face), Rauffenstein goes to a closet, gets a bottle and takes a drink, is called by the nurse, walks back to where Boeldieu lies on a bed. In a closer pan, the camera then follows his hand as he closes Boeldieu's eyes. In longer shot, he paces the room, looks out the window at the snow, takes out a pair of scissors and snips off the geranium he has carefully nurtured amid the sterile rocks of the prison, the one flower of nobility remaining. Another pan shot then moves over the snow-covered fields outside, finally picking up Marechal and Rosenthal, in dark and shabby civilian clothes, as they hide before fleeing.

The geranium is one of several props that embody the last illusory flourish of nobility. At the shooting of Boeldieu, both he and Rauffenstein are wearing their white gloves. Boeldieu is in confusing shadow at the top of the prison wall, playing a flute. Rauffenstein's neck is clamped in a metal brace that exaggerates his ramrod dignity. Injured in a plane crash, he too has been

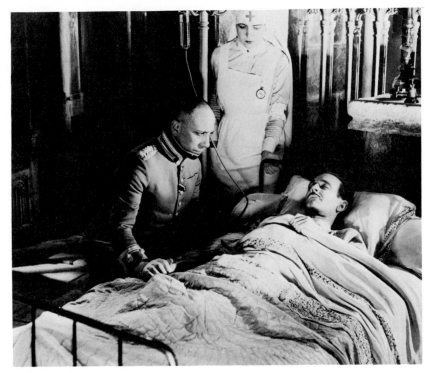

La Grande Illusion

imprisoned by the war. He looks up stiffly, painfully to Boeldieu; then he stays the rifle of an underling and shoots at Boeldieu with his pistol, intending to injure him slightly but mortally wounding him instead. Earlier, another telling pan had captured the poignancy of the carefully selected objects in Rauffenstein's room: the geraniums, binoculars, several daggers, a champagne bucket, a leather-bound book with a pistol lying on it, a framed portrait of a young woman. Then, the commandant's orderly blowing into his master's white gloves, preparatory to Rauffenstein's donning them. Erich von Stroheim gave his finest performance in this role of the obstinate, doomed idealist—a role with ironic ties to his own life and career as a director.

The Rules of the Game   Two years later, at the collapse of France's government and exposure of the insufficiency of its traditional social patterns, *The Rules of the Game* is no longer idealistic regarding class, honor, or even love. Though still marked by Renoir's generosity toward a wide variety of imperfect characters, it is also more satirical. The masterpiece of his social films, it opposes tones and techniques in a balance that is outstanding among the works of the period, Renoir's or anyone else's. It is a balance that foreshadows the ambiguous mixtures of the films of the sixties, just as its refinement of Realist nonobtrusiveness and nonintervention points ahead to the natural form and flow of the Italian Neo-Realists. The film combines Renoir's most intricate theatrical ordering (directly and lovingly modeled after the patterns of classic

French comedy) with a continuing sense of the natural flow of action and scene. It is spontaneous and mannered, tightly plotted and visually imaginative, by turn humorous and serious in audacious shifts of mood.

This time the rules that kill are those that compose the hypocritical shell of the aristocratic values of Boeldieu and Rauffenstein. The game of the "moderns" depicted, both of the upper and (mirroring) servant class, denies the earnestness and sincerity of the old aristocracy while maintaining its forms and perquisites. Only the two anachronistic loners are immune—the gamekeeper, Schumacher, who still lives with a doggedly loyal attachment to the echoes of the old way of life, and the pilot-hero Jurieu, who innocently expects to live by the ideals of the new. Exasperated by the mad minuet of shallow coquetry and romance (which Renoir proffers as the dance of death of a bankrupt culture), Jurieu cries out, futilely, to his mistress, "Christine, there are certain rules after all. . . ."

Even the good Octave (played by Renoir himself), who understands (like Renoir himself) their frailties—"Everyone," he says, "has their own good reasons"—even Octave profits from living by the rules, drifting through life as everyone's friend and houseguest. And it is he who, with the best of intentions, provokes the final confused and destructive encounter between the two idealists in which the airman is mistakenly shot by the gamekeeper.

The shooting knots together the two theatrically complex, comic love plots with a sudden wrenching seriousness. The plots run parallel but are mirror images of each other. The idealistic Jurieu is naively in love with the married Christine. She and her husband, La Chesnaye, have affairs, but with no serious intentions. La Chesnaye, a Jew, precarious and insecure in society despite his wealth, must play by the new rules of artifice even more fervently than the others. Nonetheless, as treated by Renoir (and delicately portrayed by Marcel Dalio), he maintains sensitivity and dignity. On the lower-class level, the situation is reversed. The obsolete idealist is the cuckolded gamekeeper. His wife, the maid Lisette, the direct image of her mistress, dallies with the vagrant outsider Marceau. The parallel between Marceau and La Chesnaye is developed in several ways—by their instinctive understanding of one another; La Chesnaye's helping of Marceau when Schumacher is chasing him; Marceau's toying with one of La Chesnaye's mechanical birds, paralleling earlier shots of La Chesnaye doing the same; Marceau's grappling with Schumacher, paralleling La Chesnaye's brief tussle with Jurieu.

La Chesnaye's passion for the artificial—reflecting his reductive need for the artifice of the game—is one of the chief symbolic motifs developed by Renoir's careful attention to things: La Chesnaye, in the hunt, leads the needless destruction of real fowl and rabbits, but treasures his mechanical birds; the long, climactic party sequence at his chateau involves a number of pageants in which the guests don costumes and, in one, do a dance of death dressed as skeletons. His crowning moment is the display of his electrical organ, on which three mechanical figures move and add to the music, while he stands beside the contraption, shyly proud of its wonders.

The Rules of the Game

Similarly, Octave's well-intentioned scheme climaxes a symbolic motif involving costumes. Christine is wearing Lisette's cape, and when Octave sends Jurieu out to meet her, the maddened Schumacher thinks Jurieu, too, is now courting his wife and shoots him. Earlier, when all the upper-class guests had worn costumes for the party's entertainments, Octave had had great difficulty in shedding his cumbersome bear's costume in a symbolic enactment of his clumsy scheming, his ridiculous position, his own victimization—like the animals—by the rules of the game. Renoir's basing of the final action on the old theatrical device of mistaken identity is one last delineation of the parallels between his own theatrical plot, the entertainments of La Chesnaye's party, and the counterfeit life of the chateau.

The witty intricacy of Renoir's plotting is capped by the use of the comic chase that figures throughout the party sequence. Earlier, at the close of the introductory sequence (before the weekend at the chateau), Octave has playfully and with little real interest chased Lisette around a room, while music is played on La Chesnaye's phonograph. The hunting sequence at the chateau serves as brutal counterpoint. The beaters chase the fowl and rabbit from their hiding places into the waiting guns of La Chesnaye, Schumacher, and the guests. This four-minute sequence is sharply edited, in contrast to Renoir's usual emphasis on the longer shot and movement in the shot and of the camera. Here the rapid shots of the harried animals not only accentuate the cruelty of the shoot but suggest, with the shift of editing tone, the release of the callous cruelty usually hidden by the façade of the game. The relation of the hunt to the callousness of the human relations is indicated by the immediately preceding dialogue between Octave and Jurieu, captured in one long moving shot during which the two friends joke about the fickleness of women, both mistresses and maids, and the danger of loving.

At the party, Schumacher chases and fires at Marceau as they race through rooms full of uncomprehending guests like two Marx Brothers, Marceau at one point even joining the dancers and attempting to hide in the arms of a large dowager, much as Groucho might have with Margaret Dumont. The naturally fluid, witty grace with which Renoir uses the moving camera to capture the movements and juxtapositions of the chase is typified in the sequence in which Schumacher is finally restrained: In the first shot of the sequence, several changes of room, direction, and protagonists are climaxed when the camera reverses from one pan, and, panning back across a hall, catches sight of Marceau as he runs by at its end, followed by Schumacher and then Lisette. At a gunshot, there is a cut to the main drawing room, where the guests, on hearing the shots, raise their hands. The camera then tracks sideways along the line of them, finally discovering Marceau hiding behind a woman. With another cut, Renoir turns to a group in front of the stage set up in the drawing room, as the electric organ emits loud discordant wails. Then, without a cut, the camera turns away from the stage and, panning, encounters Schumacher, tracks forward toward him as he raises his rifle, Lisette screams, and servants wrestle him out of the room.

After the chase, with a final ironic reversal, Schumacher's comic hunt turns deadly. Jurieu, in one last parallel, is jolted backward when Schumacher's bullet strikes him—as we earlier saw a rabbit jolted when hit by a guest's bullet.

When the film was released, neither the government nor the French audience was willing to laugh at the games it played with the rules and themselves. Shown briefly in mutilated form, it was quickly banned, then almost literally bombed out of existence in an Allied air raid. It was not until 1958 that 200 cans of the original film were found and, with the help of Renoir, reconstituted into a complete version of the original masterpiece.

The American Productions

During World War II, Renoir worked in America. Of his five American films, *The Diary of a Chambermaid* (1945) is the best, the closest to his work in France. Earlier he had dealt with the picturesque in the Deep South in *Swamp Water* (1941) and *The Southerner* (1944), the latter especially displaying his usual sensitivity to place and to the interaction of men with it. Without intrusive, heavy Hollywood plotting, it traces the fortunes and misfortunes of a family on the land but leaves an impression of forcing, of unintended artificiality.

With *The Diary of a Chambermaid,* Renoir returned to a French setting and to one of his favorite French authors, Octave Mirbeau. In his rendering of Mirbeau's novel (later to be used by Luis Buñuel), Renoir again draws a parallel between masters and servants, again blends a surface humor—though more muted, less farcical than in *Rules*—with an underlying soberness. Here, the hypocritical pretensions are more shallow, less fun, the middle-class repressions and emotional distortions more ugly.

Europe
Again:
*The
River
and Others*
After his American period, Renoir returned to Europe seemingly with a greater interest in the formal surfaces, the theatrical illusions, the impressionistic esthetics to which the motion picture lends itself readily. He shifted his emphasis from blending realistic and primarily social material with theatrical artifice to lending reality to materials that are basically ornamental and abstract. The British-produced *The River* (1951), his first film in color, marks the transition to this late period. Focusing on the impressions of a young British girl responding to the beauty and chaos of India, it offers some of Renoir's loveliest lyrical evocations in fluid patterns of color and movement. Three further films reflect even more his turning to spectacle, to the dreams of theater, and to the beauty in nature and in art. These became the means of giving body to his more abstract notions and his sympathetic, spiritual, calm optimism.

The Golden Coach (1953), made in Italy, is the best of these. With a vibrantly natural core in Anna Magnani's wonderful portrayal of the actress Camilla, the film reflects on the interfusion and confusion of theater and reality, ornament and representation, questioning which plane of existence touches on the deepest sources of human emotion. *French Cancan* (1954) again toys with the theatrical motif, though its intentionally conventional backstage-life plot seems a miscalculation. Blending music, impressionistic color, and spirited movement, it is primarily intended as a sensual experience. Its final affirmation of the fullness of life, as embodied in the form-giving playfulness of art, is a last twenty-minute cancan dance. *The Picnic on the Grass* (*Le Déjeuner sur l'Herbe*, 1959) finds this fullness in nature and the natural life. As Renoir's use of the title of the Manet painting suggests, however, the evocation of the natural flow of life is shaped by the form of art, by the composition, coloring, and toning of many of the nature scenes in brilliant evocation of the style and textures of the French Impressionists (including Renoir's father, Auguste Renoir). In the film this double sensuousness is merged with an abstract allegory that poses the natural against the mechanical artifice of industrial civilization—all energized, in a not totally successful blending, by the stratagems and frenetic action of farce. This kind of comic gaiety also becomes the texture and vehicle for the later *The Vanishing Corporal* (1961), Renoir's lighthearted reprise of the prison camp materials of *La Grande Illusion*.

It is a direction of stylistic development whose beginnings, in retrospect, can be seen in the intricate theatricality and more subtle use of farce in *Rules*. The earlier film remains, like Welles's *Kane*, both a monument of the independent style and an influence on more recent film-making.

3

NEW

CONSOLIDATIONS,

NEW

DIRECTIONS

CHAPTER FIFTEEN

Modifying Realism and Expressiveness

In the midst of the worldwide changes and consolidations of the years immediately following World War II, key developments within the film world presaged reconsolidations and new directions in the medium's two basic tendencies of Realism and expressiveness. This third era of the motion picture was to bring a new area of consensus, a new set of common denominators in the basic equations of content and technique, representation and expression. The result, showing the effects also of increased crossbreeding of international influences, was a distinctive *open* style, an opening up of Realism and verisimilitude, an opening up of expressive possibilites and stylization.

ITALIAN NEO-REALISM

One of the first signs of change to attract worldwide attention was the movement of Italian neo-Realism. Its approach was prefigured, at least in part, by Luchino Visconti's *Ossessione* (1942), pirated and adapted from James M. Cain's novel *The Postman Always Rings Twice* and somehow sneaked past Mussolini's censors. The peak of popularity of the movement was during the period 1945 to 1949, which saw Roberto Rossellini's *Open City* and *Paisan*, Vittorio De Sica's *Shoeshine* and *The Bicycle Thief*, Luigi Zampa's *To Live in Peace*, Visconti's *La Terra Trema*, Alberto Lattuada's *Senza Pieta* (*Without Pity*), Giuseppi De Santis's *Caccia Tragica* and *Bitter Rice*. By 1950, its momentum was slowed by the establishment of a new government bureau of control over the film industry.

Visconti's *Ossessione* offered a Realism of harsh and specific detail that directly rebelled against the empty and false ornamentation of conventional Italian movies. The films that followed developed a definition—more social and political, more concerned and committed—of the terms of that rebellion and its confrontation with the conventions of the realistic social film.

This definition stressed honesty and simplicity, a sympathetic humanism, hopeful, even sentimental. It sought to modify the social content of motion pictures: As Rossellini saw it, it bespoke an attempt ''to see man without faking the unusual''; Cesare Zavattini, who wrote many of the major films of the movement, insisted that its aim must be ''to take any moment of human life and show how 'striking' that moment is: to excavate and identify it, to send its echo vibrating into other parts of the world.'' In the films of Rossellini that dealt with World War II, that attention to the usual and real did include the major crises and tests of humanness during the wartime situation. In the films written and influenced by Zavattini, attention was paid to more minor reflections, the more commonplace human offshoots of major social crises. In De Sica's *Shoeshine* (1946), the impact of war and the transition to peace are seen in the low-keyed actions and situations surrounding two homeless shoeshine boys, who find a stray old white horse. In De Sica's and Zavattini's *Shoeshine,* the nature of the social examination, of the social protest changed. Instead of an emphasis on the concrete terms of a specific social problem, neo-Realist films emphasized the human terms of the problem, the revelation of character and response within the social situation, the look and feel of the way people lived their personal lives in society, how much that society influenced—restricted or warped—those lives.

Some later critics have found a limitation in this focus on the quietly common, a failure to explore fully the political implications of the material. Certainly the limits are there. Of this group of films, Visconti's *La Terra Trema* (1948) is the most direct in exploring economic exploitation and social oppression—in this case, of fishermen in a small Sicilian village—and more direct in calling for action to combat it. But the new dimension of social drama that is emphasized in all these films has its own value. While Rossellini's *Open City* (1945) can, with hindsight, be said to be politically naive in its failure to see the long-range impossibility of its temporary comradeship in heroism of Catholic priests and Communists, it was not Rossellini's point to predict or not predict any continuation of that partnership. Rather, what he is concerned with is the indomitable spirit of men to rise to the occasion, whatever the specific political realities of any period. Whether idealistic or naive, this emphasis did serve an important function in freeing the course of Realist films from the stereotypes of time- and issue-bound treatment of political and social materials.

In pursuing their concerns, the neo-Realists revivified certain tendencies of the Realist style, loosened others, opened ways to new dramatic structures and cinematic techniques, even to new methods by which expressive forms might mix with and arise from realistic materials. Going out into the streets for locations, often using nonprofessional casts, they revitalized the Realist style's documentary immediacy and spontaneity. This transparency before the free flow of reality was further intensified by the natural, sometimes rough and awkward quality of their visual images. In breaking free from the tightly knit plotting of the conventional problem film, they strengthened tendencies toward a freer structure, expanding and remaining in single scenes, enlarging small situations, building looser sequences of separate vignettes, reducing cause-and-effect plotting and character development, modulating clearly defined plot and character resolutions. These modifications in dramatic structure proved to be central in later developments in both Realist and stylized approaches. And in seeking the "echoes" that small acts produce, the neo-Realists encouraged development of the kind of visual symbolism that rises naturally from realistic material and investigated as well the possibilities of mixing Realism with comedy, fantasy, and stylization.

Zavattini
and
De Sica

With *The Bicycle Thief* (1947), Zavattini and De Sica produced the epitome of the style. Its simplified plotting centers on the search by an unemployed father for the stolen bicycle that is a necessity for the modest job he has

The Bicycle Thief

been offered. In the final irony, he discovers the thief is a pitiable epileptic and, when he becomes a bicycle thief himself, is caught immediately and publicly shamed in front of his son. It does not preach about postwar economic problems but captures them in discrete visual references: a panning shot of row upon row of pawned bridal sheets; the contrast between the giant crowd of soccer fans (who can afford to go to the match in the new stadium) and the wretched man caught outside stealing a bicycle. Its structure orders a series of relatively separate vignettes that develop the relationship of the father and his son as it is affected by his plight and search: the boy urinating in the street; the father caught in an uproar at a brothel; the boy and father angry, the boy walking apart from him across the street; the boy envying but empathetically enjoying a rich boy's extravagant lunch; the climactic deepening of awareness of both when the father is caught; the final hesitant, understanding clasping of their hands as they walk off—discreetly photographed, not in close-up but in medium shot, and then in long shot as they are swallowed up again in the crowd. The treatment of these details has a purity, a humility before the image, a transparency beyond earlier Realist methods.

With *Umberto D* (1952), the reduction is even more marked, the whole film concerned with the small details of the struggle of an old man, lonely but stubbornly dignified, facing eviction from his apartment: small events and a deep human resonance.

In the Silvana Mangano episode of the omnibus *Gold of Naples* (1952), the last image becomes a symbolic culmination of this period of their work and of the way in which a realistic visual detail can accumulate echoes. A prostitute has accepted the marriage proposal, offered through intermediaries, of a wealthy client. She is first made to appear awkward at the wedding festivities, then discovers the proposal was a perverse one, the result of the man's desire to punish himself for the betrayal of a former fiancée, now dead. She leaves, but once in the street her courage departs and, giving in to this more subtle form of degradation, she returns. But she has been locked out and is last seen, irrevocably an outcast, beating futilely on the giant door of the house, the cold wind of the street blowing behind her.

In subsequent years, the comic toying with the elements of Italian life (which comprises the rest of *Gold of Naples*) became the chief staple of De Sica's popularized anthology films. But the year before, in 1951, De Sica and Zavattini had, in *Miracle in Milan,* employed a more compassionate and meaningful whimsy, blending Realist concern for the plight of the dispossessed with humorous fantasy and touches of Expressionist grotesqueness: At the cavernous office of a business magnate, a man hangs outside as a kind of human weather vane that is brought in to report on the state of the weather; in the double-edged "affirmation" of the close, the poor, driven from their shanty wasteland, no longer helped even by miracles on earth, rise up on the brooms of street-cleaners to heaven, the only place they have a chance for happiness.

Two Women (1961), though more commercial and melodramatically plotted, did revive the moral seriousness and convincing texture of De Sica's earlier films. And ten years later at the age of 70, De Sica, in *The Garden of the Finzi-Continis,* created his most lyrical and psychologically sophisticated depiction of the human meaning of political events. With evocative use of décor and natural settings and deft character development, he unobtrusively captures not only the passing of a time of insulated innocence but the disturbing, complex mixture of human goodness and weakness that produced the harrowing persecution of the Jews in Italy.

Rossellini   Despite critical and popular fickleness, Roberto Rossellini maintained and developed the longest career within the boundaries of the neo-Realist style—and, in retrospect, the most substantial. Insisting throughout on the possibility of a kind of happiness, through spiritual or inner growth, in the face of the world's assaults, Rossellini tended to build to greater crises and greater extremes of melodrama than De Sica. Still, his impressive total body of work stubbornly holds to a fidelity and freeing transparency toward the details of immediate reality that his camera encounters but refuses to obtrude upon.

In *Open City,* the plotting is still traditional, yet the camerawork and editing produce a sense of immediacy and spontaneity; the jagged, uneven

Open City

actions of his characters become the central tonality of the movement. In the freer form of the six independent episodes of *Paisan* (1946), the variety of human response to war is revealed with less plot manipulation, despite occasional flourishes of melodrama and awkward sentimentality. Long-held shots and camera movements remain humble before the movements of the characters and maintain their meaningful interaction with the physical data of their environment. Yet the elements that confer the sense of immediacy have been carefully selected and unified by Rossellini's grasp of what is essential visual and character detail. In the Florence episode, a man and woman seeking their lost families are followed through the empty halls and surroundings of the Uffizi Gallery, encountering random yet cumulatively telling events that image the confusion and horror of war; finally, a dying partisan, held in the woman's arms, reveals, in a credibly built coincidence of the dirty tricks of war, the death of her fiancé. In the final Po River episode, the futile but courageous stand of the partisans is given a powerful visual correlative in the cold, foggy, empty marshlands of the valley.

Harsh images of brutality in postwar Germany mirror the human frailties that lead to wars in his *Germany, Year Zero* (1947), but then Rossellini turned to a series of films that focus on personal relationships and on women who carry the spark of the human spirit through a ravaging world.

One of the finest of these (many of which starred Ingrid Bergman), is *Europa 51* (also titled *Greater Love* and *No Greater Love,* 1952), which foreshadows his later interest in the emotional and spiritual emptiness of the prospering middle class. In the film (which reveals the influence of Simone Weil on Rossellini), Bergman rejects her comforts and pleasures and seeks to help the dispossessed, finally discovering her potential to love in the insane asylum in which she has been placed, supposedly temporarily, on a legal ruse. In the latter portions of the film, Rossellini employs a subjective expressiveness in capturing the world of the asylum with dislocating transitions, distorted perspectives, and looming, naggingly off-center close-ups. But it was not to be an approach he pursued. In the comparable *Voyage in Italy* (*Viaggio en Italia,* 1953), which, virtually unknown for years, may well be his finest achievement in the conventional dramatic film, he purifies further the techniques of carefully structured, subtle transparency before reality.

In fact, *Voyage* is in part about remaining or becoming open to the impact of external reality. Its civilized but nerve- and emotion-deadened bourgeois couple (Bergman and George Sanders), drifting through a series of seemingly aimless encounters with the raw life and the ancient wonders around them, begin to awaken to themselves and the world. In delineating their subtle change of spirit, Rossellini uses a free structure that is actually highly selective of telling detail yet maintains the sense of ambiguity and randomness. His long takes of the characters' interaction with objects, events, and people show increased understanding of the psychological significance of duration. His moving camera not only stays doggedly with them but creates rhythms of harmony and disharmony, equilibrium and disequilibrium that are part of the mood of the situations. Here is an important movement toward the indirect revelation of response, the externalization of inner reality that Antonioni and others would pursue further but again Rossellini turned restlessly elsewhere.

With *The Flowers of St. Francis* (1950), he treated history in terms of simplified legend, in lyrical, humorous vignettes, realistic in texture but abstract in implication, that show St. Francis and his followers overcoming the forces of brutalty. His most successful film in many years, *General Della Rovere* (1959), returned to the materials of the war years, this time with a new texture and tone of irony. In the loosely episodic first half, Rossellini captures the feel of the life of the confidence man—gum chewing and food nibbling, gambling, empty sex, false promises and sapphires, complicated deceits and empty justifications. In the second half, the plotting is more linear and melodramatic, but the ironic wit continues even as the sentiment builds. Overreaching, the con man is forced by the Nazis to impersonate a partisan hero; now, feeling some community with fellow prisoners, who look up to him (as the "General"), he can find himself and some honor—but only as he sincerely attempts to assume another false identity, that of the real hero, General Della Rovere. The mixed irony and sentiment of his regeneration is typified in one of the film's few close-ups: After being beaten by his captors, he is shown a letter and picture sent to "him" by the real general's wife. We see the battered face of the "General" and the tears in his eyes as he looks at the photo of "his" wife and children and seems to know, at last, who he really is.

But one last direction remained for Rossellini's career. He turned to a series of historical films. First through traditional dramatic formats—*Viva l'Italia* (1960), *Vanina Vanni* (1961)—and then through an amazingly inventive kind of epic documentary, he sought to record significant events faithfully and to analyze and interpret them, not through external commentary but through selection and juxtaposition of the concrete details and the words of their re-creation. *The Rise to Power of Louis XIV* (1966) focuses on a small segment of time. With a deceptively simple, but brilliantly selective, mosaic of the tangible—the things and acts, both domestic and public—of Louis's court, he analyzes a significant turning point in the history of government. In several films made in collaboration with his nephew Renzo Rossellini, Jr., vast stretches of human history are synthesized in multiwork sequences. In *Socrates* (1970), he illuminates the humanist significance in the major years and the culminating act of Socrates' life. In these films (originally shown on television), using a mobile camera of his own design, Rossellini accentuates and expands the capacity of the long take to remain open to the flow of unimpeded action and dialogue.

AMERICAN ROMANTIC REALISM (*FILM NOIR*)

In America at this time, the overripe romantic Realism that the French later characterized as the *film noir* was another sign of shifting style. From one point of view, these films of the later forties and early fifties reveal a growing sophistication of content, foreshadowing the content explosions of the sixties and seventies. In them, the thirties' genres of tough-guy films and social-protest films are given a new tone, more psychoanalytical, more cynical, more brutal. In them, the corruption of society is taken as a given condition beyond direct protest. But while their depiction of human frailties and perversities and social corruption is more extreme, it is embedded in a cleverly commercial context that emphasizes the tricks and turns of the audience-engaging, entertaining plot. The films are basically displays of manner, rather than matter, whatever the social and psychological implications of their portrayal of the destructive lust for power and wealth or the distortions of emotion and sexuality. The distinctive hothouse lushness of their manner betrays a decadence of style that matches the decadence of their contents—a cynical and florid stylization within the confines of the commercial production system.

In these films, Realist observation, subjects, and details are given one more expressive turn of the screw, touched with the romantic moodiness of the French school, the gothic shadows and opulence of the German Expressionists, the rococo and gauzy sheen of von Sternberg, the flourishes of Mamoulian. Harsh materials are turned soft, distanced into sentimentality by plotting and mannerisms. They are films of nighttime darkness and desperation, cruelly expert in their manipulation of violent emotion and depravity. They are filled with the vividly sordid, the cluttered, the pervasive shadows and sudden contrasts of this night world—murky, threatening, sometimes seedy and run-down, sometimes showy and crass: desperate low-life on the streets of New York (Robert Siodmak's *Cry of the City*, 1948), at the dead ends of Chicago (Edmund Goulding's *Nightmare Alley*, 1947), on the entertainment fringes of London (Jules Dassin's *Night and the City*, 1950), or in the cheap diners and shacks of California (Tay Garnett's *The Postman Always Rings Twice*, 1946); the desperate and heartless decadence of the bars and homes of the wealthy or the middle class (Michael Curtiz's *Mildred Pierce*, 1945, and *The Unsuspected*, 1947; Fritz Lang's *Woman in the Window*, 1944, and *Scarlet Street*, 1945).

The later moody, brooding Bogart takes on the *noir* tone, still somewhat jaunty in Howard Hawks's *The Big Sleep* (1946), frayed and driven in Nicholas Ray's *In a Lonely Place* (1950). In the *noir* films, the tough gangster was joined by the tough cop and private eye, their killings and beatings more sadistic, their emotional deformities more visible (but still only a pale foreshadowing of later excesses). Among the earliest was Edward Dmytryk's fast-paced brutality and lingering sentimentality in *Murder, My Sweet* (1944), with Dick Powell as Raymond Chandler's Philip Marlowe. Marlowe became the subjective eye of the camera in Robert Montgomery's *Lady in the Lake* (1946), an experiment in first-person narration. In Dmytryk's *Cornered*

Mildred Pierce

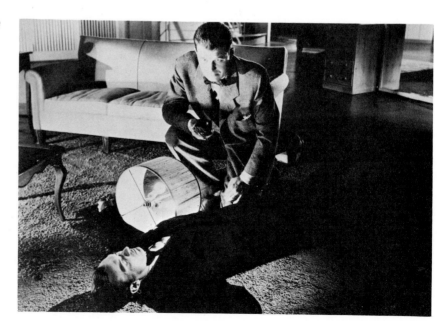

(1945), Powell and the sentimental brutality are transferred to Buenos Aires, merged with the leftover threat of Nazis; in his *The Dark Corner* (1946), the viciousness is genteelly upholstered in middle-class trimmings; in *Crossfire* (1947), interlaced with legitimizing touches in its theme of the psychopathy of anti-Semitism. (Compare the straight-message treatment of the same subject in Elia Kazan's *Gentlemen's Agreement* of the same year.) The psychopathic core of this violence was more openly faced in Richard Widmark's giggling sadist in *Kiss of Death* (1947), directed by Henry Hathaway, and in the baroquely overblown, mother-obsessed derangement of Jimmy Cagney in *White Heat* (1949), directed by Raoul Walsh. (In its final hyperbole, Cagney dispatches himself in a gigantic gas tank explosion.) Nicholas Ray's version of the Bonnie and Clyde Barrow story, *They Live by Night* (1949), maintained more of the late thirties' sympathetic conception in the midst of the moody flourishes of the new form. Robert Wise's *The Setup* (1949) provided a more underplayed renovation of the social implications of the boxer-gambler motif. Though still marred by period mannerisms, Lewis Milestone's *The Strange Love of Martha Ivers* (1946), written by Robert Rossen, developed direct social implications from the emotional tangles and machinations of its compulsive, unscrupulous heiress (Barbara Stanwyck). In 1955, Robert Aldrich's *Kiss Me, Deadly,* based on the Mickey Spillane novel and distinguished by its jabbing editing, was a sadistic reprise of this substyle.

Wilder   With ten films in six years, Robert Siodmak was the most prolific practitioner of the *noir* style; its most substantial achievements, however, were the four toughly realistic films of Billy Wilder, the first three also eminently commercial. In these, his sardonic wit found a more direct, corrosive, and unblunted expression than in his later comedies. In 1944, his *Double Indemnity*, with script by Wilder and Chandler, was an early and influential model, possessing all of the *noir* ingredients: its first-person narration by the doomed insurance agent (Fred McMurray), cynical and articulate, sentimentally tough; its pervasive shadows invaded by shafts of light or contrasted with the empty brightness of Los Angeles streets; the neon emptiness of a supermarket (in which the conspirators mutter dark plans). The brightness is only a cold, slickened form of the darkly driven desires. The pattern of shadow and light is carried like a motif from the chilling light smoothness of Barbara Stanwyck, in bleached-blond wig and often in white sweater, to a single close-up after the murder when, full of distaste and selfish fears, McMurray and Stanwyck kiss in a car, he leaning into the shadow that slants across them, blocking out part of their heads, the side of her face and bright hair still in the light, and down to the double shootout, the blinds on the window making broken patterns of meaningless light and shadow.

The Lost Weekend (1945) captures the terrors of the alcoholic, though save for a couple of expressionistic, subjective distortions these are oddly restrained. Despite the convincingly sordid milieu, the impact is vitiated by a conventional problem approach.

Double Indemnity

In *Sunset Boulevard* (1950), the surface savagery and terror give way to a clever dissection, satirical and moody, of the pathetic emptiness under the upholstery and the veneer of glamor of an industry that rapaciously capitalizes on the corruptions of its society. Its offscreen narrator is more weak than predatory, passive in accepting the risks of his own corruption. His narration is the epitome of cynical toying with screen conventions, for he is first seen, not wounded as was the insurance agent of *Double Indemnity*, but floating dead in a swimming pool. Its predatory has-been actress is the victim of a system more selfish than she, one that deals in illusions and lives and that breaks her finally as she insanely plays the reality of her arrest for murder as if it is one more big scene.

With *Ace in the Hole* (or *The Big Carnival,* 1951), Wilder more openly ties the exploitative cupidity of the mass media to the audience, to the society that seeks the glamorizing of despair and death. A washed-up reporter, Kirk Douglas, capitalizes on the plight of a man trapped in a mine; but before he and the man are both dead as a result, the selfishness and viciousness, petty and great, of almost everyone involved is caught in unrelenting focus. The shadows and flourishes are gone, but the blackness is even deeper, for it is more honestly felt, more inevitably revealed by the vehicle of the plot. *Ace in* the Hole was a box-office failure, Wilder's first; after it, he was always sure to hedge his cynicism, blunt his satire with the softening, alternating currents of comedy and cynical compromise.

NEW TECHNOLOGY, NEW TECHNIQUES

In the early fifties, the technological refinement of wide-screen production and its rapid adoption and standardization (impelled by the new threat of television) also brought modifications in film technique. Twentieth-Century Fox's CinemaScope was the first application of the new process to have a significant commercial impact. (Its release of The Robe in 1953 scuttled the temporary competition of 3-D movies.) The entrance of other studios into wide-screen production further established a change in the heighth-to-width screen ratio from the traditional 1:1.33 to ratios ranging from 1:1.85 to 1:2.55. The greater width carried important implications for film technique, though only modifying not upsetting earlier positions. The chief contribution of the wide screen was to strengthen the tendency toward transparency, toward including more of the materials in a carefully arranged single shot rather than analyzing these materials into separate points of emphasis and showing them in a sequence of shots. It did not, however, as was first feared (or hoped by some), make editing impractical. Instead, it gave a new potency to the single shot, a new flexibility in combinations of the shot and edited sequences.

With the wide screen, not only was a greater quantity of materials possible in a single composition, but so was a greater responsiveness to and use of the space between and around materials. Shots past foreground elements to others in the rear continued to be used, but these shots could now be varied so as to spread the elements more widely along the horizontal, even while still maintaining a progression into distance, one element still closer than the others. In a shot typical of the exploitation of this new potential—in Budd Boeticher's Ride Lonesome (1959)—a man who is about to be hanged is seen at the right of the composition and toward the rear. To his left is the tree, then a small gap, then the man who is preparing to hang him, turned to face a rider who has entered from the far left. The rider is closer to the viewer, but, importantly, a large horizontal gap is maintained between him and the other two, thus avoiding the artificial necessity of arranging the composition in more of a straight-line pattern from front to rear. Similarly, in Sam Peckinpah's Ride the High Country (1961), more impact is achieved through amassing more concrete detail horizontally, as in a scene where a frightened girl moves from screen right to left past a man, a space, another man, a horse, two men (in depth), and a horse and wagon. Moreover, the greater width also helps create a stronger impression of depth. In general, the wide-screen ratios encourage organization of a complex image, so that the spectator is induced to participate more directly (and the camera to intrude less openly) in the free flow of the reality of the materials.

It was at first feared that the potentialities of the close-up would also be greatly reduced, but this too has not proved to be the case. Rather, what has been developed is a greater variety of close-up possibilities—from shots with complete emphasis on the close-up face or object, to shots in which other important elements of the scene can be maintained along with the emphasized close-up. Nicholas Ray's *Rebel without a Cause* (1955) and Elia Kazan's *East of Eden* (1955) and *Wild River* (1960) provide excellent examples of holding close-ups of faces even as actors move across the screen and are kept in direct interaction with their surroundings.

In subsequent years, the perfection of the zoom and telephoto lenses also brought more opportunities to hold within a single take. Both, however, tend to diminish the sense of space and of separate planes of vision—especially the zoom, which, in focusing in on isolated elements brings those elements artificially forward (toward the viewer) rather than producing a sense of movement of the camera toward the subject, as in a tracking shot. Despite increased use, the stylistic implications of these lenses—their denial of the reality of space and their potential for abstraction—have often received less careful attention than their expediency.

NEW EXPRESSIVENESS

Dreyer   Through these same postwar years, the work of several veteran directors provided signs of the kind of modifications that were forthcoming in screen expressiveness. One of them, the Dane, Carl Dreyer, returned to production in 1944 with *Day of Wrath* after an absence of more than a decade. In the film, he continues developing his kind of quiet, personal epic, an evocation and celebration of intangible dimensions of spirit beyond the realms of objective fact, yet built on the commonplace objects and surfaces of the literal world and the Realist film. As in his *Joan of Arc,* he examines the spiritual flowering of a young woman accused of witchcraft in the seventeenth century who surmounts her persecution even as she paradoxically accepts her guilt. More psychological in its approach than *Joan,* the film is also much more concerned with the plastic possibilities of film form. Its typical lengthy close-ups are this time much more dramatically composed, its faces often patterned carefully with shadows and varieties of subtle light and with the objects of their surrounding world. In contrast to *Joan,* its images are Rembrandt-like in their emphatic chiaroscuro and highlighting, more mannered yet still severe, rigorously selective. Within the darkness, stasis, and silence that pervade, light, movement, and words achieve telling force: After several close, static shots of a witch being prepared for the fire, the camera moves back, and the woman, on the ladder to which she has been tied, falls in an arc across the entire frame to the fire below.

Day of Wrath

After *Day of Wrath*, Dreyer's isolated career went through another decade before producing another unique expression of the inexplicable spiritual dimension of existence in *Ordet* (*The Word*, 1955). More matter-of-fact and laconic of manner, it sets up a world of the commonplace acts and things of a society ruled by formal religion, against which are posed the transcendental intuitions of the mad young man Johannes. But at the climax, while his sister-in-law is about to have a baby, Johannes collapses, then rises freed from his madness. When the woman dies in childbirth, a small daughter asks Johannes to call her back to life. In the final paradox, transcendence is made manifest in the physical world as Johannes performs the miracle. Not in madness, but in lucidity, does he become the true bearer of the miraculous.

After yet another decade, Dreyer pushed his concern for purification—both in the souls of his protagonists and the means of his film-making—to a different extreme. In *Gertrud* (1964), there is a reduction of both plot continuity and the usual signs of dramatic development, although this development does occur. The film has a lingering slowness in focusing on the way form can reveal the inexpressible nuances of the inner life—human form and face, the modulation of movements, the stylization of dress and décor, the exactness of formal composition. Even the close-ups are less emphatic, more moderately distanced, the takes long, allowing the scene to send forth its vibrations, a purified Realism in which the camera is passive before more than the mere surfaces of things. It is a demanding, even frustrating film, insistent on its own kind of indirections, its oblique revealing of the inner by the intensity of its focus on patterns of the outer. Its style is one with its theme:

As Gertrud begins her realization of the possibilities of the soul and love, she chooses to renounce its human forms, accepting the losses inherent in the loneliness that is also her triumph.

Cocteau   The stylized approach to film-making of Jean Cocteau had been established in the early sound-film *The Blood of a Poet* (1930) but was not consolidated until his sequence of films in the postwar years. Like Dreyer, Cocteau was intrigued by the movies' possibility of giving tangible form to the evanescent ambiguities of the imagination and spirit—that other world reached, so often in his films, through the motif of mirrors. But unlike Dreyer, Cocteau chose in the main to break with the surfaces of things, to present the audience directly with images of a fantasy that was more than real, that was "Surreal." Like the Surrealist playwrights—but with less emphasis on wildness and moral anarchy—Cocteau wanted to pitch his symbols at a level of immediate, if confusing, apprehension, following the flow of dreamlike free associations, establishing a new continuity between the conscious and the unconscious, unifying contraries. He sought to startle and open, "to prevent images," as he said, "from flowing" in normal patterns of expectation, "to oppose them to each other, to anchor them and join them without destroying their relief," their separate, immediate impact and uniqueness.

In the earlier *Blood of a Poet,* he had composed a set of separate vignettes —a fantasy odyssey that builds an ambiguous allegory of the poet's attempts to fuse the contraries between the artist and his work, his imagination and his literal existence, his present and his past, his life and his death. In *Beauty and the Beast* (1946), he organized a more conventional narrative, an innocently pure fairy tale concerning the triumph of romance and imagination, its ornateness and airiness calmly presented in a variety of manners— farcical depiction of the real world, extreme stylization for the transition to the world of romance of the beast, ornate and symbolic décor in this world approached with a matter-of-fact simplicity of camera and editing. In *Les Parents Terribles* (1948), the tragic emotional entanglements of a family are conceived with a literal psychological surface but abstracted within the oppressive walls of the apartments, theatrically heightened by the acting and classic plot development, all magnified further by constant close-ups.

Orphée (1950) is more complex and the high point of Cocteau's film-making. Its mythic allegory is presented with a relish for the kind of conjuring tricks that Georges Méliès had early shown the cinema was capable of; yet, it is moored to reality by a witty use of the trappings and things of the contemporary world. In it, Orphée, the poet, forsakes the ease of domesticated love and disciplined, domesticated art for the princess who represents the liberating but dangerous allure of ultimate beauty in art and its strange partnership with death. He journeys back and forth (always through a mirror, penetrating the image of the self to something beyond) between the world of life, literal reality, and the world of the "Zone," the unconscious, the

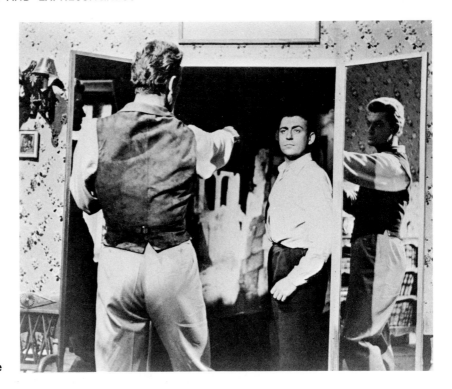

Orphée

imagination, death. Even the Zone, however, has its restricting order, against which passion and spirit must finally rebel. The setting of the Zone is the bombed-out ruins of the town of Saint-Cyr; the princess travels in a black Rolls Royce, whose car radio emits orphic utterings like "The bird sings with its fingers." Her messengers of death are black-leather-clad motor-cyclists with machine guns. Unique and personal, *Orphée* is nonetheless a film that shows others the way to a new blending of the Realist things of the surface world and the stylized expressiveness of something more.

In *The Testament of Orpheus* (1959), his last film, Cocteau's use of cinema magic, free association of transitions, and idiosyncratic symbolism is more playful, less structured; he returns again to vignette sequences of a poet's strange quests (with himself this time as the poet and with references to his own works and friends), again seeking to bridge the fragmented worlds of man.

Ophuls   The forties and fifties also saw the full flowering of the talent of Max Ophuls, like Dreyer and Cocteau, a film-maker in the early days of silence and sound but, unlike them, a constant worker within the commercial system of film production. Yet Ophuls too is concerned with a world beyond the mundane surfaces. As his spokesman, the master of ceremonies in *La Ronde,* says, "I am the incarnation of your desire to know everything. Men never know more than a part of reality. Why? Because they see only one aspect of things." The other aspects of things that Ophuls wanted to catch did not have the spirituality of Dreyer or the metaphysical and esthetic ambiguities of Cocteau; they were the sensuous beauties and pleasures—and the inevitable pains—of romance, precariously moored to a world of unwieldy, unyielding reality.

Thus, in Ophuls's stylized approach, even the data of this world are given a greater expressiveness, the Realist surfaces made to shine with the presence of the sentiments, always harassed but enduring. Though always a romantic, sophisticated yet gently tender, Ophuls did not begin to perfect the freer, expressive form for his evocations until the last four films of his career. In France in the thirties and America in the late forties, his materials had been more conventional in story and structure, always with a Lubitsch elegance and sheen of romance. Two of his American films, *Caught* (1948) and *Reckless Moment* (1949), shared in the ambience of the *noir* substyle yet showed a greater decorative elegance. *The Exile* (1947) and *Letter from an Unknown Woman* (1948) had costumed European settings. The latter was a typical Ophuls triumph of décor, movement, and tone over the trivial emptiness of story line, evoking the bittersweet nostalgia of a lost time of sensitive sufferers for romance.

In these films, as in the next four, the key to the Ophuls expressiveness is in décor and movement. Within the ornamentally full but clearly patterned settings, Ophuls orchestrates the movements of his characters in expressive designs, their movement and the décor toned by the constant movement of his camera. It is most typically a smooth glide, a flow of lyricism that frees the materials from the mundane world yet maintains their tie with it by avoiding the interruption of a cut. There is no nicer example than the scene in the foyer of the opera in *Letter:* In one long, continuously moving take, Ophuls first establishes the flux of the crowd in the foyer; then, without emphasis, he edges toward one of his favorite giant staircases, follows the heroine and her husband up the staircase with a graceful, gliding arc, turns to survey the crowd below, and moves slowly to the face of the heroine as she hears the gossips below mention the name of her lover. In the movement itself is caught the doomed connection of the sensitive romantic to the world below and the grace of her sentiments in soaring above it.

Back in France, Ophuls freed himself from conventional structure with his version of Arthur Schnitzler's *La Ronde* (1950). Its 10 vignettes of blighted romance are interlocked by ironic coincidences of plot, interrupted by the playful machinations of the ringmaster (the director), who is free of the traps that art and life set for the characters.

Le Plaisir (1951) is a less successful anthologizing of three separate tales by de Maupassant, but *The Earrings of Madame de . . .* (1953) deepens and enriches the use of the cyclical structure of *La Ronde.* In it, he traces the passage of a pair of earrings from owner to owner, but focuses on the romantic defeat of Madame de . . . , who is so much a part of the spinning world of surface glitter (heightened by Ophuls's always moving camera) that she subverts the growth of the love that has made her more sensitive but also more vulnerable. In one telling sequence, in which montage is used so subtly as to disguise itself, the movement and changing pattern of her life are part of the movement of the dancing of Madame de . . . and her lover and the camera's equivalent grace, the subtle flow of shots—even between long shots and close-ups—as they move around many dance floors, which seem to be one floor despite the changes of clothing and the increasing intimacy of their attitudes toward each other.

Ophuls's final work, *Lola Montes* (1955), is, with a fittingness uncommon in the history of the motion-picture industry, a culmination of his earlier themes and techniques and the vehicle of an important new development. No longer content merely to toy with extending reality into expressiveness, Ophuls creates a new blend of Expressionist allegory and stylization of the literal that is a perfect expression of his themes. The film is a last subtle statement about the ambiguous powers of love and art, which may be illusions, temporary, defeated, defeating, but nonetheless ultimately rise, however trapped, above the mediocrity of everyday life.

The redeeming power of woman as bearer of love and artistic sensibilities comes, however, only from a network of ironies and her ostensible defeat. The structure of the film enforces these ironies. Lola is a notorious attraction in a circus, whose baroque, ornate grotesqueness is treated as fantasy allegory. It is a world of harsh, commercialized misuse of the artist and the work of art and of the crass reality of the audience that seeks titillation. Yet out of it, and despite her defeat by it, Lola's power as an image of beauty and love (and of the artist-director's power to invoke them) does grow. This circus world (with its demanding ringmaster who is, nonetheless, not immune to Lola's power) is the framework for a series of memories of her love affairs. These memories are treated with the innocence of sentimental romances, colored delicately to match their seasons in contrast with the interlaced freakishness and violent colors of the circus framework. But even in Lola's past, her rise leads only to her downfall, the assertion of her feminine freedom trapping her in the circles of courtesanship, all of her sumptuous rooms finally cell-like around her—an effect achieved by draping or blocking out portions of the CinemaScope frame, the moving camera trapped within or (in responding to her entrances and exits) accelerated to hectic oscillations unusual for Ophuls.

The scenes of her career as a courtesan are intercut with scenes of the circus, in which she is now commercially exploited as a freak of romance. As her amorous adventures lead her up the social ladder, in the circus she climbs to higher and higher platforms, while questioned by the audience about her past. At her downfall, at the time of her one true love, in the circus

Lola Montes

parallel she must dive into a tank of water. Though dizzy and sick, she performs her act, seems to die. But then she magically rises once more in one last paradox. She is seen sitting in a sideshow cage like some exotic animal. The ringmaster of the circus has thus triumphed over the reality of her death, uses her once more as men line up to kiss her hand for a dollar. In a similar but contrasting manner. Ophuls, the director, manages once more to resurrect her romantic power from defeat, even fom commercial misuse. For even the circus audience is shown to sense the wonder of coming near, even for a moment, the power of the sentiments. The men of the audience stand in a line that seems to recede endlessly, all ready to pay (like the movie audience) for the kiss that can triumph over reality. And with the last moving shot of his career, Ophuls tracks back over the heads of the line of men, Lola getting smaller and smaller, until the two audiences seem to merge, hers and his.

Unfortunately, the film did not find its audience immediately. Although its stature and innovative influence have grown through the years, it was mutilated on its release, much to Ophuls's anguish, and not shown in its full original version until 1961. But by then Ophuls was dead.

CHAPTER SIXTEEN

NEW DIRECTIONS OUT OF OLD

The dominant open style of the contemporary period can be seen as a movement of synthesis, reconciling in new, interacting equations previously antithetical tendencies. As such, it represents an incorporation into the popular mass art of the movie esthetic and stylistic developments that came earlier in twentieth-century art, literature, and drama. But this incorporation has accommodated the bedrock sensory fact of motion pictures—the immediacy, the impact, the psychological reality of the film image (turning anything that is so imaged into an independently real sensory fact). As a result, any umbrella term to cover the various individual styles of the period would need to be a compound—such as expressive Realism, realistic expressiveness, or realistic Expressionism—embracing the readily discernible tendency toward a more expressive form of Realism more open to the intangible, or the equally discernible tendency toward a neo-Expressionism that is more flexible and realistic. Both tendencies share much common ground in approach and style; both seek new, multifaceted ways to use the realistic face of the film image—while intensifying its sensory impact—in contrast to the complete break with representation seen in many of the current styles in other arts.

NEW VIEWS OF REALITY

In all the arts, these new attitudes toward the realistic image are connected to fundamental changes in attitudes toward reality itself. The techniques that go against or beyond traditional Realism are attempts to give shape to, find a form for a sense of a reality that is elusive, ambiguous, even contradictory, and finally, ungraspable. In this view, the external world is too paradoxical, too much in flux to be susceptible to a closed pattern; similarly, man's perception and consciousness are too undependable, too subjective, too problematic to allow for any accurate, objective relationship of man and reality. Even the newer formulations of science itself—which was one of the prime shapers of the Realist attitude—have taken us beyond viewing physical reality as a neat, completely classifiable and perceivable monolith. The new physics, for example, allows for randomness, uncertainty, indeterminacy, insists that our very examination of phenomena must alter them and thus make them, in final terms, unknowable. Psychology, too, in its continuing examination of the human psyche—the unconscious, perception, knowledge and memory— has moved in the same direction of ambiguity and subjectivity.

Much that is new in recent attempts to go beyond literal imitation, beyond objective representation in art can be traced to concepts of subjectivity, especially as popularized by the varied, and even contradictory, breeds of existentialism. From this perspective, life is seen as a random set of separate points of existence—not continuing ultimate essences—perceived by a highly fallible single consciousness at single moments of existence, a consciousness that seeks to create its own, necessarily impermanent, meanings.

Similarly, current styles in art have attempted to find techniques that capture and suggest the irrational and inexplicable, that whole realm of experience that lies beyond conscious control and reasoned, logical understanding. They have attempted to give form to the unconscious.

The ambiguity of the flux of things and events, the ambiguity of man's inner world of identity, motivation, choice—these, too, are concepts that have had a major impact on artists and their aims and techniques. In a landmark study of 1908 entitled *Abstraction and Empathy: A Contribution to the Study of Style,* Wilhelm Worringer was among the first to point out that empathy (and thus artistic immersion, identification, illusion) rises from ease and security and results in styles of representationalism, while the urge to abstraction (and thus distortion, dislocation) is the product of a great inner unrest inspired in man by the phenomena of the outside world. "In the face of the intractable nature of these phenomena," he wrote, "the artist through abstraction seeks to wrest the object of the world out of its natural context, and in so doing gain some new hold on it."

Still, as existentialism also suggests, even at best this hold on reality must be incomplete. The philosopher Husserl spoke of the need "to place the world in brackets"—to reduce existence arbitrarily to artificial patterns of visible and tangible phenomena in order to understand and say something about it, while recognizing constantly that existence is beyond being actually captured in this way. A similar awareness of the limitations of his own tools to shape life into form has led the modern artist to seek techniques that come to terms with these limitations. The film director, too, recognizes that his images, for all their seeming realism, are an incomplete suggestion, an arbitrary if necessary reduction of an actuality that cannot be fixed, contained, or categorized. Thus, he is led to seek new ways to use the tangible details of acts, appearances, possessions, surroundings, movements, looks—the concrete materials of the film image.

THE NEW STYLE: OPENNESS

The new consensus of film style exhibits several forms of openness. It is more open than the conventional Realist style in obtruding, in exposing—even flaunting—its devices, its power to manipulate, whether the flourishes and the lively flamboyance of effect are appropriately tied to content or more renegade in running roughshod over content in a display of stylishness.

It is more open, too, to symbolism, one that shows greater diversity. The diversity is manifest in the kinds of things that are symbolized—with increased attention given to embodying the ambiguities of mood and situation, the intangibles of personality, unconscious impulses and motives. It is also seen, however, in the kinds of symbols developed—avoiding, for example, the Eisensteinian simile in which the second term is extraneous to the situation and, instead, embedding the symbols in the dramatic development of the scene.

But in turn this symbolism may be bizarre, grotesque, a distortion of commonplace reality and yet a part of the dramatic context; for a greater openness has also been developing in film-makers' conceptions of workable dramatic contexts and in the audience's abilities and expectations. We have witnessed the wide acceptance of allegorical modes, especially those that disfigure and distort the normally perceived surfaces of reality for the sake of expressing the tensions and traumas of the inner life. This emphasis on the figurative feel of a situation and its objects, rather than on accurate literal representation of its surface only, has led to an intensive and open use of the projective, externalizing devices of Surrealism and Expressionism even greater than in the film world of the twenties. In contrast to traditional Expressionist drama, these contemporary attempts to give visual body to abstractions of emotion or idea are regularly merged with Realist methods; this merging maintains the direct identification and validation of literal representation along with the indirect suggestiveness of distortion and hyperbole.

This blending is in line with the eclectic openness of contemporary styles with respect to approaches and devices, moods, tones, and emotions as used in an individual work or the whole body of work of a director. This can lead to ambiguities of tone in a single scene or to striking shifts and juxtapositions between scenes, to mixing the trivial and the significant, the stereotyped and the subtle, the comic and the tragic, the brutal and the amusing, the pitiable and the awesome, the ironic and the sincere.

The new audacious blends of the contemporary style have been fittingly applied to the screen's equally audacious advances in social content. Protest and criticism of society have become more extreme, and concurrently, the treatment of these issues has broken free of the limitations of linear plotting and unbroken representationalism that prevailed in the "serious" social films of the thirties and forties. Harsh comedy, allegory, antinarrative Brechtian structures have joined Realist representation as accepted media for social messages.

In Character and in Plotting

In terms of dramatic content, the most important increase in complexity of the period has occurred in the depiction of character, whether in Realist or non-Realist works. This increase has continued the medium's constant progress in capturing the elusiveness of human personality—the contradictions of personality, the tentativeness and confusion of motivation, the precariousness of identity. This development of greater subtlety in the psychology of film narrative has been especially noticeable in an openness to the vagaries of character change—whether in delineating abrupt (even inexplicable) change, limited change, or the inability to change. As a result, one of the key uses of the surface phenomena that the Realist image can reproduce has been expanded to provide projections of indeterminate states of personality beyond these phenomena—as metaphors of consciousness, whether literally imitative or distorted.

To match the shifting conception of character, concepts of the nature of dramatic plotting have also become more sophisticated. Conflict has become more flexible, allowing less precisely defined clashes of desire, taking greater account of the contradictions and ambiguities of desire and its goals. In turn, the tight cause-and-effect development of traditional Realist drama has been loosened to allow for the loose end, the sudden, the inexplicable, and, as mentioned above, the character change without a cause, character stasis despite cause. We have seen, as well, a reaction against the clear-cut resolution, against the sharply defined growth of awareness or its absence. This breakthrough toward a fuller realism than the conventional Realist patterns allowed has, however, led to its own kinds of reductive clichés and fads —in the same way that the advance into new areas and complexities of subject matter has not been without its own paradoxical kind of commercialized falsity and emptiness.

In
Structure

The loosening of the bases of plotting—conflict, cause and effect, and resolution—is but one aspect of a general loosening of structure in the open style; other changes are apparent in both overall patterns and internal patterns of editing. Even when a basic plot line is maintained, the new Realist approach allows for more flexible relationships between scenes and sequences, less tightly organized, straight-line orchestration in the overall arc of the plot elements—something seen tentatively in the early films of Italian neo-Realism. On the one hand, these patterns are more elliptical, omitting more, focusing on distinct, separable vignettelike sequences that epitomize the states of the characters, without direct causal connections; on the other hand, there has been a tendency to include more in the sequences that are used, staying within scenes longer, letting scenes flow with less internal conflict and explicit cause-and-effect dynamics.

Whatever the degree of Realist representation, the new styles have employed dislocation of normal plot patterns. This more complex structuring of continuity varies from the abrupt jolting of transitions between scenes, though still maintaining the sense of dramatic illusion, to more complete Brechtian alienation techniques. The Brechtian devices of distancing intrude on the dramatic illusion, intermittently breaking the audience's immersion in, and identification with, the reality of the playacting. In more extreme cases, they can deny that immersion completely, producing new modes of audience involvement.

Dislocation of conventional audience expectation is also a basic characteristic of the open style's more flexible approaches to editing. In contemporary editing patterns, transitions between scenes, places, and times are generally more abrupt and unexplained—the "jump cut" of juxtaposition rather than the guiding cut of overt, direct relationship. This elliptical tendency is found *within* scenes, as well, where traditional sequences of establishing shots are disregarded and greater concision is used within the developing scene. Yet, at the same time, there has been an equally strong emphasis on long takes, with both a moving or stationary camera. The combinations are thus left freer, more open, more adaptable to the demands of individual scenes and moods than was the case in the main body of work within earlier conventions. This kind of synthesis has made the contemporary movement rich in invention and creative verve—insightful, sophisticated, consciousness-shaping in ways that surpass the contributions of earlier periods—and yet peculiarly susceptible, within its times' unique combination of individual license and commercial pressure, to a facile mannerism, a decadence of excess.

CHAPTER SEVENTEEN

Antonioni
and
the
Newer
Realism

The modification in the Realist style initiated by the Italian neo-Realists continued to gain impetus in film production in a number of countries. In Italy itself, one of the most influential, and continually evolving, definitions of the new directions in open, expressive Realism has been made by the films of Michelangelo Antonioni. After five earlier films, the first showing of his *L'Avventura* in 1960 set up ragged ripples of confusion, even scorn, but established in perfected form a new kind of film consciousness.

ANTONIONI

In his first five features, Antonioni had already begun to develop, though unevenly, a distinctive technique for making vivid new images of a real world—one that is refracted through his consciousness and, in turn, that of his characters. Although the neo-Realists had shifted the focus of the social film from the direct analysis of social problems to the effects of them on individuals, they had to a great degree remained outside their characters. While never severing the ties to encompassing social situations and problems, Antonioni was concerned from the start with going further into the individual, to seeing the intimate, interior consequences of all that was happening in society. This dramatization of the inner crisis of emotion and spirit, of subjective consciousness, was to be achieved, however, by staying with representational means and not by projecting inner states through the distortions of Expressionism or by the objective exemplification of them in allegory. *Le Amiche* (1955) is the best of these early films, still one of Antonioni's most ambitious attempts to balance the delineation of a milieu with the sympathetic observation of the emotional states of its characters. Its observation of a group of women and their interleafing relationships with men revolves around three parallel stories and thus involves more detailed, intricately articulated plotting than his later films.

L'Avventura   With *L'Avventura*, the results of his experimentation burst forth fullgrown; it is a masterpiece of inner, indirect, symbolic Realism, an expressive Realism. In it, the socioeconomic aspect of neo-Realism is still present but in a new form. It is not merely that Antonioni has shifted his attention from the lower classes. His evocation of the values and pressures of the upper class is full and precise, but those values are of interest to him in terms of their internalization—how they become part of the inner web of character, part of the shaping structure for the particular arcing of tensions between men and women today. It is meaningful that Claudia (Monica Vitti) is of a lower class than the others in the film; but though that is a factor in the complex of emotions she brings to her relationship to them and to Sandro, it is not a determining factor. When Sandro, the architect turned successful cost consultant, betrays her at the elaborate, crowded aristocratic hotel, he does so by failing to break with his boss Ettore (as he had promised Claudia) and by staying all night with the tramp starlet in the deserted lobby. Both acts are part of the wracking contradictions within him, though not merely as symbolic social criticism. His economic capitulation, intertwined with his denial of satisfying work, is both cause and symptom, an interacting part of personality. It is indicative of Antonioni's subtlety of personality delineation through action and image that Sandro (Gabriele Ferzetti) stays in the lobby with the tramp, does not go to her room, debases himself (in vivid visual imagery, including a shot of her toes picking up the money he has scornfully thrown down). It is a climactic gesture, typical of the self-destructiveness of his impotent self-awareness, in response to the intractableness of his love for Claudia, which he fears, and his guilt about capitulating to Ettore.

The complex forms of this inner unease, this uncertainty of ego and unwieldy welter of sentiments, are Antonioni's chief concern, especially as externalized in relations between the sexes and between the individual and his or her social milieu. In the cool but sympathetic delineation of this unease, he has redefined the terms of dramatic conflict. Not only has he reduced the importance of external patterns of conflict (there is less plot event, less emphatic action), but he has changed the relationship between action and inner conflict. Diffuse contradictions of inner needs and motives and the fluctuation of mood and feeling are now the subtle and complex terms of conflict. External actions and conflict between characters do reflect these inner contradictions, but not in the traditional one-for-one, exact plotting of cause and effect. But cause and effect is still present, if more indirectly revealed because more inwardly complex.

The looser overall structure of L'Avventura and subsequent Antonioni films —with less articulation of the steps of dramatic plotting and more abrupt transitions—is a part of the new way of defining dramatic cause and effect. In L'Avventura the basic structural shift from examination of the character of Anna, whose disappearance is never explained, is a part of the abrupt shifting and confusion of emotion in the characters, especially Claudia and Sandro. Their search for Anna is indecisive, dramatically diffuse, psychologically uneasy, parallel to the disturbed reluctance of their growing desire for each other. Guilt about Anna is only a part of that inner disturbance, a symptom of something deeper, yet it becomes a point of focus for it. Its equivocal role is given form by the continued nagging discrepancy between maintaining the expectation of developing the search for Anna and constantly digressing from it.

In that structural tension, the search for Anna becomes a search for emotional balance. The scenes that carry out the tension between the two searches, and reveal the tensions of the inner life, are indicative of Antonioni's distinct method of using dramatic scene. The scenes do build a subtle cause-and-effect sequence, not of plot narrative but of emotional narrative, remaining open to the nuances of shifting, confusing need and impulse by excising the normal linking devices for transitions, whether in terms of individual shots or plot development. In the central sequence of Claudia and Sandro acting upon their feelings and accepting them, but with an acceleration and fluctuation in the tensions of those feelings, we first see them, in long shots, in the confusing isolation of a lovely mountain village that is completely uninhabited, an externalization of their own floundering amid perspectives gone awry. Immediately following is a series of close shots of Claudia's joyful face, as they impulsively make love in an open field. After a train goes by, seen past them in longer shot in the aftermath of their love-making, Claudia is next shown having a mixed reaction to the hungry stares of a group of men in a small town. Then in the counterpointing setting of a tawdry small shop of the town, she and Sandro grow closer. The possibilities of their relationship are strengthened on the roof of the church, in a scene amid church bells and the open sky, intersected, however, by confusing lines of ropes and wires. Claudia's relaxation into happy feelings is next shown as she playfully sings and dances in the hotel room, but to a song harshly blaring from a political sound truck outside, which abruptly cuts off. The disturbing counterpoint is carried on in Sandro's unease, his abrupt withdrawal from closeness. He leaves Claudia in the room, intentionally spills ink on a young architect's drawing, invites a fight; when he returns to the room, he says he is sorry, tries to make love to her coldly and demeaningly, but then relents.

In addition to working together in an intricate geometry of emotional tensions, scenes also stand as variations in a general pattern of motifs. Thus throughout *L'Avventura*, scenes serve as variations on the theme of debasing sexuality, arising compulsively from unease, guilt, boredom: Anna's going to bed with Sandro while Claudia waits below; the cold, jaded sexual mannerisms displayed on the yacht; the response of the crowd of men to the whorish starlet; the guilty, sneaking sexual innuendo of the small-town druggist, in front of his jealous wife; Giulia's pathetic coquetry with the young artist; Sandro's final self-abasement with the starlet.

All the scenes illustrate as well Antonioni's method of using the images and actions within scenes as objective correlatives, visual embodiments of pervasive mood and specific psychological states. These visual correlatives form motifs of background setting—whether the craggy rocks of the island, the white walls of rooms, or the elaborate furnishings of the wealthy—but also work in terms of individual objects within scenes. After Anna's disappearance and before the sequence with Sandro mentioned above, Claudia is in a state of indecision and troubling emotional openness. As she waits for Sandro at the estate of his friends, this is shown by her participation in their activities, but also by specific objects. In Patrizia's room, Claudia tries on one of Patrizia's wigs (of dark hair, like Anna's), examines herself in the mirror, walks out with the wig before she realizes she still has it. The implications of the wig are carried out further, obliquely, in the next scene, as she is forced to watch Giulia's coquetry with young Gioffredo, framed by his paintings of nude women, interrupted (as Claudia turns from them and looks out the window) by one shot of a forest and mountain, which picks up the nature motif used throughout. When they crudely embrace, knocking his painting materials onto the floor, Claudia leaves. On a landing, she checks her hair in a large mirror, as though comparing her own hair with the wig of the role (projected in Giulia's actions) that she is afraid she is assuming.

The film was Antonioni's first in wide screen, and the new height-to-width ratio allowed him to maintain an emphasis on faces while keeping them in medium shots with other faces or surrounding objects. But while the held shot of relatively long duration, with changing interaction within the composition, is his basic approach, the film exhibits telling close-ups: Claudia's face in the joyous love scene in the fields; the money between the legs of the starlet; in the final sequence, Claudia's anguished face, and her hand white against Sandro's black hair, exquisitely blended with longer shots of them on

L'Avventura

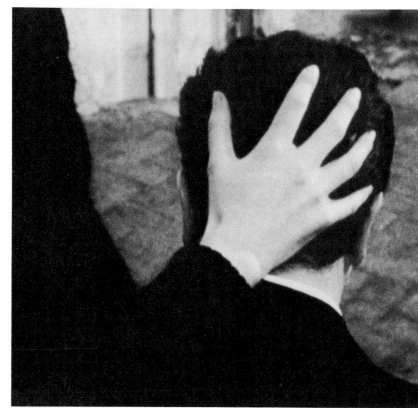

the hotel terrace, moving to the final long shot of them, photographed from behind, against a landscape that mirrors the ambiguous state of their troubled emotions, but that, like her hand still caressingly on his head, enigmatically gives some sense of misty, morning possibility.

La Notte The two films that followed constitute with *L'Avventura* an unofficial trilogy on the basis of both approach and theme. In *La Notte* (1961), the amorphous crisis is related to maintaining an emotional relationship rather than initiating one. Since the emotional thrust out of the malaise of ennui is more muted and deflected, some of Antonioni's actions and images, aimed at giving form to the inner decay, are contrived and lack the perfect balance of experiencing and symbolizing of *L'Avventura*: the husband, Giovanni (Marcello Mastroianni), momentarily responding to the pathetic sexual advances of the woman in the hospital (against a white wall); the artificial sexuality of the nightclub show; the rainstorm that interrupts Lidia's (Jeanne Moreau's) indecisive attempt at infidelity; her reading of an old love letter from Giovanni in the final scene, and his failure even to remember it. Even the details (at the long party) of the ornate display of wealth that cannot dispel emptiness are less telling, since characterizations are less individualized; the paralleling of Giovanni's emotional deadening with his sense of waste at the successful publication of his new novel seems schematic and didactic.

But still *La Notte* abounds with examples of the oblique rendering of troubled consciousness that embody its living, ambiguous disorder. The composition of a single shot captures the diminution of sexual attraction: Lidia, in her bath, asks Giovanni for the sponge. Abstractedly, he gives it to her; we see only the lower part of him as the shot is held on her disappointed response in the tub. The yearning and sense of loss that nag at Lidia are given a fascinating, indirect revelation in her seemingly digressive walk through the city. In this much debated sequence, the seemingly aimless occurrences and images that maintain a spontaneous flow of experiencing are selected and patterned to reveal a microcosm of the world outside that of Giovanni and Lidia, with its sheltered emotional clutter and the whole assortment of her unfaced needs and regrets. The sequence is intercut with two sets of images that evoke Giovanni's concurrent sense of deep, unfaced despair. The two moods are brought together when she calls him to pick her up; but as they walk through an area they used to frequent, they are caught in isolating shots, he unable to act on the sense of necessary change that she feels to a greater degree.

To the end, the possibility of change, after each flirts briefly with adultery, is still open but unsure. In the morning, the two sit in a sand trap of a golf course, next to the mansion, then desperately embrace and roll in the sand, as the camera backs up and away to place them, petty and ambiguous, in the surrounding grass and trees of what is after all an artificial slice of nature; their passion in the sand trap may be also. The question is left open.

The Eclipse Their trap is given a counterpoint in the figure of Valentina (Monica Vitti), with whom Giovanni has flirted and in whom both Giovanni and Lidia sense a glimmering of a more affirmative and active attitude. In the next film, *The Eclipse* (1961), the unshaped potential for awareness, sensitiveness, and openness that Vitti represents throughout the trilogy is at the center. It opens with the morning of a false new beginning and closes with the evening of sudden, unexplained, but inevitable failure of emotional connection. At the opening, the shots emphasize the things of the apartment in which Vittoria (Vitti), for reasons she will not and cannot explain, is breaking off an affair with Riccardo; all is fragmented, isolated. At the close, her romance with the stockbroker Piero (Alain Delon) has proved untenable even as it has developed, and we abruptly discover it is over when the characters do not appear at the corner of their regular meeting place. Instead, in a long and daring montage of shots of setting, objects, and passers-by, the dislocation, the loneliness of missed emotional connections are given a supreme oblique representation, concluding with a last objective correlative of the emotional impasse—an enlarging close-up of the streetlamp, blurring all into diffused blankness, even as it lightens the night's deepening darkness.

While the male character is this time too obviously a blocked, shallow representative of the moneyed classes, and thus too obviously insufficient for Vittoria, the film is at its best in taking the time to delineate the possibilities and limiting alternatives of the world in which the unfocused vitality of Antonioni's bearer of the flow of sentiment must find its fulfillment.

Red Desert With *Red Desert* (1964), the crisis of sensitivity is intensified to the point of crippling neurosis; yet in it, Giuliana (Vitti again) is attempting to reintegrate herself in a more fulfilling way with the people and things of her surroundings, and her attempts have a fullness of psychological detail that makes her far more than a case history. The complexity of her attempt at a more flexible adaptation is seen in the terms of the conflicts, with less judgmental analysis of the male protagonists than in the previous work. For all the elements have their values and weaknesses, their rights and wrongs, but all are dislocated. Thus, the industrial and masculine milieu is frightening and destructive but has its wonders and its own beauties; in shots of it, frequently a lovely abstract composition is discordantly invaded by a human figure, from the side, from below, from above, or left behind when the figure disappears from the frame.

This sliding past, this missing of connections, is part of Giuliana's relationship with the three male figures—her husband, her child, her temporary lover Corrado. Their limitations bump against hers, keeping her distanced.

The film is Antonioni's first in color. While always credibly realistic, the color is subtly manipulated to externalize Giuliana's subjective responses; it becomes the key device in Antonioni's fullest attempt to date to follow and project the consciousness of a single character, to capture the subjective reality of a moment. The tones, and even the beauties, of the masculine world

Red Desert

are full of strident contrasts yet overall have a coolness, a blue-gray efficiency. Giuliana's own dreams of a rocky island refuge are toned in yellow and creamy pink. When she is inspirited by the possibilities of love with Corrado, their car ride is toned in natural sunlit hues. When they make love, the heavy somber colors of the hotel room are transformed into pinks. But always the colors are used in conjunction with things, shapes, and patterns to externalize mood: the clutter of things and bodies all hued a garish red for the titillating but disturbing sexual gamesmanship in the dockside cabin; the black hull of a ship suddenly blotting everything else out as all stand perplexed by the plague that the ship has brought, and a gray fog covers them, separating them from each other.

Blow-Up *and* *Zabriskie* *Point* While the color in *Blow-Up* (1966) is just as pointedly symbolic—and also works in conjunction with the other elements of the image—its use differs in a way that reflects the different intentions of the movie. The approach here is to give form to an abstract conception with a new kind of balance struck between Realist representation and expressive allegorical embodiment of abstract themes. While its central young photographer is given a full set of personal characteristics, he and his interactions with others are not developed with a concern for full psychological density. He is clearly a vehicle for something more. That something more, elusive as it is, involves an audacious

Blow-Up

attempt to fuse a delineation of current and social and personality tendencies with more timeless dilemmas about art and the artist, perception, and the ambiguities of reality.

In the garish colors and contrasts—full of purples and other rich tones—of the mod, cool world of London, the photographer takes part in a number of variations on sex acts, interpersonal acts, socially concerned acts that all remain distanced and exploitive, artificial, without full personal commitment. Yet he also mirrors the dilemma of the artist in manipulating both people and reality while attempting to be true to them. In the striking natural yet mysterious greenery of the park, he encounters an enigmatic event of raw reality that bursts through the protective coloration of his world. He can only perceive its truth in stages, by blowing up (in black and white, which again opposes the surface colors of his life) his artistic images of what turns out to be a murder. But his black-and-white images do not really conquer his colors; he evades, he wanders through scenes of bright colors, and he does nothing. At the close, he is surrounded by green again as he seems, for the moment, to understand (by throwing back the imaginary tennis ball) that there is something intangible beyond the easy reality of his surfaces of color and even of black and white. It is an understanding about perception and art, but also about the personal ethics of acting beyond those safe, cool surfaces of indifference.

In *Zabriskie Point* (1970), Antonioni takes another tack. Even more abstracted than *Blow-Up* in treating characters as part of conceptual patterns, it at the same time imposes less on the enigmatic flow of strong surface images. These images are part of an attempt to remain open to the immediate currents, with all their exaggerations, of a place—America—new to Antonioni. While placing them in a pattern of ironies that may be cautionary, he is not basically concerned with taking sides. The film's basic pattern involves a number of parallels, posed around the sensitive central consciousness of a young, Vitti-like woman, but without the fullness of characterization of the Vitti roles, or her acting presence. The parallels set up similar, though seemingly opposing, actions by both of the extremes depicted—the youthful rebels and the business-police establishment: differing but equally fruitless group discussions, antagonism, violence. The girl's fantasy turns the lowest point of the desert, Zabriskie Point, into a paradise of communal, loving sex, but a temporary and illusory one. The boy must act out the unplumbed ritual of rebellion. The businessmen want to turn the desert into a housing development, live on it in an ornate, modern mansion. Yet the mansion is not without its beauty, and its culture. When the girl is finally pushed to hatred (by the shooting of the boy), her visions of exploding the house include destruction of its books as well as its frozen food and gadgets. That last ride of hers into the orange Western sunset, rock music blasting, poses enigmatic ironies typical of the film's difficult blend of critical, questioning detachment and openness to the surface symptoms of a time, place, and culture.

BELLOCHIO, BERTOLUCCI, AND OTHERS

Through this same period, a remarkable array of other expert Italian directors has also been working through the modifications in screen Realism suggested by the neo-Realist movement. These include, among others, Mauro Bolognini, Valerio Zurlini, Damiano Damiani, Franco Rossi, Mario Monicelli; Francesco Rosi and his direct approach to political issues; Elio Petri and his merging of elliptical Realist editing with the conventions and materials of entertainment genres in his social indictments; Pietro Germi and his extension of the Realist surface into the extremes of harsh comedy, most wildly and pointedly in *Seduced and Abandoned* (1963). Among the younger directors, Marco Bellochio jars the precise rendering of objective data with a jocularly despairing wit, creating an ambiguous realm between Realism and distortion, straightforward seriousness and satire. His *China Is Near* (1967), Marxist-oriented satire, ties individual flaws and weaknesses to those of the social system, interweaving the two levels and the details of setting and individual actions with abruptly shifting patterns of editing and changes of tone. The earlier *Fists in His Pocket* (1965) takes a more ambiguous stance, with a piling up of vivid details of suffering and degradation that borders on bizarre caricature, yet maintains an air of sympathetic objectivity.

In contrast, Bernardo Bertolucci, whose first film was produced when he was 21, has thus far produced a more significant body of work by extending the subtle, sophisticated Realism of Antonioni into more direct ideological subjects and by applying a more obtrusive heightening of emphatic technique. In *Before the Revolution* (1967), made when he was 22, he provides an electric, eclectic display of visual virtuosity that energizes, but often helps to blur, his drama. It is an acid but contradictory portrait of a young ideologue whose righteous intellectualizing keeps him from responding fully to others or to his Communist party commitment and finally leads to his self-pitying compromise with the society he had idealistically denounced. The long treatment of the young man's love affair with his emotionally disturbed aunt is excellently handled but does not serve to illuminate the political issues of the film. In the later *The Conformist* (1970), the sexual disturbances of the protagonist are fused, in an intricate dramatic structure, with a rather simplistic exposure of the psychological roots of authoritarianism in Fascist Italy. *The Conformist* is visually impressive. Its rich compositions, which often border on the surreal, deepen mood and tension; its fluid camera movements function dramatically, as in the revealing dance at the nightclub that brings to a climax the tensions within and between the characters. In *The Spider's Strategy* (1970), the intricate subjective structure again joins dilemmas of the personal emotional life—this time more directly involving relations to the father alluded to in the other films—with the complexities of political action. In *Last Tango in Paris* (*Dernier Tango à Paris,* 1972), he turns from the past and politics to the harsh ironies of a misbegotten love affair, using explicit images of sexuality as integral elements in exposing the psychological lacerations of the protagonists, especially the American, Paul (Marlon Brando).

OLMI

Ermanno Olmi most approximates the approach of Antonioni in using the slow, unforced, elliptical unfolding of surface event and image. In his observation of ordinary surfaces, he poetically selects and arranges details to reveal the interior life of the characters.

In many ways, Olmi remains closer to neo-Realist unobtrusiveness, not only in his partial use of nonprofessional actors and concern for lower-class subjects, but in his tendency to schematize less and to deal with simpler, less sophisticated, less psychologically intricate aspects of the sentiments.

As he moved to features from documentaries, his first full-length film, *Time Stood Still* (1959), added to the documentary treatment of building a dam in the mountains the human element of the initiation into manhood of a youth under the tutelage of an older man. Ten years later, he was to treat a similar pattern more subtly in *The Scavengers* (1969), in which a young man who works with a very old man in scavenging war relics breaks with him and the social implications of the job.

In his second and third film, Olmi traced the early career of a similarly ingenuous, persistent, and sensitive young man attempting to find a place for himself in postwar Italy. In *Il Posto* (also called *The Sound of Trumpets* or *The Job*, 1961), the quiet scenes of minor triumphs and painful defeats are enveloped in a humorous melancholy for the plight of the boy and those he seeks to join, whose horizons are no broader than the security and machinery of the large, depersonalizing company. At the close, after a typically poignant office New Year's party during which the boy's awkwardness and loneliness are temporarily conquered when he becomes drunk, he doesn't get the girl but does get a promotion—to the rear desk in a room full of pathetic clerks. He seems almost to think himself happy as we hear the mimeograph machine whirr and clatter on.

In *I Fidanzati* (*The Fiancées*, 1963), there is a similar attention to the accumulation of quiet, everyday scenes of work and diversion, loneliness and sharing, beginning with a wonderfully constructed dance hall sequence that reveals both the social milieu and the crisis in the lives of a young couple. To get enough money to marry, he must go with a construction company to Sicily for several years. They fear the separation may destroy the possibility of a life together. But by the end, they seem to be enduring, as are the others affected by the demands and the enticements of the company. In one sequence, as the young man reads his fiancée's letters, Olmi moves from the literal as he tenderly images the suggestions of her words.

There is a cooler quality, a distancing, despite the color, in *One Fine Day* (*Un Certo Giorno*, 1968), with its more striking combination of abrupt, fast cutting and long-held scenes. For the tone of the color serves to heighten Olmi's ironic assessment of the life of people approaching the other end of the line from that of the young couple—the precarious dilemma of a successful advertising executive, at the peak of his career and power, wealthy, still attractive to women, married for many years. We first sense an unshaped dissatisfaction in the fast pace of the scenes of his professional world and deceitful love life. Then suddenly, he inexplicably runs down and kills a man on a highway. The scenes slow to nagging insistence on detail and duration to capture his painful reappraisal of his comfortable trap, but he eventually succumbs to the comforting patterns and momentum of law, career, and marriage. By the end, responsibility, not only for the accident but for his own life, is blurred again, and we are ironically distanced from his final slight gestures toward reformation: At the close, as his wife sags in sleep against him, his eyes, already bored and trapped, stare at the images on a television screen.

In sharp contrast, the rendering of the surface details of the seemingly pathetic, small-time forger of family emblems of nobility in *In the Summer-*

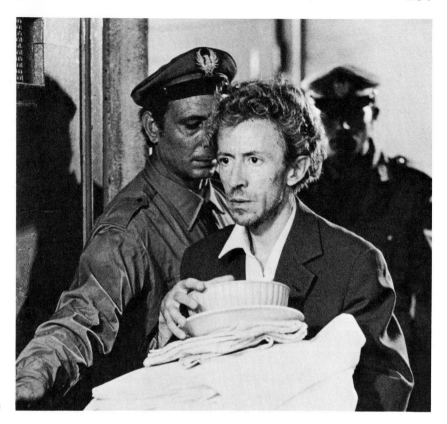

In the Summertime

time (*Durante l'Estate,* 1971) reveals an inner life whose richness surmounts the realities of the surface. The film is the most impressive of Olmi's career. Its technique is a lovely, tenderly humorous embodiment of its theme and an illustration of expressive tendencies in the contemporary Realist film. For this lonely little man, how things express an inner feeling matters more than literal or practical truth: He quits a job as mapmaker because he is not allowed to color the provinces of Italy in ways that express their qualities to him.

Throughout, Olmi uses color to delicately manipulate our response to the truths of the man's inner world. To the law, he is a forger and duper of old men for their money; to himself, to the girl he befriends, and to us, he is a bearer of the inner nobility that defies facts. (There are echoes here of the fragile comic dignity of Chaplin's Little Tramp.) But he is not without his weaknesses: After a wonderful natural flowering of colors during his visit with the girl to the floral park, he goes too far, kicks an interfering attendant, then flees in panic. Back at his apartment, the muted colors express his fright, the pathetic weakness of his collapse. But in the total grayness of the jail and court, he pulls together his strengths, as the girl, in lovely flowering dress, conquers the gloom of weakness and drabness of surface authority, showing that she is indeed the "Princess" he has dubbed her. At the close, he smiles brightly through the bars of his cell, and her smile in the street below lights the drab surfaces of the world.

VISCONTI

From *La Terra Trema* on, Luchino Visconti has pursued his unique extensions of the Realist style. In Visconti's work, the Realist detail and social concern, the transparency before the tensions within the shot are joined, sometimes contradictorily, by an ornateness of décor, composition, and camera movement, and by an operatic intensification of emotions and monumental passions. The elaboration and proliferation, the occasional excesses produce a more mannered Realism, touched by the expressiveness of epic.

Visconti's first three films after *La Terra Trema* indicated the sometimes contradictory directions he was moving in but sought to combine. His *Bellisima* (1951), with Anna Magnani, has a harsh naturalism, with a tendency toward melodramatic exaggerations controlled by an underlying irony. *Senso* (1953) traces the inevitable doom of misguided passion with elegant, appropriately patterned color and composition, placing its tragic love affair in the midst of an epic evocation of an era of historical transition, but not fully integrating the individual and social themes. *White Nights* (1957) is intimate artifice, all muted, moony operatic doom and hothouse romance, its lovers pursuing their fate amid mannered compositions of settings that are correlatives of their moods: snows and fogs; tiny, lonely squares; old bridges and streams; wretched apartments and other touches of the contemporary world.

The Leopard (1963) more fully captures the feel and meaning of an historical epoch, again at a time of change and struggle, but it is beset by contradictions. Its sweep and detail, its elaborate décor and composition do render, with Visconti's always present concern for beauty itself, the aristocratic world of the Lampedusas. At the same time, however, it has too many epic grandeurs, too many ramifications of the personal plots that interweave somewhat clumsily throughout. These blur Visconti's analysis of the betrayal of the Garibaldi revolution as an interaction of socioeconomics and individual psychology, the latter, in turn, shaped by the former. The set piece of the final ball, posing the details of the elegance and decadence of the rich against their blind denial of historical necessity, is a fine example of Visconti's use of décor and the sweep of camera and action to render the feel of social crisis.

Rocco and His Brothers The lavishness of epic detail and heightening of emotionality are applied to the harsher details of contemporary industrial life in *Rocco and His Brothers* (1960), a grandiose, romanticized enlargement of neo-Realism. But again the terms of the social theme—the impact of industrial society on a family—are blurred by other elements, especially the central personal interaction of the vicious, animalistic brother and the saintly Rocco. Their abnormally intense love-hate conflict seems to have little to do with the social

**Rocco and His
Brothers**

setting; and the acting out in violent and extended detail of their Grand Guignol passions through the latter part of the film overbalances the earlier incisive depiction of the impact of social environment on their family.

Perversities and untrammeled passions are carried even further in *The Damned* (1969), accompanied by Visconti's usual emphatic, sensuous rendering of the sumptuous clutter of corruption in the setting. All are treated as symptoms of the social decay that nurtured the rise of Nazism in Germany. But the unity achieved is reductive of the full implications of the social content; there is a disturbing deflection from the broader issues as a result of Visconti's lingering, hyperbolic elaboration of the acting out of twisted sexual passions.

In three other films, in which the manner and materials are more controlled, Visconti has focused on interpersonal relations and the inner life, though not without an important and careful placement of the individualized conflicts in appropriate social contexts. In *Sandra* (1965), he develops a tale of surface suspense while approaching the mysteries of emotion, desire, and identity—this time in triangle of brother, sister, and husband culminating in violence. In *The Stranger* (1969), he makes a faithful, sensitive, realistic adaptation of the novel by Camus; but the very nature of the screen's representation of reality seems to doom inevitably his attempt to bridge the gap between the surfaces, accurately rendered, and the allegorical philosophizing of the novel.

Death　In *Death in Venice* (1971), he is less faithful to the letter of Mann's novel
in　but more successful in a cinematic rendering of his own response to its
Venice　spirit. It is a consummate rendering of subjective states through the objective means of representational imagery. His Aschenbach has distanced himself from the flawed emotionality and interactions of life, seeking to render
through his music a beauty untouched by life's imperfections. His personal
crisis is made one with the larger crisis of culture and society, evoked by
the imagery: The details of lavish décor, of colors, patterns, objects, and
costumes; the equally lavish movements of camera and people at the hermet-
ically cloistered upper-class beach hotel in Venice; the equally striking
scenes without movement; the sensuous shifting of lighting—all have a lovely
artifice, oppressive yet protectively pleasing, with which life and the fullness
of emotion have been sealed off. Rugged life, the disease and death of plague-
ridden Venice, intrudes upon the hotel and Aschenbach (Dirk Bogarde), but
the invasion is paralleled by a catalyst within the world of the hotel and
within Aschenbach—the ambiguous, troubling beauty of the young boy, innocent and knowing, chaste and perverse. Like an hallucination of decay and
disintegration, the frightening ugliness of death and the frightening loveliness
of emotionality, of love, of living beauty challenge and overturn the defenses
of the man, the artist, and the culture—for whom it is too late to adapt. It
seems Visconti's most effective extension of the Realist mode to unify his
own, often contradictory, concerns—the emotional, the esthetic, and the
social.

Death in Venice

CHAPTER EIGHTEEN

FELLINI,
PASOLINI,
AND
SURREAL
EXPRESSIONISM

In the later work of Antonioni, in Bertolucci, in Olmi, in Visconti, the freer rendering of the literal has strained for fuller dimensions—of schematic abstracting, of the rendering of subjective consciousness, of operatic heightening. In the work of Federico Fellini and Pier Paolo Pasolini, the liberating impulse of Italian neo-Realism has led to a greater break with the representation of the literal surface, with what Fellini has called "the fanatic aspect of sensory reality." Both began within the neo-Realist style and then moved further (in differing but complementary ways) than other contemporary directors toward Surreal Expressionism.

This tendency of the contemporary style has in general maintained a degree of representationalism, a resemblance to literal reality. But this literalness is joined to an opposite approach—making concrete, as though literal, the more extravagant metaphors of conscious and unconscious states of mind and feeling. Thus, a broader spectrum of reality—from what is normally seen and heard to what may be experienced inwardly—is treated with a similar matter-of-fact literalness; what it feels like is filmed in the same way as what it is in objective external perception. Although this projection of the intangible and the inward usually has the patterned symbolism of traditional Expressionism, it is also marked by the wilder fluctuations of free association, the intensified blurring of time and causation, of the literal, the dream world, and the fantastic of Surrealism, and often by the complex comic tones of contemporary absurdist theater.

FELLINI

The ornate, elaborately baroque, rampantly sensuous proliferation of imagery in Fellini's more recent films has its roots in his earliest works. For in these were established not only certain basic motifs of character, situation, and setting, certain basic themes, personal and moral, but also a basic set of attitudes toward the surfaces of reality.

Immediately after the war, Fellini worked with Roberto Rossellini on both *Open City* and *Paisan*, but it was in his original story for Rossellini's *The Miracle* and his screenplay for *The Flowers of St. Francis* that his unique personal conceptions were first dramatized. In contrasting ways that, in later works, would be combined or denied, they celebrate a dimension of emotional and spiritual richness that is beyond the ordinary levels of existence. The wretched madwoman in *The Miracle* who imagines a passing derelict a saint and her own pregnancy miraculous does touch a realm of being that transcends that of the mocking townspeople who have driven her to a lone mountain peak; St. Francis and his saintly fools do also transcend the brutal powers of society and bring a transcendent spirit to the world's common reality.

The evolving Surrealist fecundity of Fellini's imagery can be traced from these earliest attempts to deal with the extraordinary within the ordinary. In an interview in 1965, he traced through his films to that point a thematic motif: "the attempt to retrieve an authenticity of life rhythms, of life modes, of vital cadences, which is opposed to an inauthentic form of life." This positing of the opposing forms and the attempts to depict the possibility of their fusing in a greater, harmonizing unity find him seeking to reconcile in technique the fragmenting diversity of kinds of reality. His earlier attempts extended the look and feel of neo-Realism in ways that tried to release the exceptional and the extreme, the humanly miraculous and magical, within the commonplace. In another interview he stated, "But why should people go to the movies, if films show reality only through a very cold, objective eye? . . . For me, Neo-Realism means looking at reality with an honest eye—but any kind of reality: not just social reality, but also spiritual reality, metaphysical reality, anything man has inside him."

From the start, his liberations of the inner magic mixed a comedy and pathos that his more elaborate later works continued. in *Variety Nights* (1950), made with Albert Lattuada, the typical Fellini atmosphere is present in the wandering defeats of a tawdry group of small-time vaudevillians, their dreams of something more never quite defined, let alone reached. In *The White Sheik* (1952), the dream image of the Valentino-like hero of photographic comic strips, first seen swinging through the trees on a giant swing, glowing in sunlight, is comically deflated. (He is last seen collared and driven off on the motorcycle of his tough, shrewish wife.) But the dream, however undercut and artificially manufactured, has meant something to the inhibited young wife, come to Rome on her honeymoon. The floating afternoon with the sheik on a Fellini sea, however ironic in its outcome, has touched off vibrations that lend a new possibility to her marriage. A fresh enhancement is even given to the final conventional religious pilgrimage—her family's mass audience with the Pope.

I Vitelloni

In *I Vitelloni* (1953), the situation is typical of the neo-Realist approach— a drab small town, the pathetic waste of lives of the aging adolescents, verging on thirty, shaped and stunted by society. But it is developed with a toning and shading that breaks through the expected surfaces, a self-mocked romanticizing that embodies the impasse of their lives. Each of the bored, restless drifters has his dreams, his illusions. But while Fellini, with sympathetic humor, criticizes the destructive shape of their dreams, he also reaffirms their need for the dimension of the miraculous; his comic lyricism evokes images of its ambiguous presence in all their drab routine. Ghosts of something more hover in the images of the town and in the sudden outbursts of dance and play that seem to break free from time. Walks through the sand by the sea—the camera patiently waiting and observing—dream of something more; the same sea angrily rises when individual attempts to act out the dream are punctured.

At a climactic masquerade ball—an innocent version of later revelatory partying—the camera whirls with the frenzied movements of the crowd, all seeking that nighttime of escape before wandering out once more into a dawn that mocks their blocked beginnings. In this typical Fellini morning-after, Alfredo, the self-appointed jester (Alberto Sordi, who also played the sheik), is still wearing the dress that wittily and poignantly mocks the stunting of his maleness when he discovers his sister has run away with a lover, and he turns his grief into a comic routine. Fausto returns to his wife and child but is no more a father and husband than before. Moraldo, the only one to escape, takes the train to the city.

<table>
<tr><td>The
Myth
and
Masina</td><td>Fellini's tendency toward universalizing, transforming into metaphor his misfits and outcasts and the landscape of their everyday lives, is carried further in La Strada (1954). Later, Fellini was to characterize it as the first "complete catalogue of my mythical world." Though it is thus a drama of</td></tr>
</table>

symbolic essences, and though its central characters are extremes of human tendencies, it still maintains an unbroken Realist surface. Its actions have a possible credibility; they and the carefully refined images share a single plane of realism, do not blend (with the possible exception of the mysteriousness of Matto, the acrobat) reality with fantasy or dreams. Rather, it is the way the actions and the settings are treated that makes the film a parable. The actuality of the details is minimized, though the details are literal and engage our empathy. They are condensed to pure essence of archetypal action and setting, heightened through emphasis and selection, rather than through obtrusive formal composition, cinematic devices, or distortion.

Gelsomina (Giulietta Masina) is the essence of spirit, an unworldly fool of innocence, touched with the power of St. Francis but without his efficacy in dealing with this world. She comes from the edge of the sea, finally dies at its edge. Zampano (Anthony Quinn) is of the tangible, physical world only, the strong man who has denied all in him that is not brute or material. Together, they are without ties. With no home save the strange hut on the back of his motorcycle, they wander the lonely highways and roadsides. The settings for their actions maintain a sense of their fundamental isolation and project the conflict of their essential qualities. The sun seems as cold as the ground of the frozen no man's land they travel, as hard as the wall of rocks when Zampano abandons the dying Gelsomina, but the metaphoric mood is achieved without ostentatious lighting or patterning. Even the more picturesquely peculiar touches are handled matter-of-factly: Three men appear on

La Strada

an empty road, cheerfully playing instruments, and Gelsomina joins them. For her, all is equally wondrous, equally real.

When her impulse to love and help is regularly thwarted, brutalized by Zampano, she too knows human anger but can transcend it. It is the enigmatic aerialist Matto, who can soar above the earthbound vision, who alleviates her self-doubts with his parable of all being necessary in the world. But he is a constant threat and goad to Zampano, whose blocked emotionality explodes viciously and kills Matto.

Too late, Zampano is finally driven to face his own loneliness—the severance of himself from the "vital cadences" of a life that can harmonize the tangible body and intangible transcendental yearnings of man, as surprisingly typified in the one petty, pathetic, precariously human love he had denied. Looking for Gelsomina, he passes some mundane laundry hanging on a line, its quiet flapping a mournful domestic counterpoint to the news of Gelsomina's death. Too late, he throws himself down beside the life-giving sea—which had regularly appeared, ignored, on the periphery of his empty journeying—and cries.

The subsequent *Il Bidone* (*The Swindle,* 1955), was a less successful attempt to give the import of parable to the Realist matter of confidence men who, masquerading as priests, exploit the poor and their yearning for a spiritual magic. Its central life-denying racketeer (Broderick Crawford) is left betrayed and shot, but basically self-destroyed, unnoticed by passing humanity on a slope of harsh, cold rocks. In contrast, Giulietta Masina's further reincarnation of the Francisco life force in *Le Notti di Cabiria* (*The Nights of Cabiria*, 1957), is indestructible. Despite constant betrayal, she rebounds from her own low point of despair to walk through the woods pierced by sunlight, serenaded by young people passing on bicycles. The sentimental pathos of Cabiria's regular round of degrading defeats is counterbalanced by Fellini's comic treatment and invention: an unexpected dimension of joy in life's rhythms. Similarly, the fuller contextual detail of the materials, more realistic than in *La Strada*, is raised to a symbolic level: the unexpected release of the magically extraordinary from within the ordinary.

Fellini does succeed in making convincing the unity of these paradoxical approaches (as well as the paradoxical contributions of his contrasting collaborators, the skeptical Ennio Flaiano and the mystical Tullio Pinelli, who had first worked with Fellini on *The Miracle*). He does make of the paradoxes of Masina's sexless prostitute—a loving, friendless waif with an irrepressible pixie smile—a viable vessel of the interplay of human plight and value. But not without a cloying reduction of that plight and the means of surmounting it in the straight-line trajectory of her constant violation and unimpaired resilience.

The first and last misadventures are parallel. In both, men pretend to love her in order to get her money, but in the last she almost loses her life as well. The most broadly comic comes midway. In her encounter with the jaded world of the rich and glamorous, Cabiria finally spends the night in a sumptuous bathroom while the actor who has taken her home makes love to his returned mistress. This is followed by the harsh satire of the commercialized miracle ritual—at whose climax a crippled pimp and dope-peddler throws away his crutches but falls to the floor—contrasted against the lyricism of her true encounter with the world of spirit, her meeting with a wayfaring friar on a lonely road. Her openness to spiritual innocence is violated in the complex moods of the second-rate music hall sequence. Here the crass hypnotist does have the power to release her lost images of youthful innocence, but they are acted out before an audience that, like the world outside, derides and ridicules them.

The
Corrupted
World

Like this audience, the characters of *La Dolce Vita* (1959) have lost touch with the intangible rhythms, the transcendental oversoul whose currents do flow through Cabiria. Indeed, their world is the nightmare hyperbole of what this audience admires and seeks; it is for this audience that the *paparrazi* are endlessly shooting their photos of glamorous celebrities. For all its Realist trappings, the film is a heightened concentration of exceptional essences, bigger than life, not documentary social criticism but a satirically toned allegory of the spiritual decay that underlies the society's most cherished delights. Its compositions are more intricate and decorative than in previous Fellini films, its lighting more emphatically heightening in contrasts of light and shade, its symbolism more insistently connected to the Realist base.

It toys with and mocks the society's symbols of pleasure, revealing them as its symptoms of despair and dislocation. They are the inauthentic forms, the false symbols of sensation and sensual libertinism that are the substitute gratifications, outside of life's natural harmonies, for man's yearnings for something magically gorgeous. Against these symbols, Fellini poses the ironic implications of several symbolic patterns and motifs that figure in his recurrent personal mythology. All eight of the film's damaging encounters—six are separate though overlapping vignettes; two, the Steiner situation and the relationship of Marcello and Emma, are carried forward sequentially—develop during nighttime wandering, are exposed but not changed by the natural movement to the mocking sunlight of morning. Similarly, in most, the life-giving presence of water mocks ironically, brings no regeneration: Seeking titillation, Marcello and Maddalena use a prostitute's bed in an apartment flooded by a leaking pipe; seeking the glories of Sylvia, the movie sex symbol, Marcello joins her in the fountain, only to have the water turned off.

In all eight encounters, there is a failure or violation of the kind of intimate relations between man and man, man and woman that throughout Fellini's work are seen as the manifestation of spiritual grace. At the commercialized, televised miracle ritual, this violation occurs on a mass level, as the large crowd at the site of a supposed vision of the Virgin goes wild, all seeking some kind of personal benefit from the publicized miracle children. An angry rain breaks up the farce; in the morning, sunlight reveals one miracle-seeker killed in the crush. The other seven sequences trace this destruction on the personal level. The weakest link—the Steiner sequence—is the most serious, the one that must carry the heaviest weight of dramatic effect on the final motivations of Marcello (Marcello Mastroianni). While Steiner is the intellectual counterpoint to Marcello's denial of this part of himself, Steiner's life too is a denial, an insulating withdrawal into playing Bach in an empty church, into the sheltered artifice of talk and art, of listening to natural sounds of wind and water on a tape recorder. But his inexplicable suicide and murder of his two children bring in a degree of despair that is too discordant with the satirical tone by which the despair of the others is reduced to the petty.

The pettiness, the shallowness of response, even of despair, is an integral part of the view of the others' lives. Even in the final party sequence, when Steiner's death has helped push Marcello into a more active violation of himself and others, the party is not the height of orgiastic decadence but

La Dolce Vita

rather of listlessness, of the short-circuiting of sensuality into shallow display and titillation. Thus Marcello's riding horseback on the drunken model and beating her with a leaking pillow become the perfect epitome of the trivializing level of angry brutality he has reached, out of touch with either joy or the depths of despair.

The final morning-after imagery carries out this aimless circling on a middling level of hell. At the side of the sea, Marcello squints in the morning sunlight at the waving figure of the innocent young girl (the Franciscan figure) he had earlier met at a seaside restaurant. He cannot hear her or, seemingly, recognize her, is separated from her by some water. He shrugs and rejoins his group as they stare with dull curiosity at the frightening, giant, bloated fish. The fish is more than a mirroring of themselves; washed up by the sea, it is a part of the mixture of life, the ugly and beautiful magic from which they have become separated.

Especially in terms of Surrealist shiftings, associations, and grotesque distortions, the dazzling visual extravagances multiply in geometric progression in *8 ½* (1962) and *Juliet of the Spirits* (1965). In these films, while Fellini's fecundity of imagination appropriately matches his turn to the inner tumult under the decorative insulation of the sweet life, in some ways it outraces the neat psychological explanation and resolution of that inner crisis. In *8 ½*—which is both a satirical self-portrait and a psychological allegory—the impasse in Guido's professional (he is a movie-director) and personal life unifies within a more individualized character the dislocations of personality Fellini had earlier dealt with separately and in more extreme terms. The surrender to the allures of surface symbols (the glamor of the beautiful people at the spa, the giant "realistic" rocket-launching site for the unmade movie) is here connected to the emotional fragmenting, through family and church, of his youth; the numbing search for sensual titillation, a distorted overreaction to repression. The artificial sensuality of the movie-making business that manufactures the substitute symbols of our time invades his personal life, leading him to playacting with his pathetically gross girlfriend, to fantasies of a perfect dream girl in white, who is both innocent and sexual, who is in fact the movie star (Claudia Cardinale) whom he wants to use in his next film. This untidy fusion of the warring planes of his life climaxes, quite appropriately, in the movie-house showing of screen tests. Suddenly the actresses on the screen within a screen are trying out for the roles of the "real" women in his life, who are in the audience. At this point Claudia arrives and he flees with her; her image doubles into both actress and dream girl—though she tells him that his trouble is that he can't love and must lose her.

The full protean flow of his splintered experiencing of his own life is given meaningful psychological unity by the film's mixing of tones and moods—satiric and romantic, comic and desperate—and by its witty interplay of Guido's varied realities. Not only are dreams, memories, waking fantasies triggered by immediate reality, but the images of that reality are also heightened (the foggy steam room of hell, the satanic cardinal, the magician) and include figures that parallel those in the fantasy and memory world. The line between inner and outer life is blurred, though still generally kept distinct. Similarly, the memories are both relatively literal and distorted.

It is the memories finally that dramatize the lost clues, hold the key to the sense of warm, open emotionality that inhibition has repressed and distorted. In his last fantasy review of the joyful circus parade of his lost youth, full of all the people of his fragmented life, Guido can join the flow of humanity (he first walks against the line of people, then with it), as he reunites himself as adult director with the boy he was. But the affirmation of the ending is still part of the ironic counterpoint of the film's total texture, its truth as fantasy still not acted out in the external interpersonal area of reality.

8½

Masina
Thwarted

In *Juliet of the Spirits*, Fellini's first full-length color film, the distinctions are further reduced, and the proliferation of lavishly colored, kaleidoscopic images provide one dazzling open flow of experience. Giulietta (Giulietta Masina in a domesticated, inhibited version of the Franciscan transcendent fool) cannot bring all the terms of her existence into harmony; the discordant, distorted images of that existence are the Expressionist projections that make up the film. Her visions of past and present are one with her perception of external reality; that external reality is often seen as heightened and hectic, as grotesque as her visions. Suzy, the sexy new neighbor, is the same as the innocent beauty of a bareback rider in Giulietta's visionary memory of "Grandpa's" escape into love in the old biplane. But in Giulietta's present state, Suzy and her household of garish, decadent sexuality become the grotesque projection of all that Giulietta both longs for and fears. At the beach, Suzy comes in from the sea but triggers visions of ghastly bodies on a terrifying death raft.

The distortions of spirituality in the film are tied to the distortions of sexuality. Social mores, family inhibitions, the repressions of the church have wrenched Giulietta from the natural rhythms of life. Unable to come to terms with her body, she cannot fruitfully experience the potentials of her soul. In the too perfect Freudian symbolism of the dream work of the film's last night, it is only when she crawls back through the mind's tiny low door into the unconscious that she can finally free herself from the film's recurrent image: the convent school play in which all the terrifying repressions of the church are symbolized by her being tied to a bed of artificial flames. Once free of this, she is able to liberate herself from all the others who have threatened her self-sufficiency, even the loving positive symbol of Grandpa and his old biplane rising up into freedom.

At the close, in the warm light of dawn, she leaves the cloistered patterns of her neat doll's house. Walking past the artificial forms of the trimmed trees on her lawn (which earlier had even been protected by plastic wrappings), she walks into the forest of giant trees, which her psychiatrist had earlier said were the symbols of the harmonious life. The goal, she had said, is "to fulfill yourself spontaneously, yet without putting yourself in conflict with your desires, your passions." In these terms, the final voices she hears and accepts are not an evasion of reality. They are the sounds of those "vital cadences," those childhood intimations of immortality that Fellini's Freudian and romantic synthesis affirms can flow through and revitalize the surfaces of reality.

Hyperboles of Decay

The nightmares of Giulietta pale into domestic needlepoint before the phantasmagoric eruption of brutal grotesquerie in *Fellini's Satyricon* (1969), far removed in its violent intensity from Petronius's cool, satirical approach to the original materials. While it may be seen as an attempt to sweep aside historical preconceptions to capture the feel of a distant culture by inventing fantastic hyperboles of its known tendencies, its main thrust is in another direction. The ornate and bizarre wildness of its images and actions (counterpointed by a relatively stable and unobtrusive camera) becomes an Expressionist projection—in universal archetypes of human excess, but without an explanatory framework in our normal reality—of enigmatic matters and mysteries that are ours as well as the Romans'. Its extravagantly corrupt variations on gluttony of all sorts are symptoms of a deeper inner corruption. Out of touch with the full flow of life, its people fear the material body and its decay yet find no other form of salvation than the stuffing of that body in frantic excesses of sensuality. It is the obsessive dream-work fulfillment of the needs of the last party in *La Dolce Vita*, but a fulfillment that subverts itself.

At the core of the film's corruption, Fellini traces the path of an innocent figure, Encolpius, whose ideals of love are jolted but who passively begins to accept the diversions that surround him. As the momentum of fear, guilt, pain, and pleasure accelerates, Encolpius too moves beyond being a passive participant or victim (as in his forced marriage to the totally corrupt warlord Licias) and becomes a more active sharer in destructive gluttony. He takes part in the abduction of the weird hermaphrodite demigod—frightening, yet strangely spiritual, tender, and helpless. During the abduction, an old man is killed, the demigod dies horribly. Angry over the unexpected deaths, feeling guilty over their own roles, Encolpius and his friend Ascyltus kill the leader of the kidnapping plot. In guilt and self-disgust, Encolpius becomes impotent, threatening his only source of escapist pleasure and self-definition. In the urgency of his need to regenerate his sexuality, he does not go to the aid of Ascyltus when he is killed. In the final sequence, after many rationalizations, the stable citizens of the society eat the flesh of a dead poet, who had cynically demanded that as the price of their sharing in his legacy. Nothing is too much for them; but faced with the dead ends of selfish greed, Encolpius goes off with the young men who are seeking another isle, another way of life. Even in this most horrendous display of the underside of the dislocated life, Fellini poses the possibility or hope of an alternative.

PASOLINI

From the beginning of his career, Pier Paolo Pasolini began to criticize the limitations of neo-Realism; nevertheless, his own first films clearly have strong affinities with the work of De Sica, Rossellini, and the others. For at first, his differences were subtle, though important; later, he broke more fully not only with the neo-Realists but with the literal, representational approach in general. At both stages his material and manner are the result of a sophisticated intellectual and ideological approach to cinema.

Pasolini's films bring to bear his own particular form of Marxist ideology but combine this with what he has called his "epical-religious" view of the world. This view stresses a sense of awe and reverence for life, a sense of a mythical, transcendental dimension found in the material, quotidian commonplaces. This reverential, spiritual consciousness of a life force he finds in the lowest classes and peasantry, not in the bourgeoisie and not, as in Fellini's similar conception, in innocent, touchingly comic saintly fools.

From
Realistic
Essences . . .

His first two films, *Accattone* (1961) and *Mama Roma* (1962), as well as several episodes of anthology films, deal with the lowest, roughest edges of Italian society. While this is the typical material of the neo-Realist film, he tries to avoid the combination of sentimental warmth and comic irony, the anecdotal neatness, the intimistic detailing of scene that he found limiting in the earlier approach. He uses the facticity, the existential, unadorned details, but tries to approach them with a purer manner that releases their essences. This approach, in the early films, is an application of one of his central theoretical principles of cinema: that cinema expresses itself through and with reality, not with substitute symbols. Thus it can simply use a real tree, instead of a complex organization of secondary signs and figures, to release the significance attached to the tree, the deeper level of its treeness. In *Accattone*, the best of these earlier films, he attempts to do this by a calm, cool lucidness of composition and a symptomatic selection of dramatic event, without either sentimental pity or anger. Shorter than the basic neo-Realist shots, which he retains, those peculiarly his also have a frontal directness of setup, a fixity, an austerity that avoids ornamentation, strong lighting, or tonal contrasts. What is revealed by this steady, patient gaze is a complexity within simplicity. Accattone is aimless, trapped by the futility of slum life on the outskirts of Rome. His brashness and audacity explode fitfully, to no resolute purpose. Yet he is still in touch with a natural life force, still vaguely aware that he cannot effectuate it in his life. Even in his most callous acts, he still carries a kind of animal innocence. Typical of Pasolini's calm, underplayed release of the paradoxical essence beyond Accattone's immediate acts is the sequence of matter-of-fact shots in which Accattone stands watching a child at play, talks to him, and, with face and stance beyond expression, steals a gold religious medal from the boy, who does not know Accattone, but is his son. Accattone, when confronted with his opportunism on another occasion of it, cries—self-pitying, guilty—and takes another beer. Taking a dare, he leaps from a high bridge into the Tiber, feeding his pride, yet as much impelled by his self-destructiveness. He tries to turn a new, innocent girl into his whore, then tries to change his mind, to express some kind of love; he tries, without the heart or muscle for it, to work; he drifts into a petty, casual, almost comic crime that erupts suddenly in his gratuitous, yet inevitable death.

In *Accattone*, the counterpoint between the lucid calmness and the destructive mess of the life dramatized becomes an unsettling wedge for opening deeper responses to the material. Similarly, but more debatably, he uses the counterpoint of the music of Bach to contribute to the formal aura of an enigmatic epic celebration of a life lived and ended. In the film *The Gospel according to St. Matthew* (1964), Pasolini more directly confronts the problem of merging the mythical and the historical, of releasing the dimension of the extraordinary through the expression of the material surface.

Through some trial and error, as he has recounted, he hit upon a further intensification of this counterpoint, this formal friction, as the vehicle for releasing the ambiguities of the materials of the film. The music mixes Bach, Prokofiev, American blues, primitive African Christian Masses. More important, the visual style is equally eclectic. In dealing with the response to the miraculous of Joseph and Mary and with the recurrent appearances of the angel, Pasolini's manner is similar to that in *Accattone*—an austere innocence, reverential in the matter-of-fact calmness of the presentation. In other sequences, such as the Crucifixion, there is a more heightened, monumental approach; in some, such as the long montage series of close-ups of Christ while he speaks the Sermon on the Mount, there is a greater formal abstraction.

But the chief stylistic element is a harsh, violent, documentary composition and editing, full of zooms and rough edges, abrupt movement and cuts—all of which match his conception of both the events and the Christ. The commonplace, the petty and tawdry, and the miraculous appear on the same plane of reality. When Christ attacks the money-changers and merchants in the temple courtyard, the camera whirls and jaggedly follows his impetuous, lurching anger. When he challenges the elders, when he is tried, it reports the news event, seeking an angle, accepting a long shot.

What is involved is more than an attempt to ironically underplay the events so as to make them seem real, more than a successful making fresh of tradition-worn matters. For the frictions in the treatment give a form to the disturbing contradictions, the demanding ambiguities in Pasolini's Christ. He is a harsh, demanding figure, as contradictory and unbearable as is the very mystery of the transcendent made manifest in historical time. He strides rapidly, sternly, relentlessly, impulsively spitting out his difficult demands, angrily responding to opposition and difficulty. His face is cold, his eyes fevered with self-absorption. His beard is straggly, almost like dirt, his hair hard and straight. His only tenderness is shown toward children, but he insists they must turn against their parents if they are to follow him. Indeed, to follow him becomes an unbearably difficult, violently rupturing revolutionary act—one that strangely combines the extreme demands of an intensely radical political and religious vision of life.

. . . To Allegory

In *The Hawks and the Sparrows* (*Uccellacci e Uccellini,* 1966), Pasolini moves into a more direct embodiment of ideology in dialogue and metaphor. Onto the wandering, sometimes comic adventures of an intentionally typical neo-Realist father and son, he grafts their encounter with an allegorical crow. The crow confronts them with demanding neo-Marxist insights and, after announcing, "Teachers are made to be eaten *salsa picante,*" he is eaten by them in an ambiguous finale that suggests the necessity of their assimilating what he has to say even as they turn against him.

In *Oedipus Rex* (1967), Pasolini frames his version of the Sophoclean myth with a contemporary prologue and epilogue. The Oedipus materials are used as the archetypal essence of contemporary conflicts, but even the contemporary materials are raised beyond a strictly literal treatment.

In two strangely satirical examinations of the crisis of bourgeois society—*Teorema* (1968) and *Pigsty* (*Il Porcile,* 1969)—the themes are given concrete form by a matter-of-fact use of hyperbolic allegory. The allegorical materials have the wildness and mystery of Surrealism; but, in contrast to Fellini's images, they are presented in relatively unadorned, direct compositions, as

Teorema

though they were typical neo-Realist images. *Teorema* traces the ambiguous impact of a placid, bisexual, superterrestrial visitor (Christ, life force or devil) on a bourgeois family and their peasant maid. His transcendent force is brought to bear sexually on all of them; when he leaves, each goes through a mysterious crisis, each no longer able to continue the same closed patterns of his life, but none able to assimilate the revolutionary force into their emotional lives. In three sequences that stay closer to Realist credibility, the daughter withdraws into catatonia, the son despairs of capturing the transcendent in art, the wife embarks on a coldly obsessive promiscuity. In the film's final contrasts, the peasantry's openness to the transcendent is captured in the miraculous sainthood of the maid, who first floats in the air, then is buried alive, her tears watering the ground. The father, on the other hand, after undressing in a train station (and divesting himself of his factory as well), can only rush screaming in confused despair across the ashy slopes of a wasteland.

Pigsty continues the examination of the bourgeois impasse with more brutal metaphors. In both of the two independent fables that are intercut throughout, the ultimate metaphor of cultural dislocation is the eating of human flesh. In the spare, almost silent images of one episode, outcasts who have lived off the flesh of travelers—building not only a way of subsistence but the beginnings of a kind of central faith—are finally caught, tied to stakes, and left to be eaten by wild dogs. In the other—more verbal and formally shot—the perverse love of a German industrialist's son for pigs is tolerated and hidden for the sake of business, but ended when the pigs turn on him and eat him. Thus, though Pasolini's works are more closely tied to a Marxist criticism of specific elements of capitalist society, his metaphors and those of Fellini in *Satyricon* show a remarkably similar direction in using the nightmare images of Surrealist Expressionism to capture on film the extremity of the crisis of our times.

CHAPTER NINETEEN

BERGMAN, BUNUEL, BRESSON— THE INDIVIDUAL VOICE AND VISION

In Ingmar Bergman's *Persona* (1966), at the conclusion of the opening montage of strong film images that suggest—and mock, when some frames sputter and burn—the sensory power, the surface impact of the motion picture, a boy reaches up, troubled, groping, to touch, to get beyond, to get through the surface of the giant close-up of a woman's face that appears on the white wall of the room. In the rest of the film, Bergman attempts to find cinematic devices to get beyond the surface "seeming" to the nuances of "being" (in the terms actually used in the film). It is the summation of his attempt—so characteristic of contemporary directors—to use the realistic surfaces of the film image, especially its reflection of the human face, to get at the deeper, more intangible kinds of reality that lie beyond. The results of this effort, as well as those of the equally individual efforts of Luis Buñuel and Robert Bresson, are among the most distinctive and personal examples of the suprarealistic tendency of contemporary film.

BERGMAN

Loss in the Abstract

The nature of the reality beyond and the nature of the devices to get at it have varied in a meaningful pattern through the major phase of Bergman's career. This phase was announced with *The Naked Night* (also called *Sawdust and Tinsel,* 1953) and *Smiles of a Summer Night* (1955). The former prefigured Bergman's experiments with myth in a stylized prologue shot in silvery overexposure: A forlorn clown retrieves his errant wife from her exhibitionism before a group of soldiers on a public beach and bears her up a Calvary-like hill until he staggers and falls. The Strindbergian lacerations of love and sexuality are then dramatized in moody, symbol-studded Realism that introduces a number of Bergman's recurrent visual motifs, such as the caravan of humanity—this time circus wagons—against darkness and sky. *Smiles* is deceptively light, an intricate comedic minuet; but its graceful structure seems to mock the awkward sexual stumblings of the changing partners. Only indirectly, and through the further counterpoint of the natural sexuality of the peasants (last seen in the hayfields, rising with the lovely dawn), are the deflections of their sexuality seen as the manifestation of deeper dislocations. In the later films, the struggles of the passions—the sacredness and profanity of love and sex—would be more directly related to this deeper disturbance, this metaphysical struggle for some lost ultimate meaning and harmony, for a connection to something beyond the physical touch that is its mocking promise.

With *The Seventh Seal* (1956), Bergman turned to the metaphysical struggle and quest. His seventeenth film, it created the first big stir over his work and for many revived the possibilities of symbolic cinema. In *The Seventh Seal,* as in *The Magician* (1958) and *The Virgin Spring* (1959), Bergman

The Seventh Seal

worked within the tradition of mythic allegory. He applied to it the tangible, concrete contextual details the film can bring to bear, using the realistic texture to embody the metaphysical abstractions, the anguish of the paradoxes of man's search for meaning and God. The insistent images of darkness, pain, and brutality in it figure a futile world of death in life—the life of its church leading not to God but to more pain, violence, and darkness; the life of its taverns, to careless brutality. The only light of the film hovers about the "holy" family, the saintly fool of a juggler, his wife and child. The intellectual knight (Max von Sydow) can come to terms with the figure "Death" when he has shared their tenderness, and their wild strawberries, and helped them escape; but he is still tormented by the mysteries of God. His cynical squire, who has helped others throughout, insists to the end that the honest responses of his senses are all that there is.

The question of the meaning of such sense perceptions, however, is at the core of the ambiguities of *The Magician*. Its central figure (von Sydow) is a charlatan, pretends to deafness, wears a disguise, relies on tricks for his magical acts. Still, although his "victory" over the verifiable common-sense world of the scientist is exposed, he does, like an artist or man of religion, seem to be the vessel of some intangible power that transcends reason, of a dimension of reality that can be felt but not verified. As several parallels in the film suggest—including the joyful imposition of an artificial (but nonetheless pleasing) happy ending—the artist, the film-director, has the same power to evoke in us the dimensions of the intangible.

In *The Virgin Spring*, this ambiguous interpenetration of mystery and reality is more directly attached to the metaphysical riddle of God. While Bergman's visual patterns and tone are true to the medieval Christian myth, he plays ironic counterpoints against its innocence that maintain the tormenting enigma, do not solve it. The God-fearing father (von Sydow) purifies himself, then cruelly takes revenge on the shepherds who have raped and killed his daughter, and on a young boy (the film's real center of innocence), who is guilty of nothing. Before the revenge, a monk has described to the boy the Christian pilgrim's journey toward a distant heavenly goal, during which one must endure cruelty, raging fires, injustice. But at the last moment, the monk concludes, helpful hands will reach out to lift the pilgrim over the final impasse. During the slaughter, one of the shepherds is burned to death, and the other receives the justice of the Christ, a mock crucifixion on the rafters of the room. Finally, hands do reach out for the young shepherd, only to hurl him violently against the wall. In the context of these and other ironies, the final gushing of the miracle spring is a manifestation of an inexplicable god and his creation, not of the orthodox God for whom the father will build a church to expiate his sins.

While *Wild Strawberries* (1957) has a more realistic base, its central figure again embodies the abstract dilemma of facing death without having known the meaning of living. As old Dr. Borg journeys to receive a public honor for his long career, events of the present are interlaced with dreams, fantasies, and memories, distorted and allegorized much in the tone and manner of German Expressionism. In the central subjective sequence, three motifs are intertwined. In one, Borg's career in science and teaching is mocked as he is chastised for coldness, as he, an old man, becomes a pupil again. Intercut are his memories of the lost innocence and love associated with his young cousin Sara and of the infidelity of his wife. On awakening, he comes to much the same discovery as the knight and other recurrent alienated intellectuals in Bergman's work—"That I'm dead, although I live." At the end he faces the remainder of his life, and his death, with equanimity, for he has once again come into touch with the buried stream of human feeling.

Loss as Human Experience

The realistic framework of *Wild Strawberries* foreshadowed the transition to the new ground and approaches of his trilogy—*Through a Glass Darkly* (1961), *Winter Light* (1962), and *The Silence* (1963). In these films, the metaphysical riddle of God is still central, but now the focus is on the literal human manifestations of metaphysical loss rather than on using humans allegorically to embody the abstract paradoxes. The paradoxes of God and man's alienation from him are here embodied in the contradictions of human feeling, examined much more psychologically and fully than in previous Bergman films. Love is the humanly flawed means to retrieve some lost harmony, yet with its seemingly inevitable distortions and deflections, it is also the most significant and painful manifestation of the loss.

The three films prepared the way for Bergman's intense subjective studies of the torments of human passion and being. In all, there is a great economy of means, a reduction of dramatic scope and visual effect, as well as of spiritual and emotional possibility. *Through a Glass Darkly* is treated with unbroken literal Realism. Karin's tormented yearnings and visions of God are part of her emotional breakdown. In her final inner confrontation with the horrors of God, we see her cowering against a wall, pressing her hands between her legs. After her doctor-husband Martin has calmed her with an injection in the thigh, we hear her describe God as a spider, who, like all men, crawls demandingly up her thighs. But there is no attempt at any projection of that vision or its inner reality into visual terms; indeed, Karin's collapse is accelerated by the impossibility of bridging the gap between her inner needs and the external reality of the male world. While she is destroyed, the three male characters survive, although all share the intolerable burden of alienation. Her coldly intellectual father and sexually troubled brother find themselves in a kindling of the love that the father suggests is all we can know of God. Even if taken in the total perspective of the trilogy, the regeneration is indicative of the dramatic problems of the film, especially in terms of convincingly reconciling the father's regeneration with his earlier destructive effects on both children. Much that has happened to him is not dramatized; it occurred elsewhere and is merely talked about.

The certainty of the father's regeneration is denied in *Winter Light,* in which no one grows emotionally. Despite an even greater, and vitiating, reliance on words, it is the tightly patterned irony of the images and dramatic situations that integrate the theme of God. God is not only talked about; the basic dramatic metaphor unites the desperate, yet often self-destructive, longing for love with the longing for God. The deadened, cold minister continues the routines and rituals of the church, but they do not reduce his separation from both God and the world, do not become the vehicle of God's voice or love. Two church rituals frame the action of the film and set the basic metaphoric pattern: at the beginning, a long, empty, and ironically detailed communion service; at the end, a desperate, passionate beginning of a sermon to an empty church. His dead wife had insulated him with her unrealistic Christian loving; alone, he can communicate with no one, cannot love the imperfections of his mistress, cannot help a deeply troubled parishioner, who kills himself. At the riverside—scene of the death—Bergman stays in long shot as the minister talks to the police; no words are heard over the rushing of the rapid water. Just before the suicide, in the film's one subjective suprarealistic sequence, the minister's own torrent of tormented words to the parishioner, revealing all his own fears and guilt, would seem to have been merely a dream.

The Silence is the hyperbole of this distancing, this denial of the voice of a God that can only be experienced as human loving. It is filmed in harsh, powerfully sensory detail, yet raises these details to perverse allegorical epitome. Two sisters and the son of the younger pause on a journey at a mysterious hotel in a strange land. They cannot speak the odd, guttural language, but the dying sister tries to teach some of it to the young boy. Even among themselves, verbal communication is blocked. Love is turned to selfish outbursts of violent sexuality, observed by the younger sister in a theater, acted out by her in a hotel room while her sister listens through the door. Withdrawn from all human contact but unable to resign herself to death the older sister masturbates in her bed. A troupe of dwarfs taunts the boy and dresses him as a girl; a lone tank is a frightening presence on the empty street of the totalitarian country. Oppression is external and internal for the prisoner in the cell of self.

In the films that follow, Bergman used his expert ensemble of players— Max von Sydow, Gunnar Bjornstrand, Ingrid Thulin, Bibi Andersson, Liv Ullman, Harriet Andersson—in a variety of combinations that explore with great power and subtlety the inner world of tormented subjective experience. He mixes literal representation, Expressionist and Surrealist projection, allegorical metaphor—risking much with complex forms that reach for the unsayable.

Persona (1966), which may well be the finest work of his long career, is in great part about the frightening but necessary attempt to confront the demons of the inner world, to collect a self from all its warring impulses and enervating external pressures. And thus its drama and devices are, again, an attempt to touch the self that is beyond the surface appearances that the film image can so powerfully represent. Its central actress (Ullman) has rebelled

Persona

against all of her public and personal roles; but her attempt to reach past the seeming to her being has led to a self-imposed silence. She can only deny love in the face of its elusive deceitfulness. Her silence in turn penetrates the secure veneer of her nurse-companion (Bibi Andersson), who is driven to try to maintain her precarious identity by both dominating her patient and identifying with her enigmatic power. Her first attempts are literal; but then, sandwiched between two signaling images of her sitting in bed (and elements from the opening montage), we follow three hyperbolic subjective projections of her desperate yearning. In the first, she tricks the patient's husband (who is seen as blind, though this in no way has been established) into making love to her, while the patient's face looms large over them. In the second, she accuses the patient of not loving her son, the speech being made twice, once over a close-up of the patient, once over one of herself, the two finally merging as the nurse projects her own guilt over an abortion onto the patient. Finally, she envisions the patient having a relapse and back in the hospital finally getting her to speak, but only to say, "No, nothing," in reflection of the vision of dreadful emptiness that she has been attempting, unsuccessfully, to flee.

Hour of the Wolf (1968) reveals no mitigation of the despair at inner emptiness and the seeming impossibility of connection to another that might fill it. With some confusion and some rather flat-footed Expressionist symbolism, Bergman seeks a form for the violently destructive sickness of its central artist, the painter Johan Borg. After his suicide, his widow (who is given the same name, Alma, as the nurse in *Persona* but is played by Liv Ullman, who was the actress-patient) reads his diary and seeks an empathetic understanding of the nightmares that destroyed him, and of her complicity in them. She tells his story—with all of the distortions and hallucinations of his subjective point of view, but as refracted through hers. It proves an intractable pattern, and Borg's despair is so extreme and so clinically, insurmountably mad that his nightmare horrors do not seem to touch us and the frayed edges of our world, as do the torments of the later *A Passion*.

As though to remedy that, the two central figures in *Shame* (1969) are, in the first half of the film, drawn empathetically, realistically, normally. Even as you and I, they are besieged by the war around them and have attempted to cloister themselves from it. But what begins as a relatively realistic depiction of the evils of war, which will not let them resign from participation, develops into an allegorical portrayal of the evils within man—these two, us. Under pressure, the couple begins to reveal the personal human weaknesses and flaws that produce the public horrors. Concurrently, the texture of the film changes, the scenes and shots become more abstracted, the actions and setting more symbolic. After two deaths have resulted from the greedy instinct of self-preservation of the husband, the wife, knowing better, goes along with him, shuffles dutifully after him through a desolate rocky countryside. They wait with others, separated, uncommunicative on a cold, forbidding beach; they drift, absorbed in private horrors and memories of innocence lost, in a small boat surrounded by the emptiness of the iron-gray water and sky, but surrounded as well by the remnants of their society—dead bodies of soldiers kept afloat with life jackets.

The destructiveness of man's passions is personal in *A Passion* (also called *The Passion of Anna,* 1970), although its island setting is violated by acts of physical brutality that mirror the emotional violence in its central characters. Expressive rather than Expressionist, its images are kept literal, although its dramatic structure is highly elliptical and Bergman prevents immersion in the story by inserting Godard-like interviews with the actors. These reflect his continuing concern with the morality of using the anguish of others as objects of one's study, even in making movies. This concern is dramatized within the film in the character of the rich, powerful Elis, who maintains a skeptical aloofness from the messy flow of emotions, cataloging them elaborately in a vast collection of photographs.

Elis represents one flawed horn of the dilemma of the emotions; the remaining characters are variations on the other. Elis's wife Eva turns to affairs. Anna clings to false memories of a tormented marriage, the husband now dead. Andreas Winkelman, who has sought refuge in reclusiveness, relents, becomes involved with both women—with Anna, deeply, painfully, destructively. All three gash themselves helplessly on the jagged impossibilities of loving, of finding some terms on which to live with open, warming truth in dealing with one's self and with others. The intricate shifts and clashes of emotion in the drama are given objective correlatives in the patterning of the compositions, the heightening of natural sounds, the establishing of subtle but dominant color tones that suit the moods of individual scenes. In the final magnificent image, Winkelman paces wildly back and forth, trying to decide whether to go back to Anna. He stumbles and thrashes about in the snow, as though in lone, agonized prayer to some impossible god, slowly fading into the mixed tones of his surroundings, a bleached, emptied, trembling, ambiguous form; the impasse is devastating. Unlike the far less successful *The Touch* of the following year (Bergman's first film in English), *A Passion*'s color metaphors of the tormenting intractableness of human emotion are so exciting and resonant, its psychological penetration so acute and sympathetic that it rises to the strange exhilaration of traditional tragedy. It is one of the most outstanding explorations of the psychic territory Bergman has unmistakably made his own.

BUÑUEL

Irony
and
Ambivalence

With equal persistence, Luis Buñuel, too, has pursued his own vision of human folly, chaos, and torment through many years of film-making. Despite gaps in time, wanderings, commercial uncertainties, and a strange diversity of subjects and auspices, the results are as distinct and individual as Bergman's more controlled and orderly progression. While the vision is personal, the works have the air of the impersonal—a cool, unblinking exposure of the human comedy. Whatever else he is—rebel, anarchist, Marxist, Surrealist—Buñuel is an ironist, calmly pursuing the inevitable reversals and contradictions of all ideas, passions, and actions—even his own. However audacious, provocative, or outrageous the materials or images, the approach through the years has become calmer, more unobtrusive. His style derives its effects from the ironies and juxtapositions within the images or between the images of a carefully ordered structure, rather than from flourishes of camera or editing technique. This mixing of a Realist manner and a Surreal, Expressionist sensibility is typical of the open contradictoriness of Buñuel's dialectical response to life and art. His undercutting ambivalence complicates his rebellion, although it raises it above doctrinaire partisanship. He ridicules and sympathizes, advocates and skeptically qualifies. While, for example, consistently criticizing the repressive dangers of church and capitalist state, he does not avoid showing the unmanageable dissonances that an untrammeled release of desire and passion might produce—however much that release remains a basic principle of his comment.

Even the youthfully blatant provocation of his 17-minute silent film *Un Chien Andalou* (1927), made in collaboration with Salvador Dali, is not without these ambivalences. A much more assertive display of Surreal wildness than his later films, it is out to shock, from its first shots of a razor slitting the eye of a young woman to its last shot of the young couple buried to their waists in the sand. Its images and vignettes are like a dream work of sexual symbolism that resists totally logical patterning. Although it mocks social repression, it conveys also a sense of the antagonism and fear, of the chaos of sexual desire that is more fundamental than society's demands.

In the feature-length sound-film *L'Age d'Or* (1930), originated with Dali but chiefly the work of Buñuel, the bizarre Surreal images are part of more elaborated dramatic vignettes. These are structured to produce a series of staggering juxtapositions between the forces of repression—the church, the rituals of society, inner inhibition—and the forces of natural desire. But again even the rebellious forces are treated ambivalently: Life itself is inherently dissonant and destructive. A calm documentary treatment of the violence inherent in scorpions is followed by a futile defense of naturalness—bedraggled guerrillas resisting invading civilization led by the bishops of the church. The bishops, becoming skeletons, are paid homage by processions of society, while the two central lovers (Modot and Lyon) grapple passionately in the mud, fully clothed. The pair continue to seek consummation of their desires in a variety of grotesque defiances of custom (including a reception during which a whole series of outbursts by the wildly irrepressible pair fails to disrupt the social rituals). But they can never fully break free: At their last attempt, they sit in wicker garden chairs, his fingers mutilated, blood gushing from his mouth, while she deserts him to embrace a father-figure. Enraged, Modot tears apart his room. In a final enigmatic sequence, a sadistic debauchee who resembles Jesus and would seem to be Modot kills a prostitute—but loses his beard.

In *Los Hurdes* (*Land without Bread,* 1932), Buñuel maintains a lucid documentary approach, but the surface matter-of-factness is applied to images of extreme deprivation and degradation. The horror of these images is intensified by juxtaposition with the constant failure of the attempts to alleviate their plight, each in turn producing a new problem. By the end of the film (only 27 minutes long), these impoverished mountain people have become symbolic of those oppressed throughout the world by both society and nature; it is an oppression, the film's juxtapositions suggest, that only a total change of the political system can remedy. Made in Spain, *Los Hurdes* was banned, and led to Buñuel's long exile.

It was not until *Los Olvidados* (1950), made in Mexico 18 years later, that Buñuel was able to find the means of pursuing further the major work of his career. Strikingly, it picks up the threads of *Los Hurdes*—this time developing a dramatic story line for its apparently realistic depiction of the crushed and crushing life of the poor on the fringes of a large city. But like *Los Hurdes*, its images of the terrible alliance between the socioeconomic pressures and the inner weaknesses of humanity are so intense, build so unrelieved a pattern of excruciating detail that the whole becomes a kind of mythic nightmare. In its world, natural childlike innocence does not survive. The good boy Pedro is driven to ineffectual rage by his relationship to his cold but sexually provocative mother. The promise of help proves illusory; he is killed by his counterpart, the even more tormented, evil boy, Jaibo. Fearing accusations of complicity, the good family of the girl Meche dumps Pedro on a rubbish heap. But for all the destructiveness of his periodic violence (his killing, his leading the boys to dump a legless beggar out of his cart), Jaibo too is victim, his rage perverted from true rebellion. What survives is the hypocritical blind man, quack healer, brutal lecher, whining beggar, unctuous, vindictive man of God.

Varied Subjects, Personal Concerns

The dozen or so films Buñuel subsequently made in Mexico have a variety of subjects—including his own idiosyncratic versions of *Robinson Crusoe* (1952) and *Wuthering Heights* (or *Abismos de Pasion*, 1953). But, to varying degrees, most are mined for the emphases that illumine his personal concerns. Among these, *Subida al Cielo* (1951) is one of the gayest of Buñuel films, despite such typically sardonic touches as a passenger with a wooden leg still stuck in the mud as the bus is pulled out of it by two oxen (led on a string by a little girl). Its lighthearted tone celebrates the triumph of the natural life in the inhabitants of a small town and a delightfully wayward bus. In contrast, *El* (1952) is one of Buñuel's most sardonic elaborations of the rococo aberrations of repressed emotion and sexuality. It merges objective images (which, though extreme, are literal) with dreams and distortions of the central character, Francisco. A middle-aged virgin, Francisco—in an exquisitely Buñuelian opening—taking part in a church ritual involving the washing and kissing of young boys' feet, looks up and is smitten by the shod feet of a woman. He pursues and marries her but fails to consummate the marriage, still agitated by his neurotic desires and fears, which expand to the point that he feels threatened by an entire church during a service. Almost a companion piece is *Ensayo de un Crimen* (or *The Criminal Life of Archibaldo de la Cruz*, 1955), a lighter comic approach to the passional aberrations of the *haute bourgeoisie,* whose central figure seeks the ultimate in passion through killing his love objects. Each, however, is killed by some other agency before he can actualize his dreams.

Turning to varied international production arrangements in 1955, Buñuel dramatized revolutionary issues in three films (*Cela S'Appelle l'Aurore* being the most activist, though still embittered). Then in *Nazarin* (1959), he examined with strange ambiguity the activism of a devout priest who wishes to live fully by Christian principles but is regularly defeated by the world and his own abstract purity. At the end, while he is being led to prison, the priest is moved by the offer of a piece of fruit from a passing woman, and enigmatic drum rolls signal the rising of an undetermined new consciousness.

A fuller, more complex, and eminently sardonic view of the futility of Franciscan piety is part of the subject matter of *Viridiana* (1961), made but never shown in Spain. Made when Buñuel was 61, it is considered by many the most successful of his films and inaugurates a sequence of works that constitute his most sustained plateau of accomplishment. The film is full of Buñuelian paradoxes—of both manner and theme. Basically Realist, it is full of extremes of perverse hyperbole; essentially ironic and deftly comic, it is among Buñuel's most sympathetic delineations of human imperfection. It judges harshly, yet in exempting nothing from its judgment, it denies easy moralizing.

The elderly widower Don Jaime (the old order of church, state, and selfish wealth) who, hoarding the remnants of his lust, dons his dead wife's corsets, finds in his visiting niece Viridiana a new outlet for his passions. Dressing her as his wife, he drugs her in order to rape her—all in view of a servant's errant child and accompanied by Handel's *Messiah.* But in the end, he is too gentle to go through with it, is led instead to kill himself. Viridiana, in turn, is led to seek atonement for her feelings of guilt (and her own repressed sexuality) and leaves the convent to help people directly, à la St. Francis. Her naive, pious attempts to save the souls of the beggars she brings to the estate are set against her cousin Jorge's practical efforts to improve the place.

The wild eruption of the beggars' natural and violent sensuality is a sharp, many-pointed irony. With Handel's "Hallelujah Chorus" again on the sound track, the beggars first pose in a mock Last Supper tableau, then proceed to tear apart the bourgeois world. But the exuberant liberation turns increasingly vicious; one would-be raper of Viridiana is killed by another, who has been bought off by Jorge, but whether the second completes the job is left uncertain. But certainly Viridiana's purity has been violated, and she can only surrender to the hard trap of the world, sitting down to a symbolic three-handed card game with cousin Jorge and his concubine maid, bad American jazz blaring on the radio.

While Jorge has been earlier contrasted to the deadness of the old order and the weakness of naive spirituality, his domineering practicality consists merely in patching up the old order's estate, picking up stray dogs when it is immediately shown that there will always be another stray dog to pick up.

Viridiana

His pragmatism has less of the living warmth of Don Jaime or Viridiana, if also less of their destructive weaknesses. Freed from older inhibitions, his lusty materialism has its own objectifying limits, its own forms of subjugation.

The
Bourgeois
Character

In four subsequent films—each of amazingly different format and texture—Buñuel explored further the ambiguous dead ends of bourgeois morality and emotionality. *The Exterminating Angel* (1962) is sophisticated fantasy, an inventive, though somewhat repetitive, allegory. In it, the hypocritical veneer of society is warped and cracked by the pressure of its own contradictions and falsities. When they are mysteriously unable to leave an after-the-opera dinner, the proper behavior of a group of elegant, influential people collapses, giving way to the irrationalities normally concealed by artificial surfaces. Even cannibalism is barely averted when the freedom asserted by two young people making love allows the young couple to lead the others from the shambles they have made of the room that is the trap of their own minds. But the freedom is only temporary. They all immediately file out to give thanks in a church—one more trap. While they are inside, a herd of sheep comes down the street. In the film's last image, the sheep, too, file into the church, while there are vague sounds that suggest the possible stirring of revolution in the streets of the city.

In contrast, *Diary of a Chambermaid* (1964), is a bleak, harsh, but

**The Exterminating
Angel**

strangely cool Realist depiction of the predatory viciousness of capitalism, the sexual fetishes and dislocations this time tied to more brutal forms of violence and domination. At the center of the moral chaos is the chamber-maid, Celestine (Jeanne Moreau), practical, ambitious, ambivalent. She manages to survive, but in Buñuel's view that is not enough; it is a form of collaboration. She engages in sexual battle with the vicious gamekeeper Joseph, who talks of the extreme measures needed for the moral rebirth of France. Finding proof of his rape and murder of a young girl, she reports him to the police. But she is fired, and Joseph clears himself and goes on to the city to take part in the Fascist movement. Still unable to choose real freedom, Celestine makes a good deal for herself, a marriage with the moral-izing military man, Mauger. She dominates him, but is trapped again.

Surrealist surprise and ambiguity are joined by an impartial, cool irony in *Belle de Jour* (1967). A complex, witty toying with the emotional-sexual malaise of the bourgeoisie, it opens in the midst of a sadomasochist fantasy of the young wife Severine (the sleek but brittle Catherine Deneuve) and closes with an open-ended merging of reality and fantasy. Between, it slides elliptically in and out among Severine's fantasies, her memories, and her reality. All look and seem alike; and since, in the reality sequences, behavior is often carried to perverse extremes and Severine's perceptions of it are often distorted, all these dimensions of her emotional life assume an equal role in her consciousness.

Buñuel's attitude toward the materials is as enigmatic as his blurring of fantasy and reality, one of his more sporting displays of dialectical mockery. Severine's entrance into the brothel of Anais is seen as a kind of liberation, but the free expression of passional needs at the brothel has a compulsiveness about it, is an acting out of fantasy obsessions. She and all the clients —the gynecologist who needs to be humiliated, the giant Oriental with his credit card and strange thing in a box, the count who lays her out in a coffin and then disappears beneath it to masturbate—may find erotic fulfillment of sorts. But they, like so many other Buñuel characters, are never able fully to master the dissonances of their needs, even when they begin, through one means or another, to seek their release.

While *Tristana* (1970) is contrastingly quiet and sober, rueful in its irony, it is tied to the earlier works in delineating again the failure of hobbled, incomplete, all too human rebellion. The aging businessman Don Lope professes ideals of social justice but, to the end, sups suppliantly with archly epicurean members of the clergy. He lusts after and seduces his young ward Tristana, loses her, regains her when she is returned by her lover, apathetic, sickly, one leg amputated. When he suffers a heart attack, she opens the window and leaves him to the snow, the final freezing of all their woefully inadequate desire.

In this late period, two religious films give an indication of the concern for the paradoxes of spiritual consciousness that has underlain much of Buñuel's irreverent mockery of organized religion. *The Milky Way* (1969), a satirical pilgrim's progress, presents the innocence of two vagrant pilgrims in a series of fantasy satires that use the device of slavish adherence to the letter of Catholic dogma to toy with the idea of spiritual doctrine that is spiritually disabling. The satire in the 40-minute *Simon of the Desert* (1965) is more wildly surrealistic and more complex. It is a whirling, shifting series of bizarre symbols of the religious paradox: Seeking the absolute, Simon has divorced himself from the fully human. Literally perched atop a pillar in the desert, he is supplied by rich admirers of the society that seeks to use him. Yet the film still conveys a profound awe for the demands of the absolute—tyrannical and comically distorting, or impractical, as they are. A last irony shows the futility of Simon's saintly purity before the onslaught of the contemporary world. The female Satan who has tempted Simon throughout now leads him to a New York discotheque. Though modishly adapted in turtleneck, bangs, and beard, Simon still refuses to take part in the dance— called ''Radioactive Flesh.'' When he starts to leave, Satan stops him by telling him he can't go back to his pillar. It has another tenant.

BRESSON: TRANSCENDENCE

In the unfolding unity of his films since 1944, Robert Bresson has regularly depicted the gross trials and temptations of the world; but, unlike Bergman and Buñuel, he has found the sustenance and substance of inner fulfillment in their midst, and found as well the spare, chaste purity of a form in which to capture its subtle reflections. In the later films, the ground for mooring that fulfillment in this world has become less secure, but the deep concern remains, as does the formal purity.

Bresson's austere form is itself moored to the literal surfaces of this world. He does not employ distortion, fantasy, or direct interruption of the narrative illusion in seeking to project the essences of the inner life. His films make a careful distillation of objects that subtly refines the movies' traditional ability to invest things with significance. In discussing his film *A Condemned Man Escaped*, he has said, "I wanted all the factual details to be exact, but at the same time I tried to get beyond basic realism." His way of getting beyond, as well as his conception of his subject matter, stems from an ascetic Catholic sensibility concerned with touching on the mysteries of the transcendent within the physical properties of this world. His films and their images are highly reductive and selective, elliptical, unemphatic, dramatically understated; and yet the elements included in the carefully patterned relationships within his frames and the fluid rhythms of their sequences maintain a strong, palpable sensory feel, build calmly and quietly a deep emotional ambience.

Emblems of Spirit

While the rigorous, reflective formality of the style was clearly being developed in Bresson's first two films, the next four closely interrelated works refined it to a demanding, diamondlike, hard-edged purity. Of the first two, *Les Dames du Bois de Boulogne* (1944) is the more important, playing stylized, formal elegance against the facticity of realistic detail, using rather conventional plotting to release a classical purity of feelings. Bresson plays the touching but destructive passion of Hélène against the growth of loving grace, the acceptance of the imperfections of the conditions of loving in the two lovers Hélène has sought, in jealous rage, to destroy.

The next four films form a clear unit of work—each focusing on an individual, isolated character who, in significantly varied circumstances, moves toward an inner release, a refinement of soul within the limitations of the physical world. Consequently, there is a condensation of dramatic materials to a delicately thin linear progression. The revelatory images and scenes have a rhythmic flow, but remain more static and isolated than in the cause-and-effect aggregations of conventional structure. *Le Journal d'un Curé de Campagne* (*The Diary of a Country Priest*, 1950) inaugurates Bresson's use of a narrative commentary, played in a variety of ways against austere visual materials that focus on the essential moments of partially developed scenes or even merely allude to omitted climaxes. In one striking example of Bresson's effective reticence, the commentary reports on the priest's effort to make a "gesture of total acceptance," but we do not see him performing the ritual on the floor of his bedroom; we see only his pulling himself up by the footboard of the bed afterwards—his face revealing the failure of the gesture. Actions, relationships of forms, the shape, texture, and color of landscape (here the dank grays of spiritual dejection), and most of all faces, reveal what cannot be directly dramatized. The counterpoint between voice and image distances, lessens normal dramatic immersion but does not actually prevent it. All becomes illustrative while remaining immediate.

Anxious, guilty, lonely, mortally ill, the priest does not find the gathering of inward grace an easy task; yet by his death the images of his struggle have built Bresson's belief in the immanence of the absolute in the world—that "all is grace." In an important way, the task of Fontaine in *Un Condamné à Mort S'Est Échappé* (*A Condemned Man Escaped*, 1956) is easier, his struggles less anguished. For he is not concerned with the absolute but with the immediate, the existential; yet, in the dedication, the will, the patience, the courage, the endurance, the imagination, the good luck of his successful escape from political imprisonment there is embodied for Bresson the presence of transcendent grace. (The subtitle: *The Spirit Breathes Where It Will*.) Transcendence, however, is merely implied. Bresson's quiet, graceful, exact, reverential attention is to the mundane objects of the world, the prison, and Fontaine's use of them in transforming imprisonment and death into a thrust for freedom, into a vocation that gives that freedom meaning.

A greater sense of the untidiness of the world in which spirit moves, and of the paradox of the possibility of grace, is attempted in *Pickpocket* (1959); but in view of the materials—the crowded, cluttered streets and circumstances of contemporary Paris—the abstraction of significance from the pared, emblematic images seems more arbitrary. Out of the imperfect clay of the petty and inept thief, Michel, and the inexpressive face and awkward acting of Martin Lasalle, Bresson seeks to mold his paradox. Michel is dissonant, in flight, frightened, alienated from himself as well as others; yet while his step-by-step attempts to improve his vocation are an evasion of his true self, they play their role through indirection in leading to his beginnings of acceptance, after his arrest, of himself and of love.

In Joan of Arc, Bresson has found the purest embodiment of what he has called the "familiarity with a palpable supernatural," and in *Le Procès de Jeanne d'Arc* (*The Trial of Joan of Arc*, 1961), he produced his most intense distillation of image, rhythm, and word into emblems of spirit, of ellipsis carried so far that it demands, possibly too insistently, that we recognize dimensions we cannot see or hear. Bresson even denies himself the kind of reverential, revealing close-ups used by Dreyer in his silent treatment of the material, remaining mainly in middle distance. Closer shots are more of objects or parts of Joan's person—her feet, her hands, her eyes over a sheet—than of lingering studies of her face. Physical detail and camera movement make the spiritual meaning concrete: At the burning, the camera frames and moves with her bare feet against the rough cobblestones, focuses on the steps to the stake, sees her mount them, starts from a low position as she is bound, then rises to her face; later, the chains melt and fall, pigeons rise, the stake is finally empty against the sky. Joan has been released from the imperfections of the world; but the abstract certainty of the theology and the extreme formalism of the treatment render her tragedy something too pure to be human—finally, no tragedy at all. The abstract has this time over-balanced the careful attention to the concrete.

Despair and Denial

In four subsequent films, Bresson drew back from such total abstract affirmation of immanence and grace and such total austerity of means. These films stay, sadly but compassionately, within the things of this world, refracting the possibilities of inner grace more obliquely through the imperfect mixtures of men's physical nature. Like Bergman, Bresson plays upon the paradoxical relationship of human spiritual needs and sexual needs; but from his sternly ascetic point of view, there seems to be little possibility of a flowing together, however temporary and imperfect, of the two realms.

Of all Bresson's films, *Au Hasard Balthazar* (1966) has the fullest human texture, the most complex interplay of emotion and meaning—invoked in an appropriate enrichment of his style but still within the perimeters of his basic, scrupulous extraction and condensation. Its country life is part of our time; its evil, leather-jacketed young Gérard moves from provoking auto accidents to stronger violence; its tragedies, though still muted by the possibility of redemption, are not abstracted into heavenly release.

Around the enigmatic central figure of the donkey Balthazar, Bresson develops a web of human weakness and failure. As a foal, Balthazar is in the first shot of the film; hit by a bullet while bearing the contraband of Gérard's gang, and dying among lambs in a mountain field, he is in the last. Throughout he is a palpable physical presence; even as a symbol, his texture is complex. While he has an ongoing natural goodness, in which the transcendent lives on simply, in his purity there is a lesser order of potential than in man—though, conversely, a lesser flaw of perversion. Risking more, man errs; Balthazar plods on. In their response and relationship to him—the presence of something beyond, of soul, in the natural here and now—the other characters are delineated. Bresson suggests a continuing grace of soul in Marie, but it is strangely disassociated from the demands and acts of her body: In key shots, we see parts of her body acting as though independent. The pure balance of the sacred and profane that is maintained in Balthazar is not possible for Marie. She submits to the cruel sexuality of Gérard, tries to break away, but can't. She feeds Balthazar one last time, goes back to Gérard, endures a mass rape by his gang, runs away, possibly to her death.

The aging tramp, Arnold, whose story provides a muted parallel to Marie's, cannot resist the soothing pleasures of drunkenness. When drunk, he beats Balthazar, drives him away; when sober, he saves his life. Arnold's hands, too, are shown independently when he is drinking. At the point when the windfall of a legacy gives him the opportunity to totally satisfy his worldly needs, he dies.

Marie's sternly moral Christian of a father has little use for Balthazar or for human weakness. He survives, but the spirit is dead within him. His

Au Hasard Balthazar

destructive amoral counterpart Gérard more actively debases the transcendent that resides in the physical, exploiting the things of the world for his pleasure and profit. As he has done with Marie, he abuses Balthazar, tying a burning newspaper to his tail. But though he can use Balthazar in his smuggling, and thus get him killed, the mystery of spirit somehow endures. Balthazar dies in peace, if in sorrow; the lambs live on.

When the good, but naively unseeing Jacques leaves early in the film, his last glimpse is of Balthazar. When he returns to marry Marie, she is with Balthazar and he says, mistakenly, "Balthazar. . . . Oh, Marie, everything is just as it used to be. . . ." He goes on romanticizing about their future; the camera remains on Balthazar, whose world touches theirs but is not the same as theirs. Theirs is no longer innocent, but Jacques cannot accept this loss.

In *Mouchette* (1966), the pressures of the world weigh unbearably on a young girl, still an innocent but with a mysterious understanding beyond her years. Hers is an unfeeling, uncaring, brutal world. Bresson's many images of its things are fragmented, discordant, deny rather than yield inner resonance; a welter of noises dominates the sparse, uncommunicative dialogue. Mouchette withdraws from the cruelties of family, school, and townspeople, and finally rebels; yet she retains a strange tenderness, even gently clasping Arsène as he rapes her. The images of her final suicide have a lucidity and intense inner logic that confound and disturb. On a Sunday morning, Mouchette plays in a mud puddle. Her father chases her, literally pushes her into church. After the Mass, she finds release in a dodgem car ride, is at first frightened, then exhilarated, as a boy repeatedly rams her car. Afterwards, as a sweet rapport flows between them, they are interrupted by her father. She ends wandering in the fields, rolls down a hill and into a pond,

Mouchette

the water closing quietly over her, sun glistening on the surface. As at the end of *Balthazar*, the natural images suggest a release into a pantheistic, ongoing universe, but it is difficult to know how to take Bresson's oppressively insistent despair and its equally demanding counterpoint of heavenly release.

The same enigma attends the suicide (images of which frame the film at beginning and end) of the young wife in *Une Femme Douce* (*The Gentle Creature*, 1969), adapted from a Dostoevski story. The film does not attempt to clarify her motives but, rather, through the subjective prism of her husband's rationalizing tale, presents its ambiguous ground. It poses the clash of two incompletenesses that find or allow no way of reconciliation, two emptinesses that know no way to fill the vessel of the desiring self. With a coolly dissecting camera, Bresson fragments the trap of their tiny apartment and store into disorienting bits and pieces. Even when they talk or embrace, their glances, like their words, seem to go by each other. The pawnbroker husband is not cruel, but shallow, reduced, a man of the physical surface, self-righteous in his systematic principles. He demands she too become an object of his treasuring, an adored thing. He struggles to dominate her, even in the ways he agonizes over his jealousy or tries to help her or to make amends. At the moment that he begs her forgiveness, he is shown embracing her legs, her glance distant and alone above him. He looks down, sees the book she has dropped, pulls away from her to pick it up, get it in its rightful place.

A freer spirit (and the ambiguously sympathetic center of the film), she struggles to fulfill some need to be more than a body, an object; yet from the start she drifts in a strange apathy and despair (as though sensing the futility of her struggle), broken only by impetuous outbursts. She spills out her potential indiscriminately in all directions, showing enthusiasm fitfully, impatiently, over all kinds of art objects, academic disciplines, sensual pleasures, anything that seems to offer but does not satisfy the tangible physical form of her spiritual need. At her death, a white shawl floats upward—the soul again released from the insoluble dilemmas of the physical world? Still, that world has the last image—an undertaker's hand screwing down the lid of her coffin.

A
Gentler
Mode

As he had earlier pulled back from the extreme of abstract spiritualization, in his most recent film, *Quatre Nuits d'un Rêveur* (*Four Nights of a Dreamer,* 1971), Bresson pulls back from the despairing extremes of denial of *Mouchette* and *The Gentle Creature*. While still melancholy, it is touched by a wistful humor; its emotional impasse is pitched at a lower level of intensity; what is lost in metaphysical anguish is replaced by droll insight into the human comedy. The weaknesses, pointedly tied to contemporary youth's response to the times, lead to inevitable loss but not suicide. In fact, it begins with the girl's halfhearted attempt at suicide. The key to the approach is in Bresson's use of offscreen narration for more ironic point than in any of his previous films. The young artist idealizes and abstracts the promptings of love, endlessly rehearsing his dreams with himself, listening to their playback on his tape recorder. The visual images (Bresson's second use of color) supplement this self-circling monologue. As the boy walks through Paris, we hardly look around, see only fragments, glimpses of him walking, opening doors, moving objects. The girl, more sensual, also seeks love, but it remains an abstract ideal, not an arc of intimate, opening connection between them. They see it in the falsely romantic glow of the *bateaux mouche* that glides beneath the bridge. When other young lovers are seen, they too remain unconnected—listening to a guitarist's love song, each lying apart and staring separately; in the park, a young girl's eyes wandering as a boy's hand adventures on her body. Earlier, the central girl had stood unmoving, nude, while the artist's rival caressed her.

Neither the dream ideals—in both their traditional and contemporary clichés—nor the cool desires of the body bring these young people into touch, with themselves or each other. At the close, walking in the street with the girl, the young artist looks up to the stars, loses his girl to the bolder student, retires to the brittle, lonely solace of his abstract paintings—from which human form and texture have been almost, but not quite, abstracted out. Still, in this late, mellowed pastel of the difficulties of inward grace in the physical world, the pain of its absence does seem possible of amelioration by some means other than dying from that world.

CHAPTER TWENTY

*French
Renaissance
and
Rediscovery—
New
Wave
and
After*

In the closing years of the fifties in France, some two dozen young directors completed their first films—an unprecedented burgeoning of new talent that arose out of a ferment of critical activity, typified, but certainly not monopolized, by the journal *Cahiers du Cinéma*. Although the resulting umbrella term *nouvelle vague* (new wave) oversimplifies the diversity among these *cinéphiles*, their works did create a tremendously vital movement. Its new spirit and insistently personal approach to making movies have continued to play major roles in both the rejection and reconsideration of film conventions throughout the world. In matters large and small, they have affected alike established commercial productions and the accelerating output of iconoclasts.

The young French directors pursued a personal kind of rediscovery of film history. Working with a strong sense of the historical continuity of the language of the art, they took a fresh look at its conventional usages, employed them with a new vigor and imagination. Their flexible relationship to cinematic conventions has produced several significant paradoxes in the new wave's approach to the equations of content and form, representation and expression.

The movement has placed a great emphasis on cinematic innovation—of device, structure, tone. Yet the resultant defiant dislocation and subversion of conventional processes and conventional audience expectations has frequently been within a framework of acceptance and perpetuation, often ironic and playful, of these conventions—using traditional genres, situations, the aura and screen presence of film stars, even making specific allusions to movies, stars, directorial touches of the past. Much emphasis has been placed on spontaneity and improvisation, yet much work has been done within the traditional patterns of plot.

The breaking with and the toying with conventions has been marked by a heady display of visual pyrotechnics but also by a highly literate, often complicated, verbal element. The visual innovations have often involved new combinations between image and word, whether dialogue or offscreen narration. Within the visuals themselves there has been a flexible reworking of combinations of single shots and editing patterns. On the one hand, the most dominant stylistic development (and the most readily reproducible set of surface devices) has been extremely elliptical editing. This has led to succinct reductions of dramatic and visual components or to more extreme dislocations of vision and relationship both within scenes and in transitions between scenes. Not since the early years of cinematic discovery and enthusiasm has there been such a rapid spread of insistent manipulation of time and space relationships through innovative editing. Contemporary jump-cutting, however, is more demanding on audiences, more rapid, more fragmenting, and especially more complex in the subtlety, the wit of relationships or denial of relationships between shots.

327

On the other hand—in the tradition of Renoir, Carné, Vigo—the French style has maintained a strong emphasis on the mood and ambience that can be established through *mise en scène*—through faces, relationships between people and between people and things in the composition of the shot of greater duration.

Flexibility in visual patterns is, in turn, a part of the new wave's influential exuberance about making the act of making the film a recognizable, even intrusive presence in its viewing. Yet this expressiveness, this playfulness with the devices and forms of the medium, has in the main been linked with a sophisticated development of content—psychological, philosophical, political. When played against the patterns of conventional genres, this two-part emphasis has demanded, and achieved, changes in audience expectations about the relationship between the surface patterns and the psychological complexity of the characters. It has also generated changes in attitudes toward the materials and the characters, especially when these attitudes are expressed in dialectical shiftings, blurrings, and mixing of tones and moods. At the other pole, the double emphasis on personal expressiveness and statement has produced a toying with the relationship between reality and the conventions of representing that reality on the screen, demanding important shifts in expectations about the maintenance of the illusion of reality on the screen.

GODARD

In 1959, the year the French new wave made its startling first impact on the movie world, Jean-Luc Godard released his first film, *Breathless* (*A Bout de Souffle*). In the years since, he has made more movies than any other French director and has pushed further in breaking free of traditional ways of linking film and reality. Though his revolutionary rethinking and reworking of the uses of film itself have often seemed to take him too far, he has left strewn behind him, like watering holes of the imagination, innovations of conception, structure, manner, and individual device that have refreshed and revitalized our ways of seeing and using film.

The very speed and quantity of his work are a revealing signal of his significance. Godard's films are a working out of principles of subjectivity, of an individual consciousness perceiving and responding to its version of reality in a unique manner. For, rather than shaping a film to reveal the subjective consciousness of characters (although this was often developed along the way in his earlier stages), he shapes his films to reveal the consciousness of their director. They are a working out of his attitudes and ideas about the subjects and characters at the time of making the film, even as they spontaneously change in the making. The result is an intellectual, rather than emotional, film-making and type of film, one not precisely ordered, but dialectical, shifting, often erratic. His are films of excess, of an even intentional extremism of the moment's meaning, full of much brilliance, much hard-edged wit and cool beauty, much laxness and repetitive overdoing, much intelligence, much loose thinking.

About *Breathless,* he commented in 1964, "What I wanted to do was to depart from the conventional story and remake, but differently, everything that had already been done in the cinema. I also wanted to give the impression of just finding or experiencing the processes of cinema for the first time." This double process of remaking and discovering anew has continued but with accelerating audacity of innovation and increasing emphasis on discovering new forms. *Breathless* works nostalgically with the ambience of the gangster genre, but it blurs the romantic nostalgia of Jean-Paul Belmondo's tough-guy persona with the ambience of the new: a sense of youthful coolness, skimming along just on the skin of things and people, an amoral indifference that is, confusingly, both attractive and contemptible. While this is focused primarily in the new American expatriate Jean Seberg, who moves without much show of emotion from selling newspapers to bedding down with Belmondo to betraying him to the police, Belmondo, too, for all his constant breathless motion, is running nowhere because he has nowhere to go, cares and doesn't care. With the first of many trailblazing jobs of photography by Raoul Coutard, the film's visuals match this ambience with the first full explosion of dislocating, fragmenting, intentionally mystifying jump cuts, arresting patterns of transition, and a typical Godardian counterbalance of long-held shots of *cinéma vérité* Naturalism, as in the scene of verbal fencing in bed between Belmondo and Seberg.

Films
As
Comment

In the 10 films that follow, Godard, with developing momentum, turns to using film to comment on reality rather than merely correspond to it in the representational tradition. Through *Masculine-Feminine* (1966), these films continue to maintain some semblance of a controlling plot structure, of conventional narrative and character development. But more and more intrusively, Godard plays against this dramatic structure, distancing the audience from the material with a diverse arsenal of alienation devices. The devices he uses are clearly influenced by the theories and practice of Bertolt Brecht, yet it is indicative of the film medium that the cinematic version of these techniques has a stronger sensory impact, is more fragmenting, disruptive, distracting than Brechtian stage effects. In Godard's work after *Masculine-Feminine,* it is the rhetorical rather than the narrative devices that begin to control the work.

The welter of manipulative maneuvers used by Godard in the earlier stages of his career reveals another important difference from Brecht's devices. While the latter's call our attention to the contradictory nature of our lives, which eludes easy patterns of art, they nonetheless, didactically shape an ordered response to those contradictions—as do the different but related expressive patterns of Eisenstein. Godard's, at this point, instead reveal the shifting grounds of his own attitudes toward the material, the patently incomplete manner of his working out of the making of the work. Later, Godard becomes more insistently and narrowly didactic.

Le Petit Soldat (1960) and Une Femme Est une Femme (A Woman Is a Woman, 1961) introduce the two basic themes about which Godard is to develop his uncertain dialectic in subsequent films—whatever else they are also about. The first, still using partly a chase format, traces the indecision in the protagonist's response to his unintentional involvement in violent political actions. Its offscreen narration, while still conventionally that of the character, reveals openly Godard's own intellectual and esthetic interests. Its torture scenes are a first awkward rendition of Godard's distancing of impact, coldly artificial in action, with an intercutting of shots of the façades of buildings. The second, a technicolor play against the conventions of the musical comedy, without songs, evokes—in the most lighthearted of all Godard works—woman as fascinating mystery and power.

In contrast, Vivre Sa Vie (Her Life to Live, 1962) maintains a cool Brechtian distance in following the attempts by Nana (Anna Karina, Godard's wife at the time) to bring to full realization her own inner life. The pattern of treatment is set by the close-ups of Karina's two profiles, behind the film titles, and the middle-distance position of the camera behind Karina's back in the first scene as she tells her husband she is going to leave him. Throughout—especially in the many shots of Karina's nude back and shoulders after she turns to prostitution—the camera maintains this objective distancing toward the untouchable inner life. Twelve vignettes set up the contrast between the surface objectification and the stirrings of inner vitality (gratuitously snuffed out when she is killed in a B-movie gunfight between pimps). In each vignette, comment is developed by the contrasts between her situation and the contents of various verbal, literary, philosophic, and cinematic allusions. The continuing problem of Godard's elusive and seemingly confused ironies first intrudes here, for he would seem to intend the irony to be that, despite the surface reduction of her to a usable object, a thing, she does find an inwardness. But for many the irony may well seem to be that she is so shaped by her surrounding money- and media-centered society that the only available ways of seeking herself insure her failure. The latter, more politicized view would seem indeed to make it a sounder work.

Les Carabiniers (The Riflemen, 1963) is a grim spoofing of the capitalist basis of war, focusing on some cartoon personifications of the unliberated proletariat lured into the war. All the advertised rewards prove empty. In one scene, the promised excitement of raping captured women is reduced to the strange parody of two ineffectual soldiers staring at a woman while one dully prods her with the muzzle of his rifle. At war's end, they bring home their spoils, a bagful of picture postcards; then even those are taken from them and they are shot. Alphaville (1965), a generalized critique of the corruption of ideals and human feeling projected into an authoritarian future, is laced with humor, secret agentry, and clever use of shots of contemporary Paris's antiseptic modernity.

In Contempt (Le Mépris, 1963) and A Married Woman (1964), for all their intractableness, the women are the center of sympathy; in Pierrot le Fou

(1965) and *Masculine-Feminine*, there is a shift to the men. In both the latter, Godard insists on a gratuitous concluding suicide (slightly more plausible in *Pierrot*); but in both, the woman's role in engendering the act is abetted by the protagonist's failure to cope with social reality and come to some effectual stance of commitment toward it.

One of the themes of *Contempt* sets up the impossibility of bridging the chasm between the abstractions of ideal beauty—in art or in women—and the messiness of actuality. The problem in art is typified by a movie within the movie, being made by Fritz Lang (who plays himself). The artificial beauty of the film, which is to be on classic Greek motifs, is captured in long-held shots, slowly panned or tracked, slowly dissolved, amid wondrous natural surroundings, with artificially painted actors. But this movie will be violated by its predatory producer. In a like manner, we first see the beauties of the body of Brigitte Bardot in a series of idealized shots of long duration and modulating colors as she is being looked at in awe by her husband. But neither she nor he know what to do with her beauty. It too is finally sacrificed to the producer. In contrast, the basic visual approach in *A Married Woman* is fragmenting. Wholeness and contact are lost in a myriad of physical details —of bodies, furnishings, public buildings and signs, even the contents of ladies magazines and their emphasis on chic, salable, dehumanizing sex: The married woman, too, has become an object of consumption.

While these two—*Contempt* and *A Married Woman*—stay within a credible Realist format, *Pierrot* mixes Realism with sequences of satirical distortion and extension beyond the Realist plane. The exaggerations of *Masculine-Feminine* are within the perimeter of credibility, though pushed to the limits. The film has a number of variations on question-and-answer sessions, but all are kept within the context of the narrative. On the job, for example, the boy interviews a beauty queen; in the close quarters of a public toilet, he tries to come to some deeper understanding with his girl while she answers his questions phlegmatically, too busy staring at herself in the mirror, performing the recurrent ritual of fixing her hair.

Within these limits, Godard shifts tones constantly: in a typical sequence, from the undefined anger of the boy and girl to the comedy of another girl's selling him a feel of her breasts while they stand hidden by the curtain in a photography booth; then to the poignancy of his making a record in the next booth in a futile effort to communicate his love; then to his sudden terror at being stalked with a knife by a man he had watched playing a bowling game; and finally to the absurdist shock—typical of the recurrent jolts the world gives his innocence throughout the film—of the man turning the knife against himself. In its mixtures of ironic wit and tenderness, the film has the fullest emotional air of any of Godard's works. In 1964, *Band of Outsiders*, a last toying with the gangster genre, had shown Godard's most extensive and complicated tinkering with the flow of conventional narrative of the films of this period.

With *Two or Three Things That I Know about Her* of 1966, the balance

Masculine-Feminine

shifts. A basic narrative is no longer broken up by interruptions; the interruptions have become the controlling force in the structure. Narrative is played with, more and more parodied, and rhetorical juxtaposition, not chronology, becomes the basis of the style and structure. Visual elements are set against each other, and against narrative and speech. But as the experimentation with the discordance of collage increases, the didacticism becomes more ideologically ordered, more simplistic.

In *Two or Three Things,* the suburban woman who turns prostitute becomes a social symbol, becomes Paris. As Godard (still displaying hesitations) becomes a political film-maker, the ostensible plot and drama become a springboard for satiric hyperbole—one client has the part-time prostitutes put airline flight bags over their heads—and especially for his increasingly favored long ideological monologue or discussion. In *Made in USA* (1966), the political diatribe is also carried on verbally to a great extent—long-held shots of a tape recorder playing the sound track illustrate Godard's growing defiance of maintaining dramatic conventions—but there is as well a set of comic-strip parodies.

La Chinoise (1967) and *Weekend* (1968) are more complex ruminations about the ambiguities of political commitment. Though both maintain some momentum of plot development, dramatic expectations are constantly subverted by an amazingly abundant array of ironic and didactic devices of dislocation. The failure of rhetoric, the limitations of words in dealing with the dilemmas of reality and politics, is at the core of *La Chinoise;* yet though Godard mildly mocks the abstract verbalizing of his young summer-vacation Maoists, he obviously agrees with much that they say and, in principle at least, with their final act of political murder (which comically, has to be done twice since the girl kills the wrong man the first time), so that it becomes a confusing display of mutually canceling ironies. The brutal hyperboles of capitalist decay in *Weekend* produce a more straight-line cumulative attack on the social nightmare, though the film is also filled with alienation devices. In its last section, however, Godard undercuts easy commitment with the even more directly savage violence of the young rebels' cannibalism.

Radical
Simplifications

But following the French student revolts in 1968, Godard ended his fence-straddling and gave himself to the political simplifications of radical revolution. Rejecting all previous cinema, including his own, he attempted to find a new political form and language for film, producing the most directly propagandistic works of the commercial cinema, leaving behind all attempts to maintain the form of film as drama. In *One Plus One* (or *Sympathy for the Devil,* 1969), he interweaves a recording session of the musical group the Rolling Stones with a strange conglomeration of violent parables of revolutionary action (all kept oddly artificial), interviews, and discussions—intending, without clear success, to derive a synthesis from the dialectics of disparity. *Le Gai Savoir* (1969) ponders the problem of language and the need

Weekend

for an untainted vocabulary (and art), posing its single, abstract central dialogue against a constantly shifting, often beautiful pattern of visual images. *See You at Mao* and *Pravda* (both 1970), however, are more simplistically polemical, for all their structural fireworks. But while still polemical, *Wind from the East* (1971) gives indication of a more fruitful integration of political activism and the art of film-making, mixing the making (film within a film) of a politically allegorical Western with the usual, provocatively jarring stable of Godardian dislocations and digressions, allegorical cartoons, and windy speechifying.

Godard is too unpredictable and exploratory for any conjectures about the paths he will open in his next 20 films; it is clear, however, that his first 20 have brought an important questioning and reworking not only of film techniques but of the basic forms and uses of film itself. They have, as well, raised important questions, which Godard's work has not satisfactorily answered, about possibilities of reconstructing film form within limits of reasonable usefulness. Is, for one thing, a central sense of the dramatic—of narrative and human suspense of some sort—so readily disposed of, especially for the sake of polemics? What is the most fruitful meeting ground between film, and all art for that matter, and political action or ideas?

TRUFFAUT

The innovations in the work of Francois Truffaut do not lead to these extreme considerations. They remain within the perimeter of the traditionally dramatic; they are more concerned with emotionality, with character, than with ideology or intellectual dialectics. Yet they too have an openness of form and approach that has contributed to the current period's revitalizing of conventional forms and devices. For in his own way, Truffaut, too, has been subversive of film form, of conventional balances between content and technique. "When a film is going one way," he has said, "I cut and send it off in another. . . . I try to suppress clichés, influential characters, ready-made conclusions." And in another interview: "But I like everything which muddles the trail, everything which sows doubts . . . I enjoy unexpected details, things that prove nothing, things that show how vulnerable men are." This sympathetic concern for many-sided vulnerability, for the ambiguities of human emotion and character, when joined by a playful affection for the elements of film-making itself, has led to the mixtures that are at the core of his work. These mixtures have sometimes extended the conventional expectations of the audience, sometimes led to limiting compromises with those expectations.

The Four Hundred Blows   Many of the mixtures were introduced in his film of 1959, *The Four Hundred Blows*. While still following a traditional dramatic line, its depiction of the pressures that lead to the destruction of innocence in the life of its young protagonist, Antoine (Jean-Pierre Léaud), has the more elliptical structure

**The Four Hundred
Blows**

and abrupt transitions of the new-wave approach. More importantly, it has a mixing of attitudes, of tones and moods, that dallies with audience expectations about dramatic development and emotional response, blending the lyrical tenderness of Renoir with the abrasiveness of the fanciful satire of Vigo. The result is not only a shifting and blending of moods and comedy and seriousness, but a shifting and blending of types of dramatic and cinematic materials—Realist, documentary, grotesque, satirical, lyrical.

In patterning typical of Truffaut's capturing of the emotional complexity of the boy's situation, the fun of Antoine and René's wandering through town, climaxed by the visual excitement of his ride, splayed against the wall of the centrifugal "Rotor" at an amusement park, is immediately followed by the blow of observing his mother's rendezvous with a lover. As the blows accumulate, satirical treatment of the school is interspersed with more painful sequences both at school and at home, and with the almost fantasy heightening of René's strange isolation in his home. At the peak of the direct clashes between Antoine and his parents, all go off to the movies and enjoy themselves in a lighthearted sequence. But nothing has changed, the zigzags of tone intensify: deeper trouble at school, momentary escape at a puppet show, a comical plot to steal a typewriter, the pain and sadness of arrest and rejection, with Antoine in the police van, the camera staying outside; at the police station, the pace of the visuals slowed, with contrasts of shadows and light, projections of bars across Antoine's face. At the home for boys, Truffaut holds to close-ups of Antoine's face throughout the revealing interview, alternates close-ups of his face and his mother's at her final rejection of him, shifts to the lyrical movement of both camera and character of Antoine's final run to the sea, the momentum abruptly broken one last time when Antoine, blocked by the water, with nowhere else to run, turns back to the camera and, in a most influential, haunting final freeze, is captured in a final grainy close-up.

Shoot
the
Piano
Player

In *Shoot the Piano Player* (1960), the structure is even freer, the mixing of tones more intense and unusual, while a new element of mixing is also introduced—the blending of a conventional genre (the gangster film) with a serious development of character. Within its flexible structure and shifting texture of comedy and seriousness, three major plot strands are interwoven: a flashback of the former life of the barroom piano player, once a concert pianist, and his dead wife; a gangster chase; the beginning of a hesitant love affair between Charlie (the piano player) and the bar waitress. Yet all the scenes, as well as the seemingly digressive minor vignettes, present variations on the film's central themes. While the approach produces an ironic distancing that precludes the direct emotional involvement of *The Four Hundred Blows,* this shift, too, is consistent with the themes.

For Charlie is a man who has experienced the difficulties, and his own weaknesses, in emotional relationship, in intimate connection. He now wants out, wants merely to be the aloof, unconnected piano player (like Hoagy Carmichael in so many forties movies) in the bar. Yet, denial of emotional commitment, like the using of women as objects, leads only to destruction, and all the diverse materials of the film dramatize this dilemma. In the opening comic chase (part of the gangster chase continued throughout), Charlie's brother has a conversation with a passer-by who tells him about his love for his wife, the most affirmative element in the film. At the bar, a comic song is sung about a woman misused by men, and several visual vignettes involve men on the prowl for women. When the gangsters kidnap Charlie and the girl, the comic dialogue centers on one of the gangster's proudly callous observations about women; later when they kidnap Charlie's youngest brother, the conversation centers on their prized possessions. In the flashback, both a concert promoter and Charlie misuse Charlie's wife. Just before her suicide, she describes her own damning sense of herself as an object, a body, a thing, but Charlie cannot cope with her revelations and fails her. Even Charlie's current lighthearted relationship with the whore plays further variations on the theme.

In the film's concluding ironies, Charlie first delays too long in standing up for the girl against the bar owner's demeaning of her; when he does act, the comedy of their fight ends in sudden, half-impulsive, half-accidental

living and feeling in a present that is not only uncertain itself but irrevocably tied to the distorting pressures of memory and desire.

The
Ambiguity
of
Experience

The nagging discrepancy within the struggle for clarity, for lucidity, seems to be at the core of both the content and technique of these first five films. In *Hiroshima, Mon Amour* (1959), with a screenplay by Marguerite Duras, the subjective center is a woman (Emmanuele Riva) whose attempt at an emotional concordance also becomes a vehicle for a broader coming to terms with the meaning of the acts of society. This broader perspective does generally fuse with her own personal tensions, but there is a lingering unsolved imbalance between the social and personal themes. To come to terms with her own emotions, she must come to terms with the wartime experience of Hiroshima of her Japanese lover in their brief, broken encounter. This, in turn, forces her to come to terms with her own wartime past. The film does not attempt to blur the difference between the magnitude of the destruction of Hiroshima and the destructive ambiguities of her own wartime horror in

Hiroshima, Mon Amour

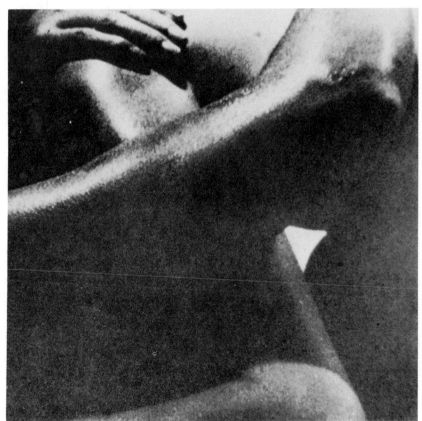

France. For her, both become personal, both part of her past and her present, and the difference becomes a part of the finally insurmountable gulf between them of both culture and personal situation. The gulf is manifest in the differences between the two technical bases of the style—montage juxtapositions for the past and for what remains associated with it (for example, the opening clash of images of their bodies in bed and of bodies after the bombing) and long scenes with long-held shots for the painful tensions of their present attempts to break free and reach out. As the repressed memories of her wartime affair with a German soldier and her guilt over his death and her ostracism surface, their depiction also builds into longer shots and scenes.

Time
and
the
Mind

For each film, Resnais has turned to a different major writer for the screenplay and taken his own emphasis from theirs. Three—Duras, Robbe-Grillet, and Cayrol—have gone on to their own particular concerns and emphases in films written and directed by themselves. With Alain Robbe-Grillet's screenplay for *Last Year at Marienbad* (1960), Resnais is at the furthest reaches of obsessive subjectivity. The film is an abstract intensification of the fanatical distortions, confusions, and torments of which mind, memory, and desire are capable. Accordingly, it is his most abstract, artificial film—its elaborate décors and patterns, its labyrinthian associations of editing an equivalent for the most highly charged and excited processes of the mind. An audacious experiment, it seems also a playful parody of the mind's raging need for order, withholding from its extremes of willful associations any final ordering of confusion. If it is, as Resnais has said, a study of persuasion, it is persuasion of the mind of the narrator himself by himself, not simply of the woman, A (Delphine Seyrig).

From the elaborate patterns of the spa and its gardens, the narrator's world and mind take not clarity of form but an empty coldness. Faced with some force outside of himself (allegorized in the recurrent match game he plays with his chief unbeatable antagonist, M), X must persuade himself of a truth he can bear, as he must persuade A that he has met her before and that she must leave with him. It is not really a question of whether he really met her last year; it is a question of whether he has met her this year. Just what takes place outside of his mind and what within—where is the boundary? And if he is speaking to her or seeing her this year, just how much of what we see and hear them doing together is outside or within his mind? A chief clue is the ritualized play that begins and ends the film, suggesting the elaboration and elongation within the mind of a single moment of time.

X's obsessive need to persuade and win A is flooded with futility and guilt. His offer of passion must save her from this deadness and her own seemingly emotional illness; but his hopefully healing passion itself suffers from guilt. All centers finally on the flashing recurrent images of her room—images that at first contradict his desires and very words. Minor discrepancies lead

Last Year at Marienbad

to two major failures of desired order: In one, he must rape her cold body to get her; in the other, she is shot by M. But finally his persuasive insistence wins out madly: In a lightened image, her arms extended like bright wings in a negligee, smiling at last, A welcomes him, and with a floating undulation as he moves toward her, the image repeats and repeats. On its own persistent terms, the mind has won. Whether he has surmounted her rebuff of him—last year or this—whether he has surmounted her murder and his guilt, whether he has overcome the intractable fact of a nonexistent relationship, X, in the images of his mind, gets her to leave with him this place of frustration, guilt, and deadness. For all its own artificial extremity, the film is a cinematic display that has proved highly influential in the embodiment of consciousness in patterns of image and highly charged editing.

The editing of *Muriel* (1964) is equally intensive, yet less directly subjective, and thus less immediately flamboyant and witty. Its mosaic dissects and reconstructs the objective surfaces of the characters' inner life rather than projecting directly their fantasy or desire. The past is talked about but not seen (except in Bernard's amateurish movies of the Algerian war). But it is a constant presence, a force in the splintering of the present that is objectified in the discordant editing of basically chronological narrative material. Again pasts of differing dimensions are juxtaposed. In his confused attempt to deal with guilt over the murder of an Algerian girl, Bernard is driven to murder. His mother, Hélène (Delphine Seyrig), unwilling to give up her destructive broken dreams of the past, is finally saved from succumbing again to lies of a former lover, brought into the present, though still without a personally felt place in it. Around them, images of the changing façades of Bologne insist on the indifferent but demanding movement of time.

Time also makes its demands on dreams and consciousness in *La Guerre Est Finie* (*The War Is Over*, 1966), written by Jorge Semprun. The longest of Resnais's films, it is his most active and straightforward dramatic narrative, allows the most direct expression of and response to emotion. Its formal elements do not distance but are part of the dramatization of Diego's (Yves Montand's) experience of his present dilemma. The unclear orientation of the first scenes of his trip back into France mirror not only the constant uncertainty of the professional revolutionary but his own new uncertainty about the value and meaning of that role 30 futile, frustrating years after the Spanish Civil War. The flashes of conjecture about future situations and memories of past begin here; they too work on both the level of surface tension and deeper disturbance and revaluation. Peak moments in this inner conflict are carried in heightened form: the contrast between the artificial montage of intercourse with the young revolutionary girl—the surfaces of passion and commitment—and the intimately realistic details of intercourse with Marianne (Ingrid Thulin); the disjunction of words and images in the frustrating meeting with party bureaucrats, the same old words unattached to faces or to reality; the climactic images in Diego's mind of the funeral of the dead comrade Ramon—in contrast to the callous fanaticism of the young leftists—with mourners and comrades flowing into a central walkway behind the casket, like tributaries into a great central river. It is this last image that embodies the motives for his resigned but reaffirming reconsolidation of his past and present on a new basis of humane realism.

Another, more tortured twist on the wheel of time is framed in the science-fiction metaphors of *Je T'Aime, Je T'Aime*. Attempting suicide, a man is mysteriously whisked away to take part in a time-space experiment. The experiment goes awry; in tormenting fragments, he must relive the tortures of the love affair that has driven him to the opening—and finally closing—moment of suicide. As in *Marienbad*, a moment is elongated, but this time only for the insistent repetition of the unconquerable past. The science-fiction frame is arguably too artificial an embellishment for the central emotional anguish; but it does serve to heighten the sense of agonizing futility in the face of some inscrutable determinism, does allow for a heightened mystery of image and editing, as in the final juxtaposition that ends by focusing on a small mouse, trapped hopelessly under the confining glass dome of the mind's past. It is a strange film of distanced despair. Equally strange, despite Resnais's important role in the French renaissance of the sixties, the film, though made in 1968, was shunted aside for years and is only slowly beginning to make its rather errant way into worldwide distribution.

CHAPTER TWENTY-ONE

Britain— Anger and After

Ihe close of the decade of the fifties brought the first signs of a renaissance among younger film-makers in Britain also—without, however, the technical audacity and innovations, the purely personal expressiveness of the French new wave. Unified by a strong social concern—a frustration-tinged anger and a newly revived conviction of commitment—the movement in its early phase led to a sharper, subtler form of Realism, but not to a break with Realist dramatic and cinematic conventions. Beginning simultaneously with the new wave in 1958 (though subsequently influenced by its techniques), the first phase revealed a rebellion not of hope and fervor but of deep and defeating frustration, a desperate lashing out at a society that won't be changed. With a striking series of films in 1963, a corner was turned to a second stage, to a sadder whimsy and wild wit, to new life styles, a troubled larking away from a society that can't be changed enough. With this shift, the path was blazed for a greater diversity in subject matter and a greater technical experimentation in blending the Realist style with the newer forms of expressiveness.

This startling break with the stolidness and conservativeness of the standard British commercial film had been prepared by the critical battles fought in the film journals *Sequence* and *Sight and Sound.* The break had also been encouraged by the success of the "angry young men" in British fiction and stage drama. Indeed, many of the early films were taken directly from materials in these other genres. While they showed some influence of the postwar American social films, they were more like the works of Italian neo-Realism, with its emphasis on viewing people intimately as they interact with a tangible environment rather than using people to prove a point about a specifically defined social problem, as in an American film like Elia Kazan's *Gentlemen's Agreement.*

Stylistically, they built on the long tradition of the British documentary, of which John Grierson, Paul Rotha, Basil Wright, Harry Watt, and Humphrey Jennings (whose wartime and postwar films had been the artistic culmination of the movement) had been the major figures. Their works and theories had balanced a transparent Realism before the facts of actuality with a strong, controlling editing, with particular emphasis on striking juxtapositions and important innovations in the relationships between sound and image. But for all its social orientation, the British documentary had been staunchly melioristic. In the late fifties, its hopeful affirmations no longer seemed tenable. Even the Socialist evolution in Britain had produced tangled dilemmas, not the social and cultural community long envisioned. For the young documentarists who were to become the leading commercial film-makers, "commitment" became the rallying cry for a stronger, more specifically defined radical basis for social films. When translated into actual production, however, the rebellion seemed a desperate one. The young rebels of these films

351

were caught between—between classes, times, clusters of values—and teased into tense, anxious irritability by the possibility of social and personal change that beckoned everywhere but got nowhere.

NEGATION, DEFEAT

The early pattern is set in two films of 1958—Jack Clayton's (adaptation of the John Braine novel) *Room at the Top* and Tony Richardson's (adaptation of John Osborne's play) *Look Back in Anger.* In the former, Joe Lampton, within the cold façade of Laurence Harvey's tensely stiff face and body, keeps the storm locked in. Killing the rebel within, Lampton pays the price of social advancement with the death of his emotions; the rebel has exacted his revenge. In the last shot, more stunted than ever, he rides in the prisonlike car of the boss (now his father-in-law) up the hill to the heavy gates of his new life of wealth and success. It is a tightly plotted, polished, conventionally developed work; after it, Clayton, an industry regular, was not to play a vital part in the movement. In *Look Back in Anger,* Jimmy Porter (Richard Burton) snarls and rages, in the first dramatic scene, amid the tacky clutter of his apartment, suddenly lashing out and striking his wife Allison. He rages throughout but changes nothing, not even himself. He ends up as he remembers he had become (following the death of his father, discarded after the Spanish Civil War)—"angry . . . angry and *helpless";* all the good causes were gone. Richardson's direction is more flexible and expressive than Clayton's; he mixes the solid, documentary-inspired texture of the realistic settings with a varied pattern of long-held shots and rapid cutting. But the result exhibits early that need for flourish, that absence of a firm core of personal style that continues to beset his work, especially after 1963.

At this first stage, Richardson was to produce three effectively varied treatments of the trap of the times. *The Entertainer* (1961), also from an Osborne play, focuses on the middle-aging remnant of the dream (with a fine job by Laurence Olivier), a second-rate vaudeville performer who embodies the shoddy leftovers of the Empire and the stunted rebel who has never grown up. In one beautiful moment, after hearing of the death of his son in the abortive Suez coup, he imitates a Black woman's blues song: On stage, in a practically empty old boardwalk theater, in a double masquerade behind his grease-painted clown's face and the words of the blues, he releases the emotion he and his world have almost destroyed. He cries. In *A Taste of Honey* (also 1961), from a play by Shelagh Delaney, Richardson sets up a basic contrast in treatment: harsh satire for the world of Mum, her beau, the ubiquitous seaside amusement park; a lyrical softness for the lost struggle of the young girl (Rita Tushingham), no longer able to be a child, but with no woman that she knows how to become. In the adaptation of Alan Sillitoe's *The Loneliness of the Long-Distance Runner* (1963), the truculent toughness of the story and its central character are softened, sentimentalized, mirrored by an uneasy reaching for effects in the cross-dissolves, the tricky editing of the morning cross-country runs and the flashbacks of memory.

Look Back in Anger

Karel Reisz's first feature film, *Saturday Night and Sunday Morning* (1960), from the Sillitoe novel, is the toughest, solidest work of the set. With a strong emphasis on camera movement and electric, individual editing, he matches the moods and careening course of Arthur Seaton's (Albert Finney's) futile attempt to break free from the tight circumference of factory, jammed apartments, "tellies," crowded pubs, dance halls, and amusement parks—the world "dead," as he says, "from the neck up." Reisz shifts the pace nicely to match the differing moods, as in the differences between Arthur's two love affairs. He is particularly effective in creating editing patterns with both sound and visuals: At the closing defeat of the renegade, we hear a couple talking in dull terms about the housing development they will move into, and we think it is the conventional pair we see walking on the screen, only to be shown finally that it is Arthur and Doreen.

In 1962, John Schlesinger's first film, *A Kind of Loving* (with Alan Bates), takes a similarly abrasive look at the squelching of young spirits but with a more open possibility left at the ending and less visual excitement. In 1963, Schlesinger's *Billy Liar* was one of several films that first marked the turn to a headier visual texture and a greater diversity of treatment of the social impasse. Billy (Tom Courtenay), a clerk in an automated mortuary, is a more wistful, whimsical rebel, sweeter in his dreams but at a later stage of inner subversion: He dreams in terms of mass-media images, longs to go to London to be a TV comedy-writer. Throughout, Schlesinger cuts between Billy's literal world and the images of his comic fantasies: When he is shaving in a room just off the kitchen and can no longer stand the clatter and complaints of his family, he turns on them, his razor becomes a machine gun, and he mows them down. For all his yearnings, he does not leave on the midnight train to London with the new free spirit, Liz (Julie Christie). It is too late. The TV terms of his rebellion are still the terms of the society he is rebelling against. They are precocious parodies of that break-out into a freer, more expressive life style that in the sixties was to sweep the world in the youth revolution, even as it too became absorbed by the commercial-media culture and was retransmitted in a vicious circle of social adaptation and commercialization, even of rebellion.

REBELLION OF CONSCIOUSNESS

But it was this new romantic sensibility—obsessed with the flourishing of the inner life of subjective freedom and responsiveness, with the extension of consciousness—that became the core of subject matter not only for the British film but for mass-media productions throughout the world. And often with the strange impure mixture so typical of the mass arts—part revealing and liberating, part imitating, part commercial capitalizing, part simplifying into salable stereotype.

Richardson's 1963 entry (with script by Osborne) is typical. His *Tom Jones* (Finney again) is a rogue of the new life style, with exuberant, playful, hip, witty flourishes in the visual style of his film. While they match his verve, the flourishes are also forced, a bow to the new wave, commercially adapted to simplified material. And lingering still in a mixture that does not quite solidify is a more serious attempt to update some of the material into contemporary social criticism. Successful dabbling as it may have been, it was a jolt to the British movie industry.

In later films, Richardson was to try his hand at a variety of subjects and treatments without a sustaining center of emotional tone or vision—from the subdued subjective grotesqueries of a woman's emotional repression in *Mademoiselle* (1969) to the uncentered, veering, satiric hyperboles of *The Loved One* (1965). His treatment of *The Charge of the Light Brigade* (1968) as a metaphoric indictment of a social and cultural system has much sharp satire and irony of juxtaposition, but also errant sections of sentiment, melodrama, and epic maneuverings that flaw a coherent thrust and unity. His career was typical of the gradual diffusion of the social thrust of the movement.

To return to 1963, in that year Lindsay Anderson's first feature, *This*

This Sporting Life

Sporting Life, revealed a quite different kind of attempt to adapt a greater concern for inner subjectivity and expressiveness of style to the concerns of the committed Realist film. With sharp visual sensitivity and intricacy of editing, Anderson stays close to the subjective consciousness of the rugby star Frank Machen (Richard Harris), not only in breaking up the naturalistic time scheme with memories and associations but in seeing things in his terms and externalizing his emotional stages in visual images, such as the nightmarishly brutal, muddy sequences of the rugby game. While Anderson emphasizes the destructive failure of an emotional life style in the interaction between Machen and his widowed landlady, their emotional disfigurement is placed in a social context. Her emotions have been rigidly repressed, his deflected into sadism because he knows no real terms on which to act them out. It is further implied, however, that his inner flaws are a result of the economic system, his sport an extension of capitalistic greed, he a victim of the bosses. The exposure through the perspective of political commitment does not coalesce with the more convincingly earned exposure of the turmoil of personal inner life.

Anderson did not have another feature released until *If* in 1969. Here the British public (in America, private) school is the metaphor, a more fitting one than the sporting world, for the distorting pressures of established society that block the inner life. Here the youth rebellion is the center, both honest and fashionable, of the story. Here the style has become more openly expressive in finding ways to externalize the *feel* of things and events beyond their literal appearances, again in a manner that seems both personal and *au courant,* creating a fluid, shifting texture of sharply detailed literal drama, satire and parody, fantasy hyperbole (and even a mixing of sepia-toned black and white and color photography). Between this style and the uncertainties of Anderson's attitude toward the rebellious students, it is hard to establish the limits of the film's ironies. For, while Anderson clearly satirizes the established codes of morality and discipline and basically makes sympathetic his trio of rebels, he does seem to intend to show from the beginning the warping impact of cultural stereotypes (even of revolution) on their basically free spirits. After the literal but satirized war games of the students (which the rebel Mick and his friends upset), the rebels *seem* to then break up a charter-day ceremony by setting fire to the school and turning their guns on the entire assemblage—students, faculty, and parents alike. How is one to take this, and the final, obviously romanticizing shot of Mick blazing away like a hero out of a World War II movie? The cumulative buildup of fantasy in preceding sequences would seem to indicate this is the fantasy projection of Mick's violent rebelliousness, the romantic shot a final, countercutting irony. In this view, we do not have a didactic advocacy of violence but an understanding, as in Michelangelo Antonioni's later *Zabriskie Point,* that the cultural warp of vicious violence—so prevalent and intense through the film—cuts both ways. The film's title does more than set the parodic terms for the exposure of Kiplingesque morality; it sets the subjunctive terms for what can, and already does, happen, if and when evolutionary change does not occur, in the final extreme explosion of frustration of the angry young man.

ROMANTIC SENSIBILITY SELF-BETRAYED

Earlier, in 1965, Karel Reisz had in *Morgan* treated another facet of social deflection of inner vitality and the élan of rebellion and liberation—of what happens *if.* It is a frantic, uneven, uneasy film that wittily marks Reisz's efforts to join the sixties' search for new ''ways,'' as he has said, ''of expressing the feelings of characters in the way you show it rather than just photograph them having feelings. The important thing about technique is that it should be an expression of feeling, not something that is applied, somewhat theoretically.''

Morgan Delt (David Warner) has given up the good fight on practical, realistic terms—given up painting, given up his father's gospel of Marx and Trotsky (though he still identifies with them). He still loves, but only irresponsibly. Turning inward to the freedom of his own consciousness (the doctrine of the new life style), he nonetheless is trapped by the riches of his inner potential and his inability to shape it into viable terms. His dilemma and the collapse of his rebellion into madness are treated sympathetically by Reisz yet are countered by an ironic satire that cuts against Morgan as it does against the establishment he rebels against with zany but childishly futile zeal.

When Morgan takes his staunchly working-class mother to Marx's grave,

Morgan

the words on the gravestone mock his life. For, unlike Marx, he can no longer believe that we can do something to change the world. Instead he turns to madcap antics and fantasies for a love and humanitarianism he cannot fulfill in reality. His fantasies center on the naturalness of wild animals (and Tarzan and King Kong), seen as clips from old movies, for Morgan is after all a child of the mass media.

When Morgan tries to bridge the gap between the dream world and reality, the results are disastrous yet captured with the same central mixture of tone, the blending and shifting between ludicrousness, humor, and tenderness that is the special feel of the work. At the peak of his efforts, he breaks up his former wife's wedding, wearing his gorilla costume. But the comic chase ends suddenly. In a typically effective cut, we see Morgan, still in his costume, lying on an industrial slag heap. He can't get off the gorilla mask; his own eyes show through the mask, the lips gasp for breath. No longer comic, the grotesque mask of his defeated dreams is suffocating him. In a subsequent fantasy, he feels himself persecuted on all sides, assassinated like his beloved idol, Trotsky. Still, the screenplay grants him the last word: His ex-wife is carrying his child.

It is interesting to note that in Reisz's later film *Isadora* (1970), Isadora Duncan (Vanessa Redgrave) is killed when her scarf, the banner of her own partly self-destructive zeal for inner liberation, catches on an auto wheel. Reisz's treatment of her triumphs and her defeats, however, does not manage to unify his selection from the complexities of her biography, nor does he establish the satisfying consistency of tone or editing and camera style that would have taken this film beyond the limitations of the biography genre.

John Schlesinger's 1965 film *Darling* also takes a look—a more ironic, far less sympathetic one—at the paradoxes of the new rebellion of consciousness. Its darling (Julie Christie) is an extension of the girl who left on the midnight train in *Billy Liar.* A young woman of energy, potential, imagination, and a diffused and undifferentiated desire, she does make it in London. But the new life style, translated into the controlling forms of media and wealth, even more cruelly dissipates the potentials of her sensibilities, because it seems to be offering the means of their fulfillment.

Schlesinger exposes the incompleteness of all the ego-locked relationships of the film with the flourishes of the new cinematic style, which here can mock the false hypocrisies of the heightening of sensation and perception that the style is often used to celebrate. Within an energetic pattern of sharp juxtapositions, he skillfully employs an elliptical paring of scenes, overlapping of sound and image, enigmatic and abrupt transitions, witty visual correlatives for the destructive emotional relationships.

In his American film *Midnight Cowboy* (1970), Schlesinger intensifies the editing and the sensationalist impact of the emotional corruption of the hip New York scene. But the modish touches seem too much external embellishments, a distraction from rather than a deepening counterpoint to the moving development of the strangely desperate need in the relationship between its innocent turned stud (Jon Voigt) and the beaten but still vulnerable Ratso Rizzo (Dustin Hoffman). In the subsequent *Sunday, Bloody Sunday* (1971), the hollow brass of the contemporary scene is kept a more modulated surround. The film's intelligent but mannered inversion of the classic triangle poses the central impasse of these films—the difficult butt-ends of emotionality in the midst of the allure of sensory stimulation. Both its man and woman are nice people but ready emotional victims, left strewn in the wake of the youthful mod artist they both love, the new-style romantic egoist whose self-absorbed freedom they can neither control nor accept.

ROMANTIC SENSIBILITY CELEBRATED

Of the movies of this period, the three early films by the American-born Richard Lester are the fullest celebration of the possibilities of the new youthful sensibility. Though the first is more literal and the second a toying with superspy fantasies, his two Beatles films—*A Hard Day's Night* (1964) and *Help!* (1965)—are technically exuberant fairy tales of freedom and release. In these, the Beatles become a four-bodied mythic figure of liberation, and the best moments capture their breaking out: escaping down fire escapes; gamboling childlike, balletlike on a concrete square in the midst of an open field; Ringo, like a child going forth alone, responding to all he encounters; the four of them in the white freedom of the Alps, clad in Batman-like capes, cavorting with an inventive freedom of movement and grace of montage. And all the while, the songs.

In the more structured realistic fantasizing of *The Knack* (1965), another quartet of young rebels finds its way to subjective meaning amid the white emptiness of a boardinghouse and the uncomprehending streets of London, as typified by the lovely comic pilgrimage with the iron bed from a junkyard.

The virtuosity and frantic vitality of Lester's direction is turned to satire in *How I Won the War* (1967), toying with the conventions of movies and moviegoing as much as with the conventions of going to war, and exposing the connection between the two. In the later *The Bed Sitting Room* (1970), woefully ignored on its original release, the disturbing paradox of war films (even antiwar films) is further underscored. One of the handful of loony survivors of the two-and-a-half-minute "WWIII" has a treasure-trove of war footage and madly savors both its images of suffering and his own indignation. "Oh, the horror, the horror," he cries, but goes on, obviously excited, enjoying the pleasure of being shocked. In *his* film, Lester shows no war footage. His fusion of a shotgun mélange of stylizations is more controlled than in *How I Won the War* but still suffers from the indulgence of too many wayward antics. Its best pattern of routines is to play the comic cartoons of its cross section of humanity's inanities and insanities (as they careen inevitably toward rebuilding both their "civilization" and its weaponry) against obviously theatricalized, movie-set locations, which are nevertheless full of the real flotsam and jetsam of civilized waste. Color is used to strengthen the distancing and unsettling discordance, sometimes, for example, dividing the screen into separate layers of different colors.

In the American-made *Petulia* (1969), Lester, like Schlesinger, goes to excessive lengths with technique and the rendering of the sensory stimuli of the time. But at its center is one of the period's finest character delineations (in George C. Scott's subtly modulated performance) of the quintessential type, the man who wants to feel more but knows he can't. The straighter dramatic sequences are the best: the subtle shifting of mood in the bedroom scene between Scott and his ex-wife (including his sudden explosion by throwing at her the bag of cookies she has brought); his sudden facing of the central theme while leaning, sweating and breathing hard from a handball game, against the blinding, empty white walls of the court: "I want to feel something"; the comic underplaying of his final refusal of the risks of committing himself to Petulia.

OTHER THEMES: BROOKS, RUSSELL, LOSEY

The work of several other directors also traces the shifting of style in the British film of the sixties, though with less central attention to the thematic core of those discussed so far. Clive Donner's version of Pinter's *The Care-*

taker (also called *The Guest,* 1963), was taut, quiet, and underplayed; subsequently—in *Nothing But the Best* (1964), *Here We Go Round the Mulberry Bush* (1967), *What's New, Pussycat?* (1969)—he turned to a varying set of flamboyantly modish comedies. The film works of stage-director Peter Brooks have experimented with a variety of approaches: the tightly disciplined *Moderato Cantabile* (1960), with Jeanne Moreau; the freer form and improvisations of *Lord of the Flies* (1963); and the transference to the screen of his important stage productions, *The Beggar's Opera* (1952), the wild theatricality of *Marat-Sade* (1969), the powerful mythic starkness of *King Lear* (1971). After the ornate spy thriller, *Billion Dollar Brain* (1967), Ken Russell has pursued the frenetic form of intense emotionalism, from the disciplined modulation of passions in *Women in Love* (1970) to the unrestrained indulgences of *The Music Lovers* and *The Devils* (both 1971). A first film by Donald Cammell and Nicholas Roeg, *Performance* (1970), was equally unrestrained but used its fanatical flourishes for a provocative exercise (much maligned by reviewers) in radical psychology. Elusive and allusive (to Jorge Luis Borges, Hermann Hesse, Norman O. Brown), it probes the murky extremes of fluid, subjective identity, the enveloping quicksand of role-playing, domination and subjection, and merger, passing finally into the mystical possibilities of a collective unconscious in which all identities and performances may be shared.

Spanning this whole period, the work of the expatriate American Joseph Losey, however, provides the fullest example of the stylistic developments of the decade; and from their own separate perspective, the works obliquely make a major comment on the period's central theme of the impasse of the emotions in a time of social crisis and frustration.

After five relatively conventional movies in Hollywood, Losey was blacklisted, then moved to London in 1952. Of his Hollywood productions, *The Prowler* (1951) exhibits an early touch of his expressive use of décor and camera movement. Despite a steady strengthening of personal style, it was not until *The Criminal* (1960) and especially *Eva* (1962) that he seems to have solidified the intense, ornate style that developed, with both flexibility and excessiveness, in subsequent works. *The Criminal,* with Stanley Baker, is still within the crime, tough-guy milieu of many of his earlier films but begins to develop more meaning within the material and express it with greater visual flair. The viciousness of the prisons is mirrored in the criminals, their greed in the surrounding society. It is a world of power struggles for dominance, in which, in typically cynical fashion, victories are only illusions.

If power struggles—cruel, selfish, destructive—are at the core of much of Losey's work, the twisting aggressions are part of the generalized sense of emotional corruption and confusion, of the loss of a unifying emotional being that Losey insistently relates to social patterns and pressures, to class, money, social structuring of greed.

Lilith

emotional potential within) and Bert Gordon, the gambler (George C. Scott), are forced into a distorting and destructive framework for the assertion of their need for identity. Caught between them, Sara has an awareness of her own emotional crippling and of the value of loving; but she can do nothing with it, is even driven to contribute to her own destruction.

Eddie's regeneration after the suicide of Sara (Piper Laurie) still remains within the earlier conventions; but in *Lilith*, Rossen moves further, and without succumbing to conventional affirmations, into the difficult ambiguities of the emotions and the passions. Stylistically, he employs a number of visual motifs: Lilith (Jean Seberg) and water; the reverse parallels of the opening tour of Vincent (Warren Beatty) through the asylum and his last frenzied walk, now trapped himself; both Vincent and Lilith past bars and in shadows (related to the central symbol of the web of the insane spider). In dialogue sequences, Rossen maintains an intensifying structural motif: He regularly holds to two-shots, shooting past one character to the other and then alternating the setups, before cutting to close-up for a final climax. The lovely patterns and contrasts of the film's compositions, especially of nature, set up an ironic opposition to its emotional torments. But it is a subtle irony, for the loveliness of the images is part of the work's disturbing paradoxes about the uncertain line between beauty and violence, sanity and aberration, emotionality and aggression.

Lilith presents a sharp and significant contrast to the pat Realist psychological formulas of Frank Perry's *David and Lisa* of the same year. The latter was critically applauded, while *Lilith* was appallingly misread and mistreated by the critics. *The Hustler*, too, while it received a more favorable response, was generally praised on the wrong, reductive terms. When viewed accurately on their exact terms, they are among the most mature and penetrating dramatizations of personality and emotion in the American film.

Martin Ritt and Sidney Lumet

In the early sixties, the limits of American Realism were also being extended by a number of former TV directors. Of these, Martin Ritt has stayed more within the patterns of traditional dramaturgy and straightforward cinematic technique. His *Hud* (1962), with Paul Newman and based on the novel by Larry McMurtry, takes an abrasive new stance toward its New West materials; yet its sophisticated treatment of its caddish antihero is undercut by stereotyping and blurring of character and social issues. Sidney Lumet, in contrast, has dabbled with a variety of technical approaches to achieve an intensity of emotional content and impact, without evolving a consistently personal style. Nonetheless, his *The Pawnbroker* (1965) was an important contribution to American steps toward heightening within the conventions of Realism. Though dramatically founded on too tenuous a ground of coincidence and key weakness of motivation (Sol Nazerman's sudden rebellion against the Black racketeer because of his discovery of the latter's brothel operations), it is important and successful in its open application of expressive devices while maintaining an unbroken dramatic illusion of reality. The combination produces a greater complexity and intensity of feeling and the resonance of metaphor. The film becomes more than a film about the problem of concentration camps or of slums or of money-making: It is a film about all that men can do to themselves, for whatever reason, to dam up and deflect their emotional life and sympathy.

This crisis, centered in the subjective consciousness of Nazerman (Rod Steiger) is developed by a series of parallels between past and present—the destructive past of the camps and the destructive present of the prison of the self, the pawnshop. In a fitting use of slow-motion (with camerawork by Boris Kaufman, who first introduced the device in Jean Vigo's *Zéro de Conduite*), the last idyllic moment before the arrival of the Nazis intrudes again and again. In rapid flashes, building in completeness, as in the work of Resnais, the camp life is paralleled with images of the present—the screens of the pawnshop shadowed on Nazerman like the fences and bars of the camps. Juxtapositions are used within the present as well, the visual details striking even when the parallels are too forced in contrast: the young helper Jesus and his Black girlfriend making love on her bed, smiling, laughing, giggling, rolling around together, always moving; Nazerman rising slowly from a nap on the sofa, checking his watch, taking off his glasses, his woman taking off her apron; Nazerman above her in the bed, hardly moving, the camera just off from the monolithic immobility of his hairy shoulder, the strap of his sleeveless undershirt, his watch still ticking, his hand, moving independently, gripping the pillow, she staring away, separate, alone. And, after, the card game.

The final visual metaphor is again indicative, appropriated from the famous silent scream of Helene Weigel in Brecht's *Mother Courage*, yet personally felt and effective: Steiger's face seen from two compelling angles, as he cradles the dead Jesus on the sidewalk, crying out for this death and the causes he now understands, but unable still to make a sound.

John
Frankenheimer

For a time in the mid-sixties, John Frankenheimer seemed on the way to a personal extending and reshaping of the film of social criticism, but since 1966, he has turned his visual flair to more standard fare. Within the literal representation of a hypothetical military takeover in *Seven Days in May* (1964), his vibrant editing and strong, inventive use of images of dominating machinery created a compelling metaphoric sense of the dominating pressures of technology and especially electronic communications. With the wartime suspense of *The Train* (1965), he developed a strong network of ironies about the cost of men's crusades, on both sides: The resistance fighters have stopped the Nazis' fanatical attempt to steal the art treasures, but at great cost—in the final shot, the boxes of paintings strewn among the corpses. The ironies of the earlier *The Manchurian Candidate* (1962) were more barbed. Mixing exaggerated thriller machinations and satiric hyperbole, it has an unsettling mixture of tones, a seeming absence of moral center. For it cuts in all directions and at various levels of political crusading and conformity, while toying mischievously, if unevenly, with the conventions of political and thriller films alike: When the plotting of the good guys goes awry, the bad guy shoots the nice senator right through his morning bottle of milk, and milk, not blood, gushes forth. *Seconds* (1966) is more patterned, thematic in its central ironies. Though weak in its development of the second life of the central character, it nonetheless is an effective extension of the literal into the plausible but unlikely fantasy of science fiction. Its central allegory poses a modern Faustian variation, as an aging businessman gives himself to "The Company," which retreads him physically and psychologically. (For the rest of the film we sense him lost within the body and face of Rock Hudson.) But, within the system of "The Company," failure, obsolescence of the attractive product are built in; at the end, he is trapped into trying again and dragging others into the system. When he refuses, he is killed so that his body can be used to cover the disappearance of a new client.

Arthur
Penn

Of this group of directors whose careers began on television, Arthur Penn has moved the furthest in blending Realist conventions with new expressive approaches and developing a unified and varied body of important work.

Penn's first screen work, while maintaining strict literal representation and a straightforward tone, was a harshly characterized and insistently edited deromanticizing of the Western genre. In *The Left Handed Gun* (1958), his Billy the Kid (Paul Newman) is a psychologically troubled young outcast, a violent, extreme American relative of the frustrated rebels who begin to enter the British film during the same year.

An instinctive interest in materials—however varied otherwise—that dramatize the difficult development of a sense of self-identity continues to show itself in Penn's films through the next decade and a half. In *The Miracle Worker* (1962), he plays the small, focused drama at a high pitch of emotion, editing sharply to build intensity, reaching a peak in the physical violence of the scene in which Anne Sullivan (Anne Bancroft) and the young blind and deaf Helen Keller explode at each other. The scene is also the psychological center of the film, accenting the teacher's learning to face unresolved tensions in herself by understanding and dealing with those within Helen Keller. In *The Chase* (1965), rampant social corruption of healthy identity is treated in unrelieved crescendo, indicative of the trend in American films at this time to turn up the volume of emotionality and sensation; unfortunately, it is replete with all the stereotypes of contemporary, and here Southern, ethical and sexual decadence.

With an unusual and literate screenplay by Alan Surgal, Penn's *Mickey One* (1964) is a comic allegory of identity that holds up as one of the unique American films of the time. The work builds from the basic Social Realist convention of the young unformed American (this time a second-rate nightclub comedian) harassed by an enigmatic version of the ubiquitous racketeers, the symbol, as in so many American dramas and films, of destructive money and power-seeking materialism. But in *Mickey One*'s special mixing of melodrama, comic vignette, and Expressionist exaggeration and fantasy, they also become the symbols of Mickey's (Warren Beatty's) inner corruption. Driven by unfocused fears and guilts, he can finally stand up to the blank spotlight of the gang-run nightclub and accept the limits of his need for others and his mortality (in a world which, in comic irony, repeatedly mocks the hope of the phrase from Jeremiah, "Is there any word from the Lord?").

Typical of the film's metaphoric wit is the motif of the unspeaking, elfin junk-dealer. Throughout, the film emphasizes images of the frightening threat and misuse of things and bodies, people treated as things. But the little junk-dealer, who constantly beckons Mickey, finally gives him a ride on his wagon loaded with junk when Mickey has faced his fears and begun to come to terms with things and the body. The film's most positive symbol is the junkman's "Being" machine, a Rube Goldbergian comic contraption, built totally out of junk, that gives pleasure, and enjoys itself, even as it uses itself up, even when the uncomprehending fire department tries to bury it in a heavy sea of antiseptic white foam.

In the trend-setting *Bonnie and Clyde* of 1967 (screenplay by David Newman and Robert Benton), the mixed moods and tones of the new-wave style are applied to the Realist genre of crime and society and to the specific materials of at least four previous films (including Fritz Lang's *You Only Live Once*). In this context, the sympathetic treatment of the bank robbers and the indictment of society are not that unusual. Neither is the psychological emphasis on crime as the distorted seeking of identity ("We rob banks"), often found in the genre, as in Rossen's films, though here their weaknesses are more clinically laid out. What is unusual—and carries the tonic note of the times—is the unsettling shifting of tone that furthers our sympathy, yet complicates it beyond earlier simplified treatments, and finally distances and

Bonnie and Clyde

undercuts it. It is in this mixture—vicious and nice, funny and terrible—that the film's greater sense of the naggingly perverse mixture of human personality is chiefly felt. Bonnie and Clyde (Warren Beatty and Faye Dunaway) are cute and bumbling as they try their first robbery; yet they end by blasting (in close-up) the face off a bank guard who leaps on the car's running board. Jovial country music and family hijinks and bickering mark their constant movement; yet so does a cumulative sense of frustration, loneliness, futile desperation. The film is at its best as a comic tragedy. In the later stages, the comedy fades. Though appropriate as the inexorable fate that was always present in the illusory frolicking, the relentless brutality of the police tips the precarious balance of tones. Especially when felt in contrast to the romanticized, rather old-fashioned emotional growth allowed Bonnie and Clyde, it resentimentalizes the film's original desentimentalization of the gangster genre and its patterns of audience expectation.

Alice's Restaurant (1969) is another interesting attempt to deal complexly with audience expectations, this time in terms of the new myth and genre of the youthful break-out life style. Against the lightness of Arlo Guthrie's original ballad and the comic satire with which the film dramatizes its japes at society, Penn opposes a harder, subtler satire of the illusions of the new rebels and a somber pathos over the emotional failures of their attempts at new identity through community. The fullest psychological probing is of the youths' den mother and father, Alice and Ray, and of the mixed motives and needs behind their interactions with the youngsters—culminating in the desperation underlying the hilarity of the wedding party and a last long-held shot of Alice, after all have split for new stopovers, the camera moving in closer and closer to her in slow, sad arcs, losing her behind trees, then glimpsing her again as she stands alone in front of their old church.

Little Big Man (1972) is Penn's most elaborate attempt to work within standard genre expectations—this time the Western—yet manipulate the materials to produce an abrasive emotional impact and a deepening of theme. The zigzag course of Jack Crabb (Dustin Hoffman), White but living alternately among Indians and Whites, takes him through the central myths of the Whites' brutally tragic encounter with the Indians. Crabb's plight creates a disturbing metaphor of the contradictions within America's identity as a nation. Part realistic epic, part bitterly witty satire, part literal representation extended to the borders of fantasy, *Little Big Man* has the fashionable didacticism of its time. It pits a sympathetic and romanticized interpretation of Indian culture against a total indictment of invading White civilization. Among its most striking transpositions of genre materials is the large-scale cavalry attack on the Indian village: An eerie dislocated nightmare, it juggles lovely compositions, relentless violence, chaotic movements, bits of dialogue, all while the military band plays away in the icy fog. Many touches comically take new perspectives on traditional devices: The lone victim in the middle of a prairie is slumped over a chaise longue; an arrow kills the preacher through his bible; Bonnie and Clyde music accompanies a John Wayne stagecoach ride.

THE NEW FREE SPIRIT

By the end and turn of the decade, the cultural nerves so successfully touched by *Bonnie and Clyde* were being assaulted by a host of imitations. As the fad accelerated and then seemed to peak, the new antihero heroes became more and more youthful, or at least acted youthful, even when played by such middle-aging gentlemen as Paul Newman. They embodied the hardening stereotype of the tuned-in rebellious free spirits of the new sensibility ("Consciousness III" as finally sanctified by the middle-brow establishment in Charles Reich's evangelical book *The Greening of America* in 1970). Their films pursued new-wave mixed tones; they openly flaunted the new expressive freedom of visual and aural artifice (sound tracks pronouncing the musical succession from Alfred Newman and Miklos Rozsa, through Elmer Bernstein, to rock) and the new explicitness in depicting sex and violence; they compounded powerful sensory impact into "experiences" of emotionality as well as vehicles for dramatic content.

Hopper, Wexler, Altman

While Roger Corman's *The Wild Angels* (1966) was the first and still one of the best of the new mode of cyclist-hero films, it was Dennis Hopper's *Easy Rider* (1970), with Hopper, Peter Fonda, and Jack Nicholson, that had the heaviest impact. With the structural purity of the classic Western and a flowing grace of imagery (and the obligatory mosaics of a "trip" sequence), it propounds the stereotyped new dualism: the gentle comradeship of the outsiders and the hard violence of the "straights." With a stronger note of self-pity than *Bonnie and Clyde,* it captures the time's fashionable romantic cynicism, which gives itself the lie by still cherishing an unskeptical indulgence in the old hope of the radical innocence of the unrepressed young spirit, the new noble savage. In his second film, *The Last Movie* (1971), Hopper pursued more subtle themes and more audacious techniques. But at this point at least, his audacious reach exceeded his grasp; he could not bring under control his radical dislocation of dramatic structure and blurring of reality, illusion, and metaphor, nor finally unify such interesting material as the clash of cultures, the psychology of violence, the interaction of media and life.

Haskell Wexler's *Medium Cool* (1969), in placing youthful rebellion in a broad social context, also emphasized the impact of media itself on consciousness, especially the paradoxical deadening of response through overpowering impact. He interestingly interwove a personal dramatic plot with documentary treatment of historical reality—the Democratic convention in Chicago of 1968; but the attempt to explore film Realism stumbled over the paradox of the film's own artificiality and the limitations of its dramatic materials.

Two Paul Newman vehicles showed deft commercial treatment of the new iconography—the controlled directness of the free spirit clashing with Southern prison authority in *Cool Hand Luke* (1967), directed by Stuart Rosenberg, and the skilled articulation of the transfusion of the new ethos and visual kit into the Western structure of *Butch Cassidy and the Sundance Kid* (1969), with Robert Redford and directed by George Roy Hill, all kept savingly light and playful, free of the self-righteousness of the fashion's more serious endeavors.

Robert Altman's *M*A*S*H* (1970), with script by Ring Lardner, Jr., ostensibly placed its medical rebels in the Korean War. The bloody results of war were strikingly juxtaposed with the comic shenanigans early on but then were pushed aside for long periods of time by the parade of comic set pieces. In balance, it is less a black comedy about war than a skillful updating of traditional antiauthority comic materials, a hip admixture of the likes of Britain's *Doctor in the House* series and *Mr. Roberts.* With *Brewster McCloud* (1971), Altman tried his hand at comic fantasy. In *McCabe and Mrs. Miller* (1971), he effectively blended comedy and a harshly literal view of a Western mining town. But the film strays from developing the blocked emotionalism in the affair between Warren Beatty and Julie Christie into the pat metaphor of its showdown climax between the eccentric individualist and the relentless brutes of the economic system.

Mike Nichols and Robert Rafelson
The most successful of the comic approaches to the clash of consciousness and generations (and one of the biggest box-office successes in movie history) was Mike Nichols's *The Graduate* (1967). The year before, Nichols had forcefully but rather statically (without a strong sense of the uses of décor and movement) filmed Edward Albee's *Who's Afraid of Virginia Woolf.* In *The*

Five Easy Pieces

Graduate, however, Nichols effectively (though sometimes too obviously and eclectically) appropriates elements of the new stylistics to shape a personal attitude toward the material—satirical but sentimental, with an intelligent simplification, a professional awareness of the deft use of convention. At the close, the bland, uncertain, waifish iconoclasm of Benjamin (Dustin Hoffman) is brought to focused action in his attack on the wedding in the church: He is frustrated and the ceremony consummated. But then he runs off with the bride anyway, shoving in a handy cross to jam the door to their pursuers. But as they ride off on the bus, an enigmatic separate silence.

Though inevitably flawed in attempting to deal with the bulky verbal complexities of Joseph Heller's *Catch-22,* Nichols's film version (1970) has an unsettling strength and style of its own. In the intricacies and meaningful repetitions of its circling structure, in its balancing (with lapses into easy cartoon) of the empathetic treatment of the quietly intelligent and sensitive Yossarian (Alan Arkin) and the distancing satiric stylization of the insanities of war that surround him, its gradations of Realism into hyperbole, pathos into comedy, it gets much further into the nightmare human folly that perpetuates war than do the easy, reductive manipulations of *M*A*S*H.* But in the subsequent *Carnal Knowledge* (1971), script by Jules Feiffer, the descent from Realism into cartoon caricature is uncontrolled, repetitious, and basically unimaginative, from surface case study to simplistic symbol.

Carnal Knowledge takes another of the turn-of-the-decade's basic motifs, the emotional impotence of the male American, into its caricature in sexual impotence. In Robert Rafelson's *Five Easy Pieces* (1970), again with its key figure Jack Nicholson, the motif is dramatized realistically but is given the enigmatic patterns of freer characterization and the elliptical structure and visual correlatives of the kind of oblique inner Realism pioneered by the Italians and especially by Antonioni.

Bogdanovich,
Cassavetes,
and
Others

Moving into the seventies, Rafelson's film seems the most sophisticated and visually achieved of a number of early works by directors working within the elliptical structures of this kind of Realism, such as Paul Newman with *Rachel, Rachel* (1968), Francis Ford Coppola with *The Rain People* (1970), Barbara Loden with *Wanda* (1971), Peter Bogdanovich with the very successful *The Last Picture Show* (1971), a Renoir–Ford-oriented, densely textured evocation of the end of innocence, personally, culturally, in the smothering deadness of a smalll Texas town in the early fifties. At the turn of the decade, John Cassavetes returned to his close-in, intense, open-structured, spontaneously acted dramas of Realist intimacy, begun earlier with *Shadows* (1960). *Faces* (1968) has a verbal, visual, and emotional shrillness; prodding close-ups overbalance its often excellent long takes in deep focus; each scene is played all out for emotional highs and lows. *Husbands* (1970) is more supple in emotion and style. Both create a vivid, open immediacy, blurring the conventional line between actors and characters.

Cassavetes's characters are, in the main, played by professional actors. The characters in the films of Andy Warhol are played by his special stable of superstars, untrained as actors, but performers and role-players with a vengeance. His films—which have succeeded in knocking down the wall between underground film-making and commercial distribution—are made casually and quickly. Editing is mainly achieved by stopping and starting the camera; performers extemporize within loosely blocked-out situations, often interrupting the fictional framework to talk as themselves and about themselves. The unblinking, unfazed eye of the camera carries the transparency of the cinema to its extreme; yet the result is a complicated experience, obliterating the lines between fictional narrative and documentary, between acting and revealing, between normality and abnormality. What is unblinkingly revealed is mainly what would normally be called bizarre, perverse behavior and personality, but the films toy with all "normal" perspectives, accepting everything matter-of-factly, yet poking fun democratically at their own stereotypes and those of the straight media world they oppose yet savor, even ape. Warhol is at his best when intentionally being funny, although his intentions are not always scrutable. He surfaced with *The Chelsea Girls* (1966); it was followed, in totally chaotic distribution arrangements, by *I'm a Man, Bike Boy, My Hustler, Nude Restaurant, Lonesome Cowboys*, and *Sex*. The last—in which three transvestites play women driven to hokey Hollywood ruin—carries out the satiric expectations of its plot more elaborately than the others. It shows the stronger influence of Paul Morrissey, who had worked with Warhol all along. Morrissey was also more directly responsible for *Flesh* and *Trash*.

THE NEW VISION IN THE WESTERN

While the Western genre was not immune to new-consciousness stylization, through these same decades there was also significant evolution within the basically Realist perimeter of the traditional epic genre. In the fifties, John

Ford produced his most deeply felt work; George Stevens mounted classically styled epics of clear moral confrontation in the Old and New West in *Shane* (1953) and *Giant* (1956). A revisionist Realism from new social and psychological perspectives was initiated by Delmer Daves's *Broken Arrow*, Henry King's *Gunfighter*, Anthony Mann's *Winchester 73* (all 1950), and Fred Zinneman's *High Noon* (1952). In a number of works in the fifties, Mann especially deepened the psychological dimension while maintaining the lyricism of place and the structure of violent action of the conventional form: among them, *The Naked Spur* (1952), *The Last Frontier* (1955), and *Man of the West* (1955). Concurrently, John Sturges (working with cinematographer Charles Lang) was consolidating wide-screen compositions and techniques into a leaner, athletic surface intensity of action and rhythm in *Gunfight at the OK Corral* (1957), *Last Train from Gun Hill* (1959), and *The Magnificent Seven* (1960). Moving into the seventies, a spate of films reversed the old stereotypes: turning the Indian to hero, the cavalry to villain, bringing the heroic Black man to the West.

Sam Peckinpah

But it was Sam Peckinpah in the sixties who brought the deepest new vision to the genre and came into the seventies as one of the most significant creative figures in Hollywood—surmounting on the way several years of exiled conflict with the production system. In his first six films—including *Straw Dogs* (1971), despite its British countryside setting—Peckinpah has worked through to an original vision of the human and dramatic meaning of the myth of the West and structure of the Western, fusing a lyrical nostalgia for landscape and manly action with an increasingly harsh and vivid stylization and cynical sense of moral paradox. In his work, much that is frequently bastardized in the contemporary revolution in collective consciousness is given a tough-minded personal unity.

His second (and first major) film, *Ride the High Country* (1962), is his most lyrical and nostalgic yet is touched by a complexity of character and perspective that deepens its economical eloquence. Like Ford's late work, its perspective is set by the passing of an era, its two aging leftover gunfighters (Randolph Scott and Joel McCrea), a wistful anachronism of simpler certainties. Still, both are humanly individualized—the cynically opportunistic Scott, the dignified but rigidly righteous McCrea. McCrea's Steven Judd especially is developed with an eye to the dangers of abstract, rigid moral rightness—seen in his inflexible responses in not protesting a forced wedding in the brothel of the vicious mining town and in his moralistic turning on his errant partners Westrum and Heck. But for all their limitations and romantic anachronisms, the two men are able to act out the justifying, manly good deed in the beautifully articulated final shootout. As Judd dies, the camera is positioned tightly from his point of view as he disappears down out of the frame and takes in his last look at the simple land that he loves but that is no longer his.

In *Major Dundee* (1964), Peckinpah reached for much more—a far fuller sense of individual identity and motivation for action, a symbolic exposure of

Ride the High Country

the torn, violent, unfaced nature of American society, a detailed panorama of action and history. Much of the planned script was never shot, much was cut when the project was taken from Peckinpah's control; but it is doubtful if even under the best of circumstances he could have totally integrated the diffused, and often faulty, trajectories of the material. Still, what remains does build and visually embody his basic conception of the cavalry chase and battles. Though left fragmented, the two central characters (as well as those that surround them) do dramatize the central psychological and ethical dilemma of that conception. Unsure of his own slippery sense of self and value, Tyreen (Richard Harris) goes along and loses his own life, but not without a saving touch of awareness and sympathy for others. Dundee (Charlton Heston) will not face his own inner void, defines himself by his leadership function, defines his values—like Melville's Captain Ahab—by a rigid, punitive righteousness. His taking action against the renegade Apaches who have fled into Mexico is viewed ambiguously: The Apaches did act viciously, but so does the cavalry. The final confrontation and decimation on both sides justifies little. Worse, it is followed by a totally useless and even bloodier battle with some French forces—the battle scenes, a difficult mixture of stirring epic composition and chaotic brutality. For all the manly valor, Dundee's violent crusade against inscrutable malice—rising from the unplumbed depths of motivation—leads nowhere, into the wilds of Mexico and back, with nothing achieved but violent death.

Five years later, *The Wild Bunch*—with all the late sixties' accelerated velocity of emotion, sensation, and cinematic stylistics—grotesquely enlarges and then explodes (like a balloon in the face) all the conventions of the myth and genre; yet it does not totally extricate itself from the explosion. Its cynical ironies expose with traumatic shock the lure of savagery rationalized into moralistic violence that Peckinpah sees at the core of the Western. The deaths are made more palpable not only by their ferocity and geometric progression but by their treatment: gushing blood, shock-cutting, intensifying slow-motion. But at the same time, there is in Peckinpah's treatment of them an artificializing, a distancing from the real ugliness of dying and killing that seems to indicate and produce something other than an ironic transcending of the conventions to shock into fresh consciousness: a relishing sensationalism with new forms of the old games. In the amazing manipulation of moods and tensions of the final blood bath, Peckinpah's mastery of form and our emotions does catch us up in our own vicarious thrills, our own rooting for the Bunch. Yet despite the ironies, many of the conventions up to this point have been rather fondly indulged, including especially the lovable rascality, the warm vitality and camaraderie, the final releasing recklessness that exist among the standard types of the Bunch. So that even though Peckinpah expertly shows their viciousness and animal lust in the way each conducts his final part in the big battle, the ironies have not gone far enough in treating them. We tend to root for them because, if not the old good guys, for the moment they are at least the better guys. Is this, too, possibly part of the mordantly ironic use of the materials? Even in its, and his, uncertainties, Peckinpah's film reveals its provocative mixture of a raw intuitive power and a cynically sophisticated manipulation.

After the lighter tone of *The Ballad of Cable Hogue* (1970), all these matters are more tightly, if no less pessimistically, wound in the metal-springed tautness of *Straw Dogs*. But for all its sunnier disposition, and its focusing on a humorously flawed but winning nice guy, *Cable Hogue* pictures an absurdly comic world in which a god, when importuned, may bring you water, wealth, and the possibilities of love, but ends up getting you run over by a new-fangled car while you are impulsively trying to save a man you had vowed to revenge yourself on.

THE NEW VIOLENCE: PECKINPAH AND KUBRICK

There is no jocularity in the perverse ironies of action in *Straw Dogs*, no nice guys. Its place in the period's crescendo of screen violence bears interesting relationships to Stanley Kubrick's film of the same year, *A Clockwork Orange*.

Before looking at them together, we'll first trace Kubrick's career to this point.

Kubrick's major work (after two apprentice films) began with the humane realism of *Paths of Glory* (1957). Though it shares with Renoir's *Grand Illusion* a sympathetic sense of the common humanity that somehow survives the brutalities of war, it is much harsher in its direct depiction of these brutalities (on both battlefield and in military court) and the social rigidity and injustice that lay behind them. Similarly, its lighting, compositional use of setting, and mobile camera also show the Renoir influence; in line with its stronger anger and accusation, it employs these more emphatically, with more striking juxtapositions, heightening camera movements, patterns of rapid editing, and orchestration of sound motifs such as the varied use of military drum rolls.

One of its peaks of emphatic, intensified Realism is the sequence of the unjust execution. As the three men are being marched to their execution (one of them tied upright to a stretcher), Kubrick first tracks backward in front of them, then forward from their point of view through the lines of massed troops, shooting sideways at the troops; then he cuts to the officers' point of view, panning as the condemned men pass. Back then from behind the three again, focusing on the three poles and brick wall against which they will be shot as these loom closer and larger. When they have been tied to the stakes, he shoots from the side as the priest walks toward the camera in front of the men, keeping in the foreground the almost dead soldier still tied upright to his stretcher. Just before the shooting, we see that looming large

Paths of Glory

in the background above the troops is the large, lovely château in which their court-martial had taken place, in which the generals live luxuriously, having their meals and formal balls while the men live and die in the trenches—a harsh reprise of a recurrent symbolic motif.

Equally striking, but with a contrasting tone, is the buildup of the scene after the execution, in which the troops first taunt a German girl in an inn, then join with her in song and in tears. Kubrick intensifies the sympathetic climax by using a series of some 30 facial close-ups in a slow, steady rhythm.

Three years later, Kubrick took over *Spartacus* while production on the panoramic epic of a Roman slave revolt was underway. Though his least personal film, it demonstrates his talent for enhancing script material with a carefully structured alternation of static shots, moving shots, and emphatic editing. His version of Vladimir Nabokov's *Lolita* (1962) was too early for the sexual frankness needed to capture the novel's erotic flavor and verve; one can only imagine what Kubrick would have done with it 10 years later. As a result, its best comic mixtures of perverse satire and sympathy are intermittent, less fulfilled in the central Humbert Humbert–Lolita scenes than in the Quilty scenes (with a series of acid impersonations by Peter Sellers) and in scenes with Lolita's mother and the surrounding middle-class society. Despite its lack of central thrust, it was at the time the strongest American dose of mixed tones and black humor and the first indication of Kubrick's penchant for bizarre satire, an ironic incongruity between approach and material.

The driving central thrust was found for *Dr. Strangelove* (1964). Here the human weaknesses that lead to the destructive rigidity of social power structures and the trap of technological advancement are stylized into madcap caricature, raised to a zany ludicrousness that is still tough-minded satire. The incongruity between the wild comedy and deeper horror here has the fully textured synthesis that was not present, for example, in Robert Altman's later *M*A*S*H*. The synthesis is built on a series of "turns," vignettes that reveal the caricatured perversities of character type yet create as well a cumulative tension. One of the strongest of the unifying devices is the repeated play on sexuality gone astray: the opening undulating shots of a fuel plane copulating with a bomber in midflight, the syrupy World War II ballad "Try a Little Tenderness" on the sound track; General Jack D. Ripper's pathological fear of losing his "precious bodily fluids," his "purity of essence"; Major Bat Guano's concern over the "*preverts*"; General Buck Turgidson's locker-room "manliness" both in bed and in the war room, his excitement over Dr. Strangelove's plan for atomic survival—many women for each man in the underground retreat; Strangelove's own growing excitement that fuses his technological sadism and sexuality in the final uncontrollable thrusting of his atrophied arm in Nazi salute that turns into self-choking; Colonel King Kong's final ride on the bomb sticking out like a giant phallus between his legs. Each is not only an excellent comic turn but contributes to

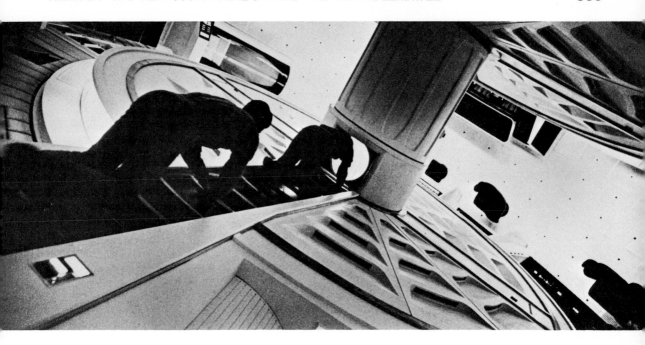

2001

building a central satiric hyperbole: that very fusing of sexuality and sadism, that warping of emotionality and motivation that is the weak and frightening human element in the dangerous rigidity of governmental and technological systems.

In *2001*, made in 1968, the satire that centers on man's inner flaws and outer technological "progress" is more muted and only part of a more complicated, and somewhat confused, larger structure. For here, Kubrick attempts to mix the satire on man and society's foibles with a display of cinematic pyrotechnics that seeks to suggest through sensory stimulation a mystic sense of man's place in patterns of universe beyond understanding. In the central space-voyage section of the film, sterile décor, debased pettiness of action and language, the routines of things and men in the name and at the service of reason serve the underplayed satire on the inner emptiness and social hypocrisy that both results from and leads to runaway technology. Even Hal, the machine that man has shaped in his own image, is similarly flawed, as were man's simian progenitors. Both man and the apes, when touched by the mystery of the giant slabs, are impelled to paradox: progress but also destructiveness. Yet in the final section of sensory bombardment, Kubrick and his collaborator Arthur C. Clarke soften the sardonic sense by sending the human voyager through nonintellectual realms of mystery that seem to transcend these limits with the more salutary paradoxes of the mystical unity of being.

A
Clockwork
Orange

Though utterly different in tone and approach, the mixtures of A *Clockwork Orange* (1971) also lead to an unfocused ambiguity. Its stylized sensory bombardment carries to hyperbolic extreme the current fashions of sadistic violence and vicious sexuality. Full of distancing devices that abstract beyond reality, it seeks to manipulate the audience by stirring confusing responses to the unsettling images of viciousness and violence. It uses the film's power to effect audience immersion in the materials while at the same time dislocating that immersion. In its glimpse of not-so-distant future results of current trends, it knowingly uses contemporary fads and fashions, art and décor, and the pseudolife of media stimulation to indict the deadening and brutalizing of emotion that these gaudy sensory-stimulating surfaces mask and nurture.

Yet the final denominator of its disturbing ironies is less than the potentials of its parts. In the first half, the brutality of the youthful gang (the pleasures "in a bit of the old ultra-violence") is treated with highly stylized, dislocating irony: slow-motion, speeded motion, balletlike grace; contrasting musical numbers (typified by Alex's singing and soft-shoeing of "Singing in the Rain" while beating the writer and raping his wife); comedy turned into sudden horror (the chase with the mod-art giant phallus climaxing with the bashing in of a woman's face with it). In the second half, however, the hypocrisy of society and the violations of free will by thought control are treated with more conventional and often too easy satire; the brutality toward Alex is direct and undistanced. While the earlier distancing styling had produced its own disturbing tensions, the net result of the two ways of treating violence is a growing sympathy for Alex, so that by the end it almost has the feel, more modishly frenetic and disturbing to be sure, of another conventional pattern of expectation—the young prankster beset by unfair authority. If all have a bit of the old evil in them, Alex is at least more knowing and honest about it, and charming—as were Peckinpah's Wild Bunch. Thus, the film does not maintain the toughness of the troubling impasse its own terms really dictate: acts against evil are often *equally* evil; in the film, they—at least certain kinds—are more so. It is indicative that in the whole second half Alex does nothing untoward; Kubrick even eliminates the murder in prison that Alex had committed in the Anthony Burgess novel. The clichéd exposure of government authority and hypocrisy does not really come to terms, then, with the disturbing violence the film unleashes and finally tends to justify for the sake of its abstract argument that it is evil to tamper with man's power to choose, even to choose evil. The argument is not earned by the actual terms of the work, which is more a stylish "hyping" of modish conventions than a transcending of them.

Straw
Dogs

Peckinpah's *Straw Dogs* is also a knowing use of conventions—of current fashions in violence and sex and traditional fashions of the Western ritual. His manipulation is achieved through a quite different mixture of stylization and Realist immersion. His basic situation has become a stylized microcosm, rather overburdened with coincidence even for metaphor. His approach is to engross us in the material, to make it compellingly credible. The shocks, the symbolic compositions, the exclamatory editing do not distance. The Realist illusion is maintained, superbly articulated through traditional tension to cathartic explosion. The basic structure is that of the Western, transplanted to the wilds of England's Cornwall coast: a small town on the distant borders of law and order, the growing threat of vicious evil, the final personal stand against it.

But the structure is turned inside out, with a cynical irony that is more simplified but more consistent than Kubrick's. On the one side of the traditional conflict the family of roughnecks (the old Western Clanton-family motif) act out a more extreme, untrammeled savagery than Western conventions ever admitted. On the other, the relationship between David, the pacifistic young mathematician (Dustin Hoffman), and his dissatisfied wife is developed with strong psychological and sexual tensions that erupt revealingly into minor savagings for the sake of the ego.

The final showdown is turned into a bleakly ironic, horrifyingly violent metaphor of the impasse of supposed moral action. While we are manipulated into rooting for Hoffman's defense of his home, its animal savagery appalls. Throughout its ferocious crescendos, Peckinpah continues to undercut our hero's evaluation of his actions and the evaluations produced by the conventional pattern of the material. David's constant reiteration of abstract principle is shaped as rationalization of emotions and motives that he has refused, or been unable to deal with. He had not dealt with the tensions between himself and his wife, with the sexual provocations of her boredom, with the escalating aggressions of the men, with the glaring evidence that she had been raped. Instead, he now acts for principle—this is his home, and he will not allow it or the rights of the village imbecile he harbors to be violated. He has let things go too far; now *he* goes too far. Yet exactly what else could he have done by this point? It is a frightening impasse, and the film faces it, does not justify one term or the other of the dilemma. The savage conquest —the explosive assertion of the instinctive territorial imperative—brings cathartic excitement and elation (to us as well as David) and a soaring of pride. This rings honestly, and unfortunately, true; but it now has none of the romantic dignity or glory given to it in the traditional Western's structure of feeling. The thrill of violence is here tied in a sickening knot to the need to thrust aside sexual insecurity—whatever abstract principles are evoked.

At the end, David rides off, not on his horse, but in his sports car. He is taking home the village imbecile, whose uncontrollable emotions had resulted in the accidental killing of a young, sexually provocative girl, and on whose just treatment David had predicated his violent stand. That we are to see them both as equal prey to uncontrollable emotion and violence is underscored by the final two-shot of them in the car: The idiot says he doesn't know his way home, and David, with a hard smile of masculine assertiveness on his face, pridefully says he doesn't either. The toughness of the irony holds firm, controls the meaningful manipulation of the fashionable screen conventions of the period.

CHAPTER TWENTY-THREE

NEW
VOICES
IN
INTERNATIONAL
FILM

At the Venice Film Festival of 1951, Akira Kurosawa's *Rashomon* was the surprising winner of the grand prize and soon was roundly acclaimed and financially successful in country after country. Its success directly accelerated the introduction of the Japanese film into the Western film world and indirectly signaled the beginnings of new national film movements in nations, both East and West, that had not previously been prominent in international cinema.

JAPAN

Kurosawa   Significantly, like much of the new work that would follow, *Rashomon* presents a fusion of the characteristics of a traditional national style and materials and those of the new international style. For, indeed, it is the earliest major example of the period's experimentation with open, flexible, expressive structures and techniques to embody the relative and subjective dimensions of reality. In his adaptation of two Ryunosuke Agkutagawa stories, Kurosawa goes beyond the originals in building an intricate structure that fragments the linear, uniform objective reality of the events centering on a rape and death (murder or suicide) into a multiple and contradictory series of subjective refractions. A woodcutter and a priest discuss with a cynical commoner what they know and what they have heard testified about the crime. Thus even the versions by the three central participants (the wife, the bandit, and the dead husband through a medium) are presented on the questionable authority of the priest or woodcutter. Finally, the untrustworthy woodcutter contradicts his earlier statements and gives his full version of the events. The unreconcilable versions not only differ but are used to reveal the prideful needs and weaknesses that impel the versions. As the priest says, "But it is because men are so weak. That's why they lie. That's why they must deceive themselves."

Kurosawa's visual approach is appropriately impressionistic in conveying the subjective immediacy of the characters' reality. More than any of his other films, *Rashomon* is a mosaic of shots of short duration; yet at the same time, it is full of strong camera movement, of careful compositions that create a tangible sense of texture and atmosphere, compositions that are particularly effective in patterning the triangular interaction among the three principals.

Rashomon was Kurosawa's eleventh film, but it clearly marks the beginning of his major period. In subsequent works, he has continued to combine the classic, relatively simple and static Japanese stylization with a freer, expressive intensity. Using both historical and contemporary materials, he deals with the moral implications of illusion and reality, conveying a lusty

387

humanism that sees growth through coming to terms with the limitations of one's personal reality.

Among his other historical films, *Seven Samurai* (1954) is a masterpiece of epic action. Its action compellingly renders a tough-minded, stoical sense of dignity and pride, the possibility of a realistic heroism that does not blink at the cost but still insists on the value of doing one's best for oneself and for others. Motion is at the core of the vibrant technique—in the scene, in the movement of the camera, in the rhythm of the editing and the striking juxtapositions of composition that it builds—whether in the dazzling ordering of the chaotic final battle in the rain and mud or in the touchingly quiet, dancelike innocence of the girls planting rice after the battle. Yet for all the emphasis on motion, separate static compositions have an unfailing power, such as the long-held shot of the naive new recruit (Toshiro Mifune), lying dead on a narrow bridge, face down, in the armor he has stolen, the rain washing away the mud from his unprotected buttocks.

Years later, in *Yojimbo* (1961) and the lesser *Sanjuro* (1962), Mifune is a cynical, aging samurai, long past holding any more illusions about himself, man, or life, but doing what he does best anyway. Both films tone the Western-like genre with comedy—in *Yojimbo,* with a harsh black comedy for its caricature vision of total corruption.

In *The Throne of Blood* (1957), Kurusawa's free adaptation of *Macbeth,* again with Mifune, the stylization of the historical genre and of the highly formalized compression and ceremony of the No drama are joined with an austere economy of visual means. All become a formal metaphor for the

The Throne of Blood

rigid, confined trap of self-delusion and obsession. All are ritualized, distanced: There are almost no close-ups. Yet there is also a textural richness, a heightening of natural objects—fogs, forests, wind, horses, birds—into symbol.

Of the contemporary works, *Ikuru* (To Live, 1952), is the masterpiece. Informed of his approaching death, the lonely civil servant Watanabe is faced with the futility of his life. In the densely detailed, vividly realized sequences of the first half of the film, we are made to share with an intimate immediacy his coming to terms with the dead ends of his reality. At the point of Watanabe's deciding to do something about a long-neglected petition for a playground, Kurosawa cuts abruptly to the second half. At Watanabe's wake, the office force conjectures about his death, mocks his attempts (seen in flashback) to fight the bureaucracy and get the park built. They still do not understand, fail to see the personal truth he has forged, even when they are told of the last sight of him. In one lovely, long-held image, Kurosawa captures the man's acceptance of the kind of action he can take to give his life meaning, his finding his place in the rhythm of things: In the falling snow, he sits on a swing in the completed park, swinging and singing gently and calmly a song of his youth.

In Kurosawa's latest work, *Dodeska Den* (1970), his abiding sympathy has a new tone and is given a new and lovely sensory form. The metaphoric tale of the pathetic misfits who live by the rubbish heap of life shows Kurosawa resigned to inevitable defeat yet able to find a kind of loving joy amid the clutter of broken hopes. It is his first film in color, and the color is used beyond realistic representation for the tones of the inner life that permeate the physical. In the sad whimsy of *Dodeska Den*, illusions become full fantasies, become a kind of reality. They are needed to supply the courage to go on.

Kinugasa, Mizoguchi, Ozu

After *Rashomon*, Teinosuke Kinugasa's *Gate of Hell* (1953) also found popular success, but its ornamental pageantry was a less significant use of the historical genre than Kenji Mizoguchi's *Ugetsu Monogatari* (1952, but released later outside of Japan). A director since the late twenties, Mizoguchi was doing his best work in the period just before his death in 1956. Mizoguchi's lovely painterly compositions derive sensuous beauty and meaning from the play of men and women against their natural environments; scenes are consistently kept in one long-held shot, often in long-distant shot as well, camera moving with lyric grace or kept imposingly stable. Blending fantasy and epic Realism, *Ugetsu* is the most complex variation on his basic concern with man and society's tragic denial of the love and spirituality offered to life through women—seen as well in historical films such as *Sansho Dayu* and *Chikamatsu Monogatari* (both 1954) and a contemporary period film like *Street of Shame* (1956).

The traditional Japanese style creates a tangible atmosphere, derived from a respectful concentration on and ordering of the details of the surface of things, leading to the suggestion of the emotional depths beyond. Mizoguchi's

Ugetsu Monogatari

sensuous lyricism is the epitome of one method of realizing this atmosphere; the films of Yasuji Ozu epitomize another. In the extreme restraint of Ozu's later films, there is a graceful purity, a sensitizing repose. Within his severe restrictions of action and setting, of camera movement and editing, within the static formal patterns of the compositions, the tangible surfaces release the interior being of his characters. The formalized, distilled Realism invokes *their* reality, the feel of their lives. Quiet, waiting observation concentrates on small, revealing actions and on meaningful relationships between man and things. Shots are mostly from a medium distance, at eye level from the front; unobtrusive, they are nonetheless varied subtly and rhythmically, linked by simple cuts only. The lives are revealed through what Donald Ritchie has aptly termed incremental structure, not plot-tightening. The emotions come from the characters, are not demanded by the camera.

Though Ozu worked with contemporary situations in his later films, most frequently with situations involving conflicts of generations and of old and new cultures, he is not basically concerned with social comment. His concern, like his style, centers on the emanations of the inner life on and through the surfaces of the everyday. His films, like those of Mizoguchi, are only now, after his death, getting their deserved attention in the West. *Tokyo Story* (1953) is the peak achievement of the final burst of creativity that includes, among others, *Late Spring* (1949), *Early Spring* (1956), *Floating Weeds* (1959), and *Late Autumn* (1961).

Masaki Kobayashi has made a fascinating adaptation of traditional fantasy-history themes in the stylized mixture of horror and beauty of *Kwaidan* (1964); but he is best known for the strong direct social statements of such works as *Black River* (1957) and the massive trilogy of wartime Japan, *The Human Condition* (1958–61).

Ichikawa and Oshima

Among the younger directors who have dealt with contemporary situations with an increasing sophistication of psychology and technique, Kon Ichikawa and Nagisa Oshima have built the most impressive body of work. Though he has often done comedies, Ichikawa's major works have been harsh, bitter tragedies, with probing psychological subtleties and a deep sense of anguished paradox. Yet his films are touched with a graphic and symbolic personal style, an intensification of the lovely classic manner. Two war films—*The Burmese Harp* (1955) and *Fires on the Plain* (1959)—present a strong contrast: The first is the quiet, dignified tragedy of a young soldier who attempts to build a separate peace; the second is composed and shot with equally dignified restraint yet builds brutal details of the physical and mental degradation of war that destroys all dignity, even that of death. In the strongly atmospheric and superbly composed *Enjo* (*Conflagration*, 1958), the anguish of human paradox is captured in the obsession of a young acolyte who must destroy the golden temple that represents all he loves and has faith in. The domestic family relationships of *Bonchi* (1960) are more commonplace, yet they too produce a destruction of love and innocence, the

Tokyo Story

human harshness again balanced by a paradoxical beauty of visual expression. *Kagi* (*The Key* or *Odd Obsession*, 1959), is Ichikawa's most sophisticated mixture of comedy and psychological distortion, this time arising from all the hypocrisies and kinks of sexuality. Though more flashy and melodramatic, the comedy of *An Actor's Revenge* (1963) again plays on sexuality in exposing personal and social viciousness.

Oshima—a prolific workman with 15 features in his first 10 years as a director—is more direct and radical in approaching social problems; he has moved from a flexible Naturalism of style to a much more eclectic and modernist mixture of approaches. His early films are bleak views of social outcasts and rebels. *The Sun's Burial* (1960) is the most pessimistic, *Shiiku* (*The Catch*, 1961), the most fully developed in drawing the selfish, destructive hypocrisies of social groups out of the story of the murder of a Black American prisoner during World War II. With *Death by Hanging* and *Diary of a Shinjuki Thief* (both, amazingly, 1968), he shows full command of a variety of supra-Realist techniques, with clear influence by Godard, and a striking grasp of intricate structural unity. In *Death,* a documentary naturalness is dislocated in several ways: by an elaborate (often bitterly comic) psychodrama fantasy in which the execution staff get the victim who wouldn't die to reenact his life and crime and end up enacting their own repressed drives —by Surrealist blurring of fantasy and reality in sequences with the victim's lover-sister, by direct Godardian discussion. *Diary,* which combines politics, sex, and theater in its treatment of social oppression and rebellion, is even more complex in structure, more varied in Brechtian and allegorizing devices. While *Boy* (1969) is more straightforward and empathetic, it still has a countercurrent of elliptical and allegorical distancing. Like Oshima's other films, it uses its individual case—a loveless family in which the boy is used to fake accidents for extortion—to expose broader social and psychological dislocations.

In *Woman of the Dunes* (1964), one of the most widely known Japanese films of this period, Hiroshi Teshigahara builds a philosophic allegory while maintaining a strong sense of textural reality. The abstracted situation of the civilized man who learns to accept the rhythms of life and the flesh when he falls into a sand pit and cannot escape is kept tangibly physical and sexual.

INDIA

Ray In India through this same period, Satyajit Ray was building an important body of work and reputation while eschewing the time's tendency toward more flamboyant expressive techniques yet nonetheless developing more sophisticated approaches through the course of his career. At one level, his work has the quiet documentary receptivity of Robert Flaherty in capturing the concrete ethnic details of a culture and way of life—though in contrast to Flaherty's usual focus on the traditional, he is concerned regularly with the dislocation of transition. As in the work of the Italian neo-Realists and Jean

Pather Panchali

Renoir, his works deal with social conflict in terms of individual character, with even less direct exposure of specific social problems. Still, these characters, for all the small, tangible details of their fully rounded development, are finally touched with an idealization, an epic epitomizing that ties his work to that of the Russian silent-film directors—yet here too, he is not concerned with directly taking sides or assigning good and evil.

The approach is at its most contemplative—least manipulative through editing or camerawork—in the slow (for some, agonizingly slow) accumulation of detail of the Apu trilogy: *Pather Panchali* (1954), *Aparajito* (*The Unvanquished*, 1956), *The World of Apu* (1959). Yet underlying the surface artlessness, the spontaneity and simplicity, is a careful selectivity. "In cinema," Ray has said, "we must select everything for the camera according to the richness of its power to reveal." The selectivity, often in terms of small, personal, domestic actions, reveals character; but it also becomes symbolic —as does the sometimes forced use of objects. Often motifs are developed through repetitions and recapitulations, as in the important use of trains— the hope and the danger of the new—and Apu's responses to them throughout the trilogy. In the trilogy, Apu is at the center of the dilemma of India's transition into the modern, industrialized world. He struggles to adjust to it, to seek some sort of personal control within it; all around him are a variety of other responses. In the final part, marred by the somewhat trite treatment of his despair as a sensitive young writer, he has come to some peace, but at great cost.

In the trilogy, Apu's father cannot adapt. In *Jalsaghar* (*The Music Room*, 1958) and *Devi* (*The Goddess*, 1960), an obsessive holding to traditional forms is seen in stronger terms of destructive decay. In the rather overly insistent, monotone symbolism of *The Music Room,* music, however valuable in itself, becomes the motif of decay. In the more complex and psychologically suggestive *Devi,* the overripe richness of the life style of the wealthy family becomes a visual parallel to the personal corruption—a young wife's succumbing to destructive superstition and the relentless domination of her father.

In *Mahaganar* (*The Big City,* 1963) and *Charulata* (*The Lonely Wife,* 1964), Ray again focuses on the family to reveal conflicts between tradition and progress, and again with a young wife as the central figure. In both, attitudes are less dichotomized and extreme, the treatment less formal and symbolic. *Mahaganar* reveals big meanings in little things and events with a good touch of humor; set in 1879, *Charulata* distills the tensions of its triangle—a young wife, her busy husband, and a visiting poet—with Ray's strongest development of character.

POLAND

Wajda
and
Others

In Europe during the fifties, film-makers in Poland provided the first display of the vitality of new film industries. They inaugurated as well a continuing paradox in countries of Eastern Europe, in which energetic creativity, spurred by state-supported film institutes, must interact with the restrictions of bureaucratic control. In Poland, the veteran Aleksander Ford continued to be an influential force, but the first major impression was made by the young Andrzej Wajda, 28 when he made his first film, *A Generation,* in 1954. *A Generation* was a straight, conventional depiction of the growth of political consciousness; but by *Kanal* (1955), Wajda was beginning to take a more distinctive ironic stance toward political consciousness, its actions and results, and beginning also to attempt more heightening of the materials within the Realist framework. In *Kanal,* the uprising against the Germans in Warsaw ends futilely in the muck of the sewers. In the more elaborate *Ashes and Diamonds* (1958), he blends Naturalism, symbolic imagery (often effective, sometimes archly poetic), and borderline touches of Surrealism—a combination that well serves the ambiguous tragic core of the film. For the young wartime activist (Zbigniew Cybulski), against his instincts, is driven in the postwar factional rivalry to kill a Communist leader. His ironic dilemma is surrounded by social ambiguity—an upsurge of patriotism, not untinged by decadence; the first sign of new selfseeking even amid the new Communist regime. The ripely poetic *Lotna* (1959) even more pessimistically reviews the degradation of ideals in war. In *Innocent Sorcerers* (1960) and the broad social canvas of *Ashes* (1964), the earlier disillusioned romanticism of imagery and statement is more cynically modulated as Wajda turns to the corruption of the postwar society. *Everything for Sale* (1968) marks a striking stylistic turn: a subjective, personal movie about a director making a movie. Unlike the somewhat comparable *8 ½* of Fellini, it stresses the dilemma that abstraction into art poses for both personal emotions and social con-

Ashes and Diamonds

science. Its intricate patterns blur the relationship between external reality, the second-level reality of the film about the director and his work, and the third-level reality of the film that he is working on. At its core is a fascinating use of the paradox of the mythic symbol that the actor Cybulski (who died in 1967) had become for Poland's youth.

In 1958, Andrzej Munk's *Eroica* had contrasted Wajda's early poeticism with an ironic counterpoint between comic hijinks and tragic defeat in wartime Poland. In *The Passenger*, which he was working on at the time of his death in an auto accident in 1961, the comedy is dropped; instead, there is a strangely restrained distancing in the treatment. Counterpointing actions in present-day Poland with heart-wrenching material from the Auschwitz death camp, Munk probes troubling and ambiguous facets of motivation, of freedom and responsibility.

In the same year, Jerzy Kawalerowicz completed his finest work, *Mother Joan of the Angels*. In striking contrast to the unrestrained sensationalism of Ken Russell's later treatment of the Loudon witch-trial material, it is an exquisitely modulated work. There is a classic, formal purity in its patterns, images, and shadings of black and white; in its deliberate rhythms and almost choreographic movements. Its style gives meaningful resonance to its psychological probing of authoritarianism and the inner drives that make men and women its accomplices. Ostensibly dealing with the church, its further implications are subtle but clear.

Similarly classic in restraint, but with more flexible application in a series of films, is the work of Wojciech Has. Though concerned with capturing mood and inner states, Has denies himself openly expressive devices. Instead, he builds long scenes, often in long-held shots, with deftly orchestrated movements and telling patterns of background décor in the composition. In varied situations, Has has explored the usually unfulfilled attempts of characters to find some kind of inner discipline and equilibrium amid corrupted and destructive environments, most notably in *One-Room Tenants* (1959), *Gold Dreams* (1961), *How to Be Loved* (1962), and *The Saragossa Manuscript* (1964), the last two featuring Cybulski.

Polanski and Skolimowski

Two younger directors have pursued more openly modernist styles; both also have moved on to make films outside of Poland. Roman Polanski's series of films have a consistency of concern with sexual antagonism and eruptions of violence. They employ a variety of expressive approaches that build to a crescendo of violence. His first feature was *Knife in the Water* (1961), a taut, elliptical, three-way power struggle. It builds its shifting sexual tensions and alliances on small details, even games, to a final exposure of the emptiness and antagonism of a man and wife. In *Repulsion* (1965), made in England, the exploding sexual confusion within a young girl (Catherine Deneuve) is built with a fusion of realistic detail and subjective fantasy, a baroque accumulation of details of décor, some literal and some distorted, to parallel her deepening emotional morass and her acts of violence. In the bitter, offbeat comedy of *Cul de Sac* (1966), also made in England, the physical violence is not a direct result of the shifting pattern of sexual hostility but a fitting cap to it. While *Rosemary's Baby* (1968), made in the United States, is primarily a clever and credible merger of devilish witchcraft and modern, Realist details, it can also be viewed in terms of two of Polanski's persistent concerns. Taken as subjective projections and distortions of the heroine, its supernatural threats become a correlative for uncontrollable sexual tensions. On another level, the action builds to the symbolic acceptance of the ineradicable taint of evil in life. In the ultraviolence year of 1971, Polanski's *Macbeth*, adapted with Kenneth Tynan, was fashionably explicit and shocking in giving form to humanity's propensity toward evil, its blood and gore rather dimming its fascinating, moody atmospheres and sporadically intriguing interpretation of the inner tensions that drive men to extremes.

Jerzy Skolimowski, an actor and screenwriter for *Innocent Sorcerers* and *Knife in the Water*, also moved abroad after his first three films but returned for a later film, the allegorical *Hands-Up* (1968), which was subsequently banned. Consistently concerned with the alienation of the young from themselves and others under the impact of materialist corruption, his films show the development of an energetic, oblique, visually dynamic style—a tough cynicism ordering a wildly surrealistic imagination. In the first three, the disillusionment of Polish youth is seen first in the elliptical Naturalism of *Identification Marks—None* (1964), then with more flamboyant use of décor and baroque imagery, often in excitingly inventive long takes, in *Walkover* (1965). *Barrier* (1966) is a more subjectively stylized (and Godard-influenced) transformation of material reality—literal images leading to surrealistic hyperbole, to outright fantasy. *Le Départ* (1967), made in Brussels with Jean Pierre Leaud, is his first fully comic treatment of the theme, with the lightheartedness of Truffaut and a dynamically paced blend of hectic movement, satiric imagery, and avant-garde devices. *Deep End* (1970), shot mainly in Munich but in English, is a harder-edged but erratic comedy; at its best, it builds its witty, semisurreal images, centering on a public bathhouse, into an ironic allegory of callous selfishness, materialism carried to the objectifying of others.

In the late sixties, the unique film-animator Walerian Borowszyk turned to live action films. In *Goto, Ile d'Amour* (1968), made in France, and *Mazepa* (1969), made in Poland, he displays a stunning interplay of stylized, sardonic distancing and intense emotionalism.

CZECHOSLOVAKIA

In 1963, a number of films made in Czechoslovakia brought to worldwide attention another national renaissance—one that in quantity and variety of excellent film-makers was not to be equaled in East Europe. The innovations in style, the outspoken frankness, the probing psychological and social insights—disillusioned, yet with a resilient assertion of humanism—managed to withstand erratic political pressures until 1968 but since have found the path of expression blocked by government censorship.

Realist Mode: Kadár-Klos, and Others

One group in this renaissance worked primarily within the Realist mode, though with the kind of extending of its borders found in other countries through the same period. Their films found wider significances in small situations or focused on small situations in the midst of larger events. In *Death Is Called Engelchen*, by the directorial team of Ján Kadár and Elmer Klos, and *Transport from Paradise* by Zbyněk Brynych (both 1963), the direct subject is Nazi brutality, but the wider subject is the degradation of war and the dangers of dictatorial control, whatever the cause or allegiance. In Kadár-Klos's widely honored *The Shop on Main Street* (1965), with slight touches of fantasy, the quiet but deep sadness of a small-scale persecution of Jews becomes a mirror for the complicity of ordinary people in totalitarian desecration of common humanity. In his 1964 film *The Fifth Horseman Is Fear*, Brynych intensifies the treatment of another tale of Nazi oppression of the Jews to nightmare levels. While not breaking the literal illusion, his intensive editing, his startling patterns of décor and objects, his vignettes reach toward the levels of parable: the haunting, wild desperation of a crowded nightclub full of Jews, seeking contacts for escape, escaping in loud drunkenness;

the hushed, painful counterpoints of sound and movement in a Jewish insane asylum; the muted irony of a scene in a brothel, the loveliness of the whores under the misty shower heads an intimation of the death-camp showers of gas. Yet, typically, Brynych asserts a counterthrust of courage and dignity against the weakness and evil.

In 1963, Milos Forman's *Black Peter* also appeared, followed in 1965 by *Loves of a Blonde*. In both, he established a blend of quiet humor and sympathetic sadness, a kind of tender irony about the pathetic pettiness of life that had by no means been obliterated by the programs of the new regime. In *The Fireman's Ball* (1967), the comedy and pathos are still blended, but Forman makes of the small details of the day and night of the ball a parable of the personal frailties and weaknesses that are the true core of official bureaucracies. His first American film, *Taking Off* (1971), starring Buck Henry, who also had a strong hand on the script, takes on the conflict of the new life styles with the old. Though it does not achieve the lyrical balance of tones of his first films, its inventive satire has an unforced naturalness and credibility of characterization. Sympathetically slicing both ways, it has a quiet humanity usually lacking in more fashionable treatments of the generation gap.

Jiří Menzel's first film, *Closely Watched Trains* (1966), also merges comedy and pathos in its delineation of a young train-dispatcher's sudden movement toward manhood—cut short by his death as he successfully blows up a German munitions train. But Menzel seeks to make of his small events a fable of compliance with and rebellion against authoritarianism, and the levels do not fully coalesce. In his first film, *Intimate Lighting* (1965), Ivan Passer employs the quiet, sympathetic satire found in his screenplays for Forman, staying with his seemingly uneventful scenes until they reveal the human foibles and stunted dreams that endure even in the postwar Socialist state. More coldly somber, Evald Schorm in his first films—such as *Courage for Every Day* (1964) and *The Return of the Prodigal Son* (1966)—also exposes the illusion that the Socialist society is immune to the moral malaise of a dedication to material progress.

Subjective and Surreal: Nemec and Others

The other major group of Czech film-makers has pursued more subjective stylization, whether into wild and grotesque comedy or haunting and ambiguous allegory, touched by the vision and tone of the Czech writer Franz Kafka. The first of these was Jan Nemec's *Diamonds of the Night* (1964), which mixes a realistic base of a pair of boys wandering through a vicious wartime countryside and city with hyperbolic vignettes and sudden surrealistic images: When the boys are given some food, their mouths are suddenly swollen and bloody, and they cannot eat it. His *Report on the Party and the Guests* (1966) has a tighter structure, all its satirical parables on the same level of unreal reality. Its stylish party guests submit to the ruler for the sake of their status and greed, finally set out to destroy the one dissatisfied guest who has refused to stay. In contrast, *The Martyrs of Love* (1967) is a gentle play of fantasy about dreamers whose dreams are futile but who find their only happiness in them.

The surreal conceits are accelerated into the wild, kaleidoscopic images and sounds of *Daisies* (1965), directed by Vera Chytilová. Two girls decide to be as rotten as everybody and go off on a madcap series of picaresque adventures, stuffing themselves with and destroying everything and everybody in sight—a witty, telling stylization of the absurdities and eventual destructiveness of the acquisitive society. In Jan Schmidt's *The End of August at the Hotel Ozone* (1966), the persuasive, destructive greed is treated in terms of a taut, austere allegory. After the next war, a surviving group of girls stops off at an old hotel, an old lady dies, an old man pleads with them to stay with him. They refuse, and when he refuses to give them his phonograph, they kill him. In the 1966 film of Antonín Mása, *Hotel for Strangers,* a crowded, Marienbad-like hotel is the allegorical center for a more ambiguous fable of the interplay of love and destruction.

HUNGARY

New talents and new approaches in the cinema of Hungary also began to emerge in 1963—the themes, like those of the Czechoslovakian movement, shaped in great part by the catastrophic upheavals of national history and the current tensions of the new system. Though under constant political pressure, the Hungarian New Cinema in the last few years has been able to maintain a level of forthrightness beyond that of the Czechs.

Jancsó and Others

Cantata (1963), was the first decisively new film of the movement's major director, Miklos Jancsó, although *My Way Home* (1964) is closer in style and approach to his later work. In the latter, however, there is still traditional attention to the personalized figures, the two young men whose brief intermission from war is finally terminated by the abrupt intrusion of violence. In the later films, individuals become part of the abstract patterns of historical forces; personal character development and cause-and-effect plot development and explanation are both reduced. Especially in Jancsó's historical trilogy, event is kept a part of a rigid and enigmatic pattern of forces. While always literal and credible, the events and situations are carried to the border of mannered unreality, the distilled essences of rituals of power and degradation through power. The images have an eerie quality, mysterious, yet not tightly symbolic. They are starkly formal, severe, the literal abstracted into the extreme and into composition that forcefully renders the mood—of what may be the bleakest vision of man in contemporary cinema.

In *The Roundup* (1965), a prison camp in a barren wilderness becomes the essence of the destructive, enigmatic complicity between the subjugating and the subjugated. In the wider war panoramas of *The Red and the White*

The Roundup

(1967), both armies (the time is the upheavals of 1918) become parallel victims, mirror-image sets of doomed puppets manipulated by blind and unseen power—the repeated and parallel patterns, often in long takes, capturing the almost mechanical acceleration of shared futility. The third of the trilogy, *Silence and Cry* (1968), has a more personal dramatic situation, but the interaction between individual figures remains elusive, slips beyond expected narrative patterns, is abstracted into haunting images. Again the issue is complicity in destructive power, the paradoxical subtleties in the ritual of victim and victimizer.

Confrontation (1969) moves up to the postwar world, is more direct in discussing the issues rising from the confrontation between officialdom and students. Less bleak in tone, less severe, even exuberant, in movement and composition, it goes beyond immediate issues to the frightening enigmas of human action that support authoritarian power. *Agnus Dei* (1971) returns to the past with an obsessive and enigmatic reprise of earlier motifs. Jancsó's typical set of figures—priests and peasants, soldiers, naked girls, and horses —cycle in an endless gyre of violation.

The same age as Jancsó, Károly Makk had come to prominence earlier, in the fifties, with a series of works, most notably the intense psychological Realism of *House under the Rocks* (1957). His *The Fanatics* (1961) was the first work to delineate a consistent motif in Hungarian films—the special individual at odds with bureaucracy and conformity—a motif subtly and lyrically modulated in Pál Gábor's recent *Horizon*. In the sixties, Makk went into eclipse, but by the end of the decade his career took on new vitality with the success of *Love,* a controlled and humane blend of comedy and pathos.

In 1963, *Current* had marked the debut of István Gáal, here more lyrical than Jancsó, but also austere in tone and image. A personal story of the impact of death on two youths, it was followed by two films more oriented to social history. In both—*The Green Years* (1965) and *Baptism* (1967)— personal stories of a return to boyhood environments set up structures that contrast the two time periods. In *The Falcons* (1970), Gáal narrows the focus of action but develops more symbolic resonance from the events and images. It is a realistic fable with several levels of overtone, focused on a young man's encounter with a trainer of falcons and his birds.

In 1964, András Kovács's *Difficult People,* a *cinéma verité* documentary, was influential in breaking through to more open and direct political discussion on screen. His *Cold Days* (1966) is more vivid narrative cinema, detailing the four accounts of Hungarian soldiers who had participated in the slaughter of hostages. While fictional, *Walls* (1968) presents politico-philosophic discussions between groupings of central characters rather than development of plot, focusing on the conflict between creativity and bureaucracy. The talky *Relay Race* (1970) goes further in trying to merge story and and documentary.

István Szsabó's first feature, made in 1964, was *The Age of Daydreaming.* But it was *The Father* (1966) that more artistically and fully developed similar themes and brought Szsabó to prominence. *The Father* intricately sets the present against a young man's romanticized memories and fantasies about his father and his childhood, drawing a parallel between his need to demythologize and come to real terms with his past and the similar needs of a nation. *A Love Film* (1970) again blends the present and idealizations of the past in the treatment of its central love affair, but here too, the personal feelings and conflicts are made interdependent with the tragedies and endurance of Hungary as a nation.

In two other approaches to political history and criticism, Ferenc Kósa's *Ten Thousand Suns* (1965) is a vast, Eisensteinian analysis of four decades of history; while Ferenc Kardos's *A Mad Night* (1969) is a Pinteresque allegory of threat and enigma, implicating a society in one night's investigation in a grocery store.

YUGOSLAVIA

Yugoslavian cinema has also experienced a renaissance, again impelled by stylistic experimentation. Aleksander Petrovíc's *I Even Met Some Happy Gypsies* (1967), for example, is a pictorially startling depiction of lusty peasant materials: Boro Drasovíc's *Horoscope* (1969) is a realistic study of small-town boredom; Zivojin Pavlovíc's *When I'm Dead and White* (1968), a harsh view of low-life in the city. In Vatroslav Mimica's *The Event* (1969), however, the realistic texture has an elliptical condensation and symbolic resonance that make its small event an elemental fable of human savagery. In *Rondo* (1966), Zvonimir Berkovíc builds an intricate and character-revealing pattern of recurrences and variations with the uneventful circumstances of a series of Sunday afternoon chess games.

Makavejev But far more important than these directors—in fact, one of the most important new spirits and influences in international cinema at the turn of the decade—is Dusan Makavejev. Makavejev's experiments in extending and reshaping the structure of the combined narrative-didactic film are like a reprise of the major stages of this type of work in the development of the film—but all with a distinctly individual verve and innovation. His work builds on Eisensteinian montage—editing by juxtaposition, by collision. But with a warmth of feeling, a humor, a playfulness of association—with the *soul* that he has stated he feels is missing in Eisenstein's cold "pile of shots." Thus he builds as well on the wildly free associations and mocking humor of Buñuel's Surrealist fantasies. His debt to Godard, and the Brechtian techniques Godard introduced to the film, is equally strong. Montage becomes a part of a larger organizing principle of collage—the blending of disparate modes of filmic discourse (fictional narrative, agitprop vignettes, interviews, speeches, original documentary footage, footage from other films, whether fictional or documentary, songs, visual and verbal gags). Juxtaposition, then, becomes more than the method of relating shots within narrative structure; it becomes the controlling rhetoric of the structure.

As in the relationship to Eisenstein, Makavejev's structure of juxtaposition is more lighthearted than Godard's, more zany, even precariously flippant at times. His ironies are more open-ended, questioning all sides of the arguments presented. For his revolutionism is less doctrinaire (though he, too, is enamored of Maoist Socialism), more questioning. Moreover, he is equally a sexual revolutionary, bringing to bear in his work an additional set of paradoxical affinities and conflicts between the two forms of revolution.

His first work, *Man Is Not a Bird* (1966), is his most straightforward narrative. Its juxtapositions are primarily made within the narrative structure but are typical of his open-ended ironies. The film introduces his seemingly contradictory treatment of the film's central themes: on the one side, the value and necessity of political commitment and community, but also the dangers of organization and dogma, the binding of the self, and the concurrent symptoms of sexual inhibition; on the other, the value of free individual expression, especially in sexuality, but also its dangers of selfishness and evasion. In a climactic sequence, the ironies are drawn. The husband—older, solid, political, inhibited—has been honored at the factory. A concert of Beethoven's Ninth Symphony is underway and is intercut with shots of the wife making love in a van, the choral "Ode to Joy" overlapping both sets of shots. In the factory, the music heightens the communal fervor; in the van, it accelerates the already irresistible abandon of the lovers.

In *The Switchboard Operator* (or *Death of a Switchboard Operator,* 1967), sex, murder, and politics are worked into a more intricate collage. The narrative is surrounded and invaded by lectures, poems, newsreel and documentary footage, footage out of chronological sequence.

The unusual *Innocence Unprotected* (1968) rescues from oblivion the sentimental innocence of a film made during the German occupation. Makavejev recuts it, tints its frames freely, intercuts recent documentary interviews of the people connected with it and older newsreel footage. His toying with the ironies of time is tied to his stance toward the ambiguities of political reality in that the innocence of the original film is contrasted not only with the new perspectives time produces but also with the political backdrop of its own time, when its makers were indicted, unjustly, for collaborating with the Nazis.

WR: Mysteries of the Organism (1971) is prime Makavejev. It is his homage to Wilhelm Reich and his theories of sexuality and the relationship of sexuality to character type and thus to politics. But it remains skeptical about the oversimplified application of the theories to either sexual behavior or politics. Its forms of expression are on the surface as untrammeled as the kind of emotional expression it advocates: exuberant, raucous in humor, sexually outspoken in word and deed. But under the wildness, and played

WR: Mysteries of the Organism

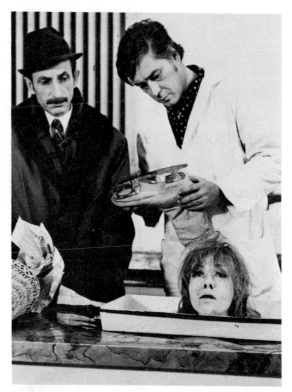

against it, is a tightly controlled pattern of juxtapositions, sometimes blatant, often subtle, always powerful. Its core narrative ties together sex and politics, opens out into direct sexual and political speeches, moves finally into fantasy, as the severed head of Milena continues its exhortations to freer sexuality. Milena had finally broken through to the frozen sexuality of the party-line Russian ice skater; but his joy had turned to guilt and murder. The narrative is intercut with documentary material about Reich; interviews and sessions with Reichian analysts, which are skeptically undercut; interviews and actions of the New York sexual underground—both sympathized with and parodied as a distortion into the same kind of fanatic fetishism that invades politics; gags, songs, poems, and brief allegories; documentary and fictional political footage.

Its flavor can be indicated by this sequence of juxtapositions: Milena is exhorting a throng of workers, intercut with shots of a couple making love. Milena wins over the throng, leads them in a triumphal, dancing march. Mao addresses a monumental throng, all waving their little red books excitedly. In a grandiose hall an actor playing Stalin walks through a small crowd, all formally dressed. He speaks, his speech intercut with shots of two mental patients, one being force-fed, one being given electric shock. Some time later, after another shot of Stalin walking through this hall, we get this montage: A plaster mold is opened, revealing an erect penis in clear red plastic. (Earlier the process of making the casting had been part of a sequence of sex fetishism in New York: Stalin and the plastic penis symbols of the two forms of calcified sexual energy.) Stalin speaks again, tinted red: "Comrades, we have successfully completed the first stage of Communism." A man in a straitjacket bangs his head against the doorjamb of his cell; in rhythm on the sound track, a song: "We thank the party/Our glorious party/For bringing happiness/To every home."

SOVIET UNION

Kalatozov and Others

In Russia itself, recent years brought no such stylistic innovation or iconoclastic statement. Standard Socialist Realism still held sway. Developments did bring realistic depiction of more personal and lyrical situations or more personalized dramatization within historical situations. Mikhail Kalatozov's *The Cranes Are Flying* (1957), Sergei Bondartchuk's *Fate of a Man,* and Gregori Chukrai's *Ballad of a Soldier* (both 1959) were among the most popular of the more personalized, but still sentimentalized, versions of postwar patriotism. Outstanding among the realistic treatment of more individualized stories and emotions, though still with sound social connections, were the works of Josip Heifitz, including *Lady with a Dog* (1959) and *In the Town of S* (1965). A uniquely formalist, Impressionist film, much influenced by silent-epic devices, was Serge Parajonov's *Shadows of Our Forgotten Ancestors* (1965). In 1955, veteran director Sergei Yutkevitch broke from a long line of historical epics to make a valuable interpretation of

Othello; even more impressive were the Shakespearean adaptations of his long-time colleague Grigori Kozintsev—*Hamlet* (1964) and *King Lear* (1971). These followed his breakthrough into classical material with *Don Quixote* in 1957.

GERMANY

In postwar Germany, renovation of the film industry and innovation in its films were slow in developing. In West Germany, the later sixties brought significant signs of resurgence, as typified in the contrasting work of Jean-Marie Straub and Ranier Werner Fassbinder. Straub's work is austere, formal, full of delicate nuance and intricate interplay between sound and image, at its best in *Nicht Versoehnt* (*Unreconciled,* 1965) and *The Chronicle of Anna Magdalena Bach* (1967). Fassbinder is more facile and flamboyant (and prolific: eleven films in four years). With an indirect Brechtian political didacticism, he is adroit at playing against conventional movie mannerisms and expectations—the gangster genre in *Gods of the Plagues* (1969) and *The American Soldier* (1970), movies about movie-making in *Warning of a Holy Whore* (1971).

BRAZIL

The political films of a number of South American directors also present a striking contrast to those of the Soviets; indeed, they mirror in cinematic terms the extreme gap between the Russians and new Third World revolutionaries. In Brazil especially, Ruy Guerra, Nelson Pereira dos Santos, and Glauber Rocha through the sixties began to build an important body of work. Guerra and dos Pereira are less vociferous in political attack, more subtle in technique. Rocha's films are florid, apocalyptic; their extreme violence is seen as a symptom of oppression and brutalization, yet touched with a romantic élan when part of the necessity of revolt. Set in various time periods on the Brazilian countryside, his first four films—*Barravento* (1961), *Deus Eo Diablo Na Terra del Sol* (or *Black God, White Devil,* 1964), *Terra em Transe* (1967), and *Antonio Das-Mortes* (1969)—are highly stylized, epic melodramas, declamatory in image and editing, operatic in character and conflict, like intensified and politicized Westerns. Of them, *Terra em Transe* is the richest in technique and political insight. Two films made in Europe in 1970—*Der Leone Have Sept Cabecas* and *Cabezas Cortadas*—seem mired in the political chaos they seek to reflect and control. Despite limitations and excesses, however, by the early seventies Rocha had become the most acclaimed of a whole new breed of Third World film-makers, committed and extreme in politics, sophisticated and rhetorical in cinematic technique.

CHAPTER TWENTY-FOUR

new worlds of entertainment and art

Whether this has been, and is, a time of radical change, or transition, or decadence, will have to be seen. The film, at least in this time, has seemed to be all three, separately and in combination; for the film, it might well be seen as a time of paradox. In a time of diminishing audiences, it has become most widely recognized as both art and social force. In a time of deepening frankness and intelligence in dealing with freer, more sophisticated subject matter, it has become increasingly sensationalized and titillating. In a time of increased audience expertise, it has fallen into ever more frantic twitchings of the pendulum of fad and fashion; yet it has also moved to richer, fuller human insights, more skilled and imaginative technical complexity and audacity. In a time of greater personal control of works of art, it has not at all been relieved of the commercializing pressures of selling products. In a time of innovation and rebellion, it has continued—often with significant adaptation and inventiveness—to make use of the entertainment conventions of the medium, such as stars and genres. What has been happening in the application of these conventions reflects definite change, even if the definite new pattern that will evolve, like that of the time itself, is still open to question.

THE STAR

Without a doubt, our stars have declined. Some persist, mainly male. Those that do still, like stars of the past, mirror the dreams and needs of their time; but there is a revealing similarity in the personas of the male stars who seem to maintain the strongest power—Paul Newman, George C. Scott, Steve McQueen, Robert Redford, Dustin Hoffman, Jack Nicholson, Jean-Paul Belmondo, Marcello Mastroianni, Warren Beatty. All have a touch of the antihero, the rebel, the outcast, but with a certain unease, an anxiety, a tension, even a neuroticism in their separateness. They too seem to be caught in equivocal paradox. What power the more traditionally glamorous stars still wield—i.e., John Wayne, Elizabeth Taylor, Richard Burton—seems touched with a campy cynicism, a playful decadence in exaggerating the implications of the persona. But in the main, it is the film and the fad that seem to pop out a star, if only temporarily in the accelerated change of fashion in the frenetic encounter between mass media and man.

THE GENRE

The genres have endured, but significantly affected by current pressures, or used sophisticatedly for innovative advances. The musical seems at low ebb: A few mammoths like *Fiddler on the Roof* or excursions into nostalgia like *The Boyfriend* (both 1971) or period *angst*, with topically explicit sexuality, like *Cabaret* (1972) cannot regenerate the form. The historical, panoramic epic has been hit hard by the economic balance sheet; but it has maintained a relative consistency, with some deepening of psychological analysis of the central characters, a greater frankness and violence. Still, one does not see any significant trend developing in such spectacles as these: *Ben Hur* (William Wyler, 1959), *The Agony and the Ecstasy* (Carol Reed, 1965), *A Man for All Seasons* (Fred Zinneman, 1966), *War and Peace* (Sergei Bondartchuk, 1964–67), *Hawaii* (George Roy Hill, 1967), *Khartoum* (Basil Dearden, 1967), *The Sand Pebbles* (Robert Wise, 1967), *Patton* (Franklin Schaffner, 1970), *Ryan's Daughter* (David Lean, 1970), *Nicholas and Alexandra* (Schaffner, 1971). Westerns, as we have seen, have undergone extensive sophisticated modulations—psychological, social, sexual, racial; but the basic genre continues, generally with increased violence—as in the successful series of Sergio Leone Italian-made Westerns beginning in the mid-sixties. Horror and science-fiction films have also been seized by fits of explicit violence and sexuality—with the exception of space films or technological exercises such as Wise's *The Andromeda Strain* (1971). The same acceleration of sensory impact and of sex and violence has been found in the gangster and suspense mysteries; the better examples have been exhibiting, to varying degrees, a more sophisticated psychology or social implication: *Point Blank* (John Boorman, 1968), *Bullitt* (Peter Yates, 1968), *The French Connection* (William Friedkin, 1971), *Klute* (Alan Pakula, 1971), *Dirty Harry* (Don Siegel, 1972), *The Godfather* (Francis Ford Coppola, 1972).

COMEDY AND THE PERSONA-DIRECTOR

Comedy, of course, continues apace but with less distinction as a genre. The best comedies have been more meaningful, more frank and devastating in their exposure of social foibles and atrocities; yet these have been, in the main, the works of versatile directors rather than of those specializing in comedy. These comedies reflect, too, the greater mixing of tones and moods, the acceleration of the grotesque that has been seen in other films. Older comic hands, like Billy Wilder, have not maintained a cumulative growth or distinctive voice.

Jacques Tati in France and Jerry Lewis and, later, Woody Allen in America have been the chief perpetuators of the comic persona or persona-director. Tati has made only five films in twenty-four years. In these he has maintained a quiet, polished whimsy and the persona of the gentle leftover man, beset but undaunted by the things of the world, and especially by rampant technology. In *Mr. Hulot's Holiday* (1953), his encounters with mutinous objects are traditional, timeless. In the earlier *Jour de Fête* (1948), in which as a country postman he brings on the "improvements" himself, and in the three later films, the encounters become more explicit satires on modernity. Though still full of deft touches, *My Uncle* (1958), *Playtime* (1968), and *Traffic* (1971) begin to seem repetitious and attenuated, materials stretched too thinly over a full-length film or over three variations on the same themes.

Lewis's persona has less of the underlying charm, the implication of deeper human significance of the traditional clowns; his is more a brash, hyperactive buffoon. His films have more proliferation than polish, more velocity than subtlety; but in their complicated plotting, occasional fantasy, and acceleration of visual gags, they do echo the great tradition. Lewis's work seemed to peak in the mid-sixties, with *The Patsy* and *The Family Jewels* (both 1964) and *Three on a Couch* (1965).

By the turn of the decade, Woody Allen had stumbled onto the scene, knocking over, as usual, everything and everyone in sight. Writing and usually directing his own material, Allen had, with his first three films (*Take the Money and Run*, *Bananas*, and *Play It Again, Sam*), established himself as a perpetuator of the tradition. His persona, a failure-prone *nebbish*, is uniquely scarred by the fashionable psychosexual neuroses of the time. His relationships to women and sex, in contrast to those of earlier clowns—even Harpo Marx—catch the deep changes that have taken place in society and the modes. His relationships to things, thus far, are less inventive, relying too heavily on his clumsiness and not enough on the unique aggressions of distinct objects and settings. His verbal wit is highly sophisticated, his blending of fantasy and literal action a promising adaptation of developments in contemporary style.

THE INDUSTRY

The state of the stars and genres reflects the state of the industry-art generally. As mentioned earlier, this state has resulted from changes within the production system and changes within society. Within the system, technological advances have been rapid and widespread; but much of the refinement and discovery of equipment and processes—some, like the multi-imaged screen, barely explored—are still to be fully assimilated. Many of these advances have been seized on in the sometimes frantic attempt to combat economic problems threatening film industries throughout the world. While income has generally tended to rise, though erratically, in the last 10 years, and while some nations have seen continued audience growth, for the major production systems actual audience totals have diminished. Since television is usually the chief competitor for this audience, much attention has thus been paid to doing in films what *they* on television can't do—both in terms of sensory spectacles and explicit subject matter.

In turn, one of the chief responses to the crisis has been adaptation of the production system itself, including more international production, more personally controlled production, more flexibility in production-planning. These last two points especially have contributed to the increased interest in seeking segmented audiences, aiming low-budget films at specific special-interest groups or hoping for enough generalized return on a reduced, relatively conservative investment. On the one hand, in the larger industries, this has meant the important encouragement and reassertion of the value of the small, personal film, although many of these films still do not get adequate distribution. Even the valuable increase in reviving older films has tended to reduce the possibilities for the newer artistic film. On the other hand, commercialized cycles and fads seem to accelerate, peak, and decline more rapidly than ever—in great part because of catering, some might say pandering—to a youthful audience. Still, from this orientation, some new genres may be emerging—bike films, films of initiation and rebellion. In America, the most successful first attempts to reach the large Black audience with pointedly Black productions have been movies like Gordon Parks's *Shaft* (1971) and Melvin Van Peebles's *Sweet Sweetback's Baadasssss Song* (1971). Typically, these have played racial variations on the conventions and expectations of the violent tough-guy film, the former rather routinely, the latter with more pointed development of Black identity and rebelliousness.

These Black films are a good example of the way that pressures within the industry and tensions and attitudes in the social context—the time's frenetic pace and change, its relativity, restlessness, and rebellion—combine to influence current cinema. The film—always sensitive to the shape and style of the cultural compositions of our lives—seems now even more sensitive a reflector of the paradoxes of the time as it struggles to adapt to the changing size and nature of its audience. While it is no longer the purveyor of entertainment to the same tremendous mass audience, it is still not ready to become only an art form for more limited audiences. There is still too much money to be made from whatever audience remains.

Thus film-producers have turned to making salable commodities out of the medium's increased power of sensory impact and out of the violence and rebelliousness, social and sexual, of our time. New clichés have replaced the old—in a rising progression of toppers, shockers, lures that go a step further to match new audience expectations. But though medium responds to social expectations—both as art and money-maker—it also shapes and reinforces them. We have still to determine accurately the extent of media influence on attitudes or actions. This social problem is more than a matter of commercial exploitation. For it is not yet clear what effect is produced by even such honest and sophisticated treatments of sexual viciousness and violence as A *Clockwork Orange* or *Straw Dogs*. How much of the sophisticated technique and attitudes are absorbed? How much more may limited responses to the sensory excitement contribute to the very callousness with which the film-makers are honestly concerned?

Yet at the same time, these elements—the acceleration of sensory impact, violence, sexual explicitness—have played a part in the esthetic and human richness of this period of film-making, its advances in technique and content. Whatever the excesses, it has been a period in which the best work individually rivals and, in many cases, betters any of the high points of the past; in which the aggregate—in the quantity, variety, and audacity of its excellence—exceeds the work of any other period.

PURPOSE

Within the welter of pressures and cross-purposes, there has developed a widespread sense of deeper purpose for the film as art and as humanist voice. A new social forthrightness and complexity of psychological probing and understanding have given the film a wider scope of concern, a deeper, denser insight, a richer, more fully human meaning.

At the same time, a growing stylistic sophistication has, with gradual evolution or sudden revolution, found an apt, just, fulfilling set of forms for this maturing content. This open, flexible style has not only broken with many conventions but also found new ways of giving them new vitality and meaning. It has certainly been marked by greater emotional and sensory intensity; yet it has also been especially sparked by a notable prevalence of wit, a quality of counterpoint and irony, a cool distancing, and a knowing playing against that are the period's most distinctive characteristics. The style has been marked by great flexibility in blending and balancing moods and tones, modes of dramatic discourse, individual techniques of camera and editing. It has loosened the patterns of narrative structure and audience expectation, enlarged the possibilities of formal and narrative logic, has even toyed with and brought into question traditions of narrative itself. Its images have given powerful and profound plastic shape to our world and our current conceptions of it.

Most important of all, the open style, in its flexible fusion of expressive and Realist techniques, has found a form, a structuring of feeling, for the interaction of the objective and subjective worlds. It has used the power of the screen's image of external life to enlarge and intensify the expression of the inner life without losing or denying the values of the tangible surfaces. This balancing of the inner and outer worlds has been one of the chief thrusts of art in the modernist period, yet in one way or the other it has been at the core of art in any period. For as Goethe saw it, his chief task as an artist was the "reproduction of the world that surrounds me by means of the world that is in me." This is the kind of reproduction the film is now able to make.

Ours is a self-conscious age; our film art is now self-conscious, knowing and knowledgeable, to the extreme, even, possibly, to a fault. It is a stage of development that can lead to sated decadence or new vitality, or possibly, in our time of paradox, to both.

INDEX

413

Picture Credits and Copyright Acknowledgments

Janus Films/The Bettmann Archive: p. 286
Astor Pictures: p. 288
Avco Embassy Pictures Corporation: pp. 290 (© 1963), 298 (© 1963), 364
American International Pictures Corporation/Audio Brandon: p. 297
Continental Division of Walter Reade-Sterling, Inc.: p. 302
The Walter Reade Organization through Continental Distributing: p. 304
Royal Films International: p. 332
Grove Press, Inc.: p. 333
Continental Distributing: p. 355
Cinema 5/The Bettmann Archive: p. 357
The Landau Releasing Organization: p. 362
Cinerama Releasing: p. 385
Photo by Dean Brown, The Nancy Palmer Agency: p. 386
New Yorker Films: p. 391
Cinema 5: p. 403

C 5
D 6
E 7
F 8
G 9
H 0
I 1
J 2